THE SCENE OF PYGMY KITABU

The tribes named in capital letters (e.g.; *TSWA*) are those which play major roles in PYGMY KITABU; those in lower case (e.g.; *Shi*) were visited by the author.

To avoid the ambiguity caused by the varying forms of traditional prefixes, all tribal names are given without prefixes, as suggested by the International African Institute.

PYGMY KITABU

PYGMY KITABU

by Jean-Pierre Hallet

and Alex Pelle

All photographs by Jean-Pierre Hallet

RANDOM HOUSE : NEW YORK

Library of Congress Cataloging in Publication Data
Hallet, Jean-Pierre, 1927– Pygmy kitabu.
Includes bibliographical references.
1.   Pygmies.   2.   Man—Origin.   I.   Pelle, Alex,
joint author.   II.   Title.
GN660.P9H34   573′.3   72-12991
ISBN 0-394-46285-8

Manufactured in the United States of America
First Edition

Special thanks and acknowledgment to the following for per-mission to reprint:
J. M. Dent & Sons Ltd.: From *The Cities and Cemeteries of
Etruria*, edited by George Dennis, and from *A Dictionary of
Non-Classical Mythology* by Marian Edwardes and Lewis
Spence (Everyman's Library Texts).
Doubleday & Company, Inc.: From *Early Man in the New World*
by Kenneth Macgowan and Joseph A. Hester. Copyright ©
1962 by The American Museum of Natural History. Copy-
right 1950 by Kenneth Macgowan.
Dover Publications, Inc.: From *The Egyptian Book of the Dead*
and *The Gods of The Egyptians* by Sir E. A. Wallis Budge,
1967 and 1969.
Farrar, Straus & Giroux, Inc.: From *The White Goddess* by Robert
Graves. Copyright 1948 by International Authors N.V.
University Books, Inc.: From *Osiris, the Egyptian Religion of
Resurrection* by Sir E. A. Wallis Budge, 1961.

To my good friends and adopted people,
the Efé Pygmies of the Ituri Forest.

Contents

List of Illustrations

PYGMY KITABU

Pygmy Genesis

Somewhere in the heart of Africa, according to a very controversial theory, the human species evolved from a troop of bloodthirsty, brutally aggressive "killer apes." The fossil bones of these ancient anthropoids bear the scientific title *Australopithecus*, which simply means "southern ape." Scientists disagree about their exact relationship to man, but there is no argument concerning their size. Like my good friends and adopted people, the African Pygmies, they averaged just about four and a half feet tall. A few years ago, at Olduvai Gorge in Tanzania, Dr. Louis Leakey unearthed a very humanoid fossil called *Homo habilis*, "the able, skilled, or clever man," who had an estimated height in life of three feet six inches. The smallest Pygmy man on record was a shade over three feet six inches tall.

Scientists and scholars such as Wilhelm Schmidt, H. Brynn, J. Kollman and Paul Schebesta have postulated that the taller human races all evolved or developed by mutation from small and anatomically primitive Pygmy-like ancestors, just as the enormous dinosaurs evolved from chicken-sized reptiles and the modern horses sprang from tiny *Eohippus*. The present-day African Pygmies have even been described as the still-surviving parent stock of *Homo sapiens*—ancestors from prehistoric times who like the coelacanth and other "living fossils" have lasted into modern times.

Anatomist Raymond Dart, who made the first Australopithecine finds, maintains that the African Hottentots and Bushmen represent the direct, little-altered descendants of the old "southern apes." These ethnic groups are short-statured; they average five feet in height and have a yellow-tan complexion. The Hottentots are a pastoral, cattle-raising people, while the Bushmen are hunter-gatherers of the savannah/desert country. The skin coloring of the Pygmies, who are hunter-gatherers of the equatorial forest, ranges from yellow-tan to red-brown. Smaller than the Hottentots and Bushmen, they are much more archaic in their anatomy and proportions; they maintain, moreover, the world's simplest level of material technology. Because their culture is so very ancient and primordial in style, the Pygmies can give us a unique insight into the manners and mores of our prehistoric ancestors. Today, in an age when other men have made computerized, transistorized journeys to the moon, some of the African Pygmies do not even make a fire by rubbing two sticks together. They carry burning brands from one forest campsite to the next and regard friction firesticks as a newfangled, rather blasphemous invention.

The Bushmen and Hottentots formerly inhabited most of southern and eastern Africa. A few thousand Bushmen currently survive in the Kalahari Desert, but they have been practically wiped out by the technologically superior Negroes, who are very modern people in comparison. Although a handful of Hottentots still drive their cattle across the sun-baked savannahs, they too have been unable to compete with the Negroes.

The Pygmies formerly inhabited a continuous belt of rain

forest that stretched across the equatorial breadth of the African continent. Today, remaining groups of Pygmies still dwell in forests that grow steadily smaller as invading Negro populations cut down the trees. In the center of Africa, a few miles north of the equator, lies the Ituri Forest of the former Belgian Congo (called Zaïre since October 1971). According to most estimates, the Ituri was invaded about three hundred years ago by a variety of Bantu and Sudanese Negro tribes. The Pygmy population is estimated to have been about two million at the time. Now some fifteen thousand pure-blooded Pygmies survive in a remnant forest that covers approximately 20,000 square miles, but most of them have been reduced to a state of wretched feudal servitude by the tall Negro invaders. In the western forests of Gabon and Cameroon only ten thousand Pygmies are left, but they have suffered just as greatly at the hands of the conquerors.

The racial relationship between the Pygmies, Bushmen and Hottentots is as yet undetermined. All three are very ancient, small, relatively fair-skinned peoples who do not belong to the contemporary world of Black Africa. Some scientists have suggested that the yellowish, rather Oriental-looking Bushmen are related to the Mongoloid peoples. Anthropologist Earnest Hooton maintained that the Pygmies' ancestors may have originated somewhere in Asia. The skin color of the Pygmies varies through Mongoloid/Caucasoid/Amerindian shades of yellow-tan, bronze, copper, brick-red and warm red-brown. Explorer Paul du Chaillu, who in 1867 discovered the Pygmies of Gabon and Cameroon, encountered many individuals with gray-blue eyes. Anthropologist Henri Trilles has described Gabon Pygmies with gray-blue eyes, auburn hair and a yellow-tan complexion so pale that they are actually fairer-skinned than some Spaniards and Italians. Today in the Ituri Forest, one occasionally sees dark blue eyes among the local Pygmy population, as well as some children who have blönd or red-gold hair that will gradually turn to dark auburn.

The range of the Pygmies' color is similar to that of the dark-to-fair Berbers, Libyans or Moors who comprise the native Caucasoid population of North Africa. The Pygmies' proto-Caucasoid traits include thin, uneverted lips, prominent eyebrow ridges, and a very heavy growth of beard and body hair. The Pygmies' large round skulls differ greatly from the typically long or dolichocephalic Negro cranium. And yet our dictionaries and encyclopedias call the Pygmies by the ostensibly scientific name Negrillos—"little blacks" or "little Negroes." The word was coined by nineteenth-century anthropologists who theorized, without benefit of evidence, that the Pygmies were degenerate, dwarfish or even shrunken Negroes. This ill-informed belief, which simultaneously libels the Pygmy and Negro branches of mankind, survives today in direct contradiction to the facts, which were thus summarized by Dr. Jean Leyder, the former administrator of the Ubangi district in the northwest Congo:

> The Pygmy constitutes a totally distinctive race, strikingly different from the Negro.
> The Pygmy is not a degenerate Negro.
> The Negro is not a Pygmy grown larger.
> The Pygmy has been thus for thousands of years: on a monument of ancient Egypt, the Egyptologist Mariette found engraved the portrait and the name of a Pygmy, "Akka," who resembled the present-day Aka Pygmies of Uele. If the strikingly original physical constitution of the Pygmies had been the result of degeneration, the Pygmy race would have disappeared a long time ago. Instead their historic existence as a population of small stature is attested to in Central Africa for millennia. And far from being a declining race, the Pygmies of the Belgian Congo are at present one of the healthiest, most vigorous, most prolific peoples . . . Grave dangers may have recently menaced their survival; these dangers come, however, from the exterior and not from the race itself.
> Medically speaking, the Pygmy is not a dwarf (degenerate, sterile).
> In brief, the Pygmies are not abnormal people. They constitute a race of normally small stature, a strongly individualized race that is entirely distinct from the Negroes . . .
> The prominent brows, the thin lips, testify to a primordial connection with the Europeans . . . [1]

Like the Pygmies, Caucasians or whites are very ancient residents of the so-called Dark Continent. Negroes are not. Dr.

[1] Jean Leyder, "Les Pygmées du Congo Belge," from the *Bulletin de la Société Royale Belge de Géographie*, No. 3–4 (Brussels, 1934), pp. 7–8, 11.

Sonia Cole discussed this topic in *The Prehistory of East Africa:*
"There were apparently three basic stocks in Africa before the
appearance of the Negro: the proto-Australoids with heavy brow-
ridges (typified by Rhodesian man, Hopefield man, and Eyasi
man); the proto-Bushmanoids; and the proto-Caucasoids, or, to
give them a more local but less accurate name, the proto-Hamites
. . . All the Upper Paleolithic peoples of Kenya were of Caucasoid or proto-Hamitic stock; they are represented by the Gamble's Cave and Naivasha skeletons, as well as the skeleton from
Olduvai in northern Tanganyika."[2]

In present-day East Africa, there are many mixed Hamite/
Negro tribes. The famous Masai people of Kenya and Tanzania
are very dark-skinned folk who sometimes have almost Grecian
profiles. The tall Tutsi* or "Watusi" of Rwanda and Burundi apparently represent another Caucasoid–Negro cross; their non-
Negroid traits include big hooked noses of the type usually
described as Semitic. In his exhaustive study of the "Watusi,"
R. Bourgeois explained that eastern and southern Africa present
"three types of fossil men who can easily be considered as ancestors of the Bushmen, Pygmies and present-day hybrid Hamite–
Blacks." What did he have to say about the Negroes? "As sur-
prising as it may seem, it is outside the area of contemporary
Black Africa that one finds fossil specimens approaching the
Negroes . . ."[3]

Some scholars have theorized that the Negroes originated
elsewhere and arrived in Africa at some unknown date, in the
manner of the Indo-European tribes who invaded India and the
Yankee colonists who invaded North America. One theory suggests that the present-day African Negroes are descended from
or related to the black people of the Melanesian archipelago.

---

[2] Sonia Cole, *The Prehistory of East Africa* (Penguin Books, 1954), pp. 111,
113.

* In this work, all ethnic names are given without prefixes (as suggested
by the International African Institute). This will avoid any ambiguity and
confusion caused by the varying forms of tribal prefixes (as "Watusi," Ba-
Tutsi, etc.).

[3] R. Bourgeois, *Banyarwanda et Barundi* (Brussels, 1957), Vol. 1, p. 16.

Anthropologists disagree about the racial status of Grimaldi Man, a quasi-Negro fossil unearthed near Menton on the European Riviera. There is, however, little doubt that the Negroes in Africa represent a rather recent racial type that did not inhabit the ancient African homeland of the Pygmy, Caucasoid and Bushman-style fossils.

In light of these facts, an incident that transpired in 1953 seems particularly ironic. *The International Anthropological and Linguistic Review*, a Miami, Florida, journal, published a paper by Raymond Dart entitled "The Predatory Transition from Ape to Man." An editorial foreword to Dart's discussion of the proposed fossil ancestors reassured racially prejudiced readers: "Of course, they [the Australopithecines] were only the ancestors of the modern Bushman and Negro, and of *nobody else*."

The Caucasoid bones of Olduvai Gorge make a mockery out of this statement. So do the racial characteristics of the people who so vainly cry "Nobody else." The white man's lips are thin and apishly uneverted. He has simian-style eyebrow ridges. Far from being a "naked" ape, he has so much beard and body hair that the smooth-skinned African Negroes very widely call Caucasians by a disparaging nickname meaning "the hairy ones" or "the hairy people." These traits, in combination with the genes for light skin, hair and eyes, are shared by Caucasoids with the African Pygmies and with *nobody else*. Under the circumstances, I am tempted to suggest that we call the Pygmies by the name Blanquitos, "little whites."

Schebesta has mentioned the Ituri Forest Pygmies' very firm tradition that their earliest ancestors were the color of white men. Trilles has reported the Gabon Pygmy legend that "there used to be white Pygmies back in the olden days." It is not unlikely, considering the pale yellow skins, gray-blue eyes and auburn hair that can be seen among the so-called "little blacks." My particular friends, the Efé Pygmies of the eastern Ituri, describe the deity himself as a very tall, elderly and sternly dignified white man with a long wavy beard. Their descriptions conjure up visions of Odin, Zeus or Michelangelo's Sistine ceiling portrait of Jehovah. They would heartily approve of any Biblical movie that starred Charlton Heston (with a beard, of course) in the role of God the Father. They would reject as wholly sacrilegious a Hollywood epic that cast Sidney Poitier or any fine black actor as the creator of mankind.

The Pygmies say in their creation stories that human beings are basically good, well-meaning characters who stand on a higher spiritual level than the rest of the fauna. This is not necessarily opposed to the theory of evolution. No one can deny that a man has more intellect, conscience and self-consciousness than a fish, fowl or hippopotamus. There are even some intriguing Pygmy legends that support the modern theories of our apish origin. The little folk say, for example, that at one time man's ancestors were covered with fur, "just like all the other creatures of the forest." But the Pygmies' insistence on the fundamental goodness of man and his ancestors would not meet with approval among the less moderate evolutionary theoreticians.

In his very influential book *African Genesis*, dramatist Robert Ardrey portrayed the Pygmy-sized Australopithecines as a gang of incurably aggressive killer apes who molded man in their ferocious and atrocious image. Mr. Ardrey puts forth the theory that the million-year-old scraps of bones he calls killer apes used antelope bones as weapons to bash in the skulls of baboon quarry. Ape, antelope and baboon bones have been found, mixed with the motley bones of many other animals, in limestone caves and fissures. Dr. Louis Leakey has commented on the Australopithecine fossils found in these African deposits: "There does not seem to be any justification for regarding these caves as their dwelling-places, and their bones, as well as those of the other fauna, were probably dragged into these caves by hyaenas and other carnivora. The relatively large numbers of 'near-men' represented in these bone breccias is probably due to the fact that they fell a fairly easy prey to the carnivora of the period."[4]

The Australopithecines may have been the victims rather than the killers. A number of paleontologists have declared, from inspections of fossil teeth, that the Australopithecines were probably vegetarians; but even if they did hunt and dine upon baboons,

[4] Louis S. B. Leakey, *Adam's Ancestors: The Evolution of Man and His Culture* (New York: Harper Torchbooks, 1960), p. 185.

there is still no reason to assume that they had a cruel and murderous disposition. We do not consider dolphins to be murderers because they eat fish. We do not censure the moral standards of cheetahs who hunt antelopes in order to live. We do not consider it an act of aggression for a man to eat a steak, chop or hamburger. So it seems rather harsh to condemn the poor little Australopithecines because they may have eaten some baboon-burgers in their time. I am inclined, however, to doubt that small and rather lightly built anthropoids armed with bone clubs ever preyed consistently on bands of baboons. These big monkeys are exceedingly tough and wary animals who organize their bands in military style. They fight like well-disciplined soldiers and are quite capable of tearing apes, men or leopards limb from limb.

There are no fossil morals in the ancient rubble of African bones. But the author of *African Genesis* unhesitatingly brands the killer apes with the mark of Cain—they murdered the innocent baboon Abels!—and concludes that human beings are Cain's children, born to fight and kill one another. This notion hardly furthers the cause of peace and progress, as M. F. Ashley Montagu and other prominent anthropologists have recently pointed out. It offers a glib and easy substitute for conscience and morality. We need not feel responsible for our crimes, since the theory of innate aggressiveness says that it is normal human behavior to exercise our built-in "killer instinct" on members of our own species—an act that differs very greatly from preying on baboons in the hypothetical style of the "killer apes" or hunting forest antelopes to feed one's family in the manner of the Pygmies. Our riots, revolutions, wars and massacres need not be blamed on decadent social structures, population pressures, poverty and the ever-growing misery of our lethally polluted environment. These things will go on unchecked, since according to the theories expressed in *African Genesis* social factors are not the cause of aggression.

Mr. Ardrey dismisses as a "romantic fallacy" the idea that "civilization must be held accountable for man's noteworthy catalogue of vices; and that human fault must therefore have its origin in human institutions, relationships, and environments." This so-called fallacy was fathered, he explains, by French philosopher and social reformer Jean Jacques Rousseau, who created

a "good-natured myth" of the "noble savage" or uncorrupted natural man. Then the fallacy was perpetuated by "the aberrations of
a Thomas Jefferson." Jefferson's mental lapses are defined by
Mr. Ardrey as "the powerful will to believe in man's essential
purity and conditioned corruption" and "the dubious proposition
that the man of the soil possesses a soul degrees purer than the
man of the city, and that a nation to remain uncorrupted must
found its strength on rural rather than urban society."[5] The tumult in our sick and rioting cities may indicate, perhaps, that
Jefferson astutely prophesied the current plight of urban industrial
society. In Africa, where the Negro man of the soil is rapidly
detribalizing and moving into cities, the rate of mental illness
among blacks has increased at least 1000 percent during the
past decade.

To support his theories, the author of *African Genesis* described the fierce behavior of New Zealand trout, European
beavers, Cuban lizards, Asiatic water buffalo and many other
interesting animals. The aggressions of the common jackdaw and
a British bird called the great tit are scrupulously detailed. There
is even a stirring account of "a territorial conflict between two
male song sparrows" that transpired in the city of Columbus,
Ohio.[6] But there is not the slightest mention of an African people
who match the Australopithecines in size, possess an anatomy so
archaic that some anthropologists have called them "ape men,"
maintain a hunter-gatherer culture that has been compared to the
way of life postulated for the Australopithecines, and employ a material technology so simple that they neither use friction firesticks
nor make artifacts from stone in the relatively modern manner of
the Great Stone Age. Mr. Ardrey never even hints that a people
called Pygmies exists, has ever existed, and may be somewhat more
importantly involved than Ohio sparrows in the "African Genesis"
of mankind.

Why?

The answer to that question can be found in some pithy

---

[5] Robert Ardrey, *African Genesis: A Personal Investigation into the Animal
Origins and Nature of Man* (New York: Delta Books, 1963), pp. 148–50.

[6] *Ibid.,* p. 48.

comments made by the explorer Henry Morton Stanley, who is much more famous for his dialogue with Dr. Livingstone. In his classic work *In Darkest Africa,* published in 1890, Stanley very perceptively described the Ituri Forest Pygmies as "the oldest types of primordial man." He even compared a Pygmy couple to those traditional human ancestors, Adam and Eve. Stanley did not, however, say or imply that those old, primordial and ancestral-style people, the African Pygmies, are at all savage and aggressive in their ways. Instead, toward the end of his pioneering trip through the Ituri Forest, he remarked: "The Pygmies showed by their conduct that they are related to all that is best and noble in human nature."

Was Stanley a muddleheaded philosopher smitten by the romantic fallacy of the noble savage? He was a tough-minded explorer who always told the facts as he found them. In 1876, while traveling through the eastern Congo, he succinctly described the manners of the local Bantu tribes. Technologically, they were several light-years more advanced than the Pygmies. Far from being primitive, their societies featured ritual cannibalism and many decadent customs entirely foreign to the Pygmies or the Bushmen. "These savages," declared Stanley, "would consider a whole congress of bishops and missionaries from only one view-point: roast beef!"

The most primitive living humans—those Pygmy Adams who are never, never mentioned by Mr. Ardrey—totally demolish any theory of man's innate aggressiveness. They are very amiable, warm-hearted, fun-loving, sometimes mischievous, but wholly non-aggressive characters who behave more like the elves of European legend than the awful killer apes of modern myth. They love to dance, sing, play the harp and flute, tell jokes, compose tongue twisters and engage in thrilling sports like the grand old game of archery-ball. (The pitcher bowls a *mukole* fruit; the batter tries to shoot it with his bow and arrow.) They loathe hard work of any kind and do their elfin best to avoid it. Americans and Europeans who are disenchanted with the ulcer-making work ethic of our society may be inclined to sympathize.

But the African Pygmies are not anything-goes hedonists in the style of Los Angeles or London "swingers." They are staunchly monogamistic, highly moral people who practice rather than preach a remarkable monotheistic religion. Some of their most important legends and customs strikingly resemble Old Testament equivalents. The Ituri Forest Pygmies, for example, recount a creation legend that almost exactly parallels the Biblical story of Adam and Eve. There is, however, no possibility that the Pygmy religion was "borrowed" from Jewish, Christian, or Mohammedan sources. Egyptian records that date back nearly five millennia—more than a thousand years before the estimated date assigned to Moses—prove that the Pygmies played a major and deeply mysterious role in shaping the earliest religion of the country whence the Israelites made their famous exodus.

Osiris, an ancient Egyptian divinity who has often been compared to the Judeo-Christian Christ, was represented as a Pygmy in faïence figurines of Ptah-Seker-Osiris, the triune god of the Egyptian resurrection. Bes, the Egyptian god of music and dancing, was pictured as a Pygmy and represented as the supreme divinity on a monument known as the Metternich Stele. Pyramid texts call the Pygmies by the pious epithet "Dancers of God." The pyramid text of the sixth-dynasty monarch Pepi I declares: "He who is between the thighs of Nut is the Pygmy who danceth like the god and who pleaseth the heart of the god before his great throne." Nut, the goddess of heaven and mother of Osiris, has been compared to the divine mother of Christian theology and to the goddess Athena, whom the Greeks anciently revered as the "Virgin Mother of Heaven." The Pygmy legend cycle features a similar personage called Matu, the mother of God.

During sixth-dynasty times, Prince Herkhuf of Elephantine led a successful expedition to the equatorial homeland of the semi-legendary Pygmies. Herkhuf's trip to the equatorial forest region was such a rare and extraordinary event that the text of Pepi II's congratulatory letter was engraved on the facade of Herkhuf's tomb. In 1870 A.D., more than four thousand years later, the next known visitor arrived: the German explorer Georg Schweinfurth officially "discovered" the Pygmies in the long inaccessible and almost impenetrable Ituri Forest. During the 4,000 years that separate Herkhuf and Schweinfurth, the Pygmies had no contact with any people who might have "diffused" to them Judeo-

Christian ideas. They nevertheless practiced a lofty monotheistic religion that closely parallels our own.

Egyptologists have been confronted by the same apparent paradox. Sir E. A. Wallis Budge commented on the scholars' dilemma: "Speaking generally, the interpreters may be divided into two classes: those who credit the Egyptians with a number of abstract ideas about God and the creation of the world and the future life, which are held to be essentially the product of modern Christian nations; and those who consider the mind of the Egyptian as that of a half-savage being to whom occasional glimmerings of spiritual light were vouchsafed from time to time."[7] The Pygmy religion creates even greater problems for orthodox theologians. At the same time it offends the more fanatical evolutionists who deny any historicity to man's ancient traditions of "the beginning." It menaces a host of scientific dogmas about the early history of man and the origin of civilization. Nevertheless, it is there—like Mount Everest —and cannot be ignored for the sake of convenience.

In his book *The Descent of Man,* Charles Darwin theorized that primitive people—or "savages," as he called them—do not and cannot envision a universal and benevolent creator. Schebesta's excellent study *Les Pygmées du Congo Belge* (Brussels, 1952) correctly explains that the religion of the Ituri Forest Pygmies is founded on the belief that "God possesses the totality of vital force, of which he distributes a part to his creatures, an act by which he brings them into existence or perfects them." There is nothing in the Old or New Testaments that equals this vision of the universal and benevolent creator. It approaches the definition of deity advanced by scientist Ernst Haeckel: "Our monistic God, the all-embracing essence of the world, the nature-god of Spinoza and Goethe, is identical with eternal, all-inspiring energy, and one, in eternal and infinite substance, with space-filling matter."

Scientists still accept or endorse the theory of religious evolution propounded by Darwin and his nineteenth-century colleagues. They maintained that religion evolved from primitive animism to fetishism to polytheism to the heights of civilized Judeo-Chris-

---

[7] Sir E. A. Wallis Budge, *The Egyptian Book of the Dead* (New York: Dover Publications, 1967), p. c.

tian monotheism. The Ituri Forest Pygmies are the most primitive living members of our species, yet far from being animistic, they pooh-pooh the local Negro tribes' fears of evil spirits. "If darkness is, darkness is good," according to a favorite Pygmy saying. "He who made the light also made the darkness." The Pygmies deplore as superstitious nonsense the Negroes' magico-religious figurines and other so-called fetishes. They would take an equally dim view of churchly huts adorned with doll-like statues of Jesus and Mary. This would be regarded as idol worship by the Ituri Forest Pygmies, who believe that the divine power of the universe cannot be confined within material bounds. The authors of the Hebrew Old Testament would certainly agree, since they observed the well-known commandment forbidding "graven images" or idols.

The missionary-anthropologist Father Henri Trilles wrote two very perceptive books, *Les Pygmées de la Forêt Equatoriale* and *L'Ame du Pygmée d'Afrique* ("The Soul of the African Pygmy"). He described the world's lowest technological primitives as people more religiously, morally and socially civilized than the Greeks, Romans, and other great nations of antiquity. Anthropologist Raoul Hartweg, who heads the Paris Museum of Man, has looked beyond the Pygmies' lack of gadgetry and praised their "civilization." In my book *Congo Kitabu*, I told of my experiences with "the most profoundly moral and religious people on the African continent," those same Ituri Forest Pygmies who had so favorably impressed Henry Stanley. Father Wilhelm Schmidt, one of the twentieth century's finest scholars, authored a monumental twelve-volume classic called *Der Ursprung der Gottesidee* ("The Origin of the Idea of God"). He interpreted the Pygmy people of the earth as the remnants of prediluvial humanity, the still-surviving ancestors of all the taller human races, and the founding fathers of monotheistic religion.

Schmidt was accused by fellow anthropologists of placing a "monotheistic halo" over the Pygmies' heads and of being "pro-Genesis." It was of course implied that his religious vocation had influenced his views. His critics apparently failed to realize that it is hardly orthodox theology to credit the Pygmies with having originated concepts that were merely echoed or inherited by Abraham, Isaac, Jacob, Joseph, Moses and a Galilean rabbi named Jesus. Since many secular investigators have relentlessly reported the proto-Biblical traditions of the Pygmies, such accusations are not only unfair but greatly hinder the advancement of knowledge. If the Pygmies are indeed responsible for the genesis of Genesis, we might well have to revise the less rational and beneficial features of organized religion.

In *Congo Kitabu* I wrote about the very strange "echoes of Genesis" I heard among the Efé Pygmies of the northeast Ituri. But I am neither a secret agent of the Vatican nor a sentimental philosopher riddled with romantic fallacies. During my eighteen years in Africa, I was a bush sociologist and agronomist for the former Belgian government of the Congo, Rwanda and Burundi. I worked with 650,000 African blacks of seventeen different tribes. I did everything from diagnosing plant diseases to delivering babies. I am the only white member of the Bwamé Secret Society, a fraternal organization of the Lega Negro tribe dwelling in the Maniema district of eastern Zaïre. I am an initiated warrior of Kenya's Nilo-Hamitic Masai tribe and a blood-brother of Rwanda's tall Tutsi or "Watusi." In 1955 I single-handedly set out to relieve a desperate famine among the pygmoid or part-Pygmy Mosso tribe of Burundi. I emerged from this episode single-handed after a dynamite explosion blew off my right hand just above the wrist. It was a very small price to pay for the lives of several hundred Mosso families.

In January of 1957 the Belgian administration stationed me at Mbau, near the eastern fringes of the Ituri Forest in the territory of Beni and the Congolese district of North Kivu. I left my post and walked into the tangled shadows of the Efé Pygmy territories— alone, unarmed, and without any equipment. For eighteen months, I lived in the eastern Ituri as an adopted member of Efé society— a 6 foot 5 inch Pygmy who at 240 pounds weighed almost as much as three full-grown Efé men. On June 26, 1957, I obtained an "emancipation proclamation" from the Nande Negro chieftains of Beni. It officially liberated every Pygmy in the territory from the bonds of feudal serfdom. An article on how these African Negroes freed their Pygmy serfs appeared in the American Negro magazine, *Sepia*.[8] Since another tall, bearded chap had been involved with another, more famous Emancipation Proclamation, the *Sepia* arti-

---

[8] *Sepia* (June 1965).

cle was much too generously entitled "The Abe Lincoln of the Congo."

During those eighteen months in the Ituri, I taught allegedly "unteachable" Pygmies how to read, write, do arithmetic, work metal, build houses and perform many other feats that would enable them to compete on a more even footing with the local Negro tribes. This work was hailed as an "ethnological revolution" by government authorities in Leopoldville (now Kinshasa). It was praised by INEAC, the National Institute for Agronomic Studies, as a "noble enterprise" and a "high humanitarian task." It was hailed in *La Presse Africaine* as "the most remarkable social achievement in recent years." It was bitterly opposed and gravely jeopardized by a misguided missionary sect, the Petites Soeurs de Jésus du Père de Foucauld.

The Little Sisters of Jesus were hellbent on clothing the little folks of the forest in garments that were much less practical than the Pygmies' traditional Ficus-bark loincloths. They distributed bras, shirts, pants, woolen baby sweaters, fedoras and so forth. In *Congo Kitabu* I wrote: "According to classic missionary traditions, clothing was supposed to make the Pygmies more 'decent' and 'moral'; instead it was constantly damp and dirty in the Grand Forest's moist heat, fostering germs and chilling the skin. The real effect, as in Polynesia and many other parts of the world, was simply to increase the incidence of pulmonary disorders."

The Little Sisters and I had many quarrels. The grand climax came when they denounced me for encouraging and even coercing the Pygmies to give indecent, degraded and shameless exhibitions. That was their interpretation of the dances which the Pygmies perform, both for pleasure and as an act of worship. My Efé friends explain that their dances please the deity: he watches from his great throne in heaven and is thereby inspired to sustain every living thing on our planet. Pharaoh Pepi I expressed the same theory, more than four thousand years ago, when he praised "the Pygmy who danceth like the god and who pleaseth the heart of the god before his great throne." The first Pygmy encountered by Georg Schweinfurth was a little gentleman named Adimokoo. He was a dancer at the royal court of King Munza, the ruler of the Ngbetu Negro tribe. The Pygmies cannot live without dancing, singing and making music. This is their greatest talent and their greatest joy. They dance through the oldest documents of Egypt's Old Kingdom. But I, Jean-Pierre Hallet, was formally accused in A.D. 1958 of "forcing the Pygmies to dance" and thereby encouraging indecency, immorality, evil, vice and so forth. The other charges included the very truthful allegation that I had made "disrespectful remarks about the missionary work accomplished by the Little Sisters of Father de Foucauld."

I could go on and on about the Little Sisters. They had, for example, a great social plan—to distribute knitting needles so that all the Pygmy residents of the equatorial forest could knit and wear highly moral woolen garments. But it should be evident that I have no interest in furthering the cause of "organized" religion. My Pygmy friends, whose religion I prefer, have never made a business out of God. They do not pass collection plates, collect tithes or sell papal indulgences. They have never fought religious wars over quibbling questions of theology. They do not attempt to convert other people to their own beliefs. They pray aloud to a heavenly deity whom they usually address by the rather familiar-sounding title "our Father." They claim to have personally received from this ostensibly barbaric deity a lofty moral code that forbids killing, lying, theft, blasphemy, adultery, devil worship or sorcery, disrespect toward old people, and other forms of antisocial or immoral behavior. Their laws are very similar to the celebrated statutes Charlton Heston brought down to a cast of thousands while Mount Sinai quaked in all its Technicolor glory. But the laws are much more faithfully observed in Pygmy society, in which there is no crime of any consequence and no war at all.

In commenting on the many parallels between Pygmy and Biblical tradition, Schebesta has repeatedly affirmed that the Pygmies "know nothing of the Bible or Christianity." The Little Sisters certainly could not have had any influence on the Pygmy religion. None of the nuns could speak more than two or three words of the Pygmies' language; their command of Kingwana, a very simple brand of Swahili spoken in eastern Zaïre, was limited to phrases used in giving orders to the houseboys. They simply puttered about on the edge of the forest, doling out brassieres and baby booties while they ranted about the Pygmies' immorality and the

Pygmies privately prayed to "our Father." After the tragic "Congo Disaster" of 1960, the Little Sisters departed; their establishment is now a patch of weeds and brush. The Pygmies, who never knew who or what the European women represented, sometimes speak wistfully of the tooth-rotting sugar and lung-eroding cigarettes that the Little Sisters charitably distributed. They find it difficult to understand, however, why such nice ladies kept magico-religious figurines in the manner of the Bantu.

It is quite impossible to use the hackneyed anthropological explanation that the Pygmy monotheistic belief must have been "borrowed from more advanced neighbors." In the Ituri Forest, the neighbors consist of Bantu and Sudanese tribes who invaded the forest during very recent times. These people are greatly advanced from a technological point of view. Their social and religious customs are equally "advanced" in the sense of being nonprimitive or even decadent.

The Budu tribe, in the Wamba area of the forest, have been credited with founding a modern Ituri institution known as the Anyoto Secret Society. It is not quite like the Elks Club or the Knights of Columbus. The Budu and other participating tribes usually stipulate that would-be members murder a close relative to fulfill the initiation requirements and become full-fledged Anyoto Leopard Men. They are then entitled to wear the society's leopard-skin regalia, practice the ritual murder of old men, women and children, ceremonially dine upon the severed breasts of female victims, and drink magical decoctions made from simmered human eyeballs. They are, however, very poorly qualified to diffuse Hebrewesque legends to the Ituri Forest Pygmies. They cannot be accused of teaching the Pygmies how to pray, since prayer is not a feature of Bantu religion. Trilles and Schebesta have both mentioned the prevalent Bantu belief that the Pygmies are "too stupid" to believe in the evil spirits, to practice sorcery, or to stage witch-hunting inquisitions and ordeals by poison, fire and water. The Negro tribes of the Ituri certainly do not try to take the credit for the Pygmies' belief that it is morally wrong to kill or even hurt a human being. According to the Pygmies' "more advanced" neighbors, this is childish nonsense.

The Aka Pygmies of the northwest Ituri have been forced into servitude by the Ngbetu, a people of Sudanese origin. Georg Schweinfurth described the nineteenth-century Ngbetu ruler, King Munza, as a "cannibal Caesar" who dined on one plump infant per day. Are the Ngbetu primitive? When Schweinfurth arrived in 1870, they had the most imposing technology to be found in all of equatorial Africa. The beautifully decorated Ngbetu houses and palaces—structures one hundred and fifty feet long with peaked roofs sixty feet high—have been praised as examples of almost monumental architecture. The royal court of their cannibal Caesar could easily compete for decadence and corruption with the establishments of Nero, Tiberius, and the other Caesars of Imperial Rome.

The Leopard Men, cannibals and company, do not behave in this manner because they are Negroes. The American Indians reached even greater heights (or depths) of civilized decadence in Mexico, where the Aztecs practiced human sacrifice and ritual cannibalism amid the architectural triumphs of their pyramid-sprouting cities. In the thirty-ninth chapter of *Germania,* Tacitus described the public human sacrifices performed by the immediate Caucasoid ancestors of Albert Schweitzer and Johann Sebastian Bach. The Greek historian and geographer Strabo told of how the northern European Cimbri tribe slit human throats and told fortunes from the blood they then collected in kettles. Only twenty-seven years ago, some "civilized" Europeans known as Nazis committed far more terrible atrocities, taking the lives of six million innocent human beings called Jews.

The Pygmies have no grand Ngbetu-style palaces and royal courts. They do not dwell in villages and tend plantations like the criminal members of the Leopard Man society. The temporary camps of the nomadic hunter-gatherers consist instead of flimsy little stick huts made of bent saplings thatched with leaves. Their architectural style should probably be described as neo-Australopithecine. Socially and morally, the Pygmies are just as "primitive" in the true, non-savage sense of a word derived from Latin *primus,* meaning "first" or "earliest." They do not indulge in cannibalism, human sacrifice, torture, mutilation, sorcery, ritual murder, intertribal war, initiation ordeals or any of the cruel customs that are associated with equatorial Africa.

Henri Trilles told of how Fang tribesmen in Gabon offered to supply his dinner table with some still-living Pygmy "meat." The cannibal Fang very humanely warned the appalled priest of the Holy Ghost Society that he might get a stomach ache from eating the meat—a tiny girl named Hummingbird Feather—since the "stinking little beasts of the forest" have a very rank smell and taste. Trilles rescued the kidnapped child and restored her to an overjoyed Pygmy family. In the Ituri Forest, Schweinfurth bought a Pygmy child at the court of King Munza. The little boy was convinced that the German explorer planned to eat him. Why else would anyone buy a Pygmy?

In Rwanda and Burundi there are pygmoid tribes known as the Twa and Mosso. These nonaggressive people were economically exploited and treated as social pariahs by the former lords of the land, the tall Tutsi or "Watusi" who are usually portrayed in tourist literature as "the Noble Giants of Rwanda." In *Congo Kitabu* I described some of the most aggressive customs that the not-so-noble giants practiced at the former royal court of Rwanda: "impalement on wooden stakes, drowning, dismemberment, blinding, scalping, bastinado, crucifixion, and amputation of hands, feet and genital organs." The Tutsi had made feudal-style vassals of the Hutu, a tribe of Bantu agriculturalists. A few years ago, the Hutu rose up against their masters. They massacred thousands of Tutsi amid hellish scenes of torture and mutilation. The Tutsi are now starting to regain their traditional status.* From the pygmoids' point of view, it matters little which side triumphs. The little folk have been degraded, humiliated and abused by both the Hutu vassals and Watusi overlords.

The Negro tribes of modern Black Africa are known in tourist-type literature as "the natives." But they are not "the natives"— they have the same relationship to the aboriginal Pygmies as the Yankee residents of the United States have to the Digger Indians. Would anyone compose a study of American prehistory that omitted any reference to the American Indian? Would anyone

---

* In May and June 1972, more than 100,000 Hutu from Burundi were slaughtered by the dominant Tutsi minority.

bring forth an "American Genesis" that portrayed the antics of Chicago gangsters, Las Vegas gamblers and Washington politicians as the primitive ancestral heritage of North America?

Yet the author of *African Genesis* depicts the very worst features of modern African culture as the built-in heritage bequeathed to every member of our species by the million-year-old African fossils. "The conscience I face in the African street bears no resemblance to my own," declares Robert Ardrey. "I am alone in the African street, lost, afraid, and without allies. I understand nothing. Yet this is the street where I was born. I too once delighted in massacre, slavery, castration, and cannibalism, and my conscience told me that these things were right."

I shall never forget the total lack of conscience displayed by captured Leopard Men awaiting trial for their crimes. One of them —a man who had murdered his sister and devoured selected portions of her body—explained that "If everyone thinks a leopard did it, the cat is guilty, not the man." I remember also how the ceremonial Tutsi drums at the former royal court of Rwanda were tastefully draped with the *ibikondo* or smoked testicles of enemies killed in battle and ceremonially castrated. Anthropologists do not, however, suggest that our species developed from the full-sized tribes of modern equatorial Africa. Since the Negro peoples of the area apparently originated elsewhere, it is particularly illogical to assume that Africa's fossil anthropoids behaved in the decadent manner of the Budu Leopard Men.

The Pygmies, on the other hand, belong to a racial stock that anthropologists Schmidt, Brynn, Kollman, Schebesta and company consider to be the oldest and ancestral form of *Homo sapiens*. Their conscience is embodied in their commandments and illustrated by their nonaggressive ways. The Bushmen are also ancestral candidates. They live in an equally peaceful, pleasant, and benevolent society. Elizabeth Marshall Thomas' very sympathetic book about the Bushmen, *The Harmless People*, sums up their peace-loving customs in its very title. Both Raymond Dart and zoologist Robert Broom represented the Bushmen and their Hottentot cousins as the immediate descendants of the Australopithecine fossils. The author of *African Genesis* hails Broom as "one of the world's great zoologists." He salutes Dart as a scientific hero who "made possible our present knowledge of human origins." But Robert Ardrey never discusses the people whom his own highly approved authorities described as the progeny of his own killer apes. Instead, in three mocking paragraphs, Mr. Ardrey dismisses the gentle little Bushmen and all of the other mild-mannered primitives with the blanket explanation that they "quite possibly suffer from nonaggressive dispositions."

Today, in 1973 A.D., hunter-gatherers like the Bushmen and the Pygmies represent 0.001 percent of the three and a half billion people who crowd our tortured planet. It has been estimated that back in 10,000 B.C., 100 percent of the earth's ten million people were hunter-gatherers.[9] Their original ancestors are believed to have been hunter-gatherer apes who originated on the African continent. One can easily conceive of the Pygmies' prehuman ancestors as good-natured anthropoids who used their highly intelligent brains to hunt rather than to prey upon the fauna. But it is very difficult to picture the Pygmies as descendants of Mr. Ardrey's "primate carnivore." No matter how hungry they are, the Pygmy hunters bring the game back to camp where it is divided up among the members of the band. This is one of the laws that the deity gave to his Ituri Forest congregation. The meat is not eaten until the Pygmies say their version of grace: a brief prayer is intoned while a little tidbit of meat is either tossed into the air (toward heaven, the traditional home of "our Father") or wrapped in a leaf and placed in the fork of a tree (an act which also raises the offering from the earth). This gesture of thanks lets the deity know that the Pygmies do not take the food and his other blessings for granted. (Unfortunately, this practice is nearly lost today.)

These very decent, even genteel customs have been mentioned in many scientific studies of the Pygmies. They are established facts. The customs of the killer apes who wend their bloody way through the pages of *African Genesis* are entirely conjectural. There is nothing sadder, T. H. Huxley once remarked, than the encounter of a beautiful theory and an ugly little fact. Here we have a very ugly theory that dares not risk an encounter with those

---

[9] John E. Pfeiffer, *The Emergence of Man* (New York: Harper & Row, 1969), p. 311.

beautiful little facts, the Pygmies. Before any judgment is passed convicting us of being "Cain's children," we are at least entitled to be informed of the evidence *for* as well as against us.

"Is there a 'killer instinct' in man—an instinct less controlled than in the most savage of animals?" asks the back-cover blurb of Konrad Lorenz' book *On Aggression*. The blurb goes on to answer this rhetorical question: "Yes, says famed scientist Konrad Lorenz, in shedding revolutionary new light on the aggressive drive held in common by both man and beast . . ." During the light-shedding process, Mr. Lorenz tells us all about the aggressive behavior of the blue triggerfish, the mandarin duck, the brown rat, the emerald lizard and a variety of other animals, including his "bitch Stasi, a Chow-Alsatian hybrid." He does not tell us anything about the Pygmies, the Bushmen or any of the nonaggressive primitives who might be able to shed a little more light on the question of man's "killer instinct" than the creature Lorenz calls "the fiercest of all the fierce territory owners"—a coral-reef fish called the sharp-toothed Abudefduf.

Primitive man is equally conspicuous by his absence from *The Naked Ape,* another sensational best seller about the origin and primitive character of man. Apparently to explain why he does not discuss the living primitives, zoologist Desmond Morris repeatedly declares that all of "the simple tribal groups" are backward, stultified and unsuccessful. Those arch-primitives, the Pygmies, are such simple folks that they do not even form tribal groups. They traditionally live in nomadic bands of five or six families. There are no Pygmy chiefs or priests. The sole civic and religious authorities are paternalistic elders. The elders have no pomp or despotic privilege. They are just old folks whose experience and knowledge are respected by the younger generation.

The Pygmy men hunt small game. They are very clever bow-and-arrow hunters who take so much pride in their skill that they refuse to use traps or snares. The women keep house and gather fruits, nuts, vegetables, roots and other edibles. They are completely devoted to their children, unlike the liberated ladies of the Western world whose offspring shuttle back and forth to Juvenile Hall. People do as little work as possible, since it is much more enjoyable to dance, sing, make music, and engage in all kinds of sports, games and diversions. Their dancing also inspires the deity, of course, to sustain the human, animal and plant life of the earth. As an agronomist, I suspect that he has also appreciated the simple fact that the Pygmies do not abuse or unbalance the ecology of their environment.

Is this way of life successful?

The Pygmies have proved that it is. They are the oldest people in recorded history, as well as the smallest and most "primitive." They were around before the founding of dynastic Egypt, roughly 5,200 years ago, and they have already outlasted, in their pure state, their Pharaonic admirers by a couple of thousand years. Relative moderns like the Babylonians, Persians, Cambodians, Romans and Mayans have arisen, had their little fling, declined, and fallen into dust. One very reasonable theory suggests that many of the great empires "farmed themselves out of existence" by overcultivating, overgrazing and exhausting the land in order to support the populations of their packed and pestilence-ridden cities. None of them, however, raped the earth as drastically as that smog-and-garbage-belching juggernaut, modern industrial society. It threatens to be so unsuccessful that none of us may survive it— even if we manage to refrain from pushing the little red buttons that will detonate the intercontinental missiles and the hydrogen bombs. The Stockholm International Peace Research Institute recently announced that the world nuclear stockpile amounts to about 50,000 megatons and represents the equivalent of "about fifteen tons of T.N.T. per person on the globe." Since each Pygmy person is so very small, he or she can be blown to bits with less explosive material than is needed to destroy a full-sized human being. The civilized world therefore possesses slightly greater powers of overkill than our clever scientists suspected.

Sir Grafton Elliot Smith, who studied the gentle primitives of the earth, told the tragic truth when he wrote, "It is important to recognize that instead of bringing enlightenment and appeasement, civilization is responsible for most cruelties and barbarities." Robert Ardrey deplores what he calls the total error of Smith's premises. If we repudiate the theory of innate aggressiveness, Mr. Ardrey declares, "our wars and our atrocities, our crimes and our quarrels, our tyrannies and our injustices could be ascribed to nothing other than singular human achievement. And we should be left with a clear-cut portrait of man as a degenerate creature endowed at birth with virtue's treasury whose only notable talent has been his capacity to squander it."

We should also be left with the moral responsibility for our wars and our atrocities. They can only be eradicated by taking appropriate social measures, not by blaming them on the hypothetical antics of ancient fossil bones that may or may not represent direct human ancestors. "But we were born of risen apes, not fallen angels," cries Mr. Ardrey, "and the apes were armed killers besides." The living African apes are shy and nonaggressive creatures. They do not recognize the Ardrey-styled "territorial imperative" that reputedly drove our apish ancestors to commit acts of mayhem and murder. The mostly Pygmy-sized Australopithecines fall considerably short of the King-Kong image Mr. Ardrey so vividly evokes. *Homo habilis* conjures up the rather pathetic vision of an armed killer thirty-six inches tall. It is rather difficult to imagine "the little chap"—as Dr. Leakey calls him—terrorizing Olduvai Gorge in the style of a simian Humphrey Bogart armed with a bone club instead of a machine gun.

Mr. Ardrey says that the ancestral weapons were not only used to procure meat but were absolutely essential for the survival of our African forefathers. He gives a thrilling description of prowling lions and leopards, implies that they are a constant menace, and dramatically inquires: "How would you have survived, O Adam, without fangs or claws or motor cars, without pointed horns or leather hide, or a snout to sniff with or feet to climb with, without even petrol to camouflage your smell—how could you have survived, O most vulnerable primate, tuskless in Paradise, had you not been created with a weapon in your hand?"[10]

In *Congo Kitabu* I told of how a tuskless, one-handed primate named Jean-Pierre Hallet was gathering mushrooms with a troop of Pygmy housewives when he unexpectedly encountered and chased away a full-grown African leopard. How? I took a menacing step forward, shook my basket of mushrooms at the crouching cat, and shouted at him, "Grandpa, get lost!" This was a somewhat

---

[10] Robert Ardrey, *African Genesis*, p. 284.

idiomatic translation of the traditional Efé leopard-chasing cry, "*Otu, ogo!*"—"Grandpa, go away!"—that has also been mentioned in Schebesta's studies of the Ituri Forest Pygmies. In his *Book of Great Jungles,* naturalist Ivan Sanderson describes his use of very similar tactics to dispose of prowling carnivores: "To all of these creatures I simply said something like 'Boo!' in a very loud and peremptory manner and they shoved off at the double . . . As a matter of fact, after nearly forty years of meandering about jungles under the most vulnerable conditions . . . I have yet to be actually jumped by anything larger than an ant."

Mr. Ardrey remarks that his "vulnerable primate" was unable to camouflage his ostensibly attractive and appetizing smell. Dr. Leakey and I have both explained that most carnivores dislike the smell and taste of ape and human flesh. It may be disconcerting, but it seems rather likely that the ancestral primates' survival was greatly aided by their chronic B.O. This is less melodramatic but much more plausible than Mr. Ardrey's claim that our pint-sized ancestors survived by battling leopards and packs of four hundred-pound African lions with a little bone club. I would never attempt such a feat although I am nearly twice as tall as *Homo habilis* and probably outweigh him five to one. Unfortunately, Mr. Ardrey has not offered to give a personal demonstration of the fighting tactics used by his Australopithecine Adam.

My Pygmy friends have an Adam story of their own. Schebesta has told this tale and emphasized that the Pygmies could not possibly have borrowed it from any outside source. It is the story of a god, a garden paradise, a sacred tree, a noble Pygmy man who was molded from the dust of the earth, and a wicked Pygmy woman who led him into sin. The bizarre and intricate details include the deity's instructions that the first-created Pygmies multiply or populate the forest with their progeny. The legend tells of the ban placed by God upon a single fruit, the woman's urging, the man's reluctance, the original sin, the discovery by God, and the awful punishments he laid upon the ancient Pygmy sinners: the loss of immortality and paradise, the pangs of childbirth, and the curse of hard work.

This is the African Pygmies' very own version of "African Genesis." A popular anthology of African folklore has described it as "an interesting African analogue" to the pre-Ardrey or Biblical version of Genesis. The Israelites brought their mirror-image story of Adam, Eve and the fatal fruit out of an African country named Egypt, where the Pygmies danced for the Pharaohs more than a thousand years before 1500 to 1200 B.C., the much-disputed date or period that is generally assigned to Moses and the exodus from Egypt.

The Old Testament tale of Adam and Eve has rightly been described as "the most influential myth or legend in the history of man." Far from being a dead issue, it is currently involved in the tragicomic drama of the Pope, the Pill and the Population Explosion that threatens to Polish off our Planet. The current edition of the *Encyclopaedia Britannica* says that this "distinctively Israelite" creation story was "unparalleled in the ancient world." The Efé Pygmy legend of the original sin has no parallel among the more than six hundred Negro tribes who currently inhabit Zaïre. It apparently dates back to the old pre-Negro Africa that was tenanted, according to the fossil evidence, by Caucasoid and Pygmy-like peoples.

For thousands of years the Caucasoid peoples known as Egyptians, Hebrews and Arabs maintained a shared tradition concerning the site of the earthly paradise or so-called Garden of Eden where the human species anciently originated. Since these legends set the opening scenes of Genesis in the land of "African Genesis," we shall inspect them in detail before proceeding to the complete Pygmy story of "man's first disobedience and the fruit of that forbidden tree whose mortal taste brought death into the world and all our woe," according to the opening lines of *Paradise Lost*.

John Milton's epic poem was based on a book called the Bible. This name is derived from the Greek word *biblíon*, book. In Arabic, the Bible and the Koran are both referred to as "the book," *el-kitab*. In the part-Arabic lingua franca Swahili, a book is known as a *kitabu*, and thus *Pygmy Kitabu* means "Pygmy Book" or, very aptly, "Pygmy Bible."

The Garden of the Gods

In the Old Kingdom of Egypt, at the dawn of African history, people cherished an already ancient tradition that the holy River Nile "flowed out of heaven" or emanated from the earthly paradise of the ancestors. Commented Sir E. A. Wallis Budge, in *The Egyptian Book of the Dead:* "From the earliest days they depicted to themselves a material heaven wherein the Isles of the Blest were laved by the waters of the Nile, and the approach to which was by way of its stream as it flowed to the north . . ."[1]

The Egyptians belonged to the so-called white or Caucasoid branch of mankind. Many ancient Caucasoid remains have been found in equatorial Africa, near the great lakes that send the

---

[1] Sir E. A. Wallis Budge, *The Egyptian Book of the Dead,* p. cxxiii.

waters of the Nile surging northward. The Egyptians placed the legendary land of their ancestors in this region. In *The Prehistory of East Africa* Sonia Cole remarks that the Caucasoid or Mediterranean stock "is apparently of very ancient origin in East Africa. There are two alternative theories as to their origin: one that they arose in Africa, the other that they came across the Red Sea area from Arabia, giving rise to the present Hamitic tribes. Hamitic languages to-day are spoken by people spread over about one-fifth of Africa. The people are divided into two groups: the Northern Hamites, including the Berbers and Tuareg, and the Eastern Hamites of the Horn, including the Galla and Somali. The Egyptians, too, belong to this stock."[2]

The Hamitic tongues are now regarded as a subdivision of the Semitic language family that includes Arabic and Hebrew. In the Hebrew language of the Old Testament, the Nile was sometimes called Gihon. Genesis 2:13 makes the quasi-Egyptian declaration that the holy river Gihon–Nile flowed out of the earthly paradise or so-called Garden of Eden in which the ancestral humans originated. In *Moses and Monotheism*, Sigmund Freud theorized that Moses, the traditional author of Genesis, was an Egyptian who brought from his native country the religion he gave to the Jews.[3] The text of Moses' book of Exodus describes him as a castaway Hebrew babe who was found by an unnamed daughter of Pharaoh in a little bulrush ark that came floating down the Nile. Genesis maintains that the paradisaical Gihon–Nile encompassed "the whole land of Ethiopia." Some modern Ethiopians still call the Nile by the only slightly altered name Gejon.

The legends of the Arabs strongly support the theory that the Caucasoid stock arose in Africa. An Arabic manuscript dated 1686 A.D. quotes the pertinent opinion of Islam's highest religious authority: "Mohammed, the Prophet of God, says: 'The Nile comes out of the Garden of Paradise, and if you were to examine it when it comes out, you would find in it leaves of Paradise.'" Many centuries before that, Arab geographers had correctly explained that

---

[2] Cole, *The Prehistory of East Africa*, p. 113.

[3] Sigmund Freud, *Moses and Monotheism* (New York: Vintage paperback, 1939).

the thrice-holy River Nile flows northward from several great lakes that are fed by the melting snows and swift-running streams of a towering mountain range, Jebel Kamar or "the Mountain of the Moon." On the border between Zaïre and Uganda, those fabulous-sounding peaks, the Mountains of the Moon, still tower far above the earth. Melting snows and streams flowing down from the peaks feed the Semliki River, Lake Edward, Lake Albert, and the emerging Albertine Nile. Farther to the east, the Victorine Nile flows northward from the enormous basin that the Arabs called *el-jamia* or "the collector"—Victoria, the largest lake in Africa. According to the Arab sages, the site of Eden lay in the immediate neighborhood of the sacred Central African mountains that feed the lakes of the Nile.

"The home of our fathers was that African highland reaching north from the Cape to the Lakes of the Nile," Robert Ardrey announced in the opening paragraph of *African Genesis*. This thesis is supposed to be irrevocably opposed to the old historico-religious legends on the origin of man. Ironically, however, every pious Jew, Christian and Mohammedan is committed to the belief that the "home of our fathers" was located near the Central African source of the Nile, in the very region where modern scientists say that mankind originated. The Biblical description of the paradisaical waters has baffled and confused generations of scholars. Here it is in its enigmatic entirety:

> And a river went out of Eden to water the garden; and from thence it was parted, and became into four heads.
>
> The name of the first is Pison: that is it which compasseth the whole land of Havilah, where there is gold.
>
> And the gold of that land is good: there is bdellium and the onyx stone.
>
> And the name of the second river is Gihon: the same is it that compasseth the whole land of Ethiopia.
>
> And the name of the third river is Hiddekel: that is it which goeth toward the east of Assyria. And the fourth river is Euphrates.[4]

The Euphrates rises in the eastern part of Turkey. The river that "goeth toward the east of Assyria" is usually interpreted as

---

[4] Genesis 2:10–14.

the Tigris. Yet the Arab geographers, who had a remarkably accurate knowledge of Central Africa, claimed that *all* of the paradisaical rivers rose from the heart of Africa. Through the ages, a galaxy of tortured theories has been offered to explain the impossible pathways taken by the Biblical waters. To the best of my knowledge, no one has proposed a very simple solution.

People have a penchant for naming rivers, mountains, towns and other geographical features after older or more famous equivalents. The River Thames, for example, simultaneously streams through England and Connecticut. The Avon flows through England and Australia. The United States has towns called Athens, Rome, Babylon and Nineveh. Could the authors of the Bible have possibly shared this very human propensity? *Langenscheidt's Pocket Hebrew Dictionary to the Old Testament* gives Gihon or Gichon as a proper name of the Nile, a river in Paradise, or a fountain west of Jerusalem. In all probability the Israelites who settled in the Promised Land of Canaan named any number of fountains, streams and rivers in honor of the paradisaical waterways.

The older Egyptian tradition states very simply that the earthly paradise lay at the source of the Nile. The Arab geographers say that the Gihon and the Euphrates both flowed from the region of the great African lakes, whence the Albertine Nile, the Victorine Nile and other tributary rivers still flow today. Could the original Euphrates have been a strictly African branch of the Nile? Why not? That little fountain near Jerusalem was named after the mighty Gihon–Nile. Similarly, a Middle Eastern stream called the Euphrates might have been christened after a branch or tributary of the African waters that comprise the longest river in the world. By the time the first historically authenticated Biblical texts were put on paper—around the sixth century B.C.—the legendary rivers of paradise could have easily been confused with neologistic Middle Eastern counterparts.

According to Genesis, in the ancient land of paradise, the deity planted a remarkable *ya'ar* or Hebrew-styled forest that is also known as Gan Eden (the Garden of Eden). Biblical scholars have attempted to derive this story from one of the world's oldest written documents, the Epic of Gilgamesh, which dates back to the fourth millennium B.C. Its authors, a Mesopotamian people called Sumerians, spoke a language of still unknown affinities. Their description of the primordial paradise features a "great waterway" or river, a forest and, in the center of the forest, a holy mountain which serves as the seat of the gods. The Arabic legends of the ancestral garden-forest identify the mountain of paradise with Jebel Kamar—the central African "Mountain of the Moon" at the source of the River Nile.

The highly volcanic geology of this region offers a rational explanation for the seemingly irrational geology of man's oldest, most important legends. The Mosaic scriptures, for example, rumble with overtly volcanic phenomena. Sigmund Freud maintained that "Jahve [Jehovah] was certainly a volcano-god. As we know, however, Egypt has no volcanoes and the mountains of the Sinai peninsula have never been volcanic; on the other hand, volcanoes which may have been active up to a late period are found along the western border of Arabia."[5] The Sumerian hero Gilgamesh had a terrifying dream or vision of erupting volcanoes when he lay down to sleep in the forest of the holy mountain. Translator N. K. Sandars explains, "A geological fault runs across Anatolia and through Armenia, and volcanoes may still have been active as late as the third millennium B.C., a fact which adds interest to the accurate description of a volcano in eruption which is contained in one of the dreams which come to Gilgamesh on the Cedar Mountain."[6]

The critics of the Sumerian and Hebrew epics rather desperately search for volcanoes that "may have been active" during the lifetime of man. If one accepts the anthropological theory that the Caucasoid stock arose in Africa and the Egyptian/Hebrew/Arabic tradition that the ancestral paradise lay at the source of the Nile, there is no shortage of unquestionably active volcanoes. Ever since modern explorers first entered the area of the Nile basin, two of the eight giant Virunga volcanoes have rumbled, smoked and vomited fiery lava. Nyamlagira erupted, on a minor scale, in 1958. Nyira-

---

[5] Sigmund Freud, *Moses and Monotheism*, p. 39.

[6] N. K. Sandars, *The Epic of Gilgamesh: An English Version* (Baltimore: Penguin Books, 1962), p. 32.

gongo sounded off in 1948.* According to geological estimates, approximately ten thousand years ago the Virungas erupted in a Krakatoa-like cataclysm which might well have inspired Gilgamesh to say, while describing his volcanic dream, that "all was turned to ashes fallen about us."

The Virungas rear their smoking cones about one hundred and twenty-five miles from the Mountains of the Moon and the emerging Albertine Nile. In this region, said the Egyptians, lay the earthly paradise of the ancestors. The book of Genesis maintains that a paradisaical forest or *ya'ar* was located at or near the source of the Nile. Did the Egyptians know of any such forest? They not only were aware of it, but also had correctly identified its residents. The old pyramid texts sometimes call these people by the rather long-winded epithet "the little men from the land of trees and spirits at the foot of the mountains of the moon." These "little men" or Pygmies still reside in the grand Ituri Forest—the "land of trees and spirits"—that is bordered on its eastern edge by the snow-capped, glacier-crowned Mountains of the Moon.

Near the northern fringes of this forest, there is a stone monument called the Pavement of Api. Some investigators argue that this so-called pavement is actually the foundation masonry of an Egyptian pyramid. In his book *Matériaux pour Servir à l'Etude de la Préhistoire de l'Uele*, Pierre Le Roy discussed this monument and the possibility that a very early Egyptian civilization flourished near the source of the Nile. Sir E. A. Wallis Budge tells us that the Egyptians "lived in imagination on the banks of the heavenly Nile, whereon they built cities." Real, not imaginary, figurines of the Egyptian god Osiris have been unearthed in present-day Zaïre. There is no telling how much precious evidence may have been obliterated when the giant Virunga volcanoes staged their Krakatoa-like eruption.

Up until a few centuries ago, the aboriginal Pygmies were the only known human residents of the equatorial forest that surrounds the Nile-spouting lakes near the Mountains of the Moon. In the past, the equatorial forest belt covered much of East Africa. A

---

* The latest eruption occurred in April 1971, forming the Shabembe, Nyamlagira's new secondary crater.

pygmoid or part-Pygmy tribe called the Dorobo or "Wanderobo" still dwell in sections of Kenya and Tanzania near Lake Victoria. "The home of our fathers was the African highland reaching north from the Cape to the lakes of the Nile," said Robert Ardrey. One of the oldest legends of this land is the great Masai creation epic "Nai-teru-Kop" (the Beginner of the Earth). Unlike Mr. Ardrey, the Masai do not exclude the Pygmies from their traditional account of man's beginning. They instead represent the Dorobo as the first, oldest, or original human race.

The part-Caucasoid Masai speak a Nilo-Hamitic language related to Egyptian and Hebrew. In his introduction to A. C. Hollis' classic work *The Masai*, Sir Charles Eliot remarked: "The traditions reported by Mr. Hollis (p. 264, etc.) seem to place the earliest history of the world in an East African setting, and convey no hint of an earlier home . . . A very different view of the past of the Masai is suggested by Merker's recent work (*Die Masai*, Berlin, 1904). He regards them as belonging to the same stock as the ancient Hebrews, and quotes a great number of traditions respecting the creation, deluge, ten commandments, etc. which resemble the Biblical and Babylonian versions of primitive history . . ."[7]

If the ancestors of the Egyptians, Hebrews, Arabs, Babylonians and other members of the Hamitic/Semitic stock originally "arose in Africa," there is no conflict or paradox in the Masai legends that simultaneously evoke Biblical counterparts and "place the earliest history of the world in an East African setting." This would also explain the quasi-Biblical traditions of the Pygmy people whom the Masai think of as the first or ancestral human race, and whom Father Wilhelm Schmidt saw as the racial and religious ancestors of mankind. The volcanic blasts of Mosaic scripture and the ash-strewn precincts of the Sumerian forest paradise support this proposition by describing geological phenomena that are typical of equatorial Africa, not the Middle East. Such legends rather strongly hint that the ancestors of the Hamitic/Semitic tribes originally came across the Red Sea area from Africa to Arabia, not from Arabia to Africa. The shared

---

[7] A. C. Hollis, *The Masai: Their Language and Folklore* (Oxford: Clarendon Press, 1905), p. xiii.

Egyptian/Hebraic/Arabic tradition that the River Nile flowed out of the earthly paradise points to an ancient African, not a Middle Eastern, homeland.

The members of the Hamitic/Semitic language family belong to the same racial stock as the Caucasoid peoples of Europe. The anthropological theory that the Caucasoids arose in Africa naturally implies that the people known as Aryans or Indo-Europeans ultimately sprang, like their Hamitic/Semitic cousins, from an Old White Africa that flourished long before the enigmatic coming of the Negro. By no coincidence, the ancient Indo-European tribes echoed the Hebrew book of Genesis in their remarkable legends of the ancestors' long-lost paradise.

Lewis Spence's *Dictionary of Non-Classical Mythology* suggests that the Eden-like residence of Indra, the king of the old Hindu gods, represents "perhaps the home whence the Indo-Aryans originally migrated." In this grand old Aryan homeland grew a lush and lovely garden. In this garden grew a very sacred tree, the *parijata* or "tree of heaven." Like the sacred tree of Hebrew and Pygmy legend, it was sinfully despoiled. Like the originally virtuous man of Hebrew and Pygmy legend, a Hindu hero named Krishna did the deed at the instigation of his wife.

According to the Hindu tale, Krishna stole the tree of heaven from the garden of the gods. An old Irish legend explains that some ancient Celtic ancestors known as the Sons of Tuireann sinfully stole the fruit of a sacred or forbidden tree. The Norse *Edda* tells us that the sacred fruit of the gods, the golden apples of immortality, were sinfully stolen by a pair of conspirators named Loki and Thiazi. In Greco-Roman legend, the golden apples were stolen by another pair of conspirators, Hercules and Atlas, from a sacred tree that grew in the famous Garden of Hesperides.

The Hebrew paradise is called the Garden of Apples in the Talmud. The stolen fruit of Genesis is traditionally associated with the Adam's apple that is still lodged in Everyman's throat. The fascinating flora of Genesis' garden forest included a tree of life whose fruit had the power to confer immortality. To steal the apples, Hercules had to embark on a long voyage to the Garden of Hesperides, located "on the borders of Ocean." To procure the magic plant of immortality, the Sumerian hero Gilgamesh voyaged to the "garden of the gods" or the "sun's garden by the shores of Ocean." This establishment, translator Sandars explains, is somehow related to the forest of the great waterway and the godly mountain throne where Gilgamesh dreamed an "accurate description of a volcano in eruption." Our Egyptian/Hebraic/Arabic tradition situates the ancestral paradise at the volcano-ridden source of the Nile. Now, how can a Central African garden possibly be reconciled with a garden on the shores or border of Ocean?

Here is a map of Africa as it was seen in Homer's day that was reproduced in Stanley's book *In Darkest Africa*. It shows the geographical concepts that were current around the eighth or ninth century B.C.

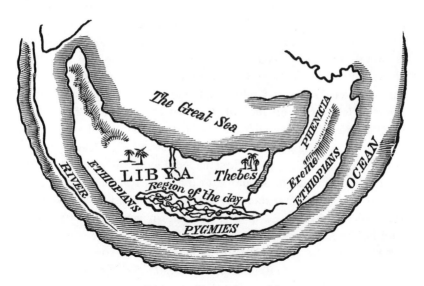

Africa in Homer's world

The Nile flows northward to the Great Sea or Mediterranean from its source in the greatly enlarged and distorted Mountains of the Moon. Beside the mountains dwell the ancient people Homer called *Oi Pygmaioi*, "the Pygmies," in the third book of his *Iliad*. Egyptian texts agree that some very small men inhabited the forested "land of trees and spirits at the foot of the mountains of the moon." In the Pygmy language of the eastern Ituri, the magnificent massif is called Baba Tiba, the Mountain of the Moon. The Pygmies are of course unacquainted with the Arabic name of Jebel Kamar, the Mountain of the Moon, and the Latin title that classical geographers used to designate the legendary Central African summits—Montes Lunae, the Mountain or Mountains of the Moon. On May 24, 1888, Henry Stanley rediscovered the fabulous-sounding lunar mountains of the ancients. He popularized a strictly local Negro name for the mist-shrouded mountains, Ruwenzori (Rainmaker). The name Ruwenzori is now used in most of our modern atlases and almanacs. To those still-surviving ancients, the Pygmies, the name remains Mountain of the Moon.

According to the Homeric map of Africa, immediately south of the Pygmies and their lunar mountains the Great Stream or River of Ocean curves around the much-truncated continent of Africa. Here, and only here, could the legendary land of paradise be simultaneously placed at the source of the Nile and the shore or border of the ocean. The ancient usage of the Greek word *okeanos*, "ocean," sheds additional light. It was mentioned in a French dissertation on the Nile, written by the Prior of Neuville-les-Dames et de Prévessin. He explained, "The Nile has changed its name, according to the times and places . . . Hesychius pretends that the Nile was at first called Egypt, and that it is this river which has given its name to the country . . . Egypt, nevertheless, is not the first name under which it was known; before it was called Oceanus . . . finally, it is known now by the Greeks as well as the Latins by the name of Nile."[8] Whichever way one interprets *okeanos*, as the ocean or the Nile, it is irrevocably associated with the Greco-Roman paradise near the borders of ocean, the Sumerian paradise on the shores of ocean, and the Hebrew/Arabic/Egyptian paradise at the source of the Nile.

The Prior's dissertation further remarks on the controversial river that the Hebrews called Gihon: "The Bishop of Avranches supports, in his 'Treatise of the Terrestrial Paradise,' that the Gihon is an easterly branch of the Euphrates, which flows from the country of Eden and passes along the country of Chus, now the

---

[8] Henry M. Stanley, *In Darkest Africa* (New York: Charles Scribner's Sons, 1890), p. 303.

Cheez-eslam. He adds that Homer makes out that it descends from Jupiter, and calls it Δητετῆ; this is what has caused Plautus to say, in speaking of a river, which he does not name, that it has its source in heaven and under the throne of Jupiter . . ."[9]

The throne of Zeus/Jupiter was traditionally situated on Mount Olympus, that lofty region which the Greeks and Romans portrayed as the home or seat of the gods. In Plato's dialogue *Timaeus* we are told that the residence of Zeus was located "at the center of the world." The Hindu version of this concept, or the so-called Indian Olympus, identifies the godly seat with a legendary mountain called Meru situated "at the center of the earth." This was the residence of Indra, the king of the gods, whose sacred tree was stolen from the paradisaical garden. The Babylonians told of a holy mountain ruled by Ishtar, the queen of the gods. The Sumerians informed us that this mountain throne or "seat of the gods" rose from the middle of the forested paradise in which Gilgamesh had his nightmare of erupting volcanoes. Now, is there any mountain that simultaneously satisfies the unique geographical and geological requirements of the lost paradise?

The waters of the Albertine Nile descend from and flow beneath the Mountains of the Moon, just like the Greco-Roman Nile that descended from Olympian Zeus/Jupiter and flowed beneath his throne. The mountains are situated almost directly on the equator, which might well be described as "the center of the earth." The remarkable knowledge of the ancient sages and their anticipation of many of our modern scientific "discoveries" easily justify this interpretation. Around 250 B.C. a Greek scientist named Eratosthenes measured the circumference of the earth. Aristarchus (c. 270 B.C.) maintained that the earth revolves around the sun. Pythagoras (c. 532 B.C.) asserted that the earth is spherical in form. A prehistoric poet named Homer (estimated dates range between 685 and 1159 B.C.) casually sang of the Pygmies whom Georg Schweinfurth "discovered" in 1870 A.D. Ancient geographers just as casually described the lunar mountains that Stanley rediscovered in 1888. He modestly remarked

[9] *Ibid.*, p. 302.

that as far as geographical knowledge is concerned, we moderns "have not much to boast of."

The mountains at the equatorial center of the earth rise from the very center of the African continent and from what once was the heart of an equatorial forest belt stretching from the west to the east coast of Africa. The mountainous Sumerian seat of the gods rose from the center of the forest in which Gilgamesh dreamed of those volcanic blasts. In the lush forest that adorns the foothills and lower slopes of the lunar mountains, one's repose might be seriously disturbed by the Virunga volcanoes. The Arabic legends state openly that the ancestral forest garden was located in the central African neighborhood of the lunar mountains and Nile-feeding lakes.

A remarkably fine drawing and description of the region appear in Stanley's pioneering book *In Darkest Africa*. West of the glacier-capped massif lies the dark expanse of the Ituri Forest. East of the lunar mountains lie a pair of apparently extinct Ugandan volcanoes. One hundred and twenty-five miles to the south, and not shown in this picture, are the eight giant cones and several hundred smaller craters of the menacing Virunga group.

> After the stories of the days of old, let us proceed to depict the Ruwenzori range—which is the modern African term among the principal tribes of the Lake regions for what was called Montes Lunae or Mons Lune by the classical and European geographers, and by the Arab compilers of travels as Jebel Kumr—Gumr, or Kammar—the Mountains of the Moon—as it was seen by us.
>
> The average European reader will perfectly understand the character of the Semliki Valley and the flanking ranges, if I were to say that its average breadth is about the distance from Dover to Calais, and that in length it would cover the distance between Dover and Plymouth, or from Dunkirk to St. Malo in France. For the English side we have the Balegga hills and rolling plateau from 3,000 to 3,500 feet above the valley. On the opposite side we have heights ranging from 3,000 to 15,500 feet above it. Now, Ruwenzori occupies about ninety miles of the eastern line of mountains, and projects like an enormous bastion of an unconquerable fortress, commanding on the north-east the approaches by the Albert Nyanza and Semliki Valley, and on its southern side the whole basin

The Mountains of the Moon: Bird's-eye view of Ruwenzori, Lake Albert Edward and Lake Albert

of the Albert Edward Lake. To a passenger on board one of the Lake Albert steamers proceeding south, this great bastion, on a clear day, would seem to be a range running east and west; to a traveller from the south it would appear as barring all passage north. To one looking at it from the Balegga, or western plateau, it would appear as if the slowly rising table-land of Unyoro was but the glacis of the mountain range. Its western face appears to be so precipitous as to be unscaleable, and its southern side to be a series of traverses and ridges descending one below the other to the Albert Edward Lake. While its eastern face presents a rugged and more broken aspect, lesser bastions project out of the range, and is further defended by isolated outlying forts like Gordon Bennett Mountain, 14,000 to 15,000 feet high, and the Mackinnon Mountain of similar height. That would be a fair figurative description of Ruwenzori.

The principal drainage of the snowy range is to the west, down into the Semliki River, and south to the Albert Edward Lake. The Katonga flowing into Lake Victoria, and the Kafur into the Victoria Nile, are both fed from the eastern face of Ruwenzori. The Mississi

River, emptying into Lake Albert direct, rises from the northern extremity of the mountains.[10]

The Old Testament repeatedly mentions a sacred mountain or "Rock of Israel" associated with the kind of pyrotechnic phenomena that led Sigmund Freud to describe Jehovah as the volcano god of some very puny little craters in Arabia that might have been active during geologically recent times. Since Freud was attempting to derive Jewish monotheism from the religion of Egypt, he might at least have investigated the Egyptians' own opinion about the site of the deity's mountain throne.

The only Egyptian deity who was ever called by the simple name God (*neter*) was the Christ-like Osiris. Egyptian texts describe him as "the god of gods, the king of kings, the lord of lords, the prince of princes, the governor of the world . . . the only one, the lord of the land on each side of the celestial Nile." His great throne in the Other World was traditionally located above "a lake of water" and near "a lake of fire." From its exalted heights, he was able to observe "the Pygmy who danceth like the god and who pleaseth the heart of the god before his great throne." This very pleasing view is still available at the source of the celestial Nile from the top of the throne-like lunar mountains that rise above the waters of Lakes Albert and Edward. A lake of boiling lava or volcanic fire seethes in the crater of Nyiragongo.

Several anthropologists have mentioned the African Pygmies' still-current and widely spread belief that from his great throne in the clouds the deity enjoys their musical performances. My Efé Pygmy friends of the eastern Ituri have a very sacred tradition that identifies the throne with the rather supernatural-looking summits of Baba Tiba, the holy Efé Mountain of the Moon. The ethereal pinnacles of these mountains reach altitudes of nearly 17,000 feet and sometimes seem to float above the clouds and thick mists that usually surround the Ruwenzori massif. The Efé tradition was unknown to Henry Morton Stanley, who in 1888 described his greatest discovery as "that lofty mountain king, clad in its pure white raiment of snow, surrounded by myriads of dark

---

[10] *Ibid.*, pp. 313, 317–18.

Ruwenzori, the Cloud King

mountains, low as bending worshippers before the throne of a monarch on whose cold white face were inscribed 'Infinity and Everlasting.' "

This "celestial castle," as Stanley called it, is simultaneously situated in the earthly paradise and the heavens above: in other words, the mountains rise from the Egyptian/Hebraic/Arabic land of paradise at the source of the Nile; the snow- and glacier-topped summits soar above the level of the almost perpetual clouds, giving the impression that the castle-like throne is entirely detached from the earth. This unique arrangement would enable the Egyptian Nile to simultaneously "flow out of heaven"—from the melting snow and ice of the heavenly throne—and emanate from the earthly paradise of the Egyptian ancestors.

The same explanation applies to the dual heaven/paradise nature of Homer's Nile-dripping Olympus. About this establishment, the *Encyclopaedia Britannica* comments: "In the *Iliad* the gods are described as dwelling on a lofty peak, rising high above the clouds of the lower atmosphere into the clear ether; in the *Odyssey* Olympus is more remote and less definite; the notions of later poets vary from a definite mountain to a vague conception of heaven." The *Britannica* article also explains that Olympus is "the name of many mountains in Greece and Asia Minor, and of the fabled home of the gods; also a city name and a personal name." As I previously remarked, people have a penchant for naming geographical localities after older or more famous counterparts. This accounts for New Zealand's Mount Olympus and the Yankee Mount Olympus that rises from the American state of Washington.

Homer's holy mountain associates the heavenly/paradisaical home of the gods with the river that the Greeks sometimes called Father Nile. The tradition that the fatherly river descended from Olympian Jupiter links these waters to the deity whose name is inseparately connected with the Sanskrit/Latin word for father, *pitar/pater*. On the basis of much cultural evidence a few daring historians have postulated that the ancestors of the Greeks and Romans originated in the neighborhood of Egypt. The Greco-Roman Nile mystique certainly gives the rather strong impression of a quasi-Egyptian fatherland that harked back to a predynastic establishment in the Nile basin near the central African Olympus that the Romans called Lunae Montes or the Mountains of the Moon.

The Hindu Olympus linked the heavenly mountain throne to the paradisaical garden of Indra, where Krishna raided the sacred tree. The Greco-Roman story of the garden whence Atlas and Hercules stole the fruit of the sacred tree mirrors both the Hindu story of Indra's plundered garden and the Hebrew/Babylonian/Sumerian tradition of the ravaged Eden-forest that was simultaneously located at the source of the Nile and on the shores of the ocean. But the Greco-Roman garden was traditionally placed "far away in the west, where the sun sets." Now, is there any way to reconcile the far western paradise of Hesperides with the southerly paradise where the waters of the Nile flow from the Mountains of the Moon?

In his book *The Greek Myths*, Robert Graves mentioned the theory that the earliest or Pelasgian residents of southern Europe "reached the mainland of Greece from Palestine about 3,500 B.C." This Middle Eastern region appears as "Phenicia" on the map of Africa in Homer's period. To anyone who dwelled in the area, an ancestral paradise at the equatorial source of the Nile would be situated in a southwesterly direction. The map greatly exaggerates the size of the mountains, extending them almost to the western coast of Africa. People who lived roughly 2,500 years before the time of Homer, such as the perambulating Pelasgians, probably had an even less accurate concept of the geography of the area. They might thus situate the southwesterly paradise in the far west, where the sun sets. Since historico-religious legends very often fossilize into sacrosanct dogmas, this traditional location might remain unchanged after the migrants moved in a northwesterly direction to the "mainland of Greece."

Graves set the date of the theoretical Pelasgian exodus from Palestine at 3,500 B.C. This places it in the period when the Sumerians inscribed the Epic of Gilgamesh. The Sumerians dwelled in the Middle Eastern region of "Phenicia," whence the Pelasgians reputedly traipsed off to Greece. Like the Greco-Roman legend of Hesperides, the Sumerian epic situates the land of paradise in the west, on the shores of Ocean. A very reasonable allowance for the imperfect geographical knowledge of the time would permit us to adjust this western location toward the southwesterly land where the Okeanos-Gihon-Nile flows from the godly throne atop the Mountains of the Moon.

From his lofty throne, Osiris gazed upon the little men who resided in this venerable neighborhood. From his towering Olympus at the source of the Nile and the center of the earth, Zeus-Jupiter might watch with equal ease the little men whom the Greeks called Oi Pygmaioi. His Germanic counterpart, All-Father Odin, might simultaneously observe the little people called *alfar* or "elves" from his high throne in the remarkable southern paradise of the Norse Eddas.

In the beginning, say the Eddas, there was a far southern world of brightness, warmth and menacing fire-giants that many critics have very plausibly interpreted as fiery volcanoes. The paradisaical land of Muspelheim was separated by a great abyss called Ginnungagap from the northern realm of Niflheim, a cold world of mist, ice and snow that was associated with Hel, the gloomy goddess of hell. The Muspelheimish continent of Africa is separated by the Mediterranean abyss from the cold northern continent of Europe. The southern world comes fully equipped with eight Virunga fire-giants that range up to nearly 15,000

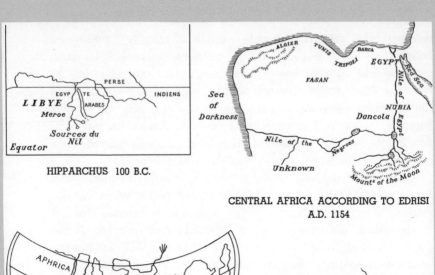

HIPPARCHUS 100 B.C.

CENTRAL AFRICA ACCORDING TO EDRISI
A.D. 1154

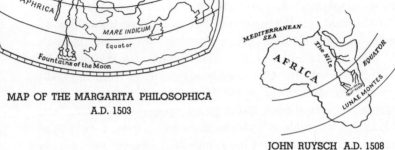

MAP OF THE MARGARITA PHILOSOPHICA
A.D. 1503

JOHN RUYSCH A.D. 1508

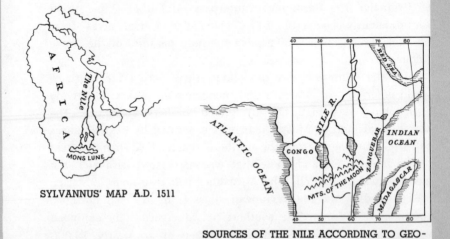

SYLVANNUS' MAP A.D. 1511

SOURCES OF THE NILE ACCORDING TO GEO-
GRAPHERS OF THE 16TH AND 17TH CENTURIES

feet tall, a Tanzanian fire-giant named Mount Kilimanjaro that is almost 20,000 feet tall, and many other cones and craters of titanic size.

In other legends, the volcanic land of Muspelheim is represented as a district of the southern paradise. Somewhere near this region lay a second paradisaical district called Alfheim (Elf-Land). One may drive in a few hours from the nearest Efé Pygmy territories of the eastern Ituri to the great Virunga fire-giants that erupted in 1948 and 1958. The part-Pygmy Twa people of eastern Zaïre, Rwanda, and Uganda, currently guide tourists and visiting scientists through the bamboo forests on the slopes of the Virungas. The pygmoid Dorobo tribe of Kenya and Tanzania are situated near the tallest African fire-giant, Kilimanjaro, which is currently dormant but erupted during geologically recent times. The western Pygmies of Cameroon live in the dangerous neighborhood of a 13,350-foot fire-giant, Cameroon Mountain, that erupted in 1959.

Alfheim was the residence of "light elves" or "fair elves" who apparently shared the pallid coloring of the so-called Nordic stock. The fairest living Pygmies have blue or gray eyes, auburn hair, and a dingy yellow-white complexion. The *Encyclopaedia Britannica* comments on the sometimes blue-eyed, fair-haired Berbers of North Africa: "The origin of this blonde element has been much discussed; it is no doubt foreign—presumably Nordic, with perhaps Alpine admixture—and it existed in Libya as long ago as the New Empire, as is shown by contemporary paintings in Egyptian tombs." A Viking invasion of the equatorial forest can scarcely be evoked to explain the Nordic element found among the Pygmies. The legends of the Norsemen very reasonably explain that the "first world" or ancestral continent was the fiery realm of Muspell "in the southern hemisphere."

The remaining district of the old Norse paradise was Asaheim or Asgard, the land of the Aesir or elder gods. This was interpreted as the ancestral homeland of the European tribes by Snorri Sturluson, the thirteenth-century Icelandic bard and historian who compiled the ancient Norse-Germanic legends of the longer *Prose Edda*. Sturluson attempted to associate Asaheim with Asia, a geographical region that bears a similar-sounding name. In his book *The Sanskrit Language* T. Burrow discusses the theory of a European homeland in Asia: "There is not the slightest trace of evidence or probability that the ancestors of the Germans, Celts, Greeks and other Europeans were ever near this area. Consequently, it is now usually held that the original home lay somewhere in Europe . . . The presence of Indo-European in the Indo-Iranian area is the result of late colonial expansion on a vast scale . . ."[11]

This colonial expansion brought the Sanskrit-speaking ancestors of the present-day Hindus into India. The so-called aboriginal tribes of this country, and of southern Asia in general, are black or very dark-skinned people. This well-known fact testifies rather strongly against the concept of an Aryan home in Asia. The theory of a European home may perhaps solve the comparatively minor problem of relationships within the Indo-European family. It fails to explain however, the much more ancient connections that unite the far-flung members of the Caucasoid stock with the ancient Caucasoid bones of equatorial Africa and the proto-Caucasoid Pygmies.

Everyman's Eden in the Mountains of the Moon satisfies the simultaneous geographical, geological and ethnological demands of the lost Hamitic-Semitic-Aryan-Sumerian paradise.* Recorded history began with the ancient Egyptian branch of the Hamite clan. From the earliest times, they placed their ancestral homeland near the southern source of the Nile. The Nilo-Hamitic Masai people likewise place "the earliest history of the world in an East African setting." The Masai know nothing of the Egyptians' little men or Pygmy people of the forest paradise near the Mountains of the Moon. They are, however, very well acquainted with the part-Pygmy Dorobo people—the hybrid de-

---

[11] T. Burrow, *The Sanskrit Language* (London: Faber & Faber, n.d.), pp. 9–10.

* The terms *Hamite, Semite,* and *Aryan* are currently used to designate linguistic communities. Pei and Gaynor's *Dictionary of Linguistics* defines Sumerian as "an extinct language, classified as *Asianic,* without any demonstrable linguistic affiliation with any known language; it was spoken in Mesopotamia, from Babylon to the Gulf of Persia, from at least 4000 B.C. till the third century B.C."

scendants of pure-blooded Pygmies—who are represented in Masai legend as the first or original human race.

There is no mention of the Negroes in the Masai legend of Naiteru-Kop, the Beginner of the Earth. There are no ancient Negro bones in the soil of equatorial Africa. Like their full-fledged Caucasoid cousins, the Masai have a very arrogant and bigoted attitude toward Negroes. They call the Kikuyu and other Bantu tribes of modern East Africa by the derogatory name *Il-Meek,* "the savages." The Dorobo people of the area are not included in that category. The ancient Dorobo are depicted in legend as the first or ancestral humans. The present-day Dorobo are uniquely qualified or entitled to preside over several major Masai socio-religious ceremonies. The seniority of the little people is even more clearly illustrated by a Masai tradition that we shall later examine in closer detail: to this day, every Masai *oibon* or priestly medicine man piously traces his descent from a legendary Pygmy prophet "no bigger than a child." Masai legend further depicts this holy personage as the direct lineal ancestor of some well-respected fellow Hamites, the East African Somali. In their own legends, the Somali claim kinship with the Semitic Arabs to whom they are linguistically, religiously and racially related.

The Masai tell their legends in the East African neighborhood of Olduvai Gorge. In this gorge, archaic Caucasoid bones are embedded in layers over fossil relics of the Australopithecines or so-called killer apes. In 1960 Dr. Leakey found the 3 foot 6 inch fossil *Homo habilis* in the bottommost bed at Olduvai. The African Pygmy stock provides an eminently plausible transition from small *Homo habilis* to small *Homo sapiens,* and thence to taller human varieties. The Pygmies' light coloring is not a highly evolved, advanced or "superior" trait. Our chimpanzee cousins have skin of a Caucasoid, not a black or Negroid, hue. The Caucasoid-style brow ridges, thin lips, hairy skins and sometimes Nordic coloring of the Pygmies rather strongly indicate that their ancient forebears sired the tall Caucasoid stock that originated in the Old White Africa of prehistoric times.

The Caucasoid peoples fan outward from equatorial Africa. Their interlocking legends of the ancestral paradise variously echo the Pygmy mystique of the godly garden, sacred tree and sinfully stolen fruit. These stories are usually dismissed as nonhistorical myths conceived by the childlike mind of "the savage." The more than six hundred Negro tribes of present-day Zaïre do not claim that their ancestors wickedly or heroically stole the forbidden fruit from the paradisaical garden of the gods. The proto-Caucasoid Pygmies, on the other hand, tell this pan-Caucasoid legend that the Semitic authors of the Old Testament echoed in almost letter-perfect style and the Aryan people of Eurasia preserved in variously fractured forms.

The Efé Pygmy narrators of this legend reside at the very site of the ancestral paradise—the only place in the world that satisfies the mutual criteria of peoples who currently dwell in Scandinavia, Masai-land, Hindustan and many other widely separated localities. The Efé say that from the beginning the ancestral Pygmies dwelled in the forest country of the northward-flowing Nile, the holy mountain and the fiery volcanoes. In apparent contradiction, they also say that the ancestral Pygmies dwelled in a glorious garden forest that was irretrievably lost when the sinful ancestors stole the forbidden fruit. Like the authors of the Old Testament, the Pygmies are a monotheistic people; their legendary Eden should therefore be called "the garden of God" rather than "the garden of the gods."

The Pygmy people of paradise thus deny that they live in the paradisaical land of the ancestors. Now, how can this last great paradox be resolved?

The Efé tell us that the original Pygmy sinners forfeited immortal life, just like the original Hebrew sinners who according to the derivative story of Paradise Lost "brought death into the world and all our woe, with loss of Eden." By examining the detailed Pygmy legend, we shall now see that death came to early man in the form of a frightful cataclysm that all but obliterated the ancestral garden paradise at the source of Okeanos–Gihon–Nile. This is why the Efé Pygmies say that they have always dwelled in the grand Ituri Forest, near the holy Mountains of the Moon, and at the same time tell us that their ancestors lived in a wonderful paradise that existed in the same geographical location. A rather poetic people, the Efé represent the coming of death as the loss of immortality. So did Moses, and the Hebrew folk whose descendants still celebrate their legendary exodus from the land where at the dawn of recorded history the Pygmies danced for the Egyptian people of the Pharaohs.

The End of the Beginning

The myths of the first ages illuminate above all the problem of the origin of death and the original sin," wrote Schebesta in his book *Les Pygmées du Congo Belge*. There are many Efé legends of the primordial transgression. One of these sagas tells the story of the stolen fruit. Other legends describe how the ancestral Pygmies stole *all* of the deity's most prized possessions, defied his will and supreme authority, broke a wide variety of commandments, and, all in all, staged a mutiny that caused the deity to leave his former residence on earth and ascend to the firmament.

From the heights of heaven, the deity still observes the doings of men with the keenest interest. He responds favorably to prayers that virtuous Pygmies piously address to "our Father."

He punishes sinful Pygmies by striking them dead with bolts of lightning, sending tempests that topple the trees, or instructing man-eating leopards to dispose of the villains who violate his eternal laws and commandments. The legends of his enigmatic ascent to the celestial residence variously describe cataclysmic events that ended the paradisaical "first ages." One such Efé story tells us, for example, that the departing deity smote the world with a giant bolt of lightning that mysteriously issued from the bowels of the earth.

In Gabon and Cameroon, a thousand miles west of the Ituri Forest, Pygmy bands tell similar legends of the deity's departure. The western Pygmies are known by many local names of Negro origin. Their own name is far more ancient and important. They call themselves Akka or Akwa, which means simply "men." The word appeared as AKKA on Egyptian monuments. The Aka Pygmies of the northwest Ituri are still known by this title. In the Efé language of the eastern Ituri, *akwi* or *agwi* means "male." Cognate words are used by many African pygmoid populations in areas all the way down to the Kalahari Desert, where the Bushmen render the word as *aukwe*.

The western Pygmy men informed anthropologist Trilles that the deity dwelled with them during the first ages of man. According to a Pygmy chant recorded by Trilles, "When he lived with us—Him, giving his orders, and us obeying Him—we were happy, we were powerful and strong, we were the Masters." The golden age of the formerly proud and mighty Pygmy nation ended abruptly when the deity departed for the heavens: "God is far away. He left us, and that is why we have become poor and miserable. Many days have passed. We are the nation that wanders . . ."[1]

The many Pygmy legends of original sin tell apparently contradictory stories concerning the downfall of the nation that presently wanders through the equatorial forest. The Efé Pygmies of the eastern Ituri, who preserve the most archaic or conservative style of Pygmy culture, possess the most complete and detailed

---

[1] Henri Trilles, *L'Ame du Pygmée d'Afrique,* "The Soul of the African Pygmy" (Paris: Les Editions du Cerf, 1945), pp. 95–96.

stock of legends. The individual stories of this "vast mythic cycle," as Schebesta called it, are variously combined in legends told by other Pygmy populations. The Kango Pygmies of the western Ituri, for example, narrate a creation epic that contains elements found in at least four separate Efé legends. As in the Efé story of the forbidden fruit, a sinful woman is depicted as the cause of the primordial disaster. For her dreadful deed, she is condemned "to bring forth children in sorrow and to do all of the hardest work." But the Kango epic makes no mention of forbidden fruit or sacred trees. It explains instead that the infamous Pygmy Eve violated a supreme commandment of an entirely different nature. After the sin was committed, the deity departed, as in the Efé legend of the earth-splitting lightning. The Kango story does not, however, describe this pyrotechnic event. The ancestors' garden paradise is instead blighted by a terrible famine that figures in yet another Efé legend.

"Why did death enter the world?" asked Trilles in his book *The Soul of the African Pygmy*. His answer was: "Because God became angry with men and retired from them. Death is the consequence of this retreat of God. The Pygmies of the West and of the East are unanimous on this point." The conflicting accounts as to *how* death entered the world apparently describe interrelated events of the primordial catastrophe. The differing accounts of the cause, or so-called original sin, inform us that the ancestral Pygmies committed many violations of the deity's diverse commandments. Their original sins collectively comprise, as Schebesta phrased it, "the rebellion against God."

The legend of the forbidden fruit is one component of the Pygmies' sinful saga. This particular story is known only from Efé versions told in the eastern Ituri. Splintered fragments of the tale are variously combined in the legends told by the other geographical-linguistic groups of Ituri Forest Pygmies. Some of them may have preserved a more or less intact account of the deity's plundered tree; the story may also survive in the far western forests of Gabon and Cameroon. The great majority of Pygmy bands have never been interrogated by anthropologists; moreover, most of the shy little forest nomads are very reluctant to discuss their religious beliefs with strangers. When Trilles asked a number of western Pygmies to tell him why the deity sent death to mankind, he received the answer: "God willed it. If God willed it thus, it is because He had his reasons. One does not judge God." In *The Soul of the African Pygmy,* Trilles expressed the hope that further research might enable him to discover a western Pygmy legend as to the nature of the ancestors' ancient crime. Then he ended his discussion of *la faute initiale,* "the initial fault," by reproducing the Efé legend of the forbidden fruit. He remarked on the obvious similarities of this legend to the tale told in Genesis, insisted on the seniority of the Pygmy story, and concluded that the Efé-Hebrew account of the forbidden fruit affair constitutes "an undeniable fact."

Father Trilles' detailed, accurate and scrupulously honest reports on Pygmy culture are not invalidated by his blatantly pro-Genesis sentiments. Such an attitude is not, however, conducive to an objective evaluation of the Pygmy legends and religion. Trilles does not comment, for example, on the only major difference to be found between the Efé and Hebrew narratives of the desecrated tree: the Pygmy story makes no mention of that arch villain, the snake in the grass of Eden, who persuaded Eve to pluck the forbidden fruit. Genesis' reptilian sinner is denounced in the Biblical book of Revelation as "the dragon, that old serpent, which is the devil, and Satan." In Egypt, he was known as Set, and in his serpent manifestation as Apepi. His Babylonian equivalent was the great dragon Tiamat. His many Indo-European analogues include the Greek serpent-monster Typhon. His Pygmy counterpart plays the villain's role in a fantastic Efé legend that Schebesta called "the myth of the savior."

The separate stories of the Efé cycle have no set order or arrangement. The savior-versus-dragon saga apparently tells, however, of events that followed the theft of the forbidden fruit. The latter legend ends with the deity's proclamation that the Pygmy sinners must die. In the myth of the savior, death enters the world in rather spectacular style. We shall later inspect the detailed texts of the major Pygmy legends. For now, a brief summary will suffice.

A gigantic dragon-like monster kills the first man and his sons. His wife manages to escape from the rampaging beast. She gives birth to a son by miraculous means. The young hero swears vengeance on the murderer of his father. He slays the monster with an iron spear that was originally obtained from God. His triumph over the dragon enables him to perform a deed that resurrects his father and the dragon's other victims. To show their gratitude, they install the savior-son as the supreme ruler or king of the primordial Pygmy nation.

Does this story sound at all familiar?

A very famous Egyptian legend tells of how the slain and resurrected man-god Osiris was murdered by the devilish man-snake Set-Apepi. Osiris' wife Isis afterwards gave birth by miraculous means to a son known as "Horus, the avenger of his father." Horus speared his evil adversary with a weapon made from "iron of the god." Then he was installed upon the throne of Osiris and endowed with "sovereignty over the world." In his book *The Gods of the Egyptians*, Sir E. A. Wallis Budge described the story of Horus' victory as "one of the sources of all the post-Christian legends of the overthrow of dragons by kings and heroes, e.g., Alexander the Great and Saint George." The *Encyclopaedia Britannica* article entitled "Dragon" remarks: "The dragon myths of the pagan East took new shapes in the legends of the victories of St. Michael and St. George . . . In this respect indeed Christian mythology agreed with that of the pagan north. The similarity of the northern and oriental snake myths seems to point to a common origin in remote antiquity . . . the slaying of a dragon is the crowning achievement of heroes—of Siegmund, of Beowulf, of Sigurd, of Arthur, of Tristram—even of Lancelot, the *beau ideal* of medieval chivalry."[2]

The Egyptian legends of the wicked devil-dragon, the murdered father and the heroic son-avenger date back to the dimly known period that preceded the founding of the First Dynasty around 3200 B.C. The belief in Osiris' death and resurrection was the foundation for the Egyptian doctrine of eternal life. Faïence figurines of Ptah-Seker-Osiris, the god of the resurrection, represent the divinity as a triumphant Pygmy standing atop the

---

[2] *Encyclopaedia Britannica*, 14th ed., Vol. 7, p. 569.

dragon-like form of a crocodile. Regarding the source of the Osiris legends, Sir E. A. Wallis Budge wrote in 1904: "The cult of Osiris, the dead man deified, and the earliest forms of his worship, were, no doubt, wholly of African origin." In 1915, René Grauwet, the Conservator of Upemba National Park, found a ninety-nine-millimeter-high metallic figure of Osiris near the Zaïrian village of Mulongo. The statuette, buried under a meter of soil, was attributed to the VII Dynasty (2181–2173 B.C.) by the Belgian Egyptologist Capart. Grauwet's find was discussed in Pierre Le Roy's study of the quasi-Egyptian masonry at Api, on the northern fringes of the Ituri Forest or the Egyptian-styled "land of trees and spirits" near the Mountains of the Moon. In the eastern Ituri, the Egyptians' "little men" or Pygmies still recount the dragon-fighting legend that was ancient in the year 3200 B.C.

This story does not prove as an "undeniable fact" that Horus, son of Osiris, plunged his trusty iron spear into Set-Apepi, that the Babylonian hero Marduk killed the primordial dragon Tiamat, that the archangel Michael fought the good fight against the wicked dragon of Revelation, or that any other legendary god, angel, saint, king or hero ever sallied forth to dispatch a dastardly dragon. The emergent fact, which Trilles fails or refuses to grasp, is that the Efé legends reveal the common origin in remote antiquity of Judeo-Christian and so-called pagan concepts. Isolated for uncountable millennia, the Pygmies tell their ancestors' versions of man's oldest, most important legends. If one concludes that the Judeo-Christian legends are "true," one must grant the same status to their pagan analogues.

Like the Efé saga of the stolen fruit, the dragon-slaying story has not been borrowed from any outside source. "[There is] no possible Biblical reminiscence, no Bantu infiltration, since these myths are unknown to the Bantu tribes," Trilles comments on the Pygmy legend cycle. On the question of borrowing, one might also remark that the Pygmies do not casually adopt alien customs and traditions. The Efé are so stubbornly conservative that they still refuse to borrow and use friction firesticks, which are banned by their religious laws. If you ask why, a Pygmy typically replies, "I do as my father did, and his father before him, and the father of his father, and the first father of the Pygmies, who was God. He told us how to live, and His way is right." That ends the discussion.

The Efé legends of the deity, the virtuous Pygmy heroes and the wicked Pygmy sinners, comprise the unwritten history of "the nation that wanders." The legends cannot be separated from the Pygmy religion. The religion in turn cannot be separated from the Pygmies' style of thought or mode of reasoning. Schebesta expressed this very beautifully when he wrote: "It is very remarkable that this religion presents only a slight degree of irrational —that is to say, magical—thoughts; the belief in a supreme Deity is of a pronounced rationalism. Its origin resides in the causal thought, and in the reasoning of these quick-witted little people . . . A striking proof of the Pygmies' supple wit is their gift for languages. If their relations with their neighbors make it necessary, they speak up to five different languages . . . The belief of the Ituri Forest Pygmies in a sole Deity as the final cause of all things and the governing power of the world rests unexplained . . . Their mental structure makes of them, in the heart of the African virgin forest, an absolutely unique human phenomenon."[3]

In their studies of the African Pygmies, Schebesta, Trilles, Wauters and other knowledgeable anthropologists, have described almost unbelievably abstract religious and philosophical ideas. Schebesta reports that by possessing and distributing the totality of vital force, the supreme deity of the Ituri Forest Pygmies brings his creatures into existence or "perfects" them. In *Congo Kitabu* I defined this all-creating deity as a holy trinity of "three divine beings who are somehow one" or one "vital force" that continuously creates the world by animating "every living thing with God's will and essence." To explain why they make no pictures or sculptures of this ineffable deity, a Gabon Pygmy elder told Trilles, "God is like the word that leaves your mouth. Make a picture of it, run after it, and bring it to me. The word? It is no more, it has passed and yet it lives always, today and tomorrow as well. God also." A discussion of Pygmy views on free will and

---

[3] P. Schebesta, *Les Pygmées* (Paris: Gallimard, 1940), pp. 87, 90.

the holy spirit of God appears in Schebesta's book *Les Pygmées du Congo Belge.* Schebesta remarks that Pygmy ideology "impresses one as being as little African as possible, while it well reflects our occidental conceptions."

The Egyptian founders of man's first historic civilization, who so deeply venerated the Pygmies, are not credited by most Egyptologists with achieving the level of "our occidental conceptions." In *The Gods of the Egyptians,* Sir E. A. Wallis Budge discusses this topic:

> The Egyptians, being fundamentally an African people, possessed all the virtues and vices which characterized the North African races generally, and it is not to be held for a moment that any African people could ever become metaphysicians in the modern sense of the word. In the first place, no African language is suitable for giving expression to theological and philosophical speculations, and even an Egyptian priest of the highest intellectual attainments would have been unable to render a treatise of Aristotle into language which his brother priests without teaching could understand. The mere construction of the language would make such a thing an impossibility, to say nothing of the ideas of the great Greek philosopher, which belong to a domain of thought and culture wholly foreign to the Egyptian.[4]

The Efé Pygmies do not speak a language that belongs to any recognized African language group. Trilles defined the Efé as a "Pygmy tribe of the equatorial region" that has conserved its "original language." The Kango Pygmies of the southwest Ituri, the Sua Pygmies of the central Ituri, and the Aka Pygmies of the northwest Ituri, speak dialects related to Efé but blended to differing degrees with the introduced tongues of the local Negro tribes. In an area stretching westward from the Ituri Forest to Gabon and Cameroon, there are many part-Pygmy and Pygmy populations who preserve words and grammatical constructions that echo the speech of the Ituri Forest Pygmies. On the Pygmy languages in general, Trilles remarks: "Our Congolese and Cameroonian Pygmies have preserved, if not their intact languages,

---

[4] Sir E. A. Wallis Budge, *The Gods of the Egyptians* (New York: Dover, 1969; originally published in 1904), Vol. 1, p. 143.

at least many words that one finds above all in the chants, the proverbs, the legends . . . and the familiar and intimate conversations. In any case, the language which they use among themselves certainly is neither by its roots nor by its grammar a Bantu dialect."

In the Ituri Forest, explains Schebesta, some Bantu and Sudanese tribes speak dialects adapted from the Pygmy language. He calls one of these pidgin tongues Bira-Sua. It contains elements from both the Bantu language of the Bira or Negro overlords and the Pygmy language of the Sua serfs. In the eastern Ituri the pidgin tongue called Lese-Efé has evolved from the Sudanese language of the Lese Negro masters and the Pygmy language of the Efé. But the old Efé language is spoken in a number of Pygmy camps.

"In all probability Efé is a Pygmy language, adopted by the Lese Negroes and their affiliates, who penetrated into the forest country of the Efé," concluded Schebesta. He also explained that it is "excessively difficult" to study the Pygmy language, since the Efé only speak this language "among themselves." To converse with their Negro masters or with the black interpreters employed by investigating anthropologists, they use the local Negro dialects.

The Efé and the other linguistic groups of Ituri Forest Pygmies are known collectively and described in many anthropological studies as the Bambuti or "Mbuti." Their languages or dialects have been lumped together under the name "Kimbuti." These are Bantu words respectively bearing the Bantu plural prefix *Ba-* (or *Woc-* or *Moc-*) (people) and the prefix *Ki-* or *Lu-* (language). Such grammar is wholly alien to Efé'ini, the pluralized "Pygmies" who add the Efé plural suffix *-ini* to the word or name Efé, which means "Pygmy" in the Efé language. In many legends, the first man or Pygmy Adam is called Efé. Since the word is also used as a collective noun for Pygmy people in general, the diminutive residents of the eastern Ituri say that all Pygmies are Efé, regardless of their dialect.

The Pygmy people, their language and their religion, have all been grossly misrepresented by academic anthropologists and travelers who have never heard the Pygmy language spoken and know next to nothing of the Pygmies' beliefs. Some of these so-called scientists are not even aware that they use as interpreters the Negro masters who claim to own the Pygmies as their personal property. Like the white slaveholders of the old American South, the Negro tribes of the Ituri Forest do not have a very high opinion of their oppressed Pygmy serfs. They tell all kinds of derogatory stories about the Pygmies, whom they represent, in general, as fiendish little morons. The visiting anthropologist swallows these stories whole. The immense treasury of Pygmy misinformation is then added to by the theorizing anthropologists of the "shrunken Negro" school, who select for use the wholly worthless "data" supplied by the tourist-type anthropologists, which apparently confirms their theories, and ignore the truly authoritative data of anthropologists who have spent decades studying the Pygmies and their culture.

A prime example may be viewed in the Fourteenth Edition of the *Encyclopaedia Britannica*.[5] The article on the Bambute (*sic*) or Ituri Forest Pygmies does not discuss the phonology, grammar or vocabulary of the Efé language, the other Pygmy dialects or the pidgin tongues that the Negro tribes have adapted from the Pygmy language. The text does not give a single Pygmy word. It instead declares that the Pygmies "speak a corrupted form of the dialects of their negro neighbours." The intellectual level of this article may be judged from its statement that the Pygmies give out a rancid odor "between the smell of a monkey and a negro." Pygmy religion is summarized as "some idea that thunder, lightning and rain are manifestations of 'an Evil Power,' and that the dead are reincarnated in the red bush-pig." Pygmy law is summarized by the statement that those seemingly subhuman creatures, the Ituri Forest Pygmies, govern themselves by "accepting as temporary lawgiver some adept hunter."

"In the beginning, God lived with men and gave them His commandments," an Efé elder informed Paul Schebesta. "He created the world. He can never die. If he did, the whole world

---

[5] The recently revised *Britannica* contains a nonpejorative article on the Ituri Forest Pygmies. Since the Fourteenth Edition is still widely used in English-speaking households, the contents of the older article still perpetrate ignorant and bigoted opinions of Pygmy culture.

would perish with Him . . . When he perceives that men do wrong or say evil things, he lets a tempest fall upon them. He kills adulterers with a bolt of lightning . . . God dwells on high, in the Firmament. God is the Lord above all things. He reigns also over men, whose actions He watches day and night. He punishes criminals."

These words are printed in Schebesta's book *Les Pygmées* (Paris, 1940). "The belief in a supreme Deity is specifically Pygmy," Schebesta comments in this same study. "This divinity, wholly anthropomorphic, is one, the creator of man and of the world; he dwells in the sky and one invokes him by the name of Father." Jesus Christ himself instructed his disciples, "After this manner therefore pray ye: Our Father which art in heaven, Hallowed be thy name." In the northwest Ituri, where the Aka Pygmies have been all but exterminated by their Ngbetu masters, they still pray aloud, Efé-style, to "our Father." Trilles' compendium of Pygmy religion, *The Soul of the African Pygmy* (Paris, 1945), describes the monotheistic faith of the Pygmies as "divine revelation dating to the origin of the world, transmitted from generation to generation."

A Reader in General Anthropology (New York, 1948) nevertheless comments on "the paucity of 'religious' phenomena in Pygmy culture." Editor Carleton S. Coon arrived at this remarkable conclusion, he explains, while editing the text of a twenty-page essay that appears in his reader. This flimsy little paper, "The Pygmies of the Ituri Forest," was written by an anthropologist named Patrick Putnam, who formerly kept an inn or motel, Putnam's Camp, near the Ituri Forest town of Epulu. Eight years prior to the publication of this essay and to Professor Coon's comment on Pygmy religion, Schebesta had deplored in the text of *Les Pygmées* the misinformed or ignorant persons who have "spread through the world the news that the Bambuti are a people without God and without religion."

Putnam's paper denigrates the Pygmies' mental powers in terms that make them seem abysmally stupid. "They do not count time," writes Putnam. "They simply respond to the practical needs of the moment, the way lower organisms respond automatically to changes in intensity of light." In *Les Pygmées* Schebesta criticizes anthropologists who use the absence of an elaborate counting system to prove the Pygmies' "mental inferiority." They rarely bother to count beyond three, he explained, but instead come equipped with an intuition of quantity: "With a glance of the eye, they seize the image of the quantity in its parts, and they note all addition or subtraction." Most Pygmies can count up to ten, some to one hundred, others to one thousand. In Southwest Africa, some of the Hottentots employ rudimentary counting methods while others use a fully developed decimal system. *Disi*, the Hottentot word for "ten," has been compared by philologists to the Sanskrit word *dasa* and the Latin word *decem*, meaning "ten" (as in "decimal").

I told in my book *Congo Kitabu* of how I taught reading, writing and arithmetic to the Efé residents of the Beni territory, District North Kivu. The territorial administrator was stunned when he walked into the classroom for the first time, "at the precise moment when thirty Pygmies held up their slates, eager to show me that $12 \times 23 = 276$." Like most representatives of the former Belgian colonial government, he had been convinced that the Pygmies were "uneducatable." This belief has been promulgated, if not originally generated, by ignorant or bigoted anthropologists.

The Pygmies' intellectual capacities are evident to anyone who takes a more than superficial look at their culture. Schebesta emphasizes their "supple wit" and ability to learn with ease "up to five languages." On their truly profound knowledge of forest botany and pharmacology, he remarks: "The Bambuti know plants that cure almost all maladies, and use them effectively." A little Efé elder named Mutuke administered surgical treatment and drugs that cured me of an otherwise fatal wound and fever. The Pygmy pharmacopoeia includes many preparations that might provide us with potent new miracle drugs.

Competent scientists should also investigate a phenomenon that Trilles discussed under the heading of Pygmy magic. He (and later I) witnessed many demonstrations by the Pygmies which rather strongly suggest that the so-called magicians are endowed with clairvoyant and telepathic powers of a superhuman order. Here is the most spectacular example. After making a three-day trip through the forest, Father Trilles and his companion, Monseigneur Le Roy, arrived at a remote Pygmy camp. The elder of the band remarked that he had watched their journey in his "magic mirror." This is a piece of polished metal or, more frequently, a reflecting pool of water. The Pygmy elder recounted the events of the trip, including the conversations of the two Europeans. "Not only had he seen us," wrote Trilles, "but he had heard us, and with my companion I spoke French, a language absolutely unknown to the magician. And this companion was Monseigneur Le Roy. He was absolutely stupefied!"[6]

These remarkable little people have an average cranial capacity of nearly 1,500 cubic centimeters. The range for European Caucasoids is 1,300-1,500 cubic centimeters. Since the average Pygmy man weighs about eighty-five or ninety pounds, he is much brainier for his size than the average Caucasoid. The extraordinary powers of his brain are verified by his many intellectual talents and by his exalted concepts of God, man and nature. These known and critically important facts are totally ignored in the anthropological theories that still attempt to derive the Pygmies from "shrunken" or degenerate Negroes.

Professor Carleton S. Coon is probably the leading exponent of the "shrunken Negro" school. In his book *The Origin of Races* he proposed an experiment to prove his theories of dwarfing mechanisms: "If we want to know what the full-sized ancestors of the Pygmies looked like, all we need do is select a group of Pygmy children, feed or inject them with the hormones the lack of which makes them small, and see what they grow into. This is a perfectly feasible experiment and the Pygmies would probably cooperate."[7] In *The Living Races of Man,* he deplored the fact that scientists have not yet "injected growth hormone into Pygmy children year after year to see what would happen." Such an experiment, he declared, "would harm no one."[8]

Heavy dosage with hormones can cause all kinds of disorders,

[6] Henri Trilles, *The Soul of the African Pygmy,* pp. 239–40.

[7] Carleton S. Coon, *The Origin of Races* (New York: Alfred A. Knopf, 1971), p. 655.

[8] C. S. Coon with Edward E. Hunt, Jr., *The Living Races of Man* (New York: Alfred A. Knopf, 1965), p. 107.

especially in children. To perform an experiment of this kind on Pygmy children—who are not "dwarfs" but perfectly normal and healthy human beings—would entail a very heavy risk of disease, deformity or death. Any scientist who proposed unpredictable and dangerous experiments to American or European parents—"Let me experiment with your baby, Mrs. Smith, and see what he turns into"—would be rather dimly regarded. If Professor Coon's proposed experiments were explained to the Pygmies, they would not cooperate. They would consider the mere suggestion to be monstrous.

When I asked an Efé elder named Mwenua to define the most atrocious violation of the Pygmy laws and commandments, he immediately replied, "To be cruel to children or old people." Among the western Pygmies, Trilles recorded a very touching little song that the mother sings to celebrate the birth of a child:

> My heart is so joyous,
> My heart flies in singing,
> Under the trees of the forest,
> The forest, our home and our mother;
> In my net I have caught
> A little, a very little bird,
> And my heart is caught in the net,
> In the net with my little bird.

This is how those so-called lower organisms, the Pygmies, feel about the children who have been proposed as candidates for irresponsible experiments. The judges at the Nuremberg trials condemned as morally infamous the "human guinea pig" experiments performed by Nazi doctors on helpless human beings who belonged to an ethnic group that Nazi anthropologists classified as inferior. In 1962, less than twenty years after Nuremberg, Professor Coon casually suggested his "perfectly feasible experiment." This proposal has appeared in eight printings of *The Origin of Races* (in the period between 1962 and 1971). To the best of my knowledge, no one has raised even a murmur of protest.

Professor Coon maintains that his experiments might enable scientists to obtain living reconstructions of the Pygmies' full-sized ancestors. The Pygmies' ancestors were represented as

Pygmies and described as "little men" in Egyptian texts that date back five thousand years. Professor Coon represents the Pygmies as Negro dwarfs or "shrunken Negroes." The historico-religious legends of the Ituri Forest Pygmies represent their ancestors as "white men."

Several such legends are recounted in Schebesta's four-volume study *Die Bambuti-Pygmäen vom Ituri* and the condensed French translation *Les Pygmées du Congo Belge*. The legends are supported by the light-colored skin, hair and eyes of the fairest living Pygmies. The religion of the Pygmies cannot conceivably be interpreted as the creed of shrunken or degenerate Negroes. The Pygmies' mode of thought has been compared to the "occidental conceptions" of the Europeans and their transplanted Yankee offspring. The anatomy of the Pygmies' skulls, their hairy skins and their other physical traits have led the most objective anthropologists to declare that they must have had "a primordial connection with the Europeans."

The Efé say that their white ancestors were created, as all children are created, in the image of their father. In *Congo Kitabu* I told of how a very tall and bushy-bearded Caucasoid named Jean-Pierre Hallet asked an Efé elder named Mwenua, "What does God look like?" Answered Mwenua, "He is wonderfully big, white and hairy—a little like you—but He is a very old man." Trilles compared the Ituri Forest deity to the Biblical "Ancient of Days." The Egyptian divinity Osiris was depicted as a bearded white man. The far-flung Indo-European pantheons were traditionally headed by patriarchal deities such as the Norse All-Father Odin. Like the Great White Father of the Ituri Forest Pygmies, he was portrayed as a wise old man with a long white beard.

The Pygmies present a wealth of physical, intellectual and religious evidence that connects them with the Caucasoids rather than the Negroes. The fossil evidence agrees, in that Caucasoid bones have been found in the equatorial and southern regions where fossil Negroes are conspicuous by their absence. The linguistic evidence has been greatly obscured by the modern Negro invasion of the equatorial forest, and by the proliferation of Pygmy-Negro pidgins or trading languages. A single Pygmy dialect has survived in fairly intact form—Efé. Its origin is described in an Efé legend that interlocks with all the other stories of the ancestors' "original sin" or rebellion against the deity's laws.

Long, long ago, say the Efé, the first men dwelled in a blessed country. They had everything in abundance, they lived in peace with one another, and they spoke a single language. Then they spoiled everything by quarreling with one another. God, the divine giver and enforcer of the law, was offended. He punished the sinners by somehow confusing their tongues, just as he did in the Biblical book of Genesis. Then He dispersed them like chaff to the wind. To each group He gave a language. To the Efé He said, "You, you must speak Efé."

Now, what kind of language is Efé, the original tongue of the African Pygmies?

It is an obscure language which has never been classified. Trilles affirms that it is not a Bantu language. Schebesta points out many profound differences between Efé and "the Negro idioms." But he does not suggest the possible affiliations of the Pygmy language, apparently because he feels that his "fragmentary researches" do not permit comparisons. Since the Pygmies have been interpreted by some anthropologists as the racial ancestors of mankind, and by others as the religious ancestors of mankind, the nature and affiliations of the Efé language should be of more than casual interest to mankind. Under the circumstances one would imagine that a whole caravan of linguistic specialists would immediately set out for the Ituri to resolve this crucial question.

The anthropologists instead debate the matter from their armchairs. Meanwhile, in the eastern Ituri, the Efé people, language and religion are being crushed out of existence by the Pygmies' feudal overlords. "With his language, the Pygmy preserves for us his primitive traditions," Trilles says of the Pygmy people in general. "With oppression or penetration, he loses them and has already fatally lost them."

In *Congo Kitabu*, I described my personal labors to improve the material welfare of 353 Efé Pygmy families whom I liberated from the bonds of feudal serfdom. I am still trying to free and help all of "my people," as I have called the Ituri Forest Pygmies. Since their speech is of great and obvious importance to the rest of humanity, I have also labored to save their language before it is irretrievably lost. During the years I lived and worked with the Efé, I compiled word lists and glossaries. In summer of 1969 I revisited the Ituri and convoked a council of twelve Efé elders who passed judgment on every word included in a preliminary dictionary of their language. In summer of 1970 I again returned to the Ituri and completed the first comprehensive dictionary of the Efé Pygmy language.

Compiling dictionaries in the remote Pygmy camps of the dark, tangled equatorial forest was not an easy task, especially for a one-handed lexicographer who had already given his right or writing hand to the pygmoid Mosso. I nonetheless managed to complete this vitally important human document, an 8,000-word English-Efé dictionary, while the scholarly anthropologists sat in their armchairs and argued about the existence or nonexistence of the Pygmy language. The accuracy and authenticity of my Efé dictionary may be confirmed in the simplest fashion possible: I will personally escort any groups of interested anthropologists, philologists or etymologists to the Ituri Forest areas where the old Efé tongue is still spoken by the Pygmies.

My literary collaborator, Alexandra Pelle, has spent more than seven years studying the legends and language of the Efé Pygmies on the basis of my notes, glossaries, dictionaries and tape recordings, Schebesta's preliminary studies of the language, and the entire body of Pygmy legend that has been recorded by me, Schebesta, Trilles and other investigators. Alex Pelle deserves complete credit for the intricately linked linguistic and religious researches, comparisons and related discoveries set forth in *Pygmy Kitabu*. Language is "inseparably connected with the religious question" and "the very soul of the people," as Trilles remarked in *The Soul of the African Pygmy*. He quoted the anthropological dictum that it is "absolutely indispensable to study the language" in order to understand any people's "spiritual culture." To understand, evaluate and compare the Pygmy legends with non-Pygmy equivalents, Alexandra Pelle not only studied the Pygmy language but plowed through endless piles of linguistic and religious studies that describe the "spiritual culture" of the Hamitic, Semitic and Indo-European peoples who tell variously fractured tales of Everyman's lost paradise in the Mountains of the Moon.

Trilles compared a handful of western Pygmy words to equivalents used in the Hamitic speech of ancient Egypt. The pygmoid Hottentots of South Africa speak a number of dialects that have well-established connections with the Hamitic-Semitic language family; the pygmoid Dorobo people of East Africa are included in the ranks of the Nilo-Hamitic Masai nation. The Masai legends have been interpreted as evidence that the East African Hamites were originally derived from early Hebrews or pre-Babylonian Semites. Such theories totally ignore the role played by the pygmoid Dorobo in the religious traditions of Masai-land.

In the Masai legend "Beginner of the Earth," the first man is represented as "the Dorobo" or the eponymous ancestor of the present-day Dorobo people. His first deed, which launches the subsequent history of the world, is the slaying of a supernatural serpent or dragon. To create the world, the Babylonian hero-god Marduk slew the dragon Tiamat. The Masai identify the dragon-killer as a "Dorobo." This name is derived from the Masai word *dorop,* meaning "short." Those very short-statured dragon-killers, the Ituri Forest Pygmies, cannot possibly be interpreted as the descendants of early Babylonians or Hebrews. Nor can the Masai people, whose priestly medicine men trace their descent from a legendary Pygmy named Mweiya.

Alex Pelle explains that the Efé legends offer almost inconceivably archaic patterns or archetypes for all the major Hamitic, Semitic and Indo-European stories of the lost paradise. These Caucasoid peoples are currently divided or defined by their language families. The Efé Pygmies say in legend that the residents of the paradisaical land spoke only "one language" prior to their quasi-Biblical dispersion. Some philologists maintain that the major Caucasoid language families indeed diverged from a common stock.

In *The Gods of the Egyptians,* Sir E. A. Wallis Budge quotes Professor J. Lieblein's opinion that "the science of languages has been able partly to reconstruct an Indo-European pre-historic language. It might be able also to reconstruct a pre-historic Semitic, and a pre-historic Hamitic, and of these three pre-historic languages, whose original connexion it not only guesses, but even commences to prove gradually, it will, we trust in time, be able to

extract a still earlier pre-historic language, which according to
analogy might be called Noahitic. When we have come so far, we
shall most likely in this pre-historic language, also find words
expressing the idea of God . . . Although the Egyptians are the
earliest civilized people known in history, and just therefore especially important for the science of religion, yet it is even there
impossible to point out the origin of the conception of the deity."[9]

The Pygmies, anthropologist A. Le Roy pointed out in *La
Religion des Primitifs*, are "older than the sphinx, older than the
pyramids, older than the texts written on papyrus, camel bones,
bronze, brick, and stone." By moral, ethical and religious standards,
they are a supremely civilized people. Since the most venerable
Egyptian documents portray the Pygmy "Dancers of God" as religious mentors or even divinities, the Pygmies rather than the Egyptians merit the title of "the earliest civilized people known in history."
One might therefore look for "the origin of the conception of the
deity" and the Noahitic tongue of prehistory in the religion and
language of the oldest group of men on earth.

Schebesta defined monotheism as a "specifically Pygmy" belief. Wilhelm Schmidt credited the Pygmies with the "origin of
the idea of God." Alexandra Pelle's researches show that they not
only practice the Noahitic religion but still possess the Noahitic
language. Here, for example, is a very basic element of Efé grammar that has close and obvious counterparts in Indo-European,
Sumerian, and Semitic-Hamitic. Any Efé noun may be pluralized
by adding the suffix *-eni* or *-ini*. Schebesta explained that the Efé
plural is "principally formed" with this grammatical device. He
did not compare it with equivalents used in any other language.
We shall cite but a few:

> Dutch *-en*, the principal plural suffix, as in Efé-Pygmeen (Efé
> Pygmies). Arabic *-in*. Latin *-enis* or *-inis*. Sumerian *-ene*. Italian
> *-ini*. Masai *-in* or *-ni*. Gothic *-ins, -ne,* or *-na*. Old Norse *-na*. Classi-
> cal Arabic *-ina*. Aramaic *-in*. Old Hebrew *-in*. Sanskrit *-in* or *-an*.
> Persian *-an*. Balochi *-an*. Avestan *-an*. Anglo-Saxon *-an* or *-en*, as
> in *oexan* (oxen). Welsh *-on* or *-en*. Greek *-ons*. Middle English *-en*,
> as in *housen, honden* and *worden* (houses, hands and words).

---

[9] Sir E. A. Wallis Budge, *The Gods of the Egyptians*, Vol. 1, pp. 69–70.

English -en, as in children and brethren. German -en, the principal plural suffix, as in Efé-Pygmäen.

The great German philosopher Gottfried Wilhelm Leibnitz (1646–1716), who founded the science of comparative linguistics, maintained that German is closer than Hebrew to the "Adamic" or "primitive root language" whence every human tongue anciently descended. Germanic legends place "the first world" in the Old White Africa (the Eddas' southern continent of Muspelheim). Here the Efé Pygmies speak a language that strikingly resembles the Indo-European tongues of the Germanic group (English, Norwegian, Old Norse, Gothic, Dutch, German, etc.). This resemblance is not a matter of isolated words that could have developed by coincidence. Entire Efé sentences have word-for-word equivalents in the Germanic tongues. Most of the individual words have obvious counterparts in other branches of the Indo-European family.

Here are some preliminary examples of simple Efé sentences and grammatical devices. Efé is a very eloquent language; these examples are on the level of a child's primer or a short course in Basic Efé. The vowels are rendered according to the spelling used in most Indo-European languages: *a = ah; e = eh; i = ee; o = oh; u = oo*. A few Egyptian and Hebrew words will be cited for purposes of comparison. All of the other languages involved in this demonstration are classified in the Indo-European family.

Afa osi èma, father sees mother. *Idè osi mai ati,* they see my family:

Norwegian *Far ser mor. De ser min aett.*

Idè osi dadi mai èma arani, they see that my mother runs:

Norwegian *De ser,* they see. Dutch *dat,* that. English *They see that my ma runs.*

Mai, my. *Maia,* mine:

French *ma,* my. Spanish *mi* and *mía,* my and mine.
Balochi *ma-i,* Old Persian *maiy,* of me, my, or mine.
Latin *mei,* of me. German *mein,* Norwegian *min,* my or mine.

Èma or *ima,* mother or a polite word for woman. Matu, the mother of God, the first woman and mother, a character in the Pygmy legend cycle:

Hebrew *em*, mother. English *ma*. Old Norse *amma*, grandmother. Sua and Kango Pygmy *ema*, mother. Egyptian *hem*, woman, wife, female organ. *Mut*, mother or Mut, a goddess who was worshiped as the great world-mother and mother of the gods. Egyptian paintings show Mut accompanied by Pygmies or "dwarfs." German *mütter*, Old Norse *mothir*, English *mother*. Latvian *mati*, mother or matrix (womb, female organ). Latin *mater*, mother; *matrona*, lady, married woman, matron; *Mater Deum Magna*, the great mother of the gods, an epithet of the goddess Cybele. Sanskrit *matar*.

Mai èma udi, my mother digs. *Mai èma odè*, my mother dies. *Idodu*, deadly, fatal:

English *My ma digs; My ma dies*. Dutch *dode*, Norwegian *dod*, German *tot*, dead.

Èma osi mau, mother sees a termite. *Mau*, termite, white ant:

Norwegian *Mor ser maur*, Mother sees ant. Armenian *mayr*, mother. *Mirciun*, ant, termite, pismire. French *mere*, mother. Dutch *mier*, ant. Swedish *myra*. Greek *myrmex*, ant. English *myrmecology*, the science or study of ants.

Idè ogo, they go. *Ogo*, to go away, move away. *A·ogo* (past form), ago. *Ogo!* Go!:

English *They go. Ago. Go!*

Idè, they. *Di*, you (singular):

Norwegian *de*, they or you (plural, polite). Low Dutch *di*, thee. English *they* and *thee*.

Mua èma, I am Mother. *Mua*, I am:

Old Norse *em amma*, am grandmother. Anglo-Saxon *am* or *eom*, am. Greek *eimai*, I am. Latin *sumus* and *sum*, we are and I am.

Mua, I am. *Muè*, me:

English *am* and *me*. Sue and Kango Pygmy *ime* or *me*, I. Gothic *im*, am. Bulgarian *ima*, Serbo-Croatian *imati*, Russian *imet*, Gaelic *me*, I or me. Sanskrit *me* or *ma*, me. Persian *man*, Balochi *ma*, I. Hittite *mu*, me. Old Bengali *mui*, I. French *me*, me or myself, *moi*, me; *C'est moi*, it is I.

Ua or *bua:* to be, to have, to comprise, to consist of ("be strong" = "have strength"):

> Egyptian *ua,* I or "I am." Old Norse *buá,* to be, live, dwell, have a household. Anglo-Saxon *búan,* to live or dwell. Lithuanian *bu.* Sua and Kango Pygmy *bu* or *bè,* to be. Anglo-Saxon *beon,* to be or become. English *be,* an irregular auxiliary verb that is not employed in its own present tense, as in Efé. (*mua,* I am, *dua,* you are, *ua,* he is, *amu·u·ua,* we are, *ami·u·ua,* you are, *a·ua,* they are)

Bèni, the participle of "to be," is related to the auxiliary Sua-Kango verb *be,* to be:

> English *been,* the participle of "to be."

Èti, to give. *Ogi,* to yield:

> Norwegian *yte,* to yield; *gi,* to give. Sua and Kango Pygmy *Gap'èmi!* Give to me! *Gap'asu!* Give to us! German *Gibt mir! Gibt uns!* English *Give me! Give us!*

Èti munè mai oro! Give me my arrow!:

> Norwegian *yte,* yield. Bulgarian *mene,* to me. Old Norse *min or,* English *my arrow.*

Oro, arrow or shaft. *Aru,* light wood or cane used for making archery equipment:

> Old Norse *or,* Anglo-Saxon *arwe,* English *arrow.* Latin *arundo,* arrow, shaft, cane, reed. Egyptian *aaru,* reed.

Ata, to take. *Ata mai oro!* Take my arrow!:

> Norwegian *ta,* to take. English *Take my arrow!*

Api, arrow. *Apili,* arrow-point. *Pilisi,* needle:

> Old Norse *pila,* arrow. Anglo-Saxon *pil,* javelin, nail, pointed object. Norwegian *pil,* arrow or shaft. Latin *pilum,* javelin. Greek *palton,* javelin. German *pfeil,* arrow. Latin *apex,* summit, point.

Di osi dadi oro, you (singular) see that arrow. *Dadi* sometimes precedes and sometimes follows the noun when used as a demonstrative pronoun or definite article. *Dadi* is employed as a relative pronoun in the sentence *Di osi dadi mai epe udi,* You see that my monkey digs:

Low Dutch *di*, thee. Dutch *dat*, that. Norwegian *det*, that or the.
English *Thee see that arrow. Thee see that my ape digs.* Norwegian
ape, Welsh *epa*, Anglo-Saxon *apa*, Dutch *aap*, Old Norse *api*, Sanskrit *kapi*, monkey or ape.

Ēdi, one, number one. *Adi*, that or the. *Ida*, it, he, she:

Gabon Pygmy *di*, one, number one. German *die, das*, or *der:* the
one, that one, that, the, it, he, she. Note the total elision of initial
vowels.

Idè osi ai arani, they see a runner. *Ai*, a, an, one who, one that, the
one who, the one that. *Ai* is mainly used to make nouns out of verbs:

English *They see a runner; a*, the indefinite article; *ae*, an archaic
form of a, an, one. Avestan *aeva*, Hittite *aika*, Gothic *ains*, one. Ger-
ran *eins*, number one; *ein*, a, an, the. Old Latin *oinos*, number one.
Greek *oi*, the (plural). Oi Pygmaoi, the Pygmies.

Efé'èni, Pygmies. *Efé*, Pygmy:

German *feen*, elves or fairies. Norwegian *feene*, "the fairies"; *fe*,
fairy; *feer*, fairies. Old French *féerie*, land of the fairies; French *fée*,
fairy. English *fairy* and *fay*. Dutch *fee*, German *fe*, Swedish *fe*, elf
or fairy.

Efé'èni osi apfo, the Pygmies see a hippopotamus. It is not necessary to use the indefinite article before every noun. *Opfo!* an excla-
mation of disgust, very curiously resembles the name of the *Apfo*:

German *Feen sehen pferd*, Fairies see horse. *Pfui!* Phooey; *pferd*,
horse; *nil-pferd*, Nile-horse, hippopotamus. Dutch *paard*, horse.
Greek *ippo* or *hippo*, pertaining to horses. Egyptian *apt*, hippopotamus. Greek *hippopotamos*, river-horse. Aristotle claimed that tiny
horses can be seen in the land of the Pygmies at the source of the
Nile. Perhaps this story originally dealt with the so-called "Pygmy
hippos" that reside in the African home of the Nile-horse.

Efé is the name of the Pygmy nation. It does not mean small or
diminutive. "*Efé*, the first man and father of all who came after,"
is the eponymous ancestor of the Pygmies (as in Israel, the patriarch and nation). Many European stories identify the fairy folk
with the ancestors or legendary heroes of antiquity. King Arthur,
for example, culminated his reign by departing for Fairyland,

where he dwells with his sister or mistress, Morgana the Fay. Efé
is the *afa* or *ava,* father of *afi*—man, mankind, Man:

> Norwegian *fe,* fairy; *far,* father; *fyr,* chap or fellow. Old Norse *afi,*
> man or grandfather; *Firar,* men or people. Anglo-Saxon *fyras,* men
> or human beings. Gaelic *fir,* men. Old Irish *fer,* man. Swedish *fe;*
> fairy; *fyr,* boy or lad; *fader,* father.

Evé, the ancestral hero or nation. *Ava,* father. *Avi,* man. The Pygmies constantly interchange the consonants *v* and *f:*

> Hebrew *Ever,* a legendary patriarch who sired the line of Abraham.
> *Av,* father, ancestor. *Avram* and *Avraham,* names of Abraham, are
> generally interpreted to mean "high father" and "father of a multi-
> tude." *Avir,* hero, protector. Latin *avus,* grandfather, ancestor. *Vir,*
> man, husband, hero. *Viri,* human beings, mortals. Sanskrit *vira,*
> man or hero. Lithuanian *vyras,* man or husband. Anglo-Saxon *wer,*
> man, husband, hero. *Werwulf,* man-wolf. *Werold,* men, people, the
> world. Old Norse *verold,* the world. *Verar* or *firar,* men. *Afi,* man or
> grandfather.

Olu, every. *Afa,* father:

> Greek *olos,* all. Norwegian *all,* all or everybody. *Far,* father. Old
> Norse *All-Föthr,* "Father of Everybody," an epithet of Odin, the
> patriarchal head of the Germanic pantheon.

Ava and *aba,* local variants of father. The consonant *v* sometimes
shifts with *b* in the *Efé* territories of the eastern Ituri:

> Latin *avus,* grandfather, ancestor. Hebrew *av* or *ab,* father, ancestor.
> Gothic *abba,* father; *aba,* man or husband. Egyptian *bah,* husband,
> male, phallus. Gabon Pygmy *baba,* Aka Pygmy *papa,* father. Greek
> *pappas,* papa. Sua and Kango Pygmy *apa, epa,* father. Egyptian *ap,*
> first ancestor. English *pa.* Latin *pater* and *Iuppiter,* father and Jupi-
> ter, the patriarchal head of the Roman pantheon. Greek *pateras,*
> father.

Matu, the first woman and mother. *Otu:* (1) forefather, grandfather, ancestor; (2) a title of God; (3) a title of his son Efé, the first
man and father of all who came after. Efé is also God the Father.
Matu and Efé are the mother and father of Efé the Savior, a character who corresponds with Egyptian "Horus the son of Isis and
Osiris" (Egyptian pictures show Horus as a Pygmy or "dwarf"):

Egyptian *mut* and *atef,* Russian *mat* and *otets,* Gaelic *mathair* and *athair,* mother and father. Old Norse *mothir,* mother. *Óthal,* patrimony, ancestral property. *Óthinn,* Odin, a divine patriarch who was called the Father of Everybody, represented as the father or son of Thor, and associated with the elves, dwarfs, or fairies.

Schebesta emphasized the fact that the Pygmy religion has not been derived from or affected by the Christian missions, whose activities are almost wholly directed toward the Negro population of equatorial Africa. His insistence is unnecessary, since the Pygmy legends have obvious Indo-European counterparts and Egyptian analogues that antedate the Christian faith by more than three thousand years. A few Pygmies who reside near the fringes of the forest have been officially "converted" by gifts of candy, salt and other delicacies. One of these "converts" explained to me that *Kilisito,* an Efé rendering of the name Christ, is a magic doll or idol to which the missionaries pray for candy.

Ironically enough, the only Christian document that has ever been translated into Efé is the Lord's Prayer or "Our Father." The text was prepared by Schebesta with the aid of a Negro missionary named Apollo. If Father Schebesta seriously intended to "convert" the Pygmies with this text, he might have much more usefully employed his time in carrying coals to Newcastle, selling iceboxes to the Eskimos, or shipping autos to the General Motors factory in Detroit. All of the local Pygmy groups, from east to west, traditionally pray aloud to the divine Father. Trilles defined this Pygmy deity as "God the Father, Chief, with no Superior." Schebesta himself explained that variants on the theme of "Father" constitute one entire class or category of the Pygmy names for God. Concerning the absence of formal or standardized prayers, Schebesta also wrote: "Your Pygmy is in everything an independent individualist, and like a poet, composes a song or prayer to suit the emotion of the moment." The spontaneous prayers of the poet-Pygmy are—at least in my opinion—far more meaningful and sincere than the fossil prayers of organized religion.

The Efé believe that their patriarchal deity commands a corps of spirits or supernatural beings. Some of these characters are personified spirits of nature, like our own Mother Earth. Some are complexly involved with the legends of the ancestors. According to Efé theology, the most outstanding ancestors were rewarded by promotion to a status intermediate between saint and angel, or angel and god. The first man, for example, ascended to the heavens after serving as the benevolent governor of the primordial Pygmy nation. Upon arriving, he established a residence on the moon, where he still assists God by serving as the god or angel of the moon.

The same legendary journey was accomplished by the Egyptian moon-god Thoth, who governed predynastic Egypt before he mysteriously ascended to the heavens. Thoth was variously represented as the grand vizier or as the brother of Osiris. According to some legends, after his earthly reign as king of Egypt, Osiris himself ascended to the moon. In Egyptian art both Thoth and Osiris are depicted wearing crescent-topped headdresses. Trilles describes as a "fetish" the crescent-shaped ornament that many local Pygmy populations wear upon a cord around the neck. Among the western Pygmies, he reports, this so-called fetish is associated with a "good spirit" or "messenger of God" who presides from the moon. "Praise be to Allah, the creator of the heavens and earth, who maketh the angels his messengers," proclaims the thirty-fifth chapter of the glorious Koran. The Islamic nations fly the emblem of the crescent moon upon their flags. The Arab geographers located Allah's garden paradise in the Mountains of the Moon, whence the lunar divinities of Egypt apparently embarked on their skyward safari.

Egyptologist E. A. Wallis Budge points out many similarities between the Judeo-Christian–Islamic angels and the Egyptian divinities, including the moon-god Thoth, whom he likened to our "recording angel." The "good spirits" of the Zoroastrian religion, a lofty theology formulated by the ancient Indo-European residents of Persia, have been compared to angels on the one hand, and to polytheistic gods on the other. Scholars have argued endlessly about the Egyptian concepts of God and the gods. These apparently conflicting ideas were maintained from the earliest known times. Hebrew analogues include the opening line of the eighty-second Psalm, "God standeth in the congregation of the mighty; he judgeth among the gods." The immense Egyptian pantheon probably included some three thousand gods. Egyptian hymns or prayers in honor of God nevertheless demonstrate a monotheistic concept of deity:

> "God is one and alone, and none other existeth with Him
> —God is the One, the One who hath made all things—God is
> a spirit, a hidden spirit, the spirit of spirits, the great spirit of
> the Egyptians, the divine spirit—God is the eternal One. He is
> eternal and infinite and endureth for ever and aye—God hath
> made the universe, and He hath created all that therein is; He
> is the Creator of what is in this world, and of what was, of
> what is, and of what shall be."[10]

"God was, He is, and He will be," say the Pygmies. The Hamitic, Semitic, and Indo-European stories of the gods correspond for the most part with the Pygmies' legends of their sainted or deified ancestors. The first man, for example, plays the role of God the Father in the Ituri Forest legend cycle. One Efé saga tells of how he slew giant monsters in the sky. In the "myth of the savior," his son defeats a dragon-like beast. A much more famous father-god, Zeus/Jupiter, fought in the sky with the monstrous serpent called Typhon. His son Hercules brawled with several hideous beasts sired by Typhon. The Egyptians' dragon-slaying son, Horus, was depicted in some legends as the offspring of the "elder Horus" or Ra-Horus, the heroic sky- or sun-god who waged his own epic battle with the devilish cosmic serpent Set-Apepi.

In Pygmy legend and theology the godly ancestors, spirits of nature, and major manifestations of God are generally arranged in trinities or triads. This mode of thought was faithfully echoed by the Indo-European, Hamitic and Semitic refugees from the Lost Paradise. Here are just a few examples:

A Norse triad that consisted of All-Father Odin and his two brothers created the world, according to the legends of the Eddas. The *Prose Edda* is itself made up of dialogues conducted by a mystical trinity called High One, Just-as-High and Third. The Hindu gods of fire, sun and wind are grouped together in the triad of Agni, Surya and Vayu; another Hindu trinity consists of Brahma, Vishnu and Siva, the Creator, Preserver and Destroyer.

According to the oldest legends of Egypt, a godly triad headed

---

[10] Sir E. A. Wallis Budge, *The Egyptian Book of the Dead*, pp. xcii–xciii.

by Thoth created the world. "Throughout Egypt generally," wrote
Wallis Budge, "the company of gods of a town or city were three
in number, and they were formed by the local deity and two gods
who were associated with him, and who shared with him, but in
a very much less degree, the honour and reverence which were
paid to him. Speaking generally, two members of such a triad
were gods, one old and one young, and the third was a goddess,
who was, naturally, the wife, or female counterpart, of the older
god. The younger god was the son of the older god and goddess,
and he was supposed to possess all the attributes and powers
which belonged to his father . . . The conception of the triad or
trinity is, in Egypt, probably as old as the belief in the gods . . .
In later times, the group of nine gods took the place of the triad,
but we are not justified in assuming that the ennead was a simple
development of the triad . . . The ennead is, however, often regarded as a triad of triads, and the three enneads of Heliopolis, as a
triad of a triad of triads. The conception of the ennead is probably
much later than that of the triad."[11]

The Judeo-Christian trinity needs no description. The members of the Babylonian pantheon were arranged in triads.
Kheper-à em neter uā neter khemt, "I became from god one gods
three," announced the Egyptian *History of the Creation of the
World and of the Gods.* This composition was attributed to Thoth,
the director of the creation trinity, who made that Pygmy-style
ascent to the heavens. The Greeks identified him with their own
deity Hermes, the angelic "messenger of the gods." The moon is
still inhabited, reported Trilles, by a Pygmy "messenger of God."

The Pygmies' extraordinary theology and cosmology do not
evoke the classic concept of a "primitive" religion. The very poorly
known beliefs of the South African Bushmen present an analogous
phenomenon. "We only know enough to detect in the Bushmen's
cosmology the traces of a rare intensity and of mental activity
and artistic creativity on a truly majestic scale," declared Andreas
Lommel, the Director of the Munich Museum of Ethnology.[12] The

---

[11] Sir E. A. Wallis Budge, *The Gods of the Egyptians,* Vol. 1, p. 114.

[12] Andreas Lommel, *Prehistoric and Primitive Man* (The Netherlands: The
Hamlyn Publishing Group Limited, 1968), p. 161.

Bushmen have been interpreted as the immediate descendants of the first human primates or so-called killer apes. During the one to two million years of their existence, we are told, these creatures never progressed beyond the pebble-tool stage of culture. Most of their "tools" are simply ordinary rocks—unflaked, unchipped, unshaped!—that differ in mineral composition from other rocks found near their fossil bones. Chimpanzees use rocks to crack open hard-shelled fruit. African vultures use rocks to crack open ostrich eggs. If the Bushmen represent the little-altered descendants of apish ancestors who never surpassed this intellectual level, how could the Bushmen conceivably come to possess a cosmology that shows traces of "majestic" mental powers?

One might logically suggest that the pygmoid Bushmen are a hybrid people who inherited these traces from the ancestral Pygmies, those quick-witted little folks whose mental endowments and astonishing religion inspired Schebesta to describe them as "an absolutely unique human phenomenon." But how, if the Pygmies represent the immediate descendants of the lame-brained killer apes, could the Pygmies conceivably come to possess majestic mental powers and a sublime monotheistic religion? Is it possible to imagine that the first human spawn of ravening "killer apes" believed in angels, saviors, divine commandments, holy trinities and other theological phenomena that evoke the loftiest beliefs of Hamitic, Semitic and Indo-European religion?

These questions are not asked or answered in *African Genesis*' detailed accounts of the fierce Ohio sparrows or Konrad Lorenz' perorations on that terrible territorial predator, the fishy Abudefduf.

The godly personalities of Efé legend are known by a number of names and epithets. The Efé concept of God is expressed in many deeply meaningful words for divine attributes, qualities or powers. Schebesta commented on the Pygmies' "disconcerting multitude of divine names," which he attempted to group in classes or categories. "His names are innumerable, they are manifold, and none knoweth their number," the ancient Egyptians commented on the being whom English-speaking peoples call "God."

Our modern churches have promoted the very false and bigoted opinion that the idea of God is a strictly Christian phenomenon. Non-Christian analogues are usually dismissed with the explanation that the so-called savages must have borrowed their religious ideas from "early missionaries." It is totally absurd to imagine that any Christian missionaries, early or recent, taught the Ituri Forest Pygmies to believe that their ancestors fought dragons and ascended to the moon. Since the Efé legend of the stolen fruit has a more conspicuous Old Testament counterpart, Trilles and Schebesta both feel obliged to insist that the Pygmy version has not been derived from Biblical sources. One might just as well deny that the Pygmies have plagiarized the Hindu, Greek and Norse accounts of the deity's plundered tree.

When the Norsemen were "converted" to Christianity, their concept of the mystical "world tree" was replaced by a Christian tree that occupied the same remarkable location: "The image of the tree that occupied the center of the world did not wholly die out. It was replaced by the conception of the Christian cross, believed to stand at the mid-point of the earth when it was raised at Calvary, at the spot once occupied by the fatal tree of Eden. No idea of this resemblance however seems to have occurred to Snorri when he wrote his description of the World Ash, taken from a number of *Edda* poems which still survive."[13]

Long ago, in the Norsemen's legendary paradise, the fruit of the gods was sinfully purloined. The gods included All-Father Odin's heroic son Thor, who battled with the giant Midgard Serpent in the classic manner of the Pygmies' hero-son.

In some territories, the elfin Efé believe that the primordial dragon will someday return. If he does, they predict, the events of the savior story will be repeated. "Thor will slay the Midgard Serpent," prophesies the apocalyptic legend of Ragnarok or Götterdämmerung, the Germanic twilight of the gods. The Zoroastrian legends of the apocalypse feature the dragon's future demise and the advent of a savior who will be born of a virgin. The apocalyptic legends of the New Testament predict that Jesus, the miraculous son of Mary, will eventually defeat "that old serpent, which is the Devil, and Satan."

---

[13] H. R. Ellis Davidson, *Gods and Myths of Northern Europe* (Baltimore: Penguin Books, 1964), p. 196.

The immaculate mother of Christian theology has very well-known connections with the Egyptian goddess Isis. The index to Wallis Budge's book *The Gods of the Egyptians* contains the terse equation: "Osiris = Christ." The text remarks that "the knowledge of the ancient Egyptian religion which we now possess fully justifies the assertions that the rapid growth and progress of Christianity in Egypt were due mainly to the fact that the new religion, which was preached there by Saint Mark and his immediate followers, in all its essentials so closely resembled that which was the outcome of the worship of Osiris, Isis, and Horus that popular opposition was entirely disarmed."[14]

The religion of Osiris, averred Wallis Budge, was "no doubt, wholly of African origin." The origin of all religion can be found in the legends and ideas of an African people who are "older than the sphinx, older than the pyramids, older than the texts written on papyrus, camel bones, bronze, brick, and stone." Throughout the equatorial forest, the Pygmies still cherish the hope that their heavenly Father will someday return or send a manifestation of himself to live among his people. They say that his spirit is always with them. They believe that he returns in visions or in dreams. "By their fault, they agree," wrote Trilles, "God no longer lives with them. He ascended on high. But even if he is on high, he returns sometimes, and above all, *he will return some day in a definitive fashion*. And that day they will be happy."

Orthodox Jews likewise await the coming of the Messiah. The Adventist sects of Christianity await his "second coming." Studies like Dr. Hugh J. Schonfield's book *The Passover Plot* interpret the events that transpired in Jerusalem during the first century A.D. as a deliberate reenactment of the ancient prophecies and legends. Pious Hindus meanwhile wait for the messianic return of Vishnu, the Preserver personage of their triune deity. His first human incarnation was Vamana or the Dwarf. He traditionally reclines upon the coils of the cosmic serpent Sesha. Wallis Budge described as a "squat pigmy" the miniature man who sometimes "stands upon a crocodile, and holds a serpent in each hand" to symbolize Ptah-Seker-Osiris, the triune god of the Egyptian resurrection. Dur-

[14] Sir E. A. Wallis Budge, *The Gods of the Egyptians*, Vol. 2, pp. 220–21.

ing the twenty-second dynasty, he reported, this divinity was "wholly identified with Osiris."[15]

Are the highly moral and ethical precepts of Osiris, the Egyptian Christ, at all affected by the question of his physical size?

Any truly rational and ethical person will agree that a man's stature cannot be gauged in inches alone. It is the measure of his soul, heart, or mind. Judged by this standard, I have known Pygmies who are ten feet tall.

---

[15] Sir E. A. Wallis Budge, *The Gods of the Egyptians*, Vol. 1, p. 507.

The Dancers of God

Osiris was a man given to mirth and jollity, and took great pleasure in music and dancing," wrote the ancient Greek historian Diodorus. The Metternich Stele, an Egyptian relic discovered at Alexandria in 1828 A.D., identifies the amiable Osiris, his avenging son Horus and other exalted manifestations of godhood with the wonderful Egyptian deity of mirth, pleasure, music and the dance. His name was Bes. He was pictured as a Pygmy or dwarf. His people were called Dancers of God by the earliest Egyptian Pharaohs. The Metternich Stele equates God's ancient congregation of gods with the Pygmies, who are depicted on this monument by portraits of Bes.

On one side of the stele, little Bes stands at the very top, surmounting all the other portraits and the hieroglyphic text (see illustration on page 86). In this picture of Bes, comments Egyptologist Budge, "we see him wearing the plumes of Shu and of the other gods of light and air, and the horns of Amen or of the Ram of Mendes, and above these are eight knives and the emblem of millions of years, and he holds in his hands all the emblems of sovereignty and dominion which Osiris holds, besides serpents, which he crushes in his grasp. He stands upon an oval wherein are grouped specimens of all the Typhonic beasts, and we may gather from his attitude that he is lord of them all."[1]

The gods of Egypt, whose attributes are combined in the figure of this deified Pygmy, were regarded as the direct ancestors of the Egyptians. As Budge explains, "they believed that they were a divine nation, and that they were ruled by kings who were themselves gods incarnate; their earliest kings, they asserted, were actually gods, who did not disdain to live upon earth, and to go about and up and down through it, and to mingle with men. Other ancient nations were content to believe that they had been brought into being by the power of their gods operating upon matter, but the Egyptians believed that they were the issue of the great God who created the universe, and that they were of directly divine origin. When the gods ceased to reign in their proper persons upon earth, they were succeeded by a series of demi-gods, who were in turn succeeded by the Manes, and these were duly followed by kings in whom was enshrined a divine nature with characteristic attributes."[2]

The ancestral gods of Egypt are summarized in the figure of the divine Pygmy, Bes. The Pygmy legends explain that God created or fathered the godly Pygmy ancestors, whose deeds are echoed by the exploits of the Egyptian ancestor-gods. Bes holds Osiris' emblems of sovereignty while he crushes serpents in his grasp and stands upon a crocodile. A "squat pigmy" is portrayed in the same heroic posture in the pottery figurines of the resurrection divinity. Like the slain and resurrected Osiris, the first man or father-god-king of the primordial Pygmy nation fell victim to the dragon. His

---

[1] Sir E. A. Wallis Budge, *The Gods of the Egyptians,* Vol. 2, p. 286.

[2] *Ibid.,* Vol. 1, p. 3.

The Metternich Stele (reverse)

resurrection was accomplished by his son, who is represented as the reincarnated image of himself in the Efé "myth of the savior." On the other side of the Metternich Stele (see illustration on page 88), the dragon-slaying hero Horus stands at bottom center in the victorious posture of his father, Bes-Osiris. The head of Bes is placed above the head of Horus, Budge explains, to show that "the two heads represent, after all, only phases of one and the same god."

The head of Bes, the deified Dancer of God, simultaneously evokes the facial features of a man and a cat. This can be seen more clearly in an Egyptian portrait that depicts the god with the rounded ears and pointed tongue of a cat:

Bes

To discover why the dragon-fighting god of music, mirth and dancing was endowed with the head of a cat, we shall consult the language and legends of the living Dancers of God who still reside in Bes's ancient homeland. It was located, according to Budge, "a few degrees to the north of the Equator." He remarked, "The knowledge of the god, and perhaps figures of him, were brought from this region, which the Egyptians called the 'Land of the Spirits,' to Egypt in the early dynastic period, when kings of Egypt loved to keep a pygmy at their courts. The earthly kinsmen of the god who lived to the south of Egypt were, no doubt, well known even to the predynastic Egyptians . . ."[3]

In the Efé language of Bes's earthly kinsmen, the small forest

---

[3] *Ibid.*, Vol. 2, pp. 287–88.

The Metternich Stele (obverse)

cats who reside in the land of trees and spirits are called *pusu:* Egyptian *basu* or *besa,* a feline animal that Budge defined as *Felis cynailurus.* He gave this as the source name of Bes, the cat-headed Dancer of God, and his Semitic analogue, the Arabic deity Buss. The cat-headed goddess Bast or Pasht presided in Bubastis, the ancient Egyptian "city of cats." According to zoologists, the domesticated cats of Europe are descended from the domesticated cats of ancient Egypt. Efé *pusu* preys on fauna that include *musese,* the little mouse, a very diminutive species of Ituri Forest rodent: Norwegian *pus* and *mus,* Armenian *pisig* and *mug,* Dutch *poes* and *muis,* English *puss* and *mouse.* Efé *pusu-pusu,* a reduplicated form of the cat name, is matched by French *pou-pous.* Efé *musese* is echoed by Latin *mus* and Greek *mys,* mouse. Old Norse *mysla* meant "little mouse."

Like the Indo-European variants of "puss," the Efé word *pusu* is generally used to designate small cats. The Pygmies admire cats as clever, alert, freedom-loving hunters, who in these respects resemble Pygmies. Like the Pygmies, the cat has sharp-sighted, large and very beautiful eyes. "Her eyes were magnificent, but absurdly large for such a small creature," Henry Stanley commented on the first Ituri Forest Pygmy he encountered. Anthropologists have remarked on the extraordinary eyesight of the Pygmies, who do not suffer from color blindness and have the keenest vision of any living humans. Their minds are also very keen: to use a favorite Efé phrase, Pygmies are as "clever as a cat."

Many Pygmy bands express this feeling of spiritual and intellectual kinship by claiming the cat or leopard as a clan emblem or symbolic representation of their ancestor. Schebesta remarked that this Pygmy leopard mystique is founded on a feeling of respect and fellowship. He erred, however, in describing it as totemism. The Pygmies do not worship leopards or animals of any variety. They have no totem feasts at which hyper-sacred animals are ritually murdered and devoured. Far from granting the leopard sacrosanct immunity, they truthfully boast that "Grandpa" runs with his tail between his legs when the mighty Pygmy hunters shout their leopard-chasing cry. When a leopard turns man-eater—a very rare event—the Pygmies courageously hunt him down and kill him without hesitation.* In most respects, the members of the Pygmy leopard clans can be compared to the American members of the Lions Club or to the exuberant college boys who call their football teams the Lafayette Leopards, the Princeton Tigers or the Pittsburgh Panthers. They cannot be described as totemistic according to any valid anthropological definition of the word.

During recent times the Pygmies' harmless leopard mystique may have been taken over and atrociously perverted by the non-Pygmy members of the criminal Anyoto "Leopard Man" Society. Back in the days of ancient Egypt, the Pygmies' views on the intellectual kinship of man and cat were very beautifully expressed in this Egyptian picture of a nameless leopard with a man's winged head:

A fabulous leopard

"The human head on an animal represented the intelligence of a man, and the wings the swift flight of the bird, and the body of the leopard the strength and the lithe motions of that animal," E. A. Wallis Budge commented on this picture. By placing the head of a man on the leopard and, conversely, by placing the head of a

---

* Man-eating leopards have been known to tear the roofs or doors off Negro huts in order to snatch and devour a child. It is a very remarkable fact that leopards almost never bother the Pygmies, who sleep in flimsy little leaf-thatched huts that have no doors. If they had doors, say the Pygmies, they would not be able to look out and see the starry sky. They feel stifled and rather claustrophobic in a Negro hut or white man's house, and will not willingly sleep behind a closed door.

cat on the Pygmy god Bes, the Egyptians worked the pictorial equation in both directions. The Efé Pygmies tell a rather charming little legend that depicts the leopard as the first man or father-god-king of the primordial Pygmy nation. In most Efé stories, this cat-clever personage is portrayed as a man. On the Metternich Stele, Bes is pictured as a cat-headed Pygmy who holds the sovereign emblems of Osiris, the father-god-king of prehistoric Egypt.

In Bubastis, the Egyptian city of cats, Osiris was the most important member of the local trinity. His wife was Bast, the cat- or lion-headed goddess whose sacred animal was the cat. She was represented as the personified "soul of Isis," the "Mother of God," and the holy "Lady of the East." The Pygmies of Gabon and Cameroon direct special prayers and offerings toward the east, reported Trilles, because they consider it to be "the side of God." A similar opinion has prevailed in many Hamitic, Semitic and Indo-European religions, as exemplified in the opening lines of an Anglo-Saxon prayer: "I stand facing the east; I pray for favour. I pray to the Great Lord; I pray to the Mighty Ruler; I pray to the Holy Guardian of Heaven."

The third member of the Bubastian trinity was Horus, the son of Osiris and Bast. Like his cat-headed mother, Horus was also known by the feline name or title Bast. To make this trinity more consistent, the cat-headed god Bes might be substituted for Osiris, whose royal emblem he holds on the Metternich Stele. The stele's several rows of small pictures include a figure of Horus equipped with the typically short legs of an African Pygmy.

The gods of Bubastis were especially dear to the Egyptian monarch Pharaoh Pepi I. In his funerary inscription, he piously declared that his heart was the heart of Bestet or Bast. Pepi undoubtedly revered Bes, the deified Dancer of God, since he expressed the humble hope that in the Other World he might achieve the ultimate honor: to dance like a Pygmy before the great throne of God. "He who is between the thighs of Nut," Pepi I affirmed in another text, "is the Pygmy who danceth like the god and who pleaseth the heart of the god before his great throne."

During this very early period in Egyptian history, the Pygmies had already become legendary characters. For this reason, Pepi II was transported with joy when he learned that a living Dancer of

God was being brought northward to Egypt by Herkhuf, Prince of Elephantine, who had boldly journeyed to the Pygmies' fabled homeland in the south. Herkhuf reported his exploits in a letter to the king. Pepi II, or Neferkare as he was also called, sent a reply that was engraved on the facade of Herkhuf's tomb.

"You announce in your letter," the king of Egypt wrote to Herkhuf, "that you have brought from the Land of Trees, and from the Land of Spirits, a Pygmy Dancer of God, similar to the one whom the Conservator of the divine Seals, Ba-Wex-Djed, brought from Punt during the days of King Isosi . . . Hail to the Dancer of God, to the one who rejoices the heart of Pharaoh, to the one King Neferkare, who lives eternally, sighs for . . . When you bring him to the ship, choose reliable men to keep watch on both sides of the vessel, lest perchance he may fall into the water. When he sleeps at night, post ten stout fellows to sleep alongside him. My majesty yearns mightily to see this Pygmy. See that you bring the Pygmy alive, hale, and sound, to my palace, and then my majesty will confer on you far higher awards than those given to the Conservator of divine Seals in the days of King Isosi."

It is a ritual performance for any anthropologist who writes a book about the Pygmies to quote extracts from Pepi-Neferkare's famous letter to Herkhuf. Having made this display of erudition, the anthropologists never mention the subject again nor do they even pause to wonder why Pharaoh Pepi II sighed so ecstatically over a single Pygmy, why Pharaoh Pepi I praised the Pygmies as the most godlike human beings, or why the Egyptians represented their divine kings' ancestors, the gods, with pictures and figures of Pygmies. The least astute anthropologists have spread the opinion that the Pygmies are descendants of "shrunken Negroes." The sainted ancestors of Efé legend are portrayed as lily-white. The ancient Egyptians, who identified the far more ancient Pygmies with their divine ancestors, were full-fledged members of the white or Caucasoid race.

To the Pharaohs of the Old Kingdom, a living Pygmy must have seemed like the reincarnated image of their ancestral gods. On the Metternich Stele, the Pygmy divinity Bes stands at the very top, incorporating the greatest gods in his image. The stele, which

The Great Sphinx of Gizeh

was found in the city of Alexandria during the building of a cistern, has the relatively recent estimated date of 378–360 B.C., but the ideas expressed on this and other "cippi of Horus" are "extremely old," as E. A. Wallis Budge averred.

The text of the Metternich Stele begins with the "Chapter on the Invocation of the Cat." The invocation is addressed to a deity who was sometimes called The Cat. His symbol on earth was the Great Sphinx of Gizeh—a gigantic stone cat with the body of a lion and the head of a man. He was the great sun- or sky-god Ra-Heru or Ra-Temu-Khepera-Heru-Khuti, who is better known to crossword-puzzle fans by the simpler appellation Ra. Both of the longer names include Heru or Horus, which was used to designate the elder Horus or god of the sky and a number of "Horus gods," including Horus the son of Ra-Heru and Horus the son of Isis and Osiris. At Bubastis, Osiris' son was sometimes called by the feline name of his mother, the cat-headed goddess Bast. The Alexandrian Metternich Stele places the wise cat head of the Pygmy divinity Bes above the head of Horus. Budge comments that "on the Metternich Stele we see the head of the 'Old Man who renews his youth,' and the Aged One 'who maketh himself once again a boy,' placed above that of Horus, the god of renewed life and of the rising sun, to show that the two heads represent, after all, only phases of one and the same god."

Horus and his father Bes-Osiris conquer the Typhonian beasts of evil on the opposite sides of the Metternich Stele. In this capacity, remarks Budge, the Pygmy divinity Bes plays the role of "the aged Sun-god." A vignette from *The Egyptian Book of the Dead* (Chapter 17) shows the god in the form of a cat, cutting off the head of the villainous cosmic serpent:

Cat cutting serpent

The accompanying text, writes Budge, tells of "a cat which took up its position by the Persea tree in Heliopolis on the night when the foes of Osiris were destroyed, and in the commentary which follows it is stated that this 'male Cat' was Ra himself . . ."[4]

Ra-Heru, a phase of the Pygmy divinity Bes, thus defeated "Apepi the prince of darkness, who had taken the form of a monster serpent." Their contest reputedly transpired beside "the sacred Persea Tree of Heliopolis," which is represented in the cat-versus-dragon picture by the rather lumpy-looking vegetable to the left of the cat. It is probable that this sacred Egyptian tree has some connection with the forbidden-fruit tree of Efé legend. The theft of the Pygmy fruit apparently generated the dragon-fight that culminated in the son-avenger's victory. A sacred tree and a supernatural reptile are found together in many similar tales of the lost paradise, including the Hebrew story of the forbidden-fruit tree and insidious snake in the grass of Eden. The Egyptian picture of the cat defeating the serpentine "prince of darkness" is echoed, moreover,

[4] Sir E. A. Wallis Budge, *The Gods of the Egyptians*, Vol. 2, p. 363.

by the expected victory of the heroic "lion of the tribe of Judah," as the fifth chapter of Revelation calls the Messiah who will someday defeat Satan, that snaky prince of darkness whose machinations caused the desecration of the deity's sacred tree.

The divine and/or royal title "Lion of Judah" is currently claimed by Emperor Haile Selassie, the two hundred twenty-fifth consecutive Solomonic ruler of Ethiopia. In the old kingdom of Israel, where King Solomon reigned, the lion was the animal emblem of sovereignty. Its many European counterparts include the royal lions of Great Britain and of my native country, Belgium. In June 1960 King Baudouin honored my humanitarian labors in the former Belgian Congo by presenting me with the Gold Medal of the Royal Order of the Lion. Zaïre uses the leopard as its national animal emblem. In the Ituri Forest, where there are no lions, the Pygmies use cats and leopards as clan emblems and symbolic representations of their ancestral father-god-king. A feminine counterpart is provided in an Efé story that casts a motherly leopardess in the role of Matu, the Mother of God. The cat- or lion-headed goddess of Bubastis was represented as the very "soul of Isis" or *mut neter*, the Mother of God whose Christian counterpart is the Virgin Mary.

In *Moses and Monotheism*, Sigmund Freud very simplistically writes of the Egyptian deities: "They have the shapes of animals as if they had not yet overcome their origin in the old totem animals." In *The Gods of the Egyptians*, Budge declares that "there is no reason for thinking that the animal worship of the Egyptians was descended from a system of totems and fetishes." His own explanation was rather simplistic, however. He maintained that "the Egyptians first worshipped animals as animals, and nothing more, and later as the habitation of divine spirits or gods." During the three-thousand-year history of dynastic Egypt, many animal-worshiping sects arose; the earliest Egyptian attitudes evoke the poetic symbolisms of Pygmy legend and theology.

Bes and Bast, the Egyptians' cat-headed father and mother gods, have rather obvious parallels among the Indo-Europeans. Down to the twentieth century, the residents of rural Europe have practiced some remarkable feline rituals: "At Briançon, in Dauphiné, at the beginning of reaping, a cat is decked out with ribbons, flowers, and ears of corn . . . At the close of the reaping the cat is again decked out with ribbons and ears of corn; then they dance and make merry. When the dance is over the girls solemnly strip the cat of its finery. At Grüneberg, in Silesia, the reaper who cuts the last corn goes by the name of the Tom-cat. He is enveloped in rye-stalks and green withes, and is furnished with a long plaited tail. Sometimes as a companion he has a man similarly dressed, who is called the (female) Cat."[5]

Some of these festivals were climaxed by the ritual killing of the cat. The death of the feline "corn-spirit" has been likened to the death of Osiris, who was also involved in Egyptian agrarian rituals that inspired Sir James George Frazer to describe him as a "corn-god" and his death as "the decay of vegetation." The feline corn-spirit and Osiris as the corn-god are united in Bes-Osiris, the cat-headed Pygmy god who stands atop the Egyptian Metternich Stele. The agrarian rituals are probably connected with the Kango Pygmy legend of the plant and animal life that dwindled away when the father-god-king departed from the primordial paradise and the Efé stories of the frightful famine that blighted the Pygmy Eden.

The European devotees of the corn-spirit donned long plaited tails for the performance of the rituals. In the Ituri Forest, the Pygmies sometimes don animal-hide sarongs or belts with long dangling tails for the performance of special religious dances. The patriarchal elders, who function as wholly nondespotic chiefs (or kings) like to wear tailed garments (without a white tie) as emblems of their dignified authority. In ancient Egypt the kings or Pharaohs wore tails, as did the gods in their pictorial representations. The modish Pygmy tail dangles from a hide garment. E. A. Wallis Budge theorized that the name of the Egyptians' Pygmy divinity "seems to have been bestowed upon him in very early times because of the animal's skin which he wore; the animal itself was called *besa* or *basu*. The Efé word for cat, *pusu*, suggests the simpler explanation that the name of the god originally meant cat or puss. The echoing name of Pasht or Bast, the cat-headed Egyptian goddess whose sacred animal was the cat, and the use of the

[5] Sir James George Frazer, *The Golden Bough: A Study in Magic and Religion*, one-volume abridged edition (New York: The Macmillan Company, 1948), p. 453.

same name to designate her son Horus certainly tend to support this explanation.

In his guise as the genial god of music, mirth and dancing, Bes is shown, complete with dangling tail, in an Egyptian picture of the divine Pygmy strumming on his harp.

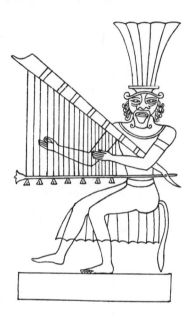

In the photo-insert section, you will find my recent photographic portraits of Pygmies making beautiful music on the Efé harp. When I showed the Egyptian drawing of Bes as a harpist to Pygmy friends in the eastern Ituri, they became tremendously excited. "Why, that is our harp," they exclaimed, "and that is the tail of a dancer or elder, and that is our most beautiful feather headdress. Who is this Pygmy?" I answered, "He was a god who was worshiped long ago by some people called Egyptians." Ebuné, the elder of the Antigbetu camp, then said, "We have never heard of them, but the man in the picture is a Pygmy. If they liked the Pygmies, they must have been good-hearted people. It is wrong, though, to worship anyone but God."

My photograph of Ebuné in the photo-insert section shows a man with bright copper skin and thin lips, who looks rather like

a broad-nosed Caucasoid. The Egyptian representatives of the
Caucasoid stock liked to call themselves "the red men" and sometimes painted their self-portraits bright crimson red to emphasize
their ethnic complexion. The skin color of the yellow-tan Pygmies
approaches that of Berbers, Arabs and southern Europeans. Anthropologists who portray the Pygmies as degenerate Negroes do not
print pictures of Pygmies such as Ebuné. Such photographic facts
might weaken the theories.

Professor Carleton S. Coon wants to prove his theories by ex-
perimenting with Pygmy children. In ancient Egypt, the Pygmy god
Bes was venerated as the "protector of children and youths, and a
god who studied to find them pleasure and amusement." The Pygmies are still devoted protectors and lovers of children. They have
no equivalents of the orphanage—that ostensibly civilized institution—since any orphaned child is immediately adopted and embraced by relatives or friendly neighbors. Cruel or neglectful treatment of children is condemned in the Pygmies' laws and commandments. When there is little food to be had, the parents go
hungry. The children are fed.

"Not have I carried off the milk from the mouth of the babe
. . . not have I carried off the food of the infant," the virtuous
Egyptian soul or heart declared in the "negative confessions" made
before Osiris in his other-worldly judgment hall. Those who could
not truthfully make these statements were damned to hellish tor-
ments. "Suffer the little children to come unto me, and forbid them
not, for of such is the kingdom of God," Jesus declared in the New
Testament. "And whosoever shall receive one such little child in
my name receiveth me. But whoso shall offend one of these little
ones which believe in me, it were better for him that a millstone
were hanged about his neck, and that he were drowned in the
depth of the sea."[6]

As the conquering "lion of the tribe of Judah," the Messiah
or Christ is the Judeo-Christian counterpart of Osiris' son Horus.
In Egyptian Per-Bast, the city of cats whose original name later
evolved into "Bubastis," Horus was called by the feline title Bast.
His cat- or lion-headed mother, Bast, was venerated at many

---

[6] Mark 10:14; Matthew 18:5–6.

other localities, including the city of Dendera, where her son was represented as the lion-headed god Ari-hes. Horus is identified on the Metternich Stele as a phase or incarnation of the cat-headed father-god Bes-Osiris. The lion Messiah in Revelation and the divine Son in the Judeo-Christian trinity, Christ is also regarded as one with his Father.

Another Christian trio, the holy family, includes the mother of Christ. Horus' miraculous mother was represented in many local Egyptian trinities by the womanly figure of Isis. In other districts, cat-headed ladies known by several local names were exalted as the mother-god. The most archetypal was Bast, the feline "soul of Isis," who would make a very fitting mother for Revelation's lion Messiah. The Jews, who have long awaited the Messiah's coming, say in the book of Exodus that their ancestors departed from Egypt, the land of the Nile, and in the book of Genesis that their ancestors originated in a paradisaical garden-forest at the source of Gihon-Nile. Here the Pygmies wait for God or a manifestation of God to descend from heaven into the equatorial forest homeland of the cat-clever Pygmy ancestors who correspond with Egypt's greatest gods. The Hindus' expected Messiah, Vishnu—the Preserver personage of the Brahma-Vishnu-Siva trinity—is represented in his fourth avatar or "down-going" as a heroic being, half man and half lion, who is called Nrisinha or "man-lion."

Man-headed and lion-bodied, the Great Sphinx of Gizeh still endures as a giant testimonial to the wisdom of the ancestral Pygmies. Concerning this monument E. A. Wallis Budge wrote: ". . . The idea of Plutarch and others that it typified the enigmatical wisdom of the Egyptians and strength and wisdom is purely fanciful. The men who made the Sphinx believed they were providing a colossal abode for the spirit of the sun-god which they expected to dwell therein and to protect their dead; it faced the rising sun, of which it was a mighty symbol." To resolve this conflict, the Pygmies will show that the Sphinx commemorates both the celestial divinity and the wisdom of the ancestors.

Ahu, the Efé leopard or big cat, is a poetic symbol of the ancestral Pygmy or wise father-god-king. In some legends the Pygmy forefather plays the role of Ahuru, the great god of heaven or the sky. Strictly speaking, this name should only be employed to describe the most important, father-creator member of the supreme Efé trinity, but it is very widely used as a name for God or the Lord in general. Schebesta gave *Ahuru* in the variant form *Ahura*:

> Egyptian Hu, the Sphinx or earthly symbol of Horus. Hur or Heru, the sky-god, God or "Horus." In the form of a cat, he fought and defeated the dragon. Avestan Ahuro or Ahura, Lord, God or Lord God. Ahura Mazda, the Wise Lord. He is the father-creator of the universe. Aided by his "good angel of obedience," he will someday defeat the dragon. Old Norse *Herran*, Lord, an epithet of All-Father Odin. He is the prime member of a creative trinity that made the universe. His son or father, Thor, fought and will fight again with the dragon. German *herr*, lord, master or mister; *herrin*, lady or mistress. Greek Hera, the goddess of heaven and queenly consort of Zeus. He is the sky-father who fought with the cosmic serpent Typhon. Heracles or "Hercules"—the son of Hera and Zeus, he battled with Typhon's offspring. Egyptian Heru-sa-Ast-sa-Asar, Horus, son of Isis and Osiris, the junior dragon-fighter. Heru-ur, the elder Horus or senior dragon-fighter.

Ahuku is the owl, the owl/eagle or the hunting bird in general. The Congo Forest serpent eagle (*Dryotriorchis spectabilis*) has the well-known habit of descending from heaven to pluck climbing snakes from the trees of the equatorial forest. In some Efé territories, Ahuku is regarded as a minor manifestation of Ahuru: Sanskrit *ghuka*, the owl; Old Norse *haukr*, the hawk, who fights the serpent in many Eurasian legends of the war with the dragon; Egyptian Hur or Heru, the hawk, the sky-god or "Horus," sometimes depicted as a hawk-headed man. In this picture, as "The God Comprehending All Gods," he has hawk wings and the head of a man (see illustration on page 102).

Compare this representation of Horus with the Metternich Stele's portrait of the Pygmy god Bes (see p. 86, top of stele) Bes is shown, explains Budge, as "the aged sun-god in the form of a man-hawk." The smaller figures on the Stele include "a hawk god, with dwarf's legs, and holding bows and arrows." The Pygmies have typically short and rather bowed legs. The bow and arrow is a traditional Pygmy weapon. In the Efé "myth of the savior," a spear is used to dispatch the dragon. The smaller figures on the Stele show Horus spearing a crocodile. Efé Ahuru, *ahu* and *pusu* are the heavenly divinity, the big cat and the small cat: Egyptian Hur and Hu, Horus and the Sphinx; *basu* or *besa*, a kind of cat. Bast is a name of Horus and his cat-headed mother; Bes is the wise old Pygmy god whose feline head surmounts the head of Horus (see page 88, bottom center of stele) to show that Bes and Horus are "phases of one and the same god."

Bes is represented with the Pygmies' characteristically short legs, long arms and long torso in an old Egyptian portrait (see illustration on page 103).

Most of the Egyptian gods are represented carrying an ankh in their hands. Bes wears a Christian-style cross at his neck. The sign of the cross was featured in many pre-Christian religions; here we see it worn by Bes, a Pygmy god whom the Egyptians identified with Osiris and Horus. Like the father and son persons of the Judeo-Christian trinity, they are forms of the same god. They are not "God."

The Osirian religion originated in Africa during prehistoric times. Today, as strange as it may seem, the African Pygmies are still far more Christian in their ways than the modern members of the assorted Christian sects or churches. "The Christian churches and Christianity have nothing in common save in name: they are utterly hostile opposites," wrote Leo Tolstoy in *The Kingdom of God Is Within You.* "The church has always been willing to swap off treasures in heaven for cash down," declared the American lawyer Robert Ingersoll. "The churches have killed their Christ," mourned the English poet Tennyson. "What! I a Christian? No, indeed! I'm Christ," declared the savior-son of organized Christian religion in a satirical poem by Ambrose Bierce.

The Egyptian pictures of Bes, or my modern photographs of the living Dancers of God may not seem particularly beautiful or inspiring to people who picture the Savior in terms of Jeffrey Hunter, the Technicolor Christ of the Hollywood epic *King of Kings.* Every group has its own local standards of beauty. "What is beautiful is good, and who is good will soon be beautiful," the Greek

The god comprehending all gods

poetess Sappho more objectively declared. Judged from a moral point of view, the Pygmies rank with the most beautiful members of our species.

"If you give a piece of your heart to things that you own," say my Efé friends, "you cannot love people with all of your heart. You become the slaves of the things that you own. We love and take care of people, not things. The Negroes and the white men think we are poor. Let them think what they please! Our ancestors, the men of the first ages, were rich and powerful. They lived in great villages. They used wonderful tools. They worked miracles. These things did not make them happy. Happiness is the smile on the face of your wife when you bring home the antelope. Happiness is the laughter of your children. Happiness is the music of the harp and the flute. Happiness is freedom. These are not things that you own—they are things you enjoy."

Schebesta described this Pygmy attitude as the "systematic renunciation of material riches," the "unimaginable poverty of material civilization," or a state of "stupefying poverty." Trilles called the western Pygmies advocates of *la vie Bohémienne*,

The god Bes

the Bohemian way of life. The Egyptians worshiped Bes-Osiris as the patron saint of music, dancing and all genial pleasures. "He is what we should call an artist and a Bohemian in His manner of life," George Bernard Shaw remarked of the New Testament Christ. Jesus' views on material riches were expressed in some very famous words: "If thou wilt be perfect, go and sell that thou hast, and give to the poor, and thou shalt have treasure in heaven: and come and follow me . . . Verily I say unto you that a rich man shall hardly enter into the kingdom of heaven. And again I say unto you, it is easier for a camel to go through the eye of a needle, than for a rich man to enter into the kingdom of God."

Christianity is currently preached by the jeweled pontiff and richly robed cardinals of the Vatican Palace. In his recent book *Worldly Goods*, James Gollin estimated that the total wealth of the world-wide Catholic organizations is at least seventy billion dollars. Christianity is preached by Protestant Revivalist ministers equipped with Cadillacs, private planes and income-tax advisers. Christianity is preached to Christian congregations who wear their "Sunday best" clothing, yawn through the sermon, put their money in the collection plate, and emerge shriven of their sins. Christianity is *practiced* by the African Pygmies, who are represented as the founding fathers of the faith in Egypt's oldest legends.

Like Bes-Osiris, the deified Dancer of God, the Pygmies enjoy the dancing, singing and gaiety of the Bohemian life. Parents and children share this life; they do not live in different worlds separated by the ever-widening generation gap of our "Christian" society. The children of the Western world courageously protest against the gross materialism, pious hypocrisy and spiritual squalor of urban life. The parents denounce the children as wastrels. The children do not consider it their sacred duty to kill and be killed in unjust or futile wars, so the parents call them cowards. The children dance and sing like Pygmies at their hippie festivals; the parents sit and push the little buttons that operate their color television sets. The children favor beards, long hair and picturesque clothing. The parents call them freaks and perverts, although those same parents revere idealized portraits of a bearded, long-haired Christ clad in a flowing robe rather than a gray flannel business suit.

The Egyptians left us portraits of a divine Pygmy dancer, singer, musician, poet, protector of children, and virtuous adversary of the Satanic powers. The Messiah of Orthodox Jewish religion will be born as the direct descendant of an ancestral hero who danced around the ark of the covenant, strummed upon the harp, composed poetic prayers or psalms, and slew wicked giants in the classic style of the hero, god or king. "Little David, play on your harp!" implores the modern folk-song. The legends of the divine hero have probably been attached to David, a semihistoric king who is represented as the traditional ancestor of the Jewish Messiah and/or the Christian Savior.

By installing their Pygmy ancestors as "gods," the Egyptians worshiped goodness incarnate. By no coincidence, the whole substance and meaning of Pygmy religion is "Be good to other people. Respect, protect and preserve. Do not destroy." These are laws, not legends. The legends are almost wholly involved with the cataclysms of the past and the apocalyptic future. Such events are prominently featured in the New Testament speeches of Jesus: "For nation shall rise against nation, and kingdom against kingdom, and there shall be famines, and pestilences, and earthquakes in diverse places . . ."

On the last page of *Adam's Ancestors*, Dr. Leakey gave Adam's descendants a warning:

> Not only has the over-specialization of our brain power made us capable of inventing the means of the destruction of our species by atom bombs, but it has also resulted in our creating for ourselves such a highly specialized material culture that we are far more—not less—at the mercy of Nature than man ever was before. We know that in the past, since man first became man, there have been very great changes both of climate and geography. Violent earthquakes such as those that must have accompanied much of the Rift Valley faulting in Africa at the end of the hand-axe times would have disturbed man of those times very little, except for the few in the immediate vicinity, but today

similar earthquakes would cause more havoc and a higher death rate than any atom bomb.[7]

The Efé "Dancers of God" dwell on the edge of the African Rift Valley. To the east of Efé territory lies Olduvai Gorge, where Dr. Leakey unearthed *Homo habilis*. Anthropologists have theorized, purely on the basis of physical evidence, that the Pygmies are the ancestors of mankind. The Egyptian founders of man's oldest historic civilization identified the Pygmies with their great ancestral gods.

The God of these beautiful Pygmy "gods" is represented as the Giver of the Law. "In the beginning," say the Pygmies, "God lived with men and gave them his commandments." The religion of the gods is practiced by every person who observes the Pygmies' Sinai-style commandments. About their legal code, Schebesta says, "The commandments and prohibitions of the Supreme Legislator are another thing from taboo, and are not merely simple economic or social precepts: they are of an ethical nature."

In *Moses and Monotheism* Sigmund Freud interpreted the legendary Hebrew lawgiver Moses as an "Egyptian prince" who converted the Jews to a relatively recent cult founded by the eighteenth-dynasty monarch Pharaoh Akhnaton. To support his theories, Freud accused the pre-Akhnaton Egyptians of practicing "unlimited polytheism" and ridiculed their veneration for "a grotesque creature like the dwarfish Bes." Freud's morally dwarfish book makes no other mention of Bes, the Pygmy Dancer of God whom the Egyptians identified with Osiris and Horus, the Father and Son of the derivative Judeo-Christian trinity. "If you love me, keep my commandments," urged the New Testament Christ. By his standards, the Pygmies are Christians. We are not.

---

[7] L. S. B. Leakey, *Adam's Ancestors: The Evolution of Man and His Culture*, p. 218.

The Angel of the Moon

The divine commandments were originally delivered to mankind, according to every pertinent Pygmy legend, by a deity who dwelled on earth before he mysteriously ascended to the heavens. Some Pygmy bands believe that God is a solemn old man who lives in the moon. Others maintain that the deity has his principal residence in the moon, but spends much of his time traveling among the stars. To keep constant watch over human affairs, he accordingly stationed his chief servant, messenger or angel on the moon. The latter theory, reported Trilles, is favored by the Pygmies of Gabon and Cameroon: "The moon, except in certain legends, is neither a divinity nor a spirit. But it is inhabited by a spirit, Rtwa, or Ndris, messenger of God, who watches men and transmits his observations to God. Even though he is not wicked, it is better to avoid exposing oneself to his gaze."

In Efé country, near the Mountains of the Moon, the Pygmies tell many wonderful stories of the celestial journeys undertaken by God and his chief assistant, the good spirit, god or angel of the moon. God is usually represented as the original source of the commandments, the lunar angel as the intermediary who transmits the deity's laws to the primordial Pygmy nation. The angel is identified with Efé, the first man and eponymous ancestor of the Efé Pygmies. Like God, Efé ascended to heaven where he took up office as the lunar angel. During his earthly reign as the fatherly ruler of the ancient Pygmy nation, he not only gave the divine commandments but invented every form of spiritual and material civilization. In this capacity, Schebesta defined him as the "civilizing hero." His career was interrupted by the murderous dragon, but he was gloriously resurrected by the dragon-slaying son-incarnation whom Schebesta called the "legendary savior."

Osiris, the Egyptian victim of the dragon and father of the savior, was likewise represented as the civilizing hero and giver of the law. Plutarch's *Treatise on Isis and Osiris* comments on this phase of his career:

> Osiris, being now become king of Egypt, applied himself towards civilizing his countrymen, by turning them from their former indigent and barbarous course of life; he moreover taught them how to cultivate and improve the fruits of the earth; he gave them a body of laws to regulate their conduct by, and instructed them in that reverence and worship, which they were to pay to the gods; with the same good disposition he afterwards travelled over the rest of the world, inducing the people everywhere to submit to his discipline, not indeed compelling them by force of arms, but persuading them to yield to the strength of his reasons, which were conveyed to them in the most agreeable manner, in hymns and songs accompanied with instruments of music; from which last circumstance, the Greeks conclude him to have been the same person with their Dionysos or Bacchus.[1]

The painted judgment scene in *The Book of the Dead* shows the other-world Hall of Double Law or Truth where the divine

---

[1] Sir E. A. Wallis Budge, *The Gods of the Egyptians*, Vol. 2, p. 187.

lawgiver Osiris presided as Judge of the Dead. Every defendant who came to trial in this supernatural courtroom had to make forty-two "negative confessions" in which he truthfully swore that he had not violated the Egyptian commandments. The lofty nature of this code may be judged by the following extract from the negative confessions:

> I have not done iniquity to mankind . . . Not have I caused pain. Not have I made to weep. Not have I killed. Not have I made the order for killing for me. Not have I done harm to mankind . . . not have I despoiled . . . not have I robbed . . . not have I spoken lies . . . not have I acted deceitfully . . . not have I raged except with a cause . . . not have I defiled the wife of a man . . . not have I stirred up strife . . . not have I judged hastily . . . not have I been an eavesdropper . . . not have I cursed God . . . not have I carried off the food of the infant . . . not have I committed faults, not have I sinned, not have I done evil, not have I borne false witness . . . I have done that which commanded men, are satisfied the gods thereat. I have appeased God by doing his will . . .[2]

Osiris' legal code rather strikingly resembles the Pygmies' Sinai-style commandments. The legendary history of Osiris echoes the Pygmy stories of the ancestral lawgiver. The Efé legends tell of how this civilizing hero ascended to heaven and assumed his role as the patron saint or angel of the moon. A similar ascent was attributed to Osiris and to another Egyptian divinity, Thoth, who may represent Osiris in the specific role of moon-god, since he was portrayed like Osiris as the civilizing hero and the "be-getter of law."

The Greeks identified Thoth with Hermes, their god of invention and the angelic messenger of the gods. In *The Gods of the Egyptians*, Budge summarizes the Greek accounts of Thoth as the civilizing hero: "They described him as the inventor of astronomy and astrology, the science of numbers and mathematics, geometry and land surveying, medicine and botany; he was the first to found a system of theology, and to organize a settled government in the country; he established the worship of the gods, and made rules concerning the times and nature of their sacrifices; he com-

---

[2] Sir E. A. Wallis Budge, *The Book of the Dead,* p. 193 et seq.

posed the hymns and prayers which men addressed to them, and drew up liturgical works; he invented figures, and the letters of the alphabet, and the arts of reading, writing, and oratory in all its branches; and he was the author of every work on every branch of knowledge, both human and divine."[3]

Like Thoth and Osiris, the ancestral Efé lawgiver is represented as the inventor of all the arts and sciences. The Pygmies' healing arts or medical and pharmaceutical science may be judged by their ability to "cure nearly all diseases." Their profound knowledge of medicinal, toxic and edible plants might be described as practical botany. As zoologists they are experts on animal behavior. According to Pygmy legend, the science of classification or taxonomy had its beginning when the first man named the plants and animals. Astronomy was launched when he named the heavenly bodies. They are still observed with the keenest interest by the Pygmies, who possess some rather remarkable knowledge of the planets and constellations.

As both the first poet-musician and the founding father of religion, the ancestral hero Efé authored the original Pygmy legends, composed prayerful songs or psalms, devised the dances that are still performed in honor of the deity, and invented traditional Pygmy instruments like the harp, flute and musical bow. Egyptian pictures show little Bes playing on his harp. On the Metternich Stele, Bes holds the sovereign emblems of Osiris, the Christlike god-king who presented his religion in the form of "hymns and songs accompanied with instruments of music." The alternate Egyptian lawgiver and civilizing hero, Thoth, invented musical instruments, along with everything else.

Some of the sciences have been abandoned or renounced by the Pygmies, who currently live on the world's simplest or "lowest" level of material technology. According to Pygmy legends, the ancient Pygmies smelted and worked metals, dwelled in "great villages" or cities, practiced agriculture and animal husbandry, sailed about in boats, manufactured pottery, and in general lived on an exceedingly high level of material technology. The survivors of the legendary cataclysms that beset the ancient Pygmy nation

---

[3] Sir E. A. Wallis Budge, *The Gods of the Egyptians*, Vol. 1, p. 414.

currently denounce complicated technology and worldly goods as unnecessary and grossly materialistic impediments to the enjoyment of the good, natural and simple life.

Evidence of every variety supports the Pygmies' legends of their ancestors' technological know-how. Smithcraft, for example, is still practiced by the pygmoid Mosso people of Burundi and many other local pygmoid populations. Ptah, the Egyptian god of smithcraft, was represented as a Pygmy in pottery figurines of Ptah-Seker-Osiris, the god of the Egyptian resurrection. Like Osiris, he was regarded as the founding father of the law. As Ptah-Osiris, he was absolutely identified with Osiris. He apparently embodied Osiris as the smith-god or ancestral Pygmy smith, while Thoth epitomized Osiris as the civilizing hero who ascended to the moon. This would explain why Ptah, Osiris and Thoth were all represented as the giver or begetter of the law. They are divergent forms of Efé, the ancestral Pygmy hero who is called by many names or epithets in different stories of the Efé legend cycle.

The Pygmies say that in ancient times their lawgiving father-god-king reigned near Ruwenzori, the Mountains of the Moon. The Arab geographers identified Thoth-Hermes with the prophet Idrisi and/or a prehistoric Egyptian ruler, King Am Kaam, who long ago reigned at Jebel Kamar, the Mountain of the Moon. In this neighborhood, according to the Pygmies, they received the deity's laws and commandments. Moses' book of Exodus locates the lawgiving scene at a mountain called Sinai. Its name has well-known connections with Babylonian Sin, the god of the moon. The *Britannica* article on this god says that "in Arabia and throughout the Semitic races of Western Asia the moon god was from the beginning the most important deity." By placing the lawgiving scene at Sinai, the mountain of Sin, the Bible seems to confirm that the commandments were handed down from the Mountain of the Moon.

Exodus' lawgiving scene features volcanic phenomena that could not possibly occur on the nonvolcanic Sinai Peninsula. Biblical critics accordingly point to problematically active craters in Arabia or Asia Minor. This simplistic "explanation" fails to resolve the great paradox of the Pentateuch or five books of Moses: the total clash between Hebrew legend and the recorded history of dynastic Egypt.

The Egyptian records make no mention of Moses, who was reputedly reared to manhood by an unnamed daughter of Pharaoh. The Egyptian records make no mention of Joseph, who supposedly ruled Egypt as Pharaoh's second-in-command. The Egyptian records make no mention of Jacob or Israel, the eponymous ancestor of the Israelites, whose Biblical funeral was personally authorized by Pharaoh and was attended by "all the elders of the land of Egypt." The Egyptian records make no mention of the miraculous Red Sea crossing, although an unnamed Pharaoh and his army allegedly drowned while pursuing the Israelites. Exodus 1:7 claims that the Israelites had waxed so "exceeding mighty" in Egypt that "the land was filled with them." Exodus 12:37 enumerates the departing Israelites as "about six hundred thousand on foot that were men, beside children." The Egyptian records fail to confirm that any people who have ever been conclusively identified as Israelites, Hebrews or Jews ever dwelled in Egypt or cataclysmically exited from the land of the Pharaohs.

Modern scholars nevertheless attempt to assign the characters and events of the Mosaic legends to a relatively recent period in Egyptian history. A variety of dates have been suggested in the assorted theories of the exodus. The *Britannica* article entitled "Exodus" gives the fifteenth century B.C. as "the earliest possible period." The article on the Biblical story of the Israelites' trip from Egypt to Mount Sinai says: "No certain reference to these events has yet been discovered in Egyptian records, unless, with Josephus and a few modern scholars, *e.g.*, Hall, we regard the story as an account of the expulsion of the Hyksos, seen from the Asiatic side. There are, nevertheless, the strongest grounds for regarding the narrative as historical in outline, although details cannot always be trusted. The whole of Israel's national and religious life was traced back to the covenant at the sacred mountain, and the memory of a divine deliverance from Egypt remained throughout history one of the most powerful factors in the national life."

At Mount Sinai, explains the *Britannica* article entitled "Michael," Moses spoke with the archangel who "holds the secret of the mighty 'word' by which God created heaven and earth." The text of this article compares Michael, the "guardian angel or 'prince' of Israel" to " 'Ahura's first masterpiece,' one of the Zoroastrian Amesha-spentas or arch-angels." An exceedingly ancient Egyptian legend declares that all things sprang into being when a divine personage spoke the word or words that launched the creation. According to the legends of many Pygmy populations, to make the universe, God merely uttered or repeated a simple little word. Trilles reported that the deity said "Be!" or "It is!" The celestial Efé creator, Ahuru or Ahura, presumably accomplished this feat by using a form of the irregular auxiliary verb *bua* or *u·a*, "to be." Ahuro or Ahura, the creative deity of the Zoroastrian scriptures or Avesta, may have employed the corresponding Avestan verb *bu*, "to be." Egyptian Heru—God or Horus—could have said *pu* (it is) to accomplish the Hamitic-Semitic creation. Like Horus, the ancestral Pygmy fought the giant monsters of the sky. As the lawgiving hero who ascended to the moon, he is the lunar divinity Thoth, whom the Egyptians identified as the mighty speaker of the mighty word. The secret of the mighty word was known to Michael, Revelation's celestial opponent of the Satanic devil-dragon that was conquered on the Metternich Stele by the Egyptians' Pygmy god Bes. At Sinai, the Mountain of the Moon, Moses apparently chatted with the Pygmy angel of the moon. According to Moses' scriptures, to create the universe God merely repeated the formula "Be" or "Let there be," as in "Let there be light."

The Efé legends identify the lunar angel as the first man or founding father of the ancient Pygmy nation. The pygmoid Tswa people, who reside in the Zaïrian province of Equator, tell a similar legend of the sainted ancestor who ascended to the sky. His name is Djakoba; his diminutive descendants call themselves the "Children of Djakoba," as Schebesta reported. Hebrew Ya'akoba or English Jacob was the original name of Israel, the first Israelite, who sired the famous Children of Israel. After his death, according to the legends of the Hebrew Talmud, Jacob or Israel went to live in the moon.

The Tswa "Children of Jacob" piously maintain that God or a spiritual force somehow intervened on their behalf to divide a body of water. This fragmentary and poorly understood tradition is summarized in Schebesta's description of "*elima*, the vital force, that parted the water (?)." His text explains that Elima probably represents the original Tswa "name of the supreme being, thus of

God."[4] In the Efé language, *ilani* or *ila* is energy, force, power, or strength. The Pygmies use this word to describe any form of energy. *Ila'tado,* "pulling energy," is the Efé name for the magnetic force embodied in lodestones. Pygmies who have seen magnets explain that these devices operate by the same principle. Such enormously abstract concepts and words are commonplace among the ostensibly "savage" Pygmies. *Ilani* or *ila* demonstrates the vast antiquity and importance of these concepts: Old Norse *eljan,* energy; Anglo-Saxon *ellen,* strength; Hebrew *el* or *il,* a strong and mighty one, a hero, a god, God; Arabic *ilah,* God; *Al-ilah,* the God, "Allah"; Phoenician *elonim* or *elim,* Hebrew *elohim,* god or gods; Tswa *elima,* the vital force or God.

Genesis 1:1 proclaims in Hebrew that Elohim created the heavens and the earth, after which the deity recited the "Let there be" formula. The book of Exodus gives a rousing account of the journey accomplished by the Children of Israel through the divinely parted waters. The pygmoid "Children of Jacob" are better known as the Tswa, a name that illustrates their close connections with the Sua Pygmies of the southern Ituri and the pygmoid Twa people of Zaïre, Burundi, Rwanda and the bordering regions of western Uganda, where a few pure-blooded Pygmy bands survive on the eastern side of the Mountains of the Moon. Egyptian records dating back to the sixth dynasty describe the Pygmies as a semi-legendary people of the far southland or equatorial "land of trees and spirits" near the Mountains of the Moon. E. A. Wallis Budge verifies that the Pygmies were undoubtedly well known to the predynastic Egyptians. The Pygmies cannot by any stretch of the imagination be interpreted as the descendants of Hebrews or Israelites who departed from Egypt no earlier than the fifteenth century B.C. or during any period of Egyptian history.

The western Pygmies of Gabon and Cameroon are in some respects the most quasi-Biblical members of the Pygmy nation. They commemorate the covenant of Noah by singing psalms and performing rituals in honor of the rainbow. They seal the covenant of Abraham by staging infant circumcision ceremonies that resemble a prayerful Jewish bris. They observe the covenant that

---

[4] P. Schebesta, *Les Pygmées du Congo Belge,* pp. 358–59.

Moses made at Mount Sinai by living in accordance with the Pygmy commandments. According to legend, their ancestors anciently fled from a paradisaical homeland called Kimi. Trilles points out that "for the Copts, the land of Kimi is Egypt." Since the records of dynastic Egypt do not mention any Pygmy exodus, we shall examine a broader gamut of names that echo the title of Kimi:

> Egyptian Kemi, Kemet or Kham—Egypt. Hebrew Cham—Egyptians, Ethiopians or the legendary son of Noah, Ham, who sired the Hamites of modern anthropology. Arabic Am Kaam—a legendary Egyptian king identified with Thoth-Hermes-Idrisi. Egyptian "Lord of Khemennu"—a title of Thoth, who reigned on earth for 3,226 years before embarking on his predynastic trip to the moon. Khemennu—the holy city of the moon-god in Upper Egypt. Arabic Kamar—the moon. Jebel Kamar—the Mountain of the Moon, where the prophetic moon-king built his predynastic establishment.

Trilles reported Ndris as a western Pygmy name for the angel of the moon. Arabic legends identify the moon-king with the prophet Idrisi. The Efé Pygmy legends identify the lunar angel with the lawgiving Pygmy ancestor who was slain by the dragon and resurrected by his son. Western Pygmy Ndris may therefore be equated with Egyptian Ntr or Neter, god, king, God, or Osiris. In the capacity of moon-god, Osiris was known as Asar Aah or the "Osiris Moon." Thoth was called Aah Tehuti or the "Moon Thoth." Together, Osiris and Thoth presided over the supernatural trials conducted in the Hall of Double Law or Truth. Osiris was the judge of the dead. Thoth acted as the recording angel who watched the scales of justice (a still-used symbol) and the lawyer who pleaded the case of the defendant. God and his chief angel are both associated with the moon in Pygmy legend. In the Egyptian judgment scenes, Osiris and Thoth apparently play the roles of God and the lunar angel.

On page 109, we saw some of the lofty ethical commandments set forth in *The Book of the Dead*. The oldest known written versions of these texts date back to the fifth dynasty. The Egyptian legends of the lunar lawgiver are older than the first dynasty (c. 3200 B.C.). At least seventeen centuries later, according to the conjectural dates assigned to the exodus, Moses and the Israelites arrived at an unidentified peak or range called Sinai, the Mountain of the Moon. To reach the lunar mountain, the Children of Israel passed through the waters that the deity miraculously divided for the pygmoid "Children of Jacob." This event enabled the Israelites to escape from Egypt while the western Pygmy ancestors fled with their quasi-Hebraic covenants from the quasi-Egyptian land of Kimi. The historic residents of Egypt—that Grand Central Station of mysterious departures!—somehow failed to notice the exodus of the Pygmies and/or the 600,000 Israelites whom Moses led from Egypt to Sinai.

The writings attributed to Moses do not deal with events that transpired during any period of Egyptian history. The Pentateuch consists instead of legends that have been edited and organized into a pseudohistorical narrative. These stories and the most basic precepts of Judeo-Christian religion echo the legends and religion of the Pygmies. The ancient Pygmies were identified by the Egyptians with their great ancestral gods. The epoch of the gods preceded the founding of dynastic Egypt. The Egyptians placed their ancestral paradise in the heart of Pygmy territory at the source of the Nile. Arab legends also place the site of prehistoric Egypt—the kingdom of the monarch Am Kaam—and the ancestral Eden-garden at the source of the Nile in the Mountains of the Moon. The book of Exodus locates the lunar mountain called Sinai in the immediate vicinity of "Egypt." In Coptic, Egypt is still called Kimi. In the language of the western Pygmies, Kimi is a name for the lost Pygmy paradise in the Mountains of the Moon.

In their original form, the Mosaic legends were probably concerned with events that occurred in this prehistoric Eden-Egypt. The pyrotechnic lawgiving scene at Mount Sinai has led many critics to declare that Jehovah must have been a volcano-god. The still-active Virunga volcanoes are located within easy reach of the Pygmy-populated forest near the Mountains of the Moon. Genesis 3:24 tells us that the deity placed on the border of his Eden garden-forest "a flaming sword which turned every way, to keep the way of the tree of life." Surt, the leader of the volcanic fire-giants, brandishes his flaming sword in the far southern paradise or elfin "first world" of the Eddas. The fire-giants of the southern continent fling fire over the world in the apocalyptic legend of Ragnarok or Götterdämmerung.

Geologists estimate that between seven and ten thousand years ago the towering Virunga fire-giants erupted with a force equal to or greater than the big blast at Krakatoa, about which *The Guinness Book of World Records* says: "The greatest explosion on earth in recorded history occurred at 2:56 A.M. G.M.T. on August 27th, 1883, with the eruption of Krakatoa, a small island lying in the Sunda Strait between Sumatra and Java in Indonesia . . . This explosion has been estimated to have had over 25 times the power of the largest H-bomb test detonation."

In his fine study *Africa: A Natural History*, Leslie Brown describes the Central African cataclysm that occurred on the edge of Efé territory near Lake Edward and the Mountains of the Moon:

> Then, probably only about seven thousand years ago, when primitive man was already living in the area, violent volcanic activity caused a series of tremendous explosions in the floor of the Rift close to Lake Edward. Huge clouds of ash and lumps of rock were blown into the air in a cataclysm that must have rivaled the greatest explosion in recorded history, the eruption of Krakatoa in the East Indies. The clouds of ash settled as a deep layer of dust at the north end of Lake Edward. The dust and poisonous volcanic substances destroyed most of the life of the area, including many of the Nilotic fish.[5]

Immediately prior to the Mosaic exodus, "Egypt" was stricken with fiery hail, dying fish, poisoned rivers, a plague of darkness that would certainly ensue if the atmosphere were saturated with volcanic dust, and other cataclysmic phenomena that are summarized in the ten plagues of Mosaic scripture. The plagues were accompanied by epic perturbations of the Yam Suf or "Sea of Reeds," traditionally identified with the Red Sea. This body of water is a part of the Rift Valley fracture system—a weblike crack in the crust of the earth that runs all the way from Mo-

---

[5] Leslie Brown, *Africa: A Natural History* (New York: Random House, 1965), p. 112.

zambique in southeast Africa to the spurs of Turkey's Taurus Mountains. Like the Red Sea, several major segments of the African Rift consist of long, narrow lakes. A water-filled crack known as Lake Tanganyika is four hundred and twenty miles long and nearly a mile deep. If measured from the lake bottom to the top of the bordering mountains, the abysmal trench of Lake Tanganyika is nearly two miles deep. The other Rift Valley lakes include Edward and Albert (the source of the Albertine Nile), which are fed by the Semliki or Ituri River and the melting snows of Jebel Kamar, the Arabic-styled Mountain of the Moon in the prehistoric land of Egypt-Eden.

If one identifies the volcanic plagues and sloshing Rift Valley waters of Mosaic legend as catastrophes caused by the prehistoric eruption of the Virunga volcanoes, the exodus from Egypt-Eden must have transpired several thousand years prior to the founding of the first Egyptian dynasty. This would certainly explain why the dynastic Egyptians left no record of the Exodus or the Israelitish people who according to the Mosaic scriptures filled and practically dominated the land of Egypt. It might appear that we have created an even greater paradox by identifying Moses' Egypt, where the Israelites dwelled for many generations, with his paradisaical land of Eden, whence the ancestors were exiled after the first generation or time of Adam and Eve. This paradox can be rather easily resolved by examining the Efé Pygmy legend of the sinful couple who plundered the sacred tree of paradise.

Unlike the stories of the Bible, the Pygmy legends have no standard or authorized versions. They are narrated by the elders of the seven or eight hundred Pygmy bands that survive in the present-day Ituri. Although greatly reduced by the agricultural and other economic activities of the Negro and European invaders, the forest is still several times larger than my native country, Belgium. In the eastern Ituri, Efé narrators tell two major variants of the stolen fruit story. In one version the first man is persuaded, like Adam, to eat the fruit of the deity's sacred tree. Here is this version of the story, just as it was told to me by Mwenua, the elder of Ebuya, a Pygmy camp in the southeast

Ituri. A photograph of Mwenua appears in the photo-insert section. His description of the domestic dispute between the Pygmy Adam and Eve evokes the Polish proverb, "What could Adam have done to God that made Him put Eve into the garden?"

> God made the first man and woman, and put them into the forest. They had no problems: there was so much food that all they had to do was bend down and pick it up. God told them they would live forever, and He let them do whatever they wanted, except for only one little thing: He said that they shouldn't pick the fruit of the *tahu* tree.
>
> The man never bothered with the tree after that, but the woman thought about it all the time. Then when she got big with a baby, she decided that she simply must eat that fruit and no other. She told the man to pick it for her, and of course he said, "No, God doesn't want us to." When she heard that, she started to argue and cry and scream and call her husband bad names. So, just to stop the noise, he picked a fruit from the *tahu* tree. He even peeled it for her. They ate the *tahu* fruit together and hid the peel under a pile of leaves.
>
> But God was very smart: He sent a big wind to blow away the leaves! He saw the peel, and He became terribly mad. He came and stood in front of the woman and He said, "You broke your promise to me! And you pulled that poor man into sin! Now I'm going to punish you: both of you will find out what it is to work hard and be sick and die. But you, woman, since you made the trouble first, you will suffer the most. Your babies will hurt you when they come, and you will always have to work for the man you betrayed."

This super-Mosaic saga ends with the thundering curses that the god of Genesis inflicted upon the thieves of the forbidden fruit: "Unto the woman he said, I will greatly multiply thy sorrow and thy conception; in sorrow thou shalt bring forth children; and thy desire shall be to thy husband, and he shall rule over thee. And unto Adam he said, Because thou hast hearkened unto the voice of thy wife, and hast eaten of the tree, of which I commanded thee, saying, Thou shalt not eat of it: cursed is the ground for thy sake; in sorrow shalt thou eat of it all the days of thy life . . . In the sweat of thy face shalt thou eat bread, till thou return unto the ground, for out of it wast thou taken: for dust thou art, and unto dust shalt thou return."[6]

The alternate Efé version of the forbidden fruit story describes man's creation out of dust, earth or clay, the command to multiply, and many other vitally important details that Mwenua omitted from his narrative. The story, as he told it, is actually an abbreviated or *Reader's Digest*-style condensation. The longer version explains that many, many years passed between the time of the creation and the theft of the fruit. As in the shorter version, the crime is instigated by a woman who persuades her husband to steal the fruit. This man is not, however, the first man or lawgiving civilizer (the equivalent of the Egyptian deity Osiris) who fathered the dragon-slaying savior. The real thief of the fruit is identified in the interlocking stories of the Efé legend cycle as the first man's younger brother.

Osiris had a devilish younger brother, Set, who corresponds with the Judeo-Christian devil Satan. Set was depicted as a man who sometimes took the form of a serpent or dragon-like monster, and in that manifestation was called by the name Apep or Apepi. The Zoroastrian devil or "Prince of Darkness," Ahriman, collaborates with the wicked dragon. Both will be defeated in the apocalyptic future, according to the legends of the ancient Persian Avesta. In the Biblical story of the stolen fruit, the devil appears in the form of his serpent manifestation. In the longer Efé legend of the stolen fruit, he appears in human form as the Set-like younger brother of Efé-Osiris.

Another Pygmy legend tells of Efé's triumph over the giant monsters of heaven. The equivalent Egyptian stories are generally interpreted as symbolic accounts of the sun-god's daily triumph over darkness or night. On the Metternich Stele, explains E. A. Wallis Budge, the Pygmy conqueror of all the Typhonian beasts, Bes, represents "the aged sun-god." Bes's earthly kinsmen have no "sun-god." Their views on the topic of sun worship may be judged from the very ironic conversation that ensued when the Jesuit missionary-anthropologist Trilles queried a western Pygmy elder:

---

[6] Genesis 3:16–19.

TRILLES: People have told me that for you, the sun which gives us light, is God.

PYGMY: Your brothers, the Whites, perhaps believe that. We others, no, never.

TRILLES: But the sun is good. It makes the trees grow. It gives life.

PYGMY: The sun is the sun. God is God. Before the sun, there was God. You, White Man, if you believe otherwise, that is your affair. All fish do not swim to the same shore. The *raha* bird flies to the top of the trees. The aardvark digs in the earth below. We, we are we. You, you are you. Enough, we are fatigued.[7]

God is regarded by the Pygmies as the heavenly source of all light. The elder Egyptian Horus, or senior dragon-fighter, was a sky-god whose two eyes were represented as the sun and the moon. Ahura Mazda, the Zoroastrian opponent of the devil and his dragon, is still regarded as the source of all light. So is Jehovah, the enemy of Satan, who created the light and saw that "it was good." He subsequently "made two great lights; the greater light to rule the day, and the lesser light to rule the night; he made the stars also." A very beautiful Pygmy legend tells an equally enigmatic story of the light-making god who reigned in the heavens before the creation or advent of the light-giving heavenly bodies:

At the beginning of things, before they existed, God dwelled in the sky, on high, in the blue where by night the stars shine and by day the sun sparkles. But that time, that was before the stars shone, before the sun gave light. Then God descended to earth and created men. He lived with them. But one day, angry with them because they no longer listened to him, He left them and reascended to the sky. That is where he dwells now.[8]

According to an exceedingly philosophic Pygmy concept, God lights the universe by continually creating the "vital force" or energy that is embodied both in material objects and—in greater quantity—in all living creatures. This vision of the world

---

[7] Henri Trilles, *The Soul of the African Pygmy*, p. 87.

[8] *Ibid.*, p. 85.

can hardly be described as a product of "the primitive childlike mind," since it agrees with our modern physicists' concepts of matter and energy and the continuous creation theory of the Cambridge astronomers. Some Pygmy legends install the light-making deity in a remote and unknowable part of the heavens, whence he wields the vital force that he creates or comprises. The ancient Greek astronomer, mathematician and philosopher Pythagoras (c. 532 B.C.) entertained similar views about the source of energy, a governing power that he placed at the center of the celestial universe: "At the centre is the central fire, called the Hearth of the Universe (among other names), wherein is situated the governing principle, the force which directs the movement and activity of the universe."[9]

Like the little people Homer called Oi Pygmaioi or "the Pygmies," the ancient Greeks told philosophical or quasi-scientific legends along with their anthropomorphic stories of the Olympian gods. The Greco-Roman legends of the lost paradise inform us that Zeus-Jupiter, the fatherly ruler of Olympus, prescribed a code of laws. As the senior dragon-fighter and lawgiving patriarch of the holy mountain, he is a form of Efé, the ancestral father-god-king who transmitted the laws of God to the ancient Pygmy nation. In the lawgiving scene at Mount Sinai— the Rock of Israel or the "great throne of God" that corresponds with the Olympian "throne of the gods"—Moses plays the role of the fatherly leader who delivers the law.

The Hebrew lawgiver is traditionally credited with the authorship of the holy Torah and the Pentateuch. Thoth, the Egyptian lord of law, was likewise credited with the authorship of the Egyptian scriptures. As the lawgiving civilizer, benevolent governor, universal inventor and ascendant moon-god, Thoth is a form of Efé, the original lunar angel who composed the original Pygmy legends. At Sinai, the lawgiving author Moses spoke with the angelic dragon-fighter Michael. They are both forms of Efé, the one-man pantheon whose incarnations play the starring roles in the vastly complex Efé legend cycle.

---

[9] "Pythagoras," *Encyclopaedia Britannica,* 14th ed., Vol. 18, p. 804.

As the first man and civilizing hero, Efé may be identified with the subject of a Vatican portrait (c. 1550 A.D.) that bears the title *Adam, divinitus edoctus, primus scientiarum et literatum inventor,* "Adam, divine educator, first inventor of science and literature." Adam is virtually deified in Hebrew and Arabic legends of the first man. According to the Koran, all the angels worshiped Adam during the balmy days that preceded the tragic Fall of Man. Genesis tells a rather fragmentary tale of how Adam named "every living creature." Efé, the versatile first man of Pygmy legend, named or classified everything. We have already seen some fascinating examples of his taxonomy (puss, mouse, ape, hippo, etc.). Here are some equally choice Efé locutions:

Méligi, queen bee; *mala,* elder, chief, or king, the civic leader and religious adviser of an Efé band. The first *mala,* Efé, ascended to heaven and became the beloved god or angel of the moon.

Arabic *malika, malik* and *malaak,* queen, king and angel. Hebrew *malka,* queen or princess; *malchuth,* kingdom; *melecheth,* queen; *melech,* king, prince, god or God; Molech, the Canaanite deity Moloch; *malach,* priest, prophet, herald, messenger, angel.

Méli, honey; *méliti,* bee; *méligi,* queen bee; *mala,* the governing official of the Efé community.

Greek *meli,* Italian *miele,* French *miel,* Spanish *miel,* Portuguese *mel,* Latin *mel,* Welsh *mêl,* Irish *mil,* Gaelic *mil,* Hittite *milit,* Gothic *milith,* honey. Armenian *meghu* and *meghr,* bee and honey. Greek *melissi,* swarm of bees or beehive; *mélissa,* honey, the bee or an enchanted princess who was turned into a bee. Her father, Melissus, was a legendary king of Crete.

Latin *mel,* honey or metaphorical sweetness. Italian *miele,* Rumanian *miere,* honey. Anglo-Saxon *merig* or *myrge,* sweet, pleasant, melodious or merry, as in Merry England and Merry Christmas. Greek *myrobolus,* sweet or fragrant; *myrodia,* perfume; *melodia,* song or melody; *meli,* honey. Welsh *mêl,* honey; *melys,* sweet; *melysion,* sweets or candy. Gaelic *mil* and *milis,* honey and sweet. Anglo-Saxon *milisc,* sweet or mild. Masai *melok,* sweet or pleasant. Greek *malakos,* mild, tender, soft. Hebrew *malats,* soft or pleasant. Masai *A-ta-melono,* I was sweet. Greek *melono,* I sweeten with honey.

Mara: (1) very great, high, eminent; (2) the elder, chief or king who governs the Pygmy bands of *méri*, the equatorial forest, that merry country near the Mountains of the Moon. The first *mara* or *mala* was Efé, the lawgiving lunar angel who battled with the giant monsters of heaven. The second was his dragon-fighting son-incarnation.

Old English *maere*, great, excellent, famous, sublime; *mara*, greater, mightier, more. Latin *maior*, elder, older, greater or major, the traditional source of French *maire*, the "mayor" who governs many European and American communities. Welsh *mawr*, great; *mawredd*, greatness, grandeur, majesty.

Pala, para and *pa*, forms of an Efé-Sua word that means town, village, inhabited place or place in general. *Mala-pa*, the Efé territory, is literally the town or place of the mayor. The present-day Pygmy community consists of twenty to twenty-five men, women and children. In the past the legendary Pygmy ancestors built enormous cities. The western Pygmies sometimes call their lost paradise "the great village of the beginning." All of the Pygmies tell grim legends of the doom that descended on this equatorial Los Angeles.

Sanskrit *palli*, village. Greek *polis*, town or city; *politeia*, state or polity. Latin *platea*, public place or street. French *place*, street, square, fortress or "place." Latin *palatium*, the Palatine hill, fortress, or palace. Sanskrit *pūr*, fortress; *pūr-pati*, lord of the town or fortress. Egyptian *per-o*, great house. Hebrew *paro*, Pharaoh, the lord of the establishment. Egyptian *pa* or *per*, house, or the prefix to the names of many ancient towns and cities; *e.g.*, Per-Tehuti, the city of the moon-god Thoth in Lower Egypt. Greek Hermo*polis*, the cities of Thoth in Lower and Upper Egypt; metro*polis*, mother city or state; megalo*polis*, big city; *politika*, politics, the affairs of the polity; *politismos*, civilization.

Pala, village, town or place. *Apulu*, mole or digging animal.

Greek *polis*, town or city; *aspalax*, mole. Welsh *palu*, to dig or delve; *palwr*, digger. Old Norse *páll*, hoe or spade. French *pelle*, shovel; *pelle mécanique*, steam shovel. Latin *pala*, spade.

Upipa, dwellers, dwellings, or population. *Upapi,* paper or grass stalks. The Pygmies traditionally make cloth out of fig bark. Those who have seen paper say that it must have been made out of grass stalks.

French *peuple* and *papier,* English *people* and *paper.* Latin *populus,* nation, district, populace, people. *Papyrus,* paper or papyrus. Greek *papyros,* a grassy plant whose stalks were used for making paper in ancient Egypt, Greece and Rome.

Gala or *gara,* reed; *agolè* or *agorè,* picture, design, or illustration. The Pygmies use reeds as drawing pens for making attractive designs on the face and body. This kind of cosmetic adornment is currently considered to be high fashion in Europe and America. The Pygmies also use reed pens to make simple geometrical designs on bark cloth.

Persian *qalam,* pen. Greek *kalamos,* reed, cane, pen. Latin *calamus,* reed, reed pen, arrow, stalk, stem, blade. Anglo-Saxon *gaers* and *graes,* blade of grass, grass. Greek *graphis,* pen or pencil; *gramma,* picture, writing, inscription, letter of the alphabet; *graphe,* picture, writing, drawing, as in "graphs" and "graphic" arts; *grapho,* I draw, write, paint, scratch, carve, engrave; *glypho,* I carve, as in hieroglyphics. Greek legends attribute the invention of writing and the alphabet to Thoth, the Egyptian version of our elfin lunar angel.

Agèru, a very poisonous Ituri Forest mushroom; *bolita,* a large edible mushroom.

Greek *agarikon,* English "fly agaric," the exceedingly poisonous mushroom *Amanita muscaria.* Greek *bolites,* Latin *boletus,* mushroom. French *bolet,* English "boletus," any club fungus of the genus *Boletus.* Thoth was represented in Greek legend as the founding father of natural history.

Osa or *hosa,* bird.

Egyptian *sa,* feathered fowl or goose. Czech *husa,* goose. Sanskrit *hamsa,* flamingo, swan, goose, the sacred bird of Brahma, Latin *ansa,* Spanish *ganso,* German *gans,* Greek *chen,*

Dutch *gans*, Norwegian *gas*, Russian *gus*, Anglo-Saxon *gos*, English *goose*.

Osa èto méli, bird and honey.

French *oiseau et miel*, bird and honey. Latin *ansa et mel*, goose and honey.

Ava, father. *Evé*, the ancestral hero Efé. *Ové*, wing.

Hebrew *av*, father. *Ever*, wing and/or the patriarch who sired the line of Abraham. Latin *avus* and *avis*, grandfather and bird. Sanskrit *vis* or *vi*, bird. Norwegian *vinge*, wing. French *avion*, airplane, as in aviation. Portuguese *ave*, bird or fowl, as in "aviary." Armenian *hav*, hen, chicken, or grandfather.

Afa and *ofé*, phonetic variants of father and wing.

Egyptian *af*, a fly. Hebrew *of*, what flies, birds or fowl. Anglo-Saxon *faeder*, father; *fether*, wing or feather. Norwegian *far* and *fjaer*, father and feather.

Tamélo, drunk or intoxicated. *Méli* or *méri*, honey.

Latin *temulentus*, drunk or intoxicated; *temetum*, wine or alcohol; *mulsum*, honey wine or mead; *mel*, honey. Greek *meli* and *melikraton*, honey and mead. Rumanian *miere*, honey. Sanskrit *mairea*, an intoxicating drink.

Emé, a mildly intoxicating beverage made from kola nuts. This Pygmy Pepsi-Cola is known in the eastern Ituri as "Efé tea." *Médéaka*, a name for plants with intoxicating or stimulating properties. Both of these words are related to the Efé name of honey.

Dutch *mee* or *mede*, the beverage called mead or the plant called madder. Sanskrit *madugha*, a plant yielding honey. *Madhu*, honey or mead, was anciently associated with the worship of the Vedic deities known as the Divine Physicians. Latin *medicamen*, drug, poison, remedy, medicine, medicament; *medicus*, physician, surgeon or "medic." Greek *methisko* or *metho*, I get drunk or intoxicated, as in methyl alcohol. Welsh *medd*, mead; *meddwyn*, drunkard; *meddig*, medic. Czech *med*, Polish *miod*, Russian *myot*, mead or honey. Old Norse *mjöthr*, mead or "dwarf's drink," was traditionally invented by the paradisaical elves.

The legends and language of the elfin Efé and their ancestral lunar angel reunite the diminutive inventors of mead with the divine physician who invented medicine. According to the legends of the Greeks, he was Thoth, the Egyptian god of the moon. As Hermes, he carried the staff or caduceus that is currently used as the emblem of the medical profession. In Kenya and Tanzania, the ancient Egyptians' present-day Masai relatives identify the divine physician as a Pygmy-sized prophet named Mweiya. The tall Masai medicine men who claim descent from this legendary sage sing parables and prophecies after imbibing and getting more than a little tipsy on honey wine. In Pygmy society, the elders prepare healing medicaments and a variety of stimulants that inspire or aid them to prophesy, divine, have visions, or "see God" and obtain his personal advice. These customs may be responsible, at least in part, for the mead-drenched aura that surrounds the divine physicians of Indo-European legend.

A number of Pygmy stories describe the lunar angel's ascents and descents, or trips between earth and heaven. According to the Masai, he came down to earth on the summit of a holy mountain about twenty miles southwest of Nairobi, one hundred and twenty-five miles northeast of Olduvai Gorge, and five hundred miles east of the Efé Pygmies' Mountain of the Moon. Europeans call his landing point by the name Mt. Ngong, after the nearby town of Ngong. To the Masai, it is *Ol-doinyo lo-'l-le-Mweiya*, the Mountain of Mweiya. A brief account of the Pygmy angel's advent is given in A. C. Hollis' book *The Masai*:

> The story of the origin of the medicine-men is said to be as follows: Ol-le-Mweiya came down from heaven and was found by the Aiser clan sitting on the top of their mountain. He was such a small person that he was first of all believed to be a child. He was taken by the Aiser clan to their kraal, where it was discovered that he was a medicine-man. He married and had issue. When he was dying he said to his children: "Do not move from this spot." On account of this the Aiser clan do not go far from their mountain . . . All medicine-men belong to the Kidongi family of the Aiser clan,

and they are the descendants of Ol-Oimooja or of E-Sigiariaishi, the
sons of Ol-le-Mweiya . . .[10]

The Pygmies, who have never heard of the Masai, would be delighted by the many local Masai legends of the ancestral Pygmy
medic.

Kula or *kura*, color. *Avi oba*, white man or fair-skinned
Pygmy. *Oba*, white, light, fair, pink or reddish. *Obu*, dawn or
morning. The legendary Pygmy ancestors were as fair as the fairest white men. Some Pygmies still have blue eyes, red hair and
a brunette Caucasoid complexion.

Polish *kolor*, Dutch *kleur*, French *couleur*, Rumanian *cu-
loare*, Italian *colore*, Latin *color*, Spanish *color*, Portuguese *cor*,
Greek *chroma*, as in all things colorful and chromatic. Latin
vir albus, white man; *albus*, white, light, pale, as in "albino";
albeo, I dawn or grow light. French *aube*, dawn. Arabic *abyad*,
white.

Esa: (1) black, dark, gloomy; (2) Black or Negro. The Negroes are newcomers to Efé territory. The Pygmies call them by
the nonpejorative title "blacks," just as we speak of blacks, black
power, and so forth. Anthropologists have pinned the title Negrillos or "little blacks" on the Pygmies. The Pygmies, ironically
enough, tell many legends of "little blacks" or black dwarfs who
dwell under the earth in subterranean caverns whence they periodically emerge to work mischief. These legendary characters,
not the Pygmies, are the "little blacks" or black dwarfs of Africa.

Sanskrit *asita*, black. Persian *siāh*, black or Negro. Danish
sort, Norwegian *svart*, Dutch *zwart*, Gothic *swarts*, black. Anglo-
Saxon *sweart*, black, dark, gloomy, swarthy. Old Norse *svartr*,
black, baneful, disastrous; *svart-álfar*, black elves or black dwarfs
who live under the ground. The Pygmies have probably been confused with their legendary dwarfs in many echoing stories of the
little people. The *Prose Edda* emphasizes the difference between the
wee Caucasoid ancestors and black dwarfs in this remarkable description of the lost Germanic paradise:

---

[10] A. C. Hollis, *The Masai: Their Language and Folklore*, pp. 325–26.

There are many magnificent places there. There is one called Álfheim, and there live the people called the light elves, but the dark elves live down in the earth and they are unlike the others in appearance and much more so in character. The light elves are fairer than the sun to look upon, but the dark elves blacker than pitch . . . In the southern end of heaven is the most beautiful hall of all, brighter than the sun; it is called Gimlé; it shall stand when both heaven and earth have passed away, and good and righteous men will inhabit that place for all time . . . "What will protect this place when Surt's Fire is burning heaven and earth?" . . . "It is said that there is another heaven to the south of and above this one, and it is called Andlang; and there is yet a third heaven above these ones which is called Vithbláin, and we think that this place [Gimlé] is there. At present, however, we think that it is inhabited only by white elves."[11]

Greek legends install a cavernous Efé-style underworld beneath the paradisaical mountain of Olympus or "throne of the gods." The Norse studies inform us that the paradisaical real estate is endangered by Surt, the chief of the volcanic fire-giants. Efé *iotani* means giant or gigantic. Old Norse *jötunn* (pronounced *yötunn*), giant. *Jötunnheim*, Giant-land, a district of paradise. The Virunga fire-giants seethe and rumble near the territories of the Efé. The Norse Eddas represent Giant-Land and Elf-Land as districts of Paradise.

Toré: (1) God; (1) Efé, the first man; (3) the first man's son-incarnation. "God is the first man," Schebesta remarked of Pygmy theology. It is more correct to say that God the Father is the first man. God is represented in the more philosophical Pygmy concepts as an ineffable cosmic force or spirit that corresponds with the "great spirit of the Egyptians." God's divinely created son, God the Father or the first man, was the "civilizing hero" and first chief or king of the ancient Pygmy nation. God the Father's miraculous son-incarnation is the "legendary savior."

God the Father, or the ancestral hero Efé, is pictured in some Pygmy stories as a radiantly fair-skinned smith who wields

---

[11] *The Prose Edda of Snorri Sturluson,* selected and translated by Jean I. Young (Berkeley: University of California Press, 1966), pp. 46–47.

a hammer and wears metal arm rings. He dwells on earth in a palatial smithy whence one hears him hammering out metal tools and ornaments. God is sometimes portrayed as a celestial smith who forged the iron weapons used in the battles with giant monsters or dragons. This anthropomorphic sky-god hurls thunderbolts at sinners who violate his commandments. He speaks in a voice of thunder. Lightning flashes from his eyes. Tempests come when he shakes his long beard and raises the winds:

Kalahari Bushman Thora, a name of God. Old Norse Thor or Thórr, Swedish and Norwegian Tor, the thundering smith of earth and high heaven. Sacred arm rings of Thor were enshrined in his temples. Miniature hammers were worn by his devotees. His son or father, All-Father Odin, prescribed a "code of laws." He did battle with giants and giant monsters. In the apocalyptic legends of Ragnarok or Götterdämmerung he fights the devilish Midgard Serpent. He was called *orms einbani,* the sole slayer of the serpent. He was a godly ancestor who dwelled in the paradisaical city of Asgard at the center of the earth. He was the sky-god. He was the god of lightning, thunder, and the thunderbolt. His eyes glared. His voice was terrifying. He raised storm winds by blowing out his long beard. His sacred day, Thors-dagr or Thursday, was the sacred day of the Roman sky-god Jupiter. He has been identified with Jupiter and the Greek sky-father Zeus.

The Efé name of "Toré" may be connected with the verb *itorè* or *itorèni,* to roar, thunder, make a loud noise: Norwegian *Tor* and *torden,* Thor and thunder; Welsh *taran,* thunder; Latin *Taranis,* a very ancient Roman deity who has been identified with Thor or with Odin. Efé "Toré" and "Otu," God and Grandfather, are alternate titles of the deity: Old Norse Thor and Othinn, Norwegian Tor and Odin, English Thor and Odin. These Germanic gods, who were represented as the fathers or sons of each other, echo the Efé mystique of the divine grandfather, father, and son-incarnation of the father. (Thor was actually called "grandfather" by some Germanic tribes.) Both Thor and Odin were inexorably involved with the little people of legend. The holy hammer of Thor and all the other great treasures of the gods were forged by the master smiths known as dwarfs, elves, or fairies. The elfin smiths were involved in ancestor-worshiping ceremonies. The anthropomorphic sky-smith Thor was represented as a divine ancestor from the lost paradise at the center of the earth.

Greek Hephaestus, the smith-god son of All-Father Zeus, had lame or deformed legs. Many ancient European smith-gods or legendary smiths suffered from lameness. The traditional and rather lame explanation is that lame people found smithcraft a suitable profession. The Greeks identified Hephaestus with the Egyptian smith-god Ptah. He is pictured in the resurrection figurines of Ptah-Seker-Osiris as a short-legged, scrawny-legged or bow-legged Pygmy. Ptah, the great "father of beginnings," was identified with the lawgiver Osiris, the "father of all the gods who begat him." On the Metternich Stele, the Pygmy god Bes was represented as the father-incarnation of Osiris' son Horus and the triumphant adversary of Thor's Typhonian enemies. The gods of Egypt were regarded as the direct ancestors of the Egyptians. The elfin ancestors were worshiped in northern Europe down into recent historic times.

Toré (1) God the Father, the ancestor of the Pygmy nation; (2) God.

Hebrew Terah, the father of Abraham; *teraphim,* household gods or idols. Terah was the grandfather of Jacob or Israel. Jacob was associated with the Biblical smiths called Kenites. The part-Pygmy "Children of Djakoba" have many pygmoid relatives who still practice smithcraft. During the course of his very colorful career, Jacob engaged in a wrestling match with a supernatural power that wounded him in the thigh. The heroic ancestor of the South African Hottentots wrestled with a supernatural power that wounded him in the knee. The Hottentot victor in this ancient African "Battle of Wounded Knee" is accordingly known by the title Tsui Goab, Wounded Knee. We thus see Biblical and pygmoid analogues of the lame European smiths. The Hottentots and Bushmen both address prayers to the moon. Since they are very kindly, gentle-mannered folk, their prayers are undoubtedly answered by the angelic Pygmy smith who ascended to the moon. After his life on earth, Jacob went to live in the moon. The pygmoid Tswa address prayers to their celestial ancestor Djakoba.

Tolé or Toré: (1) God, the immortal and continual creator of the universe; (2) Efé, the first man or God the Father; (3) Efé's son-incarnation, the "legendary savior."

Philippine Pygmy Tolandian, God, has not been forgotten by Asiatic Pygmies who live about seven thousand miles from the Ituri Forest. Andaman Pygmy Tarai, God, the first man, or the son of God. The deity is alternately described as an immortal cosmic spirit and a godly man. The theological personalities correspond with the holy Spirit, Father and Son of the Christian trinity. The Andaman Pygmies live on a forested archipelago in the Bay of Bengal, about five thousand miles from the Ituri Forest. The Andamanese language is supposedly unrelated to any human tongue. The Andaman Pygmy bands call themselves *aka* of this or that local region. Aka Pygmy *aka,* the men, people or Pygmies of the northwest Ituri.

The Efé deity is associated with the moon and the Mountain of the Moon, which is located on the border of Zaïre and Uganda. The mixed-Hamite folk of Uganda, Rwanda and Burundi call their territory by the traditional name Unyamwezi, the Land of the Moon. The divine kings of the former Watusi royal courts were regarded as successive incarnations of a good and beautiful angel who was sinfully slain and thereafter made his messianic return in the person of each Watusi king. This concept certainly appears to be connected with the Egyptian legends of Osiris, the virtuous lawgiver and benevolent king who was murdered by the devilish Set-Apepi. As the lunar divinity, he wore in his headdress the crescent moon that echoes the Pygmy crescent ornament. In Pygmy religion this is a symbol of the good spirit, god or angel of the moon. Schebesta correctly affirms that the Pygmies' moon mystique is wholly alien to the recent Negro invaders of the equatorial forest. In the Watusi Land of the Moon, the crescent is used to decorate all kinds of artifacts.

R. Bourgeois interpreted the Watusi as the descendants of "pre-Mosaic Semites." The angelic ancestor of the Watusi kings was crucified or nailed to a tree with iron spikes, according to the legends told in Rwanda and Burundi, a few degrees south of the equator. In the Norse poem of Havamal, Odin hangs on the world tree at the center of the earth. He was represented as the father-god-king of Asgard, the ancestors' paradisaical city near the center of the earth. His Greek analogue, Zeus, was wounded in the hands and feet by the devilish cosmic serpent Typhon, who attacked the Olympian paradise at the center of the earth. The New Testament Christ was wounded in the hands and feet when he was nailed to the tree of the crucifixion or fatal tree of Eden at the center of the earth. In John 19:32, he is pierced in the side by a spear. Pierced by a spear, Odin hangs on the world tree of Germanic legend. All of the wounds were healed, according to Watusi legend, when God took the crucified angel up to heaven.

The son-incarnation of Toré hangs on a tree in a major Efé legend of the ancestors' original sins. In Efé religion, Toré is also a name for God as the great spirit of the forest or trees. In this capacity, Schebesta defined Toré as *le dieu forestier* or "the forest god." The tree-spirit Toré merges with the son-incarnation of the anthropomorphic Toré; the sky-spirit Toré merges with the anthropomorphic father-incarnation. Studies of early Germanic and Greek religion describe sacred trees and groves as manifestations of the Tree and Sky God.

The sacred oaks of ancient Greece were associated with Zeus and his son Dionysus. The Greeks identified Dionysus with the great Egyptian man-god Osiris. The birthdays of Dionysus and Osiris were both celebrated on or around the local equivalents of December 25. Several hundred years after the controversial advent of the New Testament Christ, the organized "Christian" church assigned this date to the birth of Jesus and thus placated converts who insisted on celebrating the pre-Christian Christmas. The "Christian" churches have repeatedly denounced and reluctantly accepted the "pagan" Christmas tree of the European tribes. The Christmas tree rather resembles the sacred emblem of Dionysus: a wooden staff topped by a pine cone.

In the Efé "myth of the savior," the son-incarnation of Toré slays the great monster or dragon that defeated the father-incarnation, ancestral Pygmy smith or first chief of the ancient Pygmy nation. The monster arrived when the ancestors committed their many original sins. The builders of that legendary metropolis, "the great village of the beginning," must have despoiled and destroyed the sacred trees or forest of God in the irresponsible style of our modern city builders. Unlike the peaceful Pygmies of the small present-day communities, the ancestors waged a fratricidal war. This was one of their great original sins.

Thor is the smith-god who slays and is slain by the dragon in the cataclysmic legends of Ragnarok, the doom of gods and men. The Prologue to the *Prose Edda* identifies Thor or Tror as the grandson of Troan or Priam, the chief king of a town that was "built on a much larger scale than others then in existence and in many ways with greater skill, so lavishly was it equipped." Priam or Troan was the ruler of Troy, a legendary city that the *Prose Edda* identifies with Asgard, the lost Germanic paradise at the center of the earth. At Asgard Odin presided over a company of twelve ancestral gods that included his eldest son Thor. At Troy Priam reigned as the chief king or over-king of twelve Trojan kings or chieftains. His grandson Tror or Thor was the father or ancestor of Odin. Then who was Thor's father? He is identified as a king "called Múnón or Mennón" who married Priam's daughter. Greek legends identify Memnon as a king of Ethiopia who led ten thousand men to fight on the side of his uncle, Priam, in the epic conflict known as the Trojan War.

Memnon, according to Greek stories, was "black but beautiful." No black man, however beautiful, would make a suitable father for the Germanic man-god Thor. No Negroes lived in the southern continent or ancestral "first world" of Germanic legend. Its inhabitants are described as white elves who correspond with the Pygmies and underground black elves who match the black dwarfs of Pygmy legend. These stories date back to the Old White Africa that has yielded up no ancient specimens of fossil Negroes. The Asgard-Troy system of one superior chief god and twelve lesser chiefs matches the arrangements at the Greco-Roman paradise where Zeus-Jupiter presided over a company of twelve Olympian gods. Their mountainous throne was located, according to some legends, at the source of the Nile. The Egyptians placed their ancestral paradise in the same region and called the equatorial homeland of their Pygmy god Bes by the title *Ta Neteru*, the Land of the Gods.

From the godly region of Asgard-Troy, according to the *Prose Edda*, Odin traveled to Europe with "a great host" of people. He and his sons founded many nations or cities. He prescribed "a code of laws like that which had held in Troy" and modeled cities "after the pattern of Troy." These replicas might lead to confusion concerning the site of the lost paradise founded by Toré, the heroic father-god-king of the Efé Pygmies:

Greek "Tros," the legendary founder of Troy, a city that was named in his honor. Troes, Trojans. Troezen, a city about forty miles from Athens, the hometown of a legendary Athenian king called Theseus. Troezen is not the original Troy of Homer's Iliad. Neither is Troy, New York.

Troas, a region in Turkey known as the Troad. Many ancient scholars regard a Turkish region called the Troad as the original. In 1882 Heinrich Schliemann excavated the Turkish mound of Hissarlik and found ruins that have been accepted as Homer's legendary city of Troy. "No site in the Troad accords completely with all the topographical clues ingeniously derived from the text of Homer," says the *Britannica* article on Troy. Apparently misled by the traditional site of Troy, Snorri Sturluson placed the site of Asgard-Troy "near the center of the world in what we call Turkey lies." From Turkey, he maintained, Odin embarked on his city-founding safari. Other stories told in the Eddas clearly identify the ancestral paradise with the far southern land of the elves and fire-giants. The ancient cities of Turkey may have been modeled after the pattern of Asgard-Troy. The Troas is not, however, the original site of Troy. Neither is Troy, Alabama.

Troy is described in the *Iliad,* an epic poem of the Trojan War that contains the oldest known European mention of the people Homer called Oi Pygmaioi or "the Pygmies." Troy was utterly destroyed by the war. When the war ended, thunder and lightning rained down from the heights of Olympus; then came a giant lightning bolt that caused a monster earthquake and deluge. The gigantic bolt of Efé "lightning" leaped out of the earth. The Greek "lightning" struck mankind from the paradisaical mountains. This story describes the giant explosion that emanated in the bowels of the earth and blasted the ancient Pygmy nation from the thundering, fire-spewing mountains or giant Virunga volcanoes of the ancestors' perilous paradise.

The cataclysmic events of Ragnarok, the Germanic doom of gods and men, include fratricidal warfare. After many horrors, the final doom is accomplished when the Norse fire-giants of the Old White Africa fling fire over earth and high heaven. Then comes the deluge. The cataclysmic eruption of the Virunga volcanoes took place thousands of years prior to the founding of the First Egyptian Dynasty. Volcanic blasts and plagues punctuate the Biblical legends of the Israelites' bitter conflict with the "Egyptians." A pseudo-Egyptian army perished in the crazed waters of Exodus. The Israelite survivors went on to eventually found a nation in the Middle Eastern region of Palestine. Hittite, an ancient language spoken in this neighborhood, has been officially accepted into the Indo-European family. The Indo-European refugees from Asgard-Troy founded many nations. Their leader Odin "appointed chieftains after the pattern of Troy, establishing twelve rulers to administer the laws of the land." Twelve tribes of Israelites emerged from the holocaust of Exodus. An historically recent war with the Assyrians caused the demise of the famous "ten lost tribes." The twelve original tribes founded a nation divided into twelve districts or territories. The twelve tribes were represented as the descendants of Jacob or Israel. His twelve sons match the twelve chiefs of Troy, that duodecimal paradise of twelve city-states.

The primordial Pygmy nation was founded by an ancestral god or hero called Toré: Hebrew Terah, the father of Jacob or Israel. Etruscan Tarchun, the legendary ancestor of the Etruscans and founder of the twelve city-states that comprised the ancient Italian nation of Etruria. The strong Egyptian flavor of Etruscan art has led some scholars to derive the Etruscans from the North Hamitic nation of Egypt. Fragmentary legends describe the Etruscan ancestor Tarchun as a child-sized person with hoary or grizzled hair.[12] A child-sized person, the Pygmy god Bes, sums up the ancestor-gods of Egypt on the Metternich Stele. The founding father of the Nilo-Hamitic Masai religion is described as a child-sized man. His priestly descendants sing parables and prophecies. Little Tarchun sang to his Etruscan congregation, whom he instructed in the art of

---

[12] George Dennis, *The Cities and Cemeteries of Etruria* (London: J. M. Dent, n.d.) Vol. 1, pp. 397–400. Tarchun is called "Tages" in Greco-Roman legends. Dennis explains in a footnote (p. 399) that "Tagus" was a title of the Pelasgian Greek chieftains who ruled the confederated cities of Thessaly. "Tagus," he points out, has been identified by scholars as a variant of Tarchun.

prophecy or divination. His religious teachings, the code or sacred Discipline of the Etruscans, were represented as the source of Roman religion and law. Little Bes, the Egyptians' Pygmy god of the musical arts, was identified in numerous ways with the music-loving lawgiver Osiris. Osiris conveyed his religion, explained Plutarch, through the agreeable medium of music and song.

The Etruscan people of Roman times were not Pygmies. Their genealogy was complexly altered by successive waves of invaders who swept into ancient Italy. Classical legends state that shortly after the Trojan War the Etruscan people first migrated to Italy from a homeland blighted by famine. Famine and other disasters destroyed the paradisaical home of the original Pygmy sinners. Famine and plagues afflicted the sinful "Egypt" of Mosaic legend. Many Greco-Roman scholars maintained that the Etruscan people originally migrated from the nation of Lydia in Asia Minor. The very meticulous Greek historian Dionysius of Halicarnassus pointed out that the historic annals of Lydia fail to mention any such migration or exodus. The historic annals of Egypt likewise fail to mention the Israelites' spectacular exodus or even to confirm the legends of their residence in Egypt.

The people of Tarchun were known to the Greeks as Tyrrheni or Etruscans. Philologist Max Müller interpreted the Etruscans as migrants from the Lydian city of Tyrrha or Torrha. Historian George Grote remarked that Müller's theory "seems unusually slender." It is more reasonable to suggest that the Etruscans, Lydians and many other peoples derived their local variants of this name from a very ancient common source. In Etruria the people of Tarchun built a replica of Troy. The traditional site of Troy lies in the land of the Turcu or Turk. That grand old Trojan/Germanic ancestor Tor or Thor is supposed to have spent his childhood years in Thrace or "Turkey in Europe." The early history of man has been abominably confused by the renaming trick. The legends identify the first land of "Troy" with the lost Pygmy paradise of Toré.

The original sins committed in the original paradise offended every member of the supreme Efé trinity: (1) God as the god of the sky or celestial universe; (2) God as the god of the earth or terrestrial universe; (3) God as the god of the underworld or cavernous Kingdom of the Dead that the Pygmies traditionally locate under the Ituri Forest near the Mountain of the Moon. The Greco-Roman underworld was sometimes represented as a place of punishment for sinners who wage unjust wars, abuse their aged parents, commit adultery, or violate other ethical laws that resemble the Pygmy commandments. The Efé use a variety of words for laws, commandments, prohibitions and so forth. In their most philosophical concepts, God is represented as the spirit of the law and the eternal regulating power of the universe. On a more anthropomorphic level, the deity is portrayed as the grim law enforcer who hurls thunder and lightning down from the heavens or up from the thundering Efé earth.

The laws of Exodus were given during a veritable barrage of thunder, lightning, volcanic fire and earthquakes. Thor, the Germanic god of thunder and lightning, was involved with governments and legal codes patterned after the model of Troy. The Troy-Asgard-Olympus system of one supreme chief and twelve subordinate chiefs corresponds with the legal format of the judge and twelve good men of his jury. The ancient Roman legal code or the Twelve Tables of the Law seems to have been involved with the religious laws of the twelvefold Etruscans. The ancestral Pygmy lawgiver ascended to heaven and became the great god or angel of the moon. The moon has twelve months. Jacob or Israel, the ancestral hero who made the Talmudic ascent to the moon, had twelve sons whose modern Jewish descendants still use the lunar calendar. In many ancient theologies each of the lunar months had a god. The lunar calendar was of course invented by Thoth, the Egyptian lawgiver who ascended to heaven and became the great god or angel of the moon.

Tawa or Taua is the sacred bird of the lawgiving lunar angel and all of his Efé descendants. The national bird is *Ibis aethiopica,* the sacred ibis.* It nests in the Ituri Forest and frequents the

---

* The sacred ibis has black and white plumage, a black head, a long curving black bill, a black neck and black feet. In some Pygmy territories, the name of the sacred ibis is used as a slangy word for crows or prevailingly black birds. Misled by this usage, Schebesta and Trilles described the crow as the sacred bird of the Pygmies. The Efé, ironically enough, regard the

lakes near the Efé Mountain of the Moon. It makes yearly migrations to Egypt, arriving in summer and returning to the Nile basin area when the inundation of the Egyptian Nile subsides.

Western Pygmy Rtwa, another name for the lunar angel. Arabic Ta'ut, Egyptian Tahuti or Tehuti, the god who was sometimes represented as an ibis-headed man. Thoth, the law-giving god of the moon, universal inventor, divine physician and traditional author of every ancient Egyptian book on every branch of knowledge, human or divine. Hermes, the Greek equivalent of Thoth, turned into an ibis when Typhon attacked the Olympian paradise. In this magnificent Egyptian picture, we see Thoth represented as the ibis-headed author or "Scribe of the Gods" (see illustration on page 140).

Tahato, Ta'ato, Ta'to, local variants of the Efé word for ape or chimpanzee.* The ape is very correctly represented by the Pygmies as the most intelligent animal. Cats are generally ranked second. Man is not regarded as an animal. In some Efé stories, the ape plays the role of the civilizing hero.

Egyptian Tahuti or Tehuti, Arabic Ta'ut, Greek Tot or Thoth, the god whose sacred animal was the ape, dog-headed ape or baboon. In Egyptian art Thoth was sometimes portrayed as a

crow as a noisy nuisance. As Trilles himself remarked, one cannot understand any people's spiritual culture until one masters their language.

* In my books *Congo Kitabu* and *Animal Kitabu,* I gave the Pygmy name of the chimpanzee as *tseko* or *cheko.* This is a Sua, not an Efé, word.

Thoth, the scribe of the gods

baboon. Isis, the wife of the civilizing hero Osiris, was sometimes represented as a baboon. In that guise, she makes a fitting help-mate for the simian form of Thoth. A vignette from *The Book of the Dead* shows Thoth as a sanctimonious baboon wearing lunar headdress as he presides over the scales of justice in Osiris' judgment hall. To the right of the scales stands the goddess of right and truth. At the base crouches a monstrous animal, the Eater of the Dead. It devours human hearts that have been weighed in the balance and found wanting because their owners violated the Pygmy-Egyptian commandments.

The dog-headed ape is depicted as the colleague or assistant of the ibis-headed Thoth in an old Egyptian picture (see illustration on page 142).

The ancestral lunar angel, God the Father or God, is usually represented by the Pygmies as a tall, long-bearded patriarch. He is thus portrayed in a stately Egyptian picture of Thoth, the great god of Aah or the moon (see illustration on page 143). In Upper Egypt, at this holy city of Khemennu, Thoth was called by the title "Lord of Khemennu, self-created, to whom none hath given birth, god One."

Tau or Tahu, the sacred tree of the moon. In the longer Efé stories of the stolen fruit, the angel of the moon observes and brings punishment to the Pygmy sinners who plundered the forbidden tree. In a separate and entirely different story, the son-incarnation of God hangs upon a tree, ignominiously defeated by a human sinner.

Greek *tau*, Hebrew *tav*, the tau cross or letter *t*, identified in Judeo-Christian legend with the fatal tree of Eden and the tree of the crucifixion at the center of the earth. Egyptian Tehu, a name of the moon. Tehuti, Thoth, the lawgiving god of the moon. "Not have I stolen from the orchard," the deceased Egyptian swore before Thoth and Osiris in their supernatural courtroom. The original sinners stole from the orchard, forest or trees, not the forbidden "tree" of God. To build their legendary megalopolis or "great village of the beginning," they ravaged and destroyed nature. In the Efé legend cycle, they are charged with the commission of every conceivable sin. Revelation denounces "that great city, which spiritually is called Sodom and Egypt, where also our

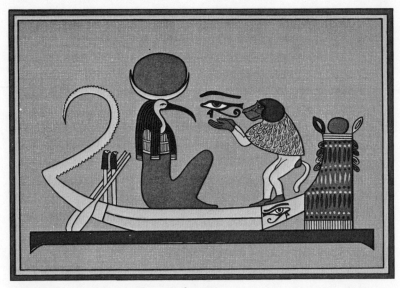

Aah-Tehuti and his associate the ape

Lord was crucified." The Arab geographers placed the prehistoric land of Egypt-Eden in the Mountains of the Moon.

The Efé legend of the forbidden tree has withered into myth. Like many Christians, the Pygmies believe in this story but do not understand it. Down through the eons, we have been unable to see the forest for the trees. All of the ancient Pygmies' original sins add up to one very real and terrible crime: they looted nature to build an urban civilization that approached the technological level of our own. Ecologists warn that we may be wiped out in less than fifty years if the present spoliation and pollution of the natural world continues unchecked. "Those who cannot remember the past are doomed to repeat it," declared the philosopher George Santayana. Now we shall try to remember by examining the detailed texts of the major Pygmy legends. These stories were originally composed by Efé, the ancestral elf of paradise and ever-watchful angel of the moon.

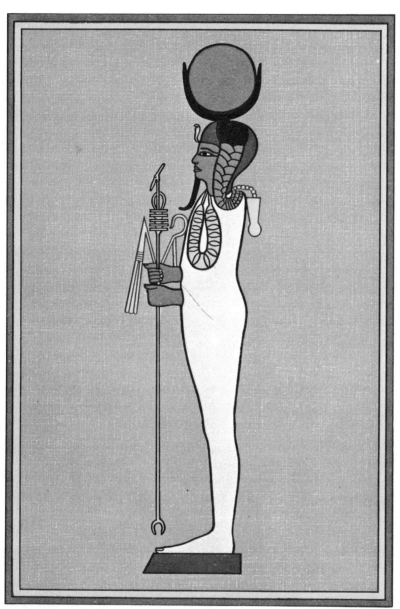

The moon-god Aah

The First Ages of Man

According to numerous Pygmy legends, God or the lunar angel descended from heaven to earth, created man, gave the commandments, dwelled for a time on earth, and returned to the sky. These events are described in the longer Efé narratives of the forbidden *tahu* tree. "God, with the aid of the moon, created the first man," begins a version recorded by Schebesta. "The moon created the first man," according to another one of his texts. In a story Schebesta obtained from "the Efé of the Kuku camp," the god of the moon performs the task of creation. God sends the angel of the moon down to earth in a saga that was narrated to me by Efé elders of the Erengeti region in the extreme north of the Kivu province:

One fine day in heaven, God told his chief helper to make the first man. The angel of the moon descended. He modeled the first man from earth, wrapped a skin around the earth, poured blood into the skin, and punched holes for the nostrils, eyes, ears and mouth. He made another hole in the first man's bottom, and put all the organs in his insides. Then he breathed his own vital force into the little earthen statue. He entered into the body. It moved . . . It sat up . . . It stood up . . . It walked. It was Efé, the first man and father of all who came after.

God said to Efé, "Beget children to people my forest. I shall give them everything they need to be happy. They will never have to work. They will be the lords of the earth. They will live forever. There is only one thing I forbid them. Now—listen well—give my words to your children, and tell them to transmit this commandment to every generation. The *tahu* tree is absolutely forbidden to man. You must never, for any reason, violate this law."

Efé obeyed these instructions. He, and his children, never went near the tree. Many years passed. Then God called to Efé, "Come up to heaven. I need your help!" So Efé went up to the sky. After he left, the ancestors lived in accordance with his laws and teachings for a long, long time. Then, one terrible day, a pregnant woman said to her husband, "Darling, I want to eat the fruit of the *tahu* tree." He said, "You know that is wrong." She said, "Why?" He said, "It is against the law." She said, "That is a silly old law. Which do you care about more—me, or some silly old law?"

They argued and argued. Finally, he gave in. His heart pounded with fear as he sneaked into the deep, deep forest. Closer and closer he came. There it was—the forbidden tree of God. The sinner picked a *tahu* fruit. He peeled the *tahu* fruit. He hid the peel under a pile of leaves. Then he returned to camp and gave the fruit to his wife. She tasted it. She urged her husband to taste it. He did. All of the other Pygmies had a bite. Everyone ate the forbidden fruit, and everyone thought that God would never find out.

Meanwhile, the angel of the moon watched from on high. He rushed a message to his master: "The people have eaten the fruit of the *tahu* tree!" God was infuriated. "You have disobeyed my orders," he said to the ancestors. "For this you will die!"

God told his chief servant or angel to make the first man. The Talmud maintains that God commanded the archangel Michael to mold man from the dust of the ground. Michael apparently manufactured Adam, man or the first man, from the Hebrew *adama* or "earth" of the earthly paradise at the source of Gihon-Nile. The Pygmies' angel is the heavenly form of Efé, the first man or God the Father. He is often called God. He came to the paradisaical garden-forest at the source of the Albertine Nile, made the earthly form of man, and "breathed his own vital force into the little earthen statue." Genesis 2:7 states: "And the Lord God formed man of the dust of the ground, and breathed into his nostrils the breath of life; and man became a living soul." Efé, the heavenly father, modeled an earthly form of himself. His children or people are also called Efé. The Efé nation includes male and female individuals. "So God created man in his own image, in the image of God created he him; male and female created he them (Genesis 1:27)." Efé was told to "beget children" who would be given "everything they need to be happy" and who would preside as the divinely ordained "lords of the earth." Genesis 1:28 avers: "And God blessed them, and God said unto them, Be fruitful, and multiply, and replenish the earth, and subdue it: and have dominion over the fish of the sea, and over the fowl of the air, and over every living thing that moveth upon the earth."

Efé descended from heaven to perform the modeling task. His career as the civilizing hero was briefly summarized in this story by the statement that he gave mankind "his laws and teachings." The Greek demigod Prometheus made the descent from heaven to earth, modeled man out of clay mixed with water, and taught his protégés all kinds of useful arts and sciences. This event presumably occurred in the lost Greco-Roman paradise at the center of the earth and the source of Okeanos-Nile. Efé expressly forbade lying, cheating, blasphemy, theft and other forms of unethical conduct in his laws and commandments. Several Pygmy legends describe the theft of fire as one of the great original sins that brought death to the world. Prometheus was portrayed as a master of cunning and fraud. He ridiculed the gods. He taught smithcraft, an art that is absolutely dependent on the use of fire, before he stole the first fire from Olympus. His crime brought death and every misery to mankind. He combines Efé, the virtuous maker of man, with the thief of fire.

The thief of the *tahu* fruit traveled to the heart of the paradisaical forest. He was a son of Efé or God the Father, the first man and father of all who came after. He was sentenced to "work hard" in the stolen-fruit story told by the Efé elder Mwenua. Zeus's son Hercules traveled to the paradisaical garden of Hesperides as one of the many difficult labors he was commanded to perform by his kinsman Eurystheus, the king of Mycenae in southern Greece. Hercules had great difficulty finding the garden that Greco-Roman legends variously placed "on Mount Atlas in the Land of the Hyperboreans; or on Mount Atlas in Mauretania; or somewhere beyond the Ocean stream; or on two islands near the promontory called the Western horn, which lies close to the Ethiopian Hesperiae, on the borders of Africa."[1] When he finally reached the garden, Hercules persuaded Prometheus' brother Atlas to steal the golden apples. A brief story told by the Greek historian Herodotus declares that Hercules attacked the Pygmies, wrapped them up in his lion's skin, and delivered them to Eurystheus. Both the golden apples and the kidnapped Pygmies that Hercules brought to Eurystheus were presumably obtained from the same source: the land of Homer's Pygmies on the shores of Okeanos-Nile, the great stream or river of Ocean.

Efé is kidnapped and imprisoned in a long and very thrilling Pygmy legend. Matu, the mother of Efé the Savior, is kidnapped in another Pygmy story. The kidnappers are associated with the thieving characters who stole the forbidden fruit and fire. A mortal son of Efé took the fruit of the sacred tree. The savior-son of Efé did not steal the fruit or kidnap the Pygmies. He is the supremely virtuous adversary of giant monsters or dragons. Hercules, a mortal son of Zeus, fought giants and dragons of every variety. He combines the prodigal son of Efé with the heroic son-incarnation of the heavenly hero.

Phoebus Apollo, a divine son of Zeus, fought with a monster called Python. The Greeks identified Apollo with the Egyptian god known as Horus the Child. He was portrayed as the son-incarnation of the Pygmy god Bes on a sacred stone stele that Muham-

---

[1] Robert Graves, *The Greek Myths* (Baltimore: Penguin Pelican, 1955), Vol. 2, p. 145.

med'Ali Pasha presented to Prince von Metternich of Austria (1773–1859). The Pygmy god of the musical arts was identified on the Metternich Stele with Rā or Rā-Horus, the dragon-fighting god of light or the sun. Apollo was the god of music, poetry, fine arts, medicine and the sun. Mount Parnassus, Apollo's sacred mountain at the center of the earth, was located at the traditional site of the Greco-Roman gods' Olympian home. Parnassus was also associated with Dionysus, the amiable god of wine and revelry whom the Greeks identified with Osiris, the music-loving father of Horus the Child. Bes, the Pygmy god of music, mirth and dancing, holds the sovereign emblems of Osiris in the Metternich Stele's portrait of Horus' saintly father.

Bes wore a stylish cat-skin sarong, the ceremonial garb of Pygmy elders and dancers, while Zeus's son Hercules wore a lion-skin garment that he apparently used to wrap up the Pygmy victims of his kidnapping safari to the land of paradise. The prodigal son of All-Father Efé was persuaded by a woman to plunder the forbidden *tahu* tree. "It is against the law," this innately virtuous but fallible man protested. "Which do you care about more—me, or some silly old law?" his wife demanded to know. Krishna, the son of the great god Vishnu, was persuaded by his wife to steal the tree of heaven from the garden of Mount Meru, the Hindu Olympus at the center of the earth. Efé's son succumbed to feminine wiles, looted the tree, and gave the *tahu* fruit to the first woman. Paris, the woman-crazy son of the supreme Trojan king Priam, gave a golden apple marked *For the Fairest* to the goddess Aphrodite. This was the ultimate cause of the Trojan War.

Efé's delinquent son was the brother of Efé's divine son-incarnation, and hence of All-Father Efé. Loki, the blood brother of All-Father Odin, engineered the theft of the golden apples from the forest outside the walls of Asgard-Troy, the ancestor-gods' paradisaical city at the center of the earth. He lured the goddess Idun, who carried the golden apples in a box or bowl, into the forest, where she was then kidnapped. The willful woman of the Efé legend tasted the *tahu* fruit. She shared the fruit with the thief and mankind in general. The women called the Hesperides were accused of lunching on golden apples. They gave three golden apples to their father Atlas. He took the apples from the walled orchard of paradise and gave them to Hercules, the man who kidnapped the Pygmies.

Atlas' brother Prometheus stole the forbidden fire of Zeus from the Olympian residence of Zeus and his company of gods. Plato's dialogues *Timaeus* and *Critias* describe Atlas as the king of Atlantis, a legendary nation that warred against the first or paradisaical city of Athens. According to Plato's story, the war occurred around or even prior to 9600 B.C. The golden "apple of strife" caused the pseudo-historical war between the Greeks and the Trojans. The golden apples were stolen from the forest of Asgard-Troy, the paradisaical city of Odin and his company of gods.

The *Prose Edda* locates Odin's residence on the southern continent at a place called Gimlé: "All righteous men shall live and be with him where it is called Gimlé or Vingólf, but wicked men will go to Hel and thence to Niflhel that is down in the ninth world." Gimlé is inhabited by "white elves" and situated "in the southern end of heaven." The elves dwell in the neighborhood of an Olympian massif called Himinbjörg, the Heaven-Mountain "at heaven's end." The mountains and Pygmies were located at the southern end of the southern continent in the map of "Africa in Homer's World." Hercules brought the golden apples from the land of the Pygmies on the shores of Okeanos-Nile. The theft of the fruit was caused by the first woman of Pygmy legend. Eve plucked the fatal fruit of Genesis from the Talmudic "Garden of Apples" or Eden garden forest at the source of Gihon-Nile.

The Jesuit missionary-anthropologist Trilles used the Pygmy story of the stolen fruit to support the "undeniable fact" of the Old Testament tale. The Biblical story of the so-called original sin has been used by the organized Christian churches to promote anile and pernicious doctrines like the dogma of infant damnation. The command to "be fruitful and multiply" is currently being used as an argument against population control. The penalty laid upon Eve—to bring forth children in sorrow—is used by Christian zealots as an ostensibly rational basis for denying anesthetics to women in childbirth. "Beget children to people my forest," God told Efé or God the Father. These instructions were addressed to the earthly incarnation of a legendary angel who founded the ancient Pygmy nation. Mortal men and women who are not angels or Pygmies need not beget children to people the Pygmy forest of paradise or the Hebrew Garden of Eden.

The first woman of Efé and Kango Pygmy legend was condemned to bring forth children in pain and sorrow. The pregnant Efé lady who caused the theft of the fruit was harried by a dragon, gave birth to the son-incarnation of Efé, and thereby became Matu the Mother of God, in the Pygmy legend that Schebesta called "the myth of the savior." Genesis 3:15 describes the son or seed of Eve, the first woman, as the future adversary of the wicked snake in the grass of Eden. The pregnant Virgin Mary was harassed by the Satanic devil-dragon of Revelation. A Greek villain named Python persecuted Leto, the pregnant mother of Phoebus Apollo. The Greeks identified her son with Horus the Child, or Horus the son of Isis and Osiris. Isis, the older Egyptian version of Mary, was known as "the lady of sorrows." Her son was pictured as the son-incarnation of the Pygmy god Bes on the pre-Christian Metternich Stele. Modern women who give birth to ordinary babies in dragon-free environments need not feel constrained to share the sorrows of Matu, the maternal parent of Efé the Savior. They may choose or reject anesthetics as they see fit and as their physicians advise.

Isis was the wife, daughter, mother and/or sister of Osiris-Horus. Such relationships have no parallel among mortal men and women. Matu was the wife, daughter, mother and/or sister of Efé and his sons. The story of the sacred tree does not mention that All-Father Efé had a wife. Other Pygmy legends reveal that Efé was the first husband of Matu. He returned to heaven when his father God urgently requested his aid. Matu waited for years. Then she married Doru, the younger son of God or of Efé. She sent Doru down the primrose path to the forbidden *tahu* tree while Efé watched from his post on the moon. A separate episode in the continuing story of the Pygmies' cosmic Peyton Place describes Efé's heroic adventures in heaven, his trip back to earth, a confrontation with Matu, and an apparent reconciliation with Doru.

The local variants of this story feature a celestial battle between Efé and one or three giant monsters. The adversary is
variously described as a titanic ogre, serpent or bull elephant. The
great heroes of pan-Caucasoid legend brawled with ogres, serpents and bulls of many different varieties. Mithra, the cat-headed
sun-god of ancient Persian theology, was the fearless foe of a
vast creature known as the "Bull of Heaven." Bes, the cat-headed
Pygmy god of light or the sun, conquered all the Typhonian
beasts of the Metternich Stele. The following account of Efé's
battle with three celestial bull elephants was recorded by Schebesta.[2] A condensed version was presented in Geoffrey Parrinder's
book *African Mythology* as "a Pygmy story of the first man, called
Efé."

> God dwelled in the sky, in a beautiful field surrounded by a
> vast forest. The forest was filled with all sorts of game. There was,
> however, no hunter to chase the game. Then God remembered the
> first man, Efé, whom he had put on the earth. He decided to bring
> Efé back to his side. So God forged three big spears, cut a long
> liana, and let it drop all the way down to earth. He trailed it along
> the ground, lassoed the Pygmy—the great hunter!—and hauled him
> up to heaven. He gave Efé the spears and the mission of hunting for
> him. But first he escorted Efé through his domain, to introduce the
> Pygmy to his household. Everyone was astonished to see this
> stranger, whom nobody knew. They asked God, "Father, whom have
> you brought here?" He explained that it was Efé, his first creature,
> whom he had left on earth and who was a great hunter. He had now
> drawn Efé up to heaven, he said, and had entrusted him with the
> hunt. Joyous, the Pygmy left on the expedition. Soon he felled an
> elephant whose tusks were as big as giant trees. Everyone came to
> cut it up. Above all, the women rejoiced. They took Efé in their arms
> and sang his praises. In the same fashion, Efé killed a second and
> third elephant.
>   God kept Efé with him for a long time. He provided for him
> richly, presented him with iron ornaments, and gave him the three
> spears for his own. Then he cut another long liana, attached it to
> the celestial vault, and swung until he had made a hole big enough
> for the Pygmy to pass through. God attached Efé to the liana and

---

[2] P. Schebesta, *Les Pygmées*, p. 73; *Les Pygmées du Congo Belge;* pp. 312–
13.

let him down to earth. But the Pygmy was caught in the top of a Borue tree.

God saw that the liana had not come to the end of its course, and that Efé had not reached the ground. So he hauled the Pygmy up again and let him down a second time. Then he heard the clinking of iron rings, and knew that Efé had made a safe landing on earth.

Efé went quickly to his hut, where his wife had long mourned his death. When his youngest child came home and saw the stranger with his iron ornaments, he ran away, frightened, to warn his mother. She did not recognize her husband. Soon the whole camp had gathered in the hut, and no one recognized the newcomer. Finally, the oldest of his children looked into his eyes, recognized his father, and cried joyously, "The stranger is our father!" The mother drew him close to her and said, "If you have seen a ghost, you will die!" The curiosity of all had reached its highest point. The brother of the man, gathering all his courage, said, "I am going to look in the hut to see who it is, even if I die." He recognized his brother and asked him with astonishment, "Is it you? Where have you been for such a long time? Where do you come from?" Efé answered, "The father who created me took me up beside him in heaven, and had me hunt on his behalf. See what he has given me."

Then there was a joyous reunion and everyone came forward to congratulate Efé.

The first man, the eldest son of God, and the first chief of the ancient Pygmy nation returned to earth through a hole in the vault of the sky. Sabizeze-Kigwa-Kimanuka—the first man, the eldest son of God, and the first divine king of the Tutsi or "Watusi" nation—fell or descended to earth through a hole in the floor of the sky. He landed on the sacred rock of Rutara Rw'Ikinani, which is located in the modern nation of Rwanda. The mixed-Hamite tribes of Rwanda, Burundi and Uganda, call their territory by the traditional name of Unyamwezi, the Land of the Moon. Mwezi was the name of several divine kings who reigned in the lunar nation of the Tutsi. My friend Mwambutsa IV, the deposed (1966) king of Burundi who currently resides in Geneva, Switzerland, claimed descent from the divine kings called Mwezi. Anthropologists have interpreted his people as the descendants of early Hebrews who migrated to equatorial Africa.

Hebrew legends situate the ancestral paradise at the source of the Gihon-Nile. The southernmost source of the Nile is located at Kasumo in Burundi, about four degrees south of the equator. The Albertine Nile flows from the Pygmies' Mountain of the Moon, where the Arab contingent of the lunar nation traditionally placed the prehistoric land of Eden-Egypt.

Efé or God the Father, the first man and the original lunar angel, modeled his earthly incarnation out of earth. His wayward woman caused the sin against the sacred tree. The first man of Tutsi legend was modeled out of clay in the sky or celestial paradise of Pygmy legend. The first woman and miraculous mother of the Tutsi nation committed the original sin and thereby caused the expulsion from paradise—a literal Fall of Man!—through the Pygmies' hole in the vault of heaven. Talmudic legends maintain that Mother Eve brewed wine from the forbidden fruit that grew in the garden of apples. The celestial mother of Tutsi legend got drunk on banana beer and then committed an original sin of an entirely different nature.

The wild Tutsi saga of the creation and fall scrambles five or six Pygmy legends. Efé-Adam is described as "the first Mututsi." *Mututsi* is the singular form of *Batutsi*. Here is the story, as it was told to me by Johanni Kashirahamwe, the Tutsi chief of Buyagoma in the nation of Burundi:

> The first Mututsi came from the sky. His father was Imana— God himself!—and his mother was named Gasani. His birth was a miracle.
>
> Life in the sky was very beautiful. There was no hunger, disease, or death. But even so, Gasani wasn't happy, for she was a barren woman. She begged Imana to help her. God listened to that weeping woman and was moved by her tears.
>
> So he took a piece of clay, wet it with the spittle from his own tongue, and shaped it into the form of a child. "You must hide it in a pot of milk," Imana told the woman. "If you keep the pot filled with fresh milk for nine months, the child will come to life. But you mustn't tell anyone how I made this child for you! Do you promise?"
>
> Gasani promised, nine months passed; then just as Imana had told her, the clay child awakened and started to cry. She gave him

the name Sabizeze. Then Imana made a brother and sister for Sabizeze so that the little boy wouldn't be lonely.

Now Gasani, the mother of God's children, had a sister who was just as barren as she was. When that woman saw Gasani's beautiful children, she gave her sister no peace, trying to find out her secret. Then one day she tricked her sister into drinking too much beer, and Gasani told her the story. She whispered very quietly, but you cannot fool Imana! He knew at once, the moment the words were spoken. Outraged, he searched through all of Heaven for the children of Gasani. He found them at last, returning from the hunt. Then Imana made a big hole in the floor of Heaven, and the poor children fell through that hole onto the barren earth.

It was a terrible world! After ten days they were so sick with hunger and cold that they begged Imana to forgive them. They thought they were dying! So God sent a streak of lightning from the clouds to make a fire in the grass. Then the next day seeds and plants fell through the hole in the sky: beans, peas, corn, sorghum and bananas. And the next day the hole opened again and tools rained down upon the earth. "Imana has helped us!" the children cried. Then they picked up the tools and started to work.

Imana looked down upon his children and he was pleased with them. So he sent a Mutabazi—a beautiful angel—to pay them a visit. When the children saw the angel fly down on wings of thunder, they were terrified. "Do not fear me!" the Angel of God told them. "Imana has sent me to help you. Ask what you wish."

The children asked for a cow, a bull, a ram, a ewe, a rooster and a chicken. Imana smiled, and the animals fell from the clouds! While they were admiring those beautiful animals, the Angel told the children that God would permit them to mate with each other, even though they came from the same womb. Then the children cried out with joy and began to people the earth.

Mutabazi, the Angel of God, stayed on the earth for many years to help people with their troubles. But then, one day, evil men seized the Angel and nailed him to a tree with iron spikes! Imana pulled out the spikes and healed the Angel's wounds. Then he sent a terrible storm from the sky which blew the poor Angel back to Heaven.

That was a long time ago. But the Angel comes back again and again. He sends his spirit into the body of each new Mwami, so that the Mwami himself is the Angel of God.

At the time of Johanni's narration (1951) Rwanda and
Burundi were each ruled by a Mwami or divine angel-messiah-
king. These royal descendants of the clay Adam were successively
animated by the spirit of a heavenly angel who anciently dwelled
in the earthly Land of the Moon. Efé, the lunar angel, breathed
his vital force or transferred his spirit into the little earthen
statue that came to life as "Efé, the first man and father of all
that came after." Thoth, the self-created god of the moon, was
the executive director of the Egyptian trinity that molded the first
man from the dank earth or mud of the holy River Nile. Thoth
was addressed by the title Tem in *The Book of the Dead*. Tem
was the self-created first man and Adam-like "father of the human race" who emerged from the primordial waters. Like Efé,
Thoth gave his laws and teachings, and embarked on the Pygmy
angel's ascent to the heavens. Efé made the trip at the request
of his father, the great smith of the sky. Ptah, the celestial smith
and potter of Egyptian theology, fathered a beloved son called
I-em-Hetep "in the image and likeness of Thoth the wise."

Ptah's son was the god of wisdom and good physician of
gods and of men. His name. I-em-Hetep, meant "He who cometh
in peace." Efé's people are still the good little physicians who can
cure all kinds of ailments with their healing herbs. Efé's peaceable
laws and commandments forbid war and murder. Efé's father, the
sky-smith, is described as the ultimate source of the law. Ptah was
the heavenly lord of right and truth "who created his own image,
who fashioned his own body." Pottery figurines of Ptah show him
in his earthly form or image—as a Pygmy.

Efé traditionally controls or operates the universe on behalf
of his father, the original and continuous creator of the universe.
Thoth controlled every power on heaven and earth. Ptah sculpted
and hammered out heaven and earth when Thoth spoke his
mighty word. Their triune partner Khnemu, the god of the Nile
flood, modeled the first man on his potter's wheel or table. He
was identified with Ptah, Thoth, Osiris and Tem, the self-created
first man and "father of the human race." Efé, the original modeler of man, returned to the sky to hunt on behalf of his father.
The elders explain that his quarry, the giant beasts, were ravag-
ing the forest of heaven. Michael, the Talmudic modeler of man,

led Revelation's celestial battle against the Satanic devil-dragon and his confederates. Bes, the Pygmy dragon-fighter of the Metternich Stele, stands in triumph on an oval cartouche that contains two serpents, a crocodile, a hippopotamus and other Typhonian monsters. A pottery Pygmy crushes serpents in his grasp as Ptah-Seker-Osiris, the god of the Egyptian resurrection.

Efé brought metal tools and ornaments when he returned from the sky. Tutsi legends boast that the ancestors brought the secret of working metal from heaven to earth. The first tools fell, like the Tutsi ancestors, through the Pygmies' hole in the vault of the sky. The ancestors descended through the heavenly hole after the deity found them "returning from the hunt." When the tools and seed rained down through the hole, the ancestors used them to cultivate the soil. The tall Tutsi do not hunt, practice agriculture, work metal, make pottery or perform manual labor of any variety. They are cattle barons who regard any other profession as unspeakably degrading. The pygmoid Mosso people of Burundi and the pygmoid Twa folk of Rwanda, Burundi, eastern Zaïre and western Uganda are versatile little hunters, potters, smiths and jacks-of-all-trades. The Tutsi despise the pygmoid peoples as lowly pariahs who not only perform manual labor but eat wild game, a kind of food that the East African Hamites typically forbid in their dietary codes.

Ironically enough, the Tutsi used their garbled versions of the ancient Pygmy legends to justify the social exploitation of the pygmoid peoples and the Bantu Negro agriculturalists of the Hutu tribe. "Twa and Hutu were already on the earth. They lived like savages in poverty and ignorance. But the Ibimanuka—those who fell from Heaven—were kindly and generous. They shared their heritage and in gratitude the savages became their servants," according to my Tutsi informant Johanni Kashirahamwe. The members of the ancient Pygmy nation dwelled on earth before Efé returned to his people through the Pygmy-Tutsi hole in the vault of heaven. When I pressed Johanni for further information about the origin of the so-called savages, he very arrogantly replied, "Imana made them too, but he was tired that day. His hand slipped as he fashioned their bodies. They were ugly and stupid, and God was tempted to destroy them. But he decided to save them to help us and to be our servants."

The Genesis-like creation out of clay and the crucifixion of the beautiful man-angel inspired me to ask, "It sounds almost as if your story came from the Bible. Johanni, are you sure that the missionaries' teachings haven't been mixed into your people's stories?"

"Oh, no," he answered quickly. "That is a very old Tutsi legend. It hasn't changed for a hundred years. The missionaries don't even like it. They say we should give up our own legends and believe in theirs, but nobody really wants to—their stories don't even mention the Tutsi!"

The story is told by back-country Tutsi who have never been exposed to Christian teachings. The quasi-Biblical legends and customs of the Tutsi and East African Hamites are responsible for the anthropologists' persistent efforts to derive their ancestors from Middle Eastern Hebrews. The ancient Egyptian representatives of the Hamitic-Semitic stock left historic records that fail to confirm even the mere existence of the Hebrews or Israelites. Numerous Egyptian texts and pictures install the Pygmies as the divine ancestors from the southern Land of the Gods or Land of Trees at the site of the Hebrew Eden forest and all the Indo-European forests, gardens and orchards located at the Olympian center of the earth.

The Tutsi Adam, his brother and his sister came to earth from the Pygmies' Edenic forest in the sky. The first man, the junior male and the woman are the principal characters of the Pygmy legend cycle. When Efé returned to earth, his brother risked death by daring to look at him: "The curiosity of all had reached its highest point. The brother of the man, gathering all his courage, said, 'I am going to look in the hut to see who it is, even if I die.' " The woman of the Kango Pygmy creation epic brought death and disaster to the world when she dared to look at God, the divine man who dwelled in the "big house" of the earthly paradise.

The Kango Pygmies of the southwest Ituri and the Sua Pygmies of the central Ituri tell many similar versions of this story. God dwells with men, gives the commandments, and departs from the earthly paradise after the curious woman commits her apparently trivial sin. The "God" of their story is Efé or God the Father. The following version was recorded by Schebesta in the western Ituri.[3]

In the beginning, God lived with men, his children, who consisted of two sons and a daughter. God had relations with men. He spoke with them, but he did not show himself to them. His supreme commandment, which they might never transgress, was that he forbade them to look at him. God lived in a big house, where you could hear him hammering and forging away. He was good to his children, who lacked nothing, lived happily and contentedly, and did not have to earn their living by the sweat of their brow since all things came to them without their having to make any real effort. The daughter had the duty of bringing firewood and water to the door of the house.

One evening while she was placing a pot of water in front of the door, she gave in to the curiosity which had gnawed at her for such a long time. She decided to try to see her father on the sly, without anyone knowing about it. In order to see at least the arm of her father, she hid herself behind a post of the house. God extended his arm, richly garnished with copper bracelets, to pick up the pot. She had seen it, the splendidly adorned arm of God! What joy was in her heart! But alas, the punishment quickly followed the crime. God, who had seen the sin, gathered his children and reproached them for their disobedience. He announced to them a cruel punishment: in future, they would live alone, without him. He would go far away from them. Tears and lamentations were in vain. God left them weapons and tools. He taught them the art of the smith and all that they would need to survive on their own. As for the daughter, he cursed her. She must become the wife of her brothers, bring forth children in sorrow, and do all of the menial work. This is the malediction which falls upon women unto this day.

God made a secret departure from his children and disappeared down the river. Since that day no one has seen him. With God also well-being and peace disappeared; yes, everything—water, fruit, game, all the foods which before had grown spontaneously—was

---

[3] P. Schebesta, *Les Pygmées du Congo Belge*, pp. 302–3; *Les Pygmées;* pp. 74–75.

taken away from men. They had to work hard to earn their living, far from God. Death came also as a punishment for this sin. The first-born child that the woman brought forth, she, full of pre-monitions, called Kukua-Kende, "Death comes." The child died two days after its birth. Since then, no man has escaped from the avenging death. Thus death came into the world.

The woman was told that she must not try to look at the godly resident of the paradisaical mansion. A very curious lady named Psyche was forbidden to gaze upon the divine being who dwelled in a legendary Greco-Roman palace. His name was Eros or Cupid. He was frequently portrayed, like the Etruscans' child-sized ancestor, as a little boy or child. He was the oldest of the gods; according to the Orphic creation legend of ancient Greece, he was hatched from the silver egg of the moon and thereafter set the universe in motion. He was alternately fathered by Her-mes or the Egyptian moon-god Thoth. He was Efé, the original lunar angel of Everyman's Lost Paradise in the Mountains of the Moon.

The best-known version of the Cupid and Psyche story was told in the *Metamorphoses* or *The Golden Ass* of Apuleius the African (c. 125 A.D.), a classical scholar who was born in the Roman provinces of North Africa. In his story Psyche travels to a paradisaical forest where she discovers "a princely Edifice" built of gold, silver, ivory and precious stones. Cupid, her invisible host, provides gourmet meals and ethereal music played by in-visible harpists. He makes love to her, sight unseen; then, like the first Efé woman, Psyche becomes pregnant. Finally, taking lamp in hand, she steals a forbidden glimpse of the god and accidentally burns him with boiling-hot oil that drips from the lamp. After this incident—which is connected with Pygmy stories of the stolen fire—Cupid rebukes her bitterly and departs.

The curious Kango woman was sentenced by the departing deity to do "all of the menial work." The pregnant lady of Efé legend received a similar sentence. Despite her pregnant condi-tion, Psyche had to perform a series of arduous tasks while she wandered over the earth searching for Cupid. As her last task, Psyche had to fetch a mysterious box from the underworld. She was warned that she must not open the box. She opened the box. When a cloud of vapors poured out, she fell to the ground in an "infernal and deadly sleep." Another Greek lady, Pandora, opened an ominous box that was originally described as a *pithos* or clay jar. When she opened her box or jar, a great cloud of miseries flew out and descended on the formerly blissful race of mankind. Zeus had previously commanded his son Hephaestus, the god of smithcraft and fire, to create "the first Greek woman," as Pandora has been called. The legends say that Zeus ordered Pandora's creation in order to avenge Prometheus' theft of the forbidden fire.

Pandora, the first woman, was herself made out of clay. Eve was created from the body of Adam, the man of *adama* or earth. Eve plucked the sacred fruit that Pandora's brother-in-law Atlas removed from the orchard of paradise. The Hebrew garden-forest was located "eastward in Eden." An apparently neighboring district, "the land of Nod, on the east of Eden," was the site of the first Biblical city and hometown of "Tubalcain, an instructor of every artificer in brass and iron." The Germanic paradise in the southern continent was the site of the garden-forest whence the apples were stolen, the primordial city of Asgard-Troy, and the home of the great smith Thor.

Thor's son or father, Odin, and the Pygmy-like elves dwelled in a place called Gimlé or Vingólf. Their smithy and an enigmatic disaster caused by women are described in Snorri's *Prose Edda*: "They built another hall that was the sanctuary of the goddesses, and it was a very beautiful building; it is called Vingólf. Next they laid the hearth of a forge and then made hammer and tongs and an anvil, and thenceforward all other tools, and went on to work in metals and stone and wood, and also in gold, so abundantly that all their household utensils and furniture were of gold. That age was called the Golden Age before it was spoiled by the arrival of the women who came from Giantland."

The elves or dwarfs of the Eddas forged the mighty hammer of Thor. They made the great spear of Odin. They made the gold ring Draupnir—also called the Ring of the Nibelungs—and all the great treasures of the gods. Hephaestus, the Greek god of smithcraft and fire, performed the same tasks in the smithy of Olympus. Plato's dialogues *Timaeus* and *Critias* portray Hephaestus as the founding father of a paradisaical Greco-Egyptian nation that was attacked by the aggressive empire of Atlantis. The war was followed by "violent earthquakes and floods." The paradisaical city of Tubalcain, the Hebrew teacher of smithcraft, was washed down the drain by the great deluge of Genesis.

Cain, the legendary ancestor of Tubalcain, had a rather famous argument with brother Abel. War-prone humans were accordingly labeled "Cain's children" in Ardrey's *African Genesis*. The ancestral weapons of "Cain's children" were depicted as the antelope bones that according to Dr. Leakey hyenas dragged into ancient African caves. The Pygmies, who are at present the most technologically "primitive" living humans, claim that their ancestors made metal ornaments and weapons. Efé *oru* is metal or metallic mineral:

> Anglo-Saxon *ora*, unwrought metal, brass, ore. Greek *orykton*, mineral. Spanish *oro*, Portuguese *ouro*, Latin *aurum*, Rumanian *aur*, French *or*, gold. Dutch *oer*, bog ore or iron ore. Cornish *hoern*, Welsh *haern*, iron, Sanskrit *hiranya*, Hungarian *aranyi*, gold. Welsh *arian* and *aur*, silver and gold. Latin *aerir*, *aurum* and *argentum*, bronze, gold and silver. Anglo-Saxon *ar*, brass, bronze, copper or ore.

Geologist Charles Hapgood and other outstanding scientists recently urged the abandonment of hackneyed theories about the Stone Age, Bronze Age, Iron Age and so forth. There is simply too much evidence of prehistoric civilizations that were destroyed by ancient disasters. This evidence is ignored by anthropologists who depict man's evolution as a slow, steady, straight-line movement "upward" from savage simpletons to our glorious selves. Many, if not most, of man's so-called creation legends tell instead of death and disaster. The Pygmy sagas typically end with a divine proclamation that the sinners must die, the advent of death, or a mass dying by unexplained means. The Efé story that Schebesta called "the myth of the savior" uniquely begins with the advent of death and ends with the resurrection.

Death comes in the form of an implacable giant that wipes out all the camps or cities of the ancient world. The race of man is extinguished. Matu, the Mother of God, uniquely survives the disaster. Typhon, the giant Greek man-dragon, attacked the Olympian paradise at the center of the earth. Athena, the Greek "Virgin Mother of Heaven," stood alone while the other members of the pantheon fled in terror. Athens stood alone, deserted by her allies, when the aggressive nation of Atlantis attacked the city of paradise. According to Greek legends about her origin, Athena was born in the African land of Libya, traveled to Crete, and moved on to Europe. All-Father Odin led the Germanic exodus from the twelvefold paradise of Asgard-Troy. During the course of his prehistoric safari to northern Europe, Odin apparently founded the twelve cities of the Attic or Athenian confederation, the twelve cities of Etruria, and a number of similar establishments that were modeled after the pattern of Troy.

The Trojan War was caused by a golden apple, the "apple of strife." Matu, the first mother, demanded the fruit of the *tahu* tree. Three supernatural mothers called Athena, Hera and Aphrodite demanded the fruit from Paris of Troy. When Paris gave the golden apple to Aphrodite, Athens and Hera went off arm in arm to plot the destruction of Troy. The blissful men of the Greek Golden Age were followed by a race of men who were "utterly subject to their mothers and dared not disobey them, although they might live to be a hundred years old." The Germanic Golden Age was destroyed by superhuman women from the land of the giants. Matu, the first woman and mother, caused the disaster that she alone survived. Who is she?

To answer that question, we shall examine the Efé "myth of the savior."

The Myth of the Savior

Bes and Horus, the Pygmy father and youthful hero of the Metternich Stele, were the virtuous foes of a monstrous man-serpent who was sometimes called the Roarer. The Egyptian fiend roars "like a tornado" in the stories told by Bes's earthly kinsmen of the eastern Ituri. Some Efé narrators say that he roars "like an automobile." This modern Pygmy metaphor has been inspired by the traffic on the Belgian-built highways that traverse the formerly paradisaical forest near the Mountains of the Moon. Like every Pygmy legend, the story of the savior's birth and battle with the monster is told a little differently by every

Pygmy elder. The following version was recorded by Schebesta in the eastern Ituri.[1]

The *lulu* monster was huge, as big as a Negro's house. He dwelled in the deep forest and menaced men. One day he came out with a terrible roar, demolished all the camps, and devoured the people. The only survivor was a pregnant woman who managed to escape unseen. When the time of her delivery approached, the unborn child spoke to his mother from her womb: "Mother, how shall I come forth unto the light of day?" He did not wish to enter the world like other children, so he opened a path through a hole under the big toe of his mother's right foot. All of a sudden, he became tall, wise, and knowing in the use of arms. "Mother, you are all alone, where are the others?" he asked, surprised. "A monster swallowed them up," answered the mother. "I was the only one who escaped, and you came into the world afterwards." Her son said, "Show me the monster. I want to kill him and avenge my own."

He already had his father's spear in his hand. Courage and audacity sparkled in his eyes. "Show me the monster!" he insisted to his hesitant mother, who did not wish to send her only son to certain death. For the *lulu* was tall as a tree, and more furious than all the animals of the forest put together.

Her son would not be placated. She had to lead him through the forest. She chanted, *"Lulu, odi avié!"* ("Lulu, killer of man!") Astonished, the *lulu* monster cocked its ear. Someone was calling it? Who could be calling it? Had it not killed all of the men? It hurtled forward, roaring like an automobile! The monster crashed down trees as it came. The mother heard the trees breaking. She saw it approach and she ran, terrified, to her son.

He stood his ground courageously, with two spears stuck in the ground beside him. He brandished the third in his mighty hand. Thus he waited for the monster. "Flee, my son, hide yourself!" begged his mother. He stood firm. The *lulu* monster opened its mouth, as big as a house, to swallow him. He brandished his spear, ready to throw it into the blood-red mouth. "Do not do it, my son!" cried his terrified mother. "It is futile!" His lance was already whistling through the air. It passed through the jaw and neck of the monster. With a frightful thud, the *lulu* fell to earth. Quickly its

[1] P. Schebesta, *Les Pygmées*, pp. 77–78; *Les Pygmées du Congo Belge*, pp. 322–23.

conqueror cut the monster's neck and took off its head. He stood in front of the dragon that had devoured all men, about to open up its belly. Then he heard voices speaking to him from the monster's belly. He heard, "Be careful! Do not pierce me! I am inside."

In the interior, there were still living men. With caution, he carried out his task. The first man whom he liberated was recognized by his mother. It was the father of the hero. Joyously the father hugged his son to his breast. All of those who came out of the monster were grateful; each of them gave the hero a young girl for a wife. He thus became chief of the country.

The son was armed with three spears, the weapons of his father. Efé fought the giant monsters of heaven with three iron spears. He brought the spears with him when he came back to earth and went to his house, expecting a hearty welcome from his wife. Matu instead refused to acknowledge or recognize Efé. Doru, the younger brother and/or prodigal son of Efé, recognized the heavenly hero without hesitation. There was a "joyous reunion" and it seemed that all parties would live happily ever after. Now we discover that Efé was apparently assassinated by a giant monster after this hypocritical scene.

Osiris likewise returned from a lengthy trip abroad to a welcome-home party staged by his brother Set, " a certain queen of Ethiopia named Aso," and seventy-two confederates who conspired to assassinate the godly king of prehistoric Egypt. Osiris' posthumous son Horus later speared and beheaded Set, the scheming man who was responsible for the murder of Osiris. After being beheaded, Set turned into the serpentine monster Apepi, known as the Roarer. Doru, the delinquent male of Pygmy legend, is identified with the infamous *lulu* monster. This creature is a giant ogre-like man who according to many Pygmy bands can transform himself into the vast serpent called *kituri* or *situri* and the other supernatural monsters of Pygmy theology.

As the brother of Matu and of All-Father Efé, this picturesque character is Set the brother of Isis and Osiris. Matu behaved in highly suspect fashion during the complex events of the dragon-fighting story. She ostensibly tried to dissuade the young hero from fighting the dragon because "she did not wish to send her only son to certain death." When the beast was about to swallow her only son with its gaping blood-red mouth, and his certain death seemed far more imminent, she tried to prevent the hero from hurling the spear that he brandished in his mighty hand. "Isis was present at the fight and because she in some way supported Set against Horus, her son turned upon her with the fury of a 'panther of the south,' and cut off her head."[2]

After the spear fight Efé's avenging son was made "chief of the country." Horus took his seat upon the throne of Osiris to the tune of this proclamation: "Horus is triumphant in the presence of the whole company of the gods, the sovereignty over the world hath been given unto him, and his dominion is in the uttermost parts of the earth." On the story of his battle with the monster, Egyptologist Budge comments: "We have no means of assigning a date to the composition of the above legend, but it must be very old, and it is easy to see that it is only a version of the older legend of the combat between Ra and Apep, and Heru-ur and Set, and Heru-Behutet and Set, and it is, of course, one of the sources of all the post-Christian legends of the overthrow of dragons by kings and heroes, e.g., Alexander the Great and Saint George."[3]

Horus of Behutet speared Set through the neck with a very long spear made of "divine iron" or "iron of the god." The hero was the "deified king of the blacksmiths" and chief god of Edfu or Behutet, the forge city of Upper Egypt. He fought Set and the monster's conspirators on behalf of his father Ra-Horus. In the form of a cat, Ra battled with the monster at the foot of the "southern sycamore tree" or "sacred Persea tree of Heliopolis," as we saw in the cat-versus-serpent vignette. Bes, the cat-headed Pygmy father-god of the Metternich Stele, originated in the southern "Land of Trees" or "Land of the Gods." According to many Egyptian texts, the throne of Osiris and his son Horus were located in the vicinity of the southern sycamore tree that was also known as the "tree of Nut." Nut, the Egyptian goddess of heaven who gave birth to the gods, was sometimes portrayed as the mother of Isis and sometimes equated with Isis; she was also

---

[2] Sir E. A. Wallis Budge, *The Gods of the Egyptians*, Vol. 1, p. 488.

[3] *Ibid.*, p. 489.

variously represented as the mother, daughter, wife and/or sister of Ra, Osiris, and the other top-ranking gods. The true identity of her divine consort was divulged in the sixth-dynasty pyramid text of the divine king Ra-Meri or Pepi the First: "He who is between the thighs of Nut is the Pygmy who danceth like the god and who pleaseth the heart of the god before his great throne."

The superhuman mother of Pygmy legend somehow managed to escape from the giant monster that swallowed mankind. The Nilo-Hamitic relatives of the North Hamitic Egyptians still tell many versions of this legend. The Taveta tribe, a branch of the East African Masai, call it "The Story of the Demon Who Ate People, and the Child." Their story begins: "There was once upon a time a demon who was greatly dreaded by the inhabitants of the country in which he lived, owing to his principal food being human beings." The demon then proceeds to devour "a large number of people and cattle—so many, in fact, that he thought he had exterminated the whole tribe." One woman escapes and hides with her child in a pit. She repeatedly urges her son to stay in the pit and avoid the demon, but the boy is determined to slay the great monster. He procures spears and arrows by unexplained means, climbs with his mother to the top of a tree, and lights a fire to attract the demon's attention. The monster rushes to the spot and starts to cut down the tree with an axe. The boy kills him with arrows, descends from the tree and resurrects the swallowed victims from the body of the monster. The cattle emerge when he cuts off the monster's fingers, one man comes out of its face, and the rest of the people return to the world of the living through the stump of its severed thumb. After holding a consultation, the grateful people "decided to appoint the boy chief."[4]

The Pygmy victims who were resurrected from the carcass of the *lulu* monster gratefully made the savior-son the chief of the country. The giant ogre is associated with Doru, the man who sinfully assailed the forbidden *tahu* tree. In several Pygmy stories, the hero climbs a tree to escape from villains, monsters

---

[4] A. C. Hollis, *The Masai: Their Language and Folklore*, pp. 221–23.

and/or cataclysmic events. Elements of these and other Pygmy
stories are ingeniously combined in the Taveta tale of the mother,
the son and the swallowing monster. Like Matu, the mother tried
to prevent the battle with the beast. If she had succeeded, there
would have been no glorious resurrection.

A mighty Masai warrior fights the monster and brings about
the resurrection in "The Story of the Warriors and the Devil."
The warriors are a pair of brothers who live together with their
parents. Their father gives them a bullock and tells them to go
and slaughter it. They travel with the bullock to "a big forest"
in which they kill the animal and cut some firewood from a tree
that cries out and rebukes them. These events apparently represent Efé's bull-slaying journey to the forest of the celestial paradise, which he made at his father's request, and brother Doru's
raid on the forbidden tree of the earthly paradise. After their encounter with the tree, the Masai brothers fall asleep. During the
night a devil comes and puts out their fire—an incident connected with the Pygmy stories of the stolen fire. The devil swallows the younger brother. "Go now, but tomorrow I will look for
you," the victim's elder brother warns the devil. Then the battle
commences:

> At dawn he started off in pursuit, and when he found the
> devil, he noticed that he had nine heads and a very big toe.
> The devil told the warrior to go away, and said he did not wish
> to hurt him as he was brave. The warrior refused, however, and
> told the devil he wanted to fight. The devil rushed at him and tried
> to kick him, but the warrior caught the kick on his shield and cut
> off one of his adversary's heads. The devil then fled, and the warrior
> called out to him that he would return on the morrow . . .
> The next day he followed the devil, and in the fight which
> ensued cut off another head. The devil ran away again, and the
> warrior told him that he would return the following morning to kill
> him.
> When he came to the spot the next day, he found the devil very
> weak from losing two of his heads, and he easily dispatched him,
> after which he cut off the big toe. Every kind of animal came out of
> the toe, and last of all came the warrior's brother . . . .[5]

---

[5] *Ibid.*, pp. 115–16.

The people emerged in the Taveta story from the stump of the demon's thumb, which is equivalent to the big toe of the hand. The Efé hero came out of a hole under his mother's big toe. Then he speared the monster, cut off its head and opened its belly. The Masai hero fought with a nine-headed devil that put out his fire. Hercules battled a nine-headed water monster that was called the Hydra. He shot fiery arrows at the monster, cut off its heads and disemboweled the beast. The Hydra was represented as a child of the giant man-dragon Typhon. Typhon or the Egyptian fiend Set was described as the son of Cronus, a titanic Greek swallowing monster, in Plutarch's treatise on Isis and Osiris.

Hercules' father Zeus resurrected five Olympian gods and goddesses—Poseidon, Hades, Hera, Hestia and Demeter—who had been swallowed by their ogre-like father Cronus. Zeus, the youngest son of Cronus, gave an emetic potion to the Titan. Cronus thereupon vomited up Zeus's elder brothers and sisters. They sprang out unharmed and expressed their gratitude by asking Zeus to be their chief in the ensuing war with the Titans. Atlas, the Titan who took the sacred fruit from the garden of paradise, led the Titans during their ten-year war with the Olympian gods. He was condemned to carry the sky on his shoulders. Cronus and the other defeated Titans were either confined in the underworld kingdom of Tartaros or banished to "a British island in the farthest west" that probably corresponds with Plato's island of Atlantis.

The Greek gods were not harmed by their sojourn in Cronus' capacious belly. The Efé swallowing monster does not chew, digest, fold, staple or mutilate its victims. On emerging, they gratefully make the son-incarnation of Efé or God their beloved chief. In another Pygmy legend, Efé is pursued by the predatory dog-dragon, a creature that the elders variously define as a form or relative of the giant swallowing monster. All-Father Odin is swallowed by the ferocious Fenris Wolf during the apocalyptic cataclysms of Ragnarok or Götterdämmerung. The canine swallowing monster was fathered by Loki, the delinquent blood brother who expedited the theft of the sacred fruit from the forest of Asgard-Troy. Since righteous men will dwell forever with Odin in the paradisaical land of the white elves, he apparently survived his hectic adventure with the Pygmies' picturesque dog-dragon.

The Greek dog serpent Cerberus was fathered by Typhon, the titanic patriarch whose monstrous brood included the nine-headed Hydra. The water serpent's victims were resurrected by an heroic Masai warrior who played the role of the Pygmies' ancestor-god. The God of the Old Testament resurrected Jonah from the belly of a giant fish or whale. The creature may have been the terrible Hebrew *tannim*—a whale, dragon, serpent, sea monster or land monster. It may have been *leviathan*—a huge sea monster, serpent or crocodile. It may have been *rahab*—a sea monster or crocodile symbolizing Egypt. Whatever it was, the thing swallowed but refrained from injuring its victim. Jonah was vomited up, unchewed and undigested, like the Greek victims whom Zeus retrieved from the belly of Cronus.

Ngoogounogounmbar, the swallowing monster of western Pygmy legend, can turn into a crocodile or dragon-like beast, but his primary form is that of an ogre-like man who resembles Lulu, the giant swallowing ogre of Ituri Forest legend: "Ngoogouno-gounmbar is very tall, as tall as the tallest trees, with enormous feet and hands, and also an enormous mouth that opens vertically instead of being horizontal. He is completely white, with a long white beard that descends all the way to his feet, but he keeps it rolled up in his belt . . . When he takes a child, he seizes it by the neck and swallows it with a single gulp, head-first. He transforms himself at will into an animal—into a crocodile by preference, or a fantastic animal midway between a serpent and a hippopotamus, and dwells in the caverns near the great waterfalls."[6]

"What if one day you met Ngoogounogounmbar in the forest, and he tried to attack you? What would you do to escape from him?" Trilles asked his Pygmy informant. "Oh, I would run him through with my lance," answered the little Sir Lancelot. Trilles remarked that his fear of the monster "did not have the air of being excessive." The fearless Efé hero speared the roaring *lulu* monster that according to most of the elders dwells in the cavernous underworld kingdom of legend. Ngoogounogounmbar is defined as

---

[6] Henri Trilles, *The Soul of the African Pygmy*, p. 168.

a "bottom spirit" or tenant of the underworld. His residence is "a big somber cavern, in a place where the waters of a great river are precipitated in roaring cataracts. An Efé legend of the war with the monster declares that the villain "dived into a deep pool and hid in the slime" to escape from the godly hero. Like the Creature from the Black Lagoon, Ngoogounogounmbar is said to "dwell by preference at the bottom of swamps, under the black and stinking slime." He is a "spirit of night" and a "spirit of cold." He came to the equatorial forest from his legendary homeland in "the faraway countries where it is always very cold, so that they are always frozen." The dire deeds of Lulu-Ngoogounogounmbar, his ghastly residence and his combat with the Pygmy hero were described with remarkable fidelity in the story of Grendel, the giant man-swallowing ogre of the Anglo-Saxon epic *Beowulf*.

Grendel was a cruel monster who "looked like a man, though greater in height and build than a Goliath." He was the night prowler or "dark death-shadow" that lurked in ambush and "prowled the misty moors in the dead of night." His homeland was described as a little-known country of swampy fens and "perilous paths across the boggy moors, where a mountain stream plunges under the mist-covered cliffs" near a very deep pool, "the lake of water monsters." The country must have been very cold, since the lake was rimmed by "trees stiff with hoar-frost." Beneath the lake there was a "vaulted chamber" or "loathsome hall," the ogre's underworld residence.

From these headquarters, Grendel sallied forth and preyed for twelve long winters on the dwellers in a paradisaical hall or palace called Heorot, where harpists played beautiful music and good king Hrothgar "gave presents of rings and treasure at the feasting." Grendel raided the hall one terrible night and carried off thirty Danish warriors whom he took to his lair for midnight snacks. His assaults continued until Beowulf, the heroic prince of a tribe called the Geats, heard of his crimes and traveled to the beleaguered hall where Grendel came by night to dine on sleeping Danes. Beowulf stayed awake and warily observed the ogre's tactics. Grendel "hungrily seized a sleeping warrior, greedily wrenched him, bit into his body, drank the blood from his veins, devoured huge pieces; until, in no time, he had swallowed the whole man, even his feet and hands." Lulu-Ngoogounogounmbar swallows the man whole, like a college boy gulping a goldfish. Lulu's victims can accordingly be retrieved in tip-top condition. Ngoogounogounmbar's victims disappear forever into his vast gullet and paunch, since the resurrection story has apparently been lost among the western representatives of the Pygmy clan. Similar divergencies account for Grendel's messy table habits and the tragic plight of his unresurrected victims.

After beholding Grendel's gourmet dinner, Beowulf rose up from his bed and wrestled with the monster. Beowulf's men struck at Grendel from every side, "unaware that no war-sword, not even the finest iron on earth, could wound their evil enemy, for he had woven a secret spell against every kind of weapon, every battle blade." The Efé hero used iron weapons that were not forged on earth. Beowulf later obtained "an invincible sword" from a supernatural source. During the wrestling match, he managed to wound Grendel with his bare hands. The ogre retreated to the swamps and dived down to his dismal lair beneath the lake of water monsters.

There was a joyous celebration at King Hrothgar's hall. Then a lady ogre arrived, attacked a sleeping warrior, and carried his macerated remains to "the terrible lake, the cold water streams" where she dwelled with Grendel, her son. Beowulf and his men tracked the female fiend to her home, where they saw "many strange sea-dragons swimming in the lake." Undismayed, the hero donned his coat of mail and dived into the lake like an armored Tarzan. He swam downward for a full day, apparently holding his breath all the while, until he reached the bottom of the lake. Then he was seized by Grendel's mother and swept into the underworld residence, a cavernous chamber stocked with treasures that included a "huge ancestral sword" or "invincible sword." He beheaded the lady ogre with the sword and attacked the body of Grendel, who had died of his previous wound. "Then Grendel's corpse received a savage blow at the hero's hand, his body burst open: Beowulf lopped off his head." The hero took the gold sword hilt, along with Grendel's severed head, "and was soon on his way, swimming up through the water."

In the Pygmy legend of Efé's trip to the underworld, the hero descends by a non-watery route. Near the subterranean river and cataracts of Lulu-Ngoogounogounmbar, he is waylaid by a hideous hag and imprisoned in the cavernous "Kingdom of the Dead" whence he subsequently returns with a load of treasure. Beowulf's trip to the underworld blends this saga with the legend of the savior who beheaded the giant ogre and with other related stories. Grendel's mother apparently combines the infernal hag with the pri-mordial mother who brings, causes or gives birth to death in many doom-packed episodes of the Pygmies' cosmic soap opera.

Beowulf beheaded the wicked mother and son. The Egyptian hero Horus beheaded his mother Isis and the man-dragon prince of darkness who was usually represented as her brother. The Babylonian hero Marduk fought Tiamat, the lady-dragon mother of the gods, and the demon who commanded the powers of darkness, her son and second husband Kingu. Tiamat had an estimated length of three hundred miles, moved in undulations six miles high, and roared with a mouth that was seven miles wide. The serpent manifestation of the Pygmies' swallowing monster has no specific sex and might be regarded as female. Tiamat combines this crea-ture with Matu, the primordial mother, who departed from the ways of righteousness when she married her brother, son and second husband Doru, the manly associate of the swallowing monster.

The fragmentary Sumerian story of the battle with Tiamat declares that the dragon can only be wounded through the mouth or the belly. Efé's avenging son speared the monster through the mouth and punctured its belly. Marduk, the son of the great Babylonian god Ea or Enki, drove the "Evil Wind" into Tiamat's mouth and shot his arrow or dart into her vulnerable belly. He then split the dragon in two, made the heavens from half of her body, and fashioned the earth from the other segment. Odin, the son or father of Thor, meanwhile created the heavens and earth by dissecting the ogre manifestation of the monster. Odin was assisted by his brothers Vili and Ve. Together they slew a giant known as "that old frost ogre Ymir," making the sky from his severed head and the rest of the world from the other parts of his carcass.

Lulu-Ngoogounogounmbar, the giant ogre from the frosty countries of legend, can change at will into a serpentine monster.

Boreas, the North Wind, turns into "the great serpent Ophion" in the Pelasgian Greek story of the beginning. The manly associate of the Pygmies' monster married Matu, the first woman and mother. They quarreled about the forbidden fruit and probably argued about other domestic affairs. Boreas-Ophion mated with Eurynome, the motherly goddess of all things. Then this remarkable couple had an argument: "Eurynome and Ophion made their home upon Mount Olympus, where he vexed her by claiming to be the author of the universe. Forthwith she bruised his head with her heel, kicked out his teeth, and banished him to the dark caves below the earth." In Genesis 3:15, the deity warns the snake who persuaded Eve to steal the forbidden fruit: "I will put enmity between thee and the woman, and between thy seed and her seed; it shall bruise thy head, and thou shalt bruise his heel."

Eurynome was the Pelasgian moon-goddess. She dwelled with her serpentine spouse at the mountain of paradise. The Efé Mountain of the Moon is the home of Matu, a superhuman mother who is further associated with mountains in general. "They describe as the mother of God, Matu who dwells in the mountains and is bright as the sun," reported Schebesta. "She was called the Mountain Mother; her sanctuaries were almost invariably upon mountains, and frequently in caves; lions were her faithful companions," the *Encyclopaedia Britannica* comments on the goddess who was worshiped throughout Asia Minor and in southern Europe as the Great Mother of the Gods. The Greek moon-goddess called Artemis asked her father Zeus for "all the mountains in the world" because she intended "to live on mountains most of the time." Rhea, the Titaness mother of Zeus, was worshiped on Mount Ida on the island of Crete and was identified with the Mountain Mother or Great Mother of the Gods.

Matu is not worshiped and cannot be described as a goddess. In the myth of the savior, this sun-bright lady of the lunar mountain gives birth to the son-incarnation of Efé or God the Father. Excerpts from the twelfth chapter of Revelation read as follows:

> And there appeared a great wonder in heaven: a woman clothed with the sun, and the moon under her feet, and upon her head a crown of twelve stars: And she being with child cried, travailing in birth, and pained to be delivered. And there appeared another

wonder in heaven; and behold a great red dragon, having seven
heads and ten horns, and seven crowns upon his head. And his tail
drew the third part of the stars of heaven, and did cast them to the
earth: and the dragon stood before the woman which was ready to
be delivered, for to devour her child as soon as it was born. And she
brought forth a man child, who was to rule all nations with a rod of
iron: and her child was caught up unto God, and to his throne.
And the woman fled into the wilderness . . . And there was war in
heaven: Michael and his angels fought against the dragon; and the
dragon fought and his angels . . . And the great dragon was cast
out, that old serpent, called the Devil, and Satan, which deceiveth
the whole world: he was cast out into the earth, and his angels
were cast out with him . . . And when the dragon saw that he was
cast unto the earth, he persecuted the woman which brought forth
the man child. And to the woman were given two wings of a great
eagle, that she might fly into the wilderness, into her place, where
she is nourished for a time, and times, and half a time, from the
face of the serpent. And the serpent cast out of his mouth water as
a flood after the woman, that he might cause her to be carried away
of the flood. And the earth helped the woman, and the earth opened
her mouth, and swallowed up the flood which the dragon cast out
of his mouth. And the dragon was wroth with the woman, and went
to make war with the remnant of her seed, which keep the commandments of God, and have the testimony of Jesus Christ.

The son is armed with "a rod of iron" and "caught up unto
God, and to his throne." Efé's savior son and the conquering son
of Egyptian legend were equipped with iron spears. Horus succeeded to the throne of Osiris, which Pharaoh Pepi the First
placed in the land of the Pygmy. Horus of Behutet, a form of the
god, was the divine king of the blacksmiths. The New Testament
Christ was associated with the itinerant smiths, tinkers and
carpenters called Kenites and Rechebites. He was traditionally
portrayed as the carpenter son of a carpenter. The several incarnations of the Efé deity are smiths. So was Thor, the smith-god son
or father of Odin, who fights the Midgard Serpent in the Germanic
apocalypse. The elves or dwarfs forged the mighty weapons of
Thor. Ptah, the Egyptian god of smiths and craftsmen in general,
was pictured as a Pygmy in the pottery resurrection figurines that
show Ptah-Seker-Osiris crushing serpents in his hands.

Revelation's predatory dragon tried to swallow or devour the woman's godly child. Cronus, the Greek swallowing monster, was identified in Plutarch's treatise on Isis and Osiris as the father of Typhon or Set-Apepi, the giant monster whom Zeus is supposed to have buried under Europe's tallest volcano, Mount Etna, on the island of Sicily. The seventeenth chapter of Revelation describes the dragon's heads as a group of mountains associated with volcanic plagues and located at the site of a city called "Babylon the Great." The historic city of Babylon in Mesopotamia had no mountains or volcanoes. Sumeria, in southern Mesopotamia, was equally devoid of volcanoes. The Sumerian hero Gilgamesh dreamed of erupting volcanoes when he journeyed with his friend or brother, Enkidu, to the garden forest of paradise. Revelation's dragon-mountains are the home of an infamous lady, the "Whore of Babylon." According to the *Epic of Gilgamesh,* a whore from the city of Uruk corrupted Endiku. According to the Pygmy legend of the forbidden fruit, Matu corrupted Efé's virtuous younger brother or son, Doru.

"Come hither; I will shew unto thee the judgment of the great whore that sitteth upon many waters," an angel declares in Revelation 17:1.

> So he carried me away in the spirit into the wilderness: and I saw a woman sit upon a scarlet coloured beast, full of names of blasphemy, having seven heads and ten horns. And the woman was arrayed in purple and scarlet colour, and decked with gold and precious stones and pearls, having a golden cup in her hand full of abominations and filthiness of her fornication: And upon her forehead was a name written, MYSTERY, BABYLON THE GREAT, THE MOTHER OF HARLOTS AND ABOMINATIONS OF THE EARTH. And I saw the woman drunken with the blood of the saints, and with the blood of the martyrs of Jesus: and when I saw her, I wondered with great admiration. And the angel said unto me, "Wherefore didst thou marvel? I will tell thee the mystery of the woman, and of the beast that carrieth her, which hath the seven heads and ten horns . . . And here is the mind which hath wisdom. The seven heads are seven mountains, on which the woman sitteth . . . And the beast that was, and is not, even he is the eighth, and is of the seven, and goeth into perdition . . . And the woman which thou sawest is that great city, which reigneth over the kings of the earth."

There are eight giant Virunga volcanoes in a land of many waters: the Rift Valley lakes and rivers that feed the world's longest river, the Nile. A dragon called the Hydra was described in many Greek stories as an immense water serpent with eight mortal heads and a ninth head that was immortal and partially made of gold. The Virunga volcanoes are mortally dangerous. The nonvolcanic Mountain of the Moon is an enormous granite fault block located at the eastern edge of the Ituri Forest, where gold is mined by the Belgian-founded Société Minière de l'Aruwimi-Ituri. The lunar massif is the home of Matu, the capricious mother of the Pygmy legend cycle. The Greek moon-goddess who dwelled on the mountains was very intimately involved with the Hydra. This creature was sometimes represented as "the sacred cuttle-fish" which had "eight snaky arms ending in heads, and one head on its trunk, together making nine in honour of the moon-goddess." Thetis, a form of the goddess, turns into the beast in the story of her marriage with Peleas.[7]

The Efé monster is called Lulu: Etruscan Lala, the moon-goddess. Sumerian *lila*, monster or demon. Babylonian Lilu and Lilithu, the male and female forms of a monster or demon. Hebrew Lilith, the night monster, was the first wife of Adam. After she left her husband, she became a demoness who by choice preyed on little children. Efé's wayward wife Matu lures children and grown men to their destruction, as Schebesta reported. She sings, dances and beckons from her lairs in mountain caves and rocky ravines. The Efé word *lulu* has the phonetic variant *luru*: Old High German *lur*, elf or demoness; German Lurlei or Lorelei, a singing river siren who lures fishermen onto the rocks.

The Babylonian Lilu or Lil was sometimes represented as a kind of incubus who enticed young ladies. En-lil, the lord of demons, was the god of the earth. "He was addressed as 'the Great Mountain' and 'Lord of the Storm,' from which it is concluded that his original habitat was a mountain-top city; as there are no mountains in the Euphrates valley, he must have been the god of a people living in a mountainous area who later emigrated

---

[7] Robert Graves, *The Greek Myths,* Vol. 2, p. 110.

to Babylonia."[8] Revelation's dragon-mountains were the site of "Babylon the Great." According to the Efé myth of the savior, Lulu demolished the camps or cities of the ancient world. The Babylonian deluge legend describes an obviously volcanic cataclysm: "All the earth spirits leapt up with flaming torches and the whole land was aflare. The thunder god swept over the heavens, blotting out the sunlight and bringing thick darkness. Rain poured down the whole day long, and the earth was covered with water; the rivers were swollen; the land was in confusion; men stumbled about in the darkness, battling with the elements. Brothers were unable to see brothers; no man could recognize his friends . . ."[9]

The Babylonian hero Marduk fights the great dragon Tiamat in a "creation" story that instead describes a re-creation after the cataclysms perpetrated by Lulu and Matu: "Tiamat, the chaos dragon, is the Great Mother. She has a dual character. As the origin of good she is the creatrix of the gods . . . As the origin of evil Tiamat personified the deep and tempests. In this character she was the enemy of order and good, and strove to destroy the world . . . Tiamat was the dragon of the sea, and therefore the serpent or leviathan . . . In various countries the serpent or worm is a destroyer which swallows the dead . . . It lies in the ocean which surrounds the world in Egyptian, Babylonian, Greek, Teutonic, Indian, and other mythologies . . . Floods are also referred to as dragons, and the Hydra, or water serpent, slain by Hercules, belongs to this category."[10]

Greek coins showed the Hydra with seven heads, like the seven-headed dragon of Revelation. A Babylonian cylinder seal portrays Gilgamesh as the heroic slayer of a seven-headed monster. Zeus's son Hercules beheaded the Hydra "which had its lair beneath a plane-tree at the sevenfold source of the river Amymome." "Plane-tree" is a name for sycamores or trees that resemble sycamores. The Egyptian god Ra beheaded a monstrous

---

[8] Egerton Sykes, *Everyman's Dictionary of Non-Classical Mythology* (London: J. M. Dent & Sons Ltd., 1961).

[9] Donald A. Mackenzie, *Myths of Babylonia and Assyria* (London: Gresham Publishing Company, n. d.), p. 192.

[10] *Ibid.*, pp. 151–52.

man-dragon whom the Greeks described as the Hydra's father at the foot of the southern sycamore tree. Bes, the Pygmy Ra of the Metternich Stele, originated in the southern "Land of Trees" near the mountainous heads of the dragon.

The eight-headed dragon of Japanese legend was cut to pieces by the god Susa-No-O. Like the valiant son of Efé, he was the son of the first man, the great god Izanagi. He disposed of a dragon that supposedly was terrorizing the residents of Izumo in western Japan. His descendants were aided by a "dwarf god" called Suku-na-Biko, a highly skilled practitioner of that great Pygmy specialty, the healing arts. The dwarf physician "arrived on the Izumo coast on a little raft, wearing moth wings and tiny feathers." He cured disease in the area, taught agriculture and ascended to heaven by climbing up a stalk of millet. "His weight, coupled with that of the ears of grain, caused the plant to bend and then fling him up to heaven. It is said that this endearing little god still appears and leads people to hot springs, an action characteristic of him because he was known for his kindly disposition as well as for his medical knowledge."[11]

Efé returned to heaven with the aid of a liana. In many Pygmy versions of the savior story, his heroic son is not formally identified as the son-incarnation of the heavenly god. A Japanese story of the battle with the Pygmies' swallowing monster describes the hero as a tiny boy, Issun Boshi or "Little One Inch," who dueled with the fiend in the city of Kyoto. There a giant *oni* or devil swallowed the hero. "Immediately the little youth drew his needle sword and began to stab the oni's stomach. Then he worked his way up into the gullet, wielding his sword as he climbed. So painful was this for the oni that it spat Issun Boshi out as soon as it could."[12] After this inside-out version of the battle with Lulu, the hero was magically transformed into a full-sized man. Efé's savior son turned into a man before his epic encounter with the giant swallowing monster of Everyman's Lost Paradise in the Mountains of the Moon.

Soon after his birth Indra, the divine landlord of the Hindu

---

[11] Juliet Piggott, *Japanese Mythology* (London: Paul Hamlyn, 1969), p. 26.

[12] *Ibid.*, pp. 88–90.

Olympus at the center of the earth, battled with the enormous monster called Vrita. "This demon was immense and his head touched the sky. He challenged Indra to combat. A horrible struggle ensued in which the demon was victorious. He seized the king of the gods, stuffed him into his mouth and swallowed him. The other gods were terrified and at a loss what to do next. Then they hit upon the idea of making the demon yawn. As soon as he opened his mouth, Indra curled up and sprang out of the gaping jaws, and the battle began afresh. But the god was put to flight."[13] Indra eventually triumphed by hurling at the monster "a huge column of foam" that rose from the sea. As the swallowed victim and conquering hero, he combines Efé the father and son.

The son inherits the ancient Chinese empire and founds the Hsia dynasty in a weird Oriental version of the Pygmy resurrection. His father, Kun, was assaulted on the Mount of the Feather while attempting to quell a flood that lasted for twenty-two years. Chu Jung, an apparently volcanic "god of fire and master of celestial justice," put the paternal hero to death. "For three years Kun's body was exposed on the Mount of the Feather without decomposing. Finally, someone (the Lord on High?) cut it open with Wu's sword. From Kun's stomach emerged his son Yu (in the shape of a horned dragon?). Kun immediately turned into a beast and threw himself into the Gulf of the Feather (or into the Yellow River). Evidence and interpretations vary greatly as to the sort of beast he became . . . The location of the Mount and Gulf of the Feather is not given in detail. It is, however, known that they were on the very edge of the world."[14]

Yu went on to battle with "a huge, nine-headed dragon, whose vomit and excrement created poisonous swamps." The nine-headed Hydra that Hercules fought was said to haunt the unfathomable Lernaean swamp. Lulu-Ngoogounogounmbar lurks under the black and stinking slime at the bottom of swamps. The giant swallowing ogre Grendel and his monstrous mother were the most prominent residents of the Anglo-Saxon swamps. The death-

---

[13] *Larousse World Mythology*, Pierre Grimal, ed. (London: Paul Hamlyn, 1969), pp. 228–29.

[14] *Ibid.*, pp. 287–88.

bringing mother of Efé legend dwells in the mountains, not the swamps or underworld abyss. She is matched by Hsi Wang Mu, the calamitous Chinese mother who dwelled in the jade mountain of the Western Paradise, a legendary establishment that has been compared to the Olympus of Indo-European legend (Efé *ema* and *afa*, Chinese *mu* and *fu*, and English *mother* and *father* are the most basic residents of the lost paradise).

The superhuman mother of Efé theology has dwellings in mountain caves. She is associated in some Pygmy stories with the leopardess. On the Chinese lady of the jade mountain the *Larousse World Mythology* says:

> She had her abode in the depths of a rocky cave, where she sat on a stool with her hair flowing round her (this is the attribute of witches) and a *cheng* ornament on her head (these two details of hair and headdress indicated the female sex). She had a human face with a leopard's tail and tiger's teeth . . . She governed the spirits of plague and calamity. Now this dread appearance and evil character of Hsi Wang Mu do not comply with later descriptions, in which she was always a goddess (a tendency in Taoism and popular religion) or a sovereign (a tendency in historical novels) of great beauty, a delicate hostess, queen of a paradise-like Kun-lun, the counterpart in the Far West of the floating isles in the Far East; she was, in addition, the possessor and dispenser of the herb of immortality. The transformation of this ogress, who was the patron of epidemics, into the guardian-goddess of the herb of immortality is rather strange. Perhaps it came about because she originally had the task of spreading malady and death, and therefore was capable of withdrawing them when she so wished . . .[15]

The goddess Idun watched over the Germanic apples of immortality. The daughters of Atlas pilfered the Grecian apples and aided their father Atlas, the mountainous giant who led the Titans in their war against Zeus and the regurgitated gods. The western Pygmy swallowing monster, Ngoogounogounmbar, is a white-bearded ogre who can turn at will into a crocodile. An identical character dwells on the continent of Australia, where ancient Pygmy fossils have been found and the aboriginal tribes are interpreted by most anthropologists as complex mixtures of the

---

[15] *Ibid.*, p. 284.

presently extinct Australian Pygmies and archaic Caucasoids.

The African Pygmies' man-dragon is described as a flood-making monster in the Australian aborigines' legend of the Croco-dile-Man: "When the floodwater comes that old man goes out along the plain. When the floodwater goes away that old man comes back. He is an old man. He has white whiskers. He is crocodile too. You can hear him when you come for water. He is in the waterhole. He calls out, 'Oi! Oi! Brrpm!' You think he's a crocodile. He's an old man." The monster is speared in the leg by a character called "my son." Later, a patriarch named Tjimarr is incarcerated by the monster "somewhere down in the water." He eventually emerges, full of water. "My son" holds him upside-down and drains him dry.[16]

The son is the hero of the Efé resurrection. He is also the elder brother of Doru, the manly form or colleague of the monster. In the Australian legend of the two brothers, the heroic elder brother and the junior male are swallowed and resurrected by their kinsman, a supernatural serpent that resembles the snake manifes-tation of the Efé swallowing monster. This event occurred when the two brothers went fishing in a country called Milingimbi:

> Then, as the brothers paddled the canoe, laden with fish, up the creek, the big snake, Kurrijarra, humped up out of the water. The elder brother stood ready with his spear. The head of the snake rose up and the brother struck him at the back of the head with his spear. Lightning zigzagged out of the sky. The big snake thrashed the water, and his tongue was like a whip. In one lunge and gulp the snake seized and swallowed the canoe, the fish, and the two men. The snake sank down under the water. He travelled under-neath the ground. "This is the saltwater country," the snake said. "I will go another way to a freshwater country." The snake came up out of the ground blowing out spray and making a rainbow. He stood up and looked around at the country. "I think I must have swallowed my own countrymen," he talked. The snake was belching and breathing hard. He lay down and heaved, and brought out the first brother. Again he heaved, and the second brother was vomited

---

[16] Roland Robinson, *Aboriginal Myths and Legends: Age-Old Stories of the Australian Tribes* (London: Paul Hamlyn, 1969), p. 46.

out. The snake kept the canoe and the fish inside him. "The canoe and the fish are mine," he said. "Only these men I bring out."[17]

The elder brother of the Masai story more correctly beheaded the monster and resurrected the junior male from its vast interior. Another Australian story sets the scene in the monster's swampy lair: "Suddenly, out of the ground, came the head and body of the great black rock-snake. Her tongue was shooting out lightning and her mouth opened showing her fangs. Her great body lashed out far across the swamp and, as she drew herself out of the ground, a huge force of water rushed out after her. The water filled the hollow of the swamp where the tribe was camped, and drowned them all."[18]

The serpent manifestation of the monster is combined with the gigantic lightning bolt that leaps out of the earth in another Efé story. Matu, the dangerous lady who dwells in the mountains, has not been forgotten in the land of the kangaroo and the platypus. Australian legends declare that "an old devil woman called Marm" dwells on the top of some rocks at a place called Munjajawa. Marm fed some plums to "a big mob of girls" who ate the fruit and "were all turned into the devils called Marm." Matu shared the forbidden *tahu* fruit with the residents of the lost paradise. She subsequently embarked on the criminal career of musical siren, like the German Lorelei and the Greek chorus of sirens who tried to lure Ulysses or Odysseus onto the rocks during his trip back from Troy. The Australian devils called Marm sing from the rocks and drive men to madness. Matu's victims die or are permanently deranged. Her Australian manifestations undoubtedly include the "wild women" who lure men into their caves and cause them to "go stupid." Like the fatally beautiful Matu, "those wild women are very good to look at."

Matu's virtuous husband, All-Father Efé, is commemorated in the Australian legend of the divine creator Pund-jel who modeled the first men out of clay and subsequently ascended to heaven: "After again smoothing their bodies with his hands, from the feet upwards to their heads, he lay upon each of them, and

[17] *Ibid.*, p. 62.

[18] *Ibid.*, p. 66.

blew his breath into their mouths, into their noses, and into their navels. Breathing very hard, they stirred. He danced about them a third time. He then made them speak, and caused them to get up, and they rose up, and they were full-grown young men—not like children."[19]

Efé, the angel, breathed his own vital force into the Adam-like ancestors of the Australian aborigines. They had many encounters with the Pygmies' giant monster, a geophysical fiend that demolished the cities of the ancient world and swallowed mankind in a cataclysmic banquet. Trilles gave an accurate description of Ngoogounogounmbar, the bearded white ogre who turns into a dragon, and very simplistically suggests in his book *The Soul of the African Pygmy:* "Ngoogounogounmbar might well be a souvenir of prehistoric animals that have disappeared from the African forests more recently than we believe. If they have indeed disappeared . . ."

In 1957, the Efé Pygmies of the Muhekuva camp in the southeast Ituri warned a very tall, heavily bearded white man that he might be mistaken for the atrocious *lulu* monster if he traveled into the deep forest to seek out the few Pygmy bands who have not yet been subjugated by the Bantu and Sudanese overlords. The suspected *lulu* would then be slain by the unsophisticated Efé people of the interior, declared the men of Muhekuva. "The *lulu* monster?" I asked, intrigued by what sounded like an Ituri Forest version of the abominable snowman. "What is it? Do I look like it at all?" My informant answered, "A little. The *lulu* monster is supposed to be as tall as a tree and as wide as a Negro's house. He is fiercer than Kituri, the giant snake-monster, and more powerful than Piobo, the elephant monster who loves to kill men. Sometimes he roars like an automobile."

The African forests are not infested with prehistoric animals that resemble me, or with relics of the dinosaur clan, as Trilles implied. The Tswa "Children of Djakoba" are probably responsible for the legend of the giant snake-elephant-dragon or so-called water elephant that dwells in the swamps of Zaïre's Lake Maji Ndombe. It has a long serpentine neck, an abbreviated two-foot

---

[19] *Ibid.*, p. 18.

trunk, no tusks and the sleek hide of a hippopotamus. A number of Europeans claim to have seen this creature, which is probably being used—like the Loch Ness monster—to promote the tourist trade. It has thus became a white man's myth. The Pygmy concepts and legends of the monster prove, ironically enough, that it originated as a white man's myth in the Old White Africa of prehistoric times.

"To avoid the attacks of this villain Ngoogounogounmbar, one should first of all spit behind oneself, then sing with all one's strength (an excellent means of chasing fear), and finally pronounce the magic words of conjuration as fast as one can, which is also an excellent means of avoiding the spirit," reported Trilles. The Egyptians would certainly agree that one should first of all spit to fend off the man-dragon Set-Apepi. The first chapter of the first book of the ancient Egyptian *Books of Overthrowing Apep* was entitled "The Chapter of Spitting upon Apep." These books of magico-religious formulas were daily recited by the priests in the temple of Amen-Ra at Thebes, the ancient capital of Upper Egypt.

"Mother, how shall I come forth unto the light of day?" asked the Efé savior. A collection of Egyptian texts called *per em hru*, "coming forth by day," is now known as *The Book of the Dead*. Chapter One begins the chapters of "coming forth by day." Many vignettes show "the god or the deceased spearing a serpent." The *Books of Overthrowing Apep* contain chapters entitled "The Chapter of Taking a Lance to Smite Apep" and "The Chapter of Taking a Spear to Smite Apep." The monster, the savior and the mother are symbolic personalities involved in a vast cosmic drama. The mother corresponds in some respects to our concepts of Mother Earth and Mother Nature. As the Mountain Mother, she brought death to the world in the fragmentary Egyptian legend called "The Destruction of Mankind."

According to this story the goddess Hathor "slew mankind on the mountain." She was assisted by the goddess Sekhet, who "waded about in their blood." Numerous Egyptian texts identify Hathor with Sekhet and with many local variants of the mother-goddess. In Egyptian stories of her exploits Sekhet, the Lady of Flame, "pours fire out of herself" and shoots pyrotechnic missiles. Scholars have astutely described "The Destruction of Mankind" as "an early myth of volcanic catastrophe followed by flood." There are no volcanoes in Egypt. Where then did this great disaster occur?

Pharaoh Pepi the First located "the Pygmy" between the thighs of the formidable Egyptian mother-goddess. The Pygmy savior emerged from the foot of Matu, the Mother of God. Like the Egyptian mother-goddess Isis, she is alternately represented as a human being and a vast cosmic power. Isis' son Horus was identified by the Greeks with their sun-god Apollo. He was born "where the sun never shone, namely underground."[20] The story of Efé's descent to the underworld and his triumphant return will shed additional light on the nature of the savior and his miraculous mother.

[20] Robert Graves, *The Greek Myths*, Vol. 1, p. 57.

The Hero's Trip to Hades

Mutuké, an old man of the southeast Ituri, told me the following legend of Efé's descent to the underworld kingdom of the dead:

> Armed with his three iron spears, Efé went hunting for meat in the forest near the Mountain of the Moon. He chased a giant black hog that tried to hide in its den. Efé, the great hunter, went into the beast's gloomy hole. He tracked his quarry through a long, winding cavern and felled it at last by hurling spear after spear with his strong right hand. Then Efé tried to carry the carcass out of the cave. It was so huge that even he could not lift it. So he went outside, cut a liana rope and returned with the intention of hauling up the carcass.
>
> Efé was amazed to discover that the beast had disappeared.

Then he saw bloody tracks leading down a side passage. The monster was still alive! No one but Efé, the Pygmy, would have dared to follow those tracks. He walked for hours through the rocky tunnel that went deeper and deeper into the earth. At the end of the tunnel, there was a mighty river that rushed over towering cliffs. Dense forest and groves of bananas stretched as far as the eye could see.

"What place can this be?" Efé said to himself. Then he heard someone cutting wood and went to investigate. Instead of a real person, he found the ghost of a sorceress in the shape of a hideous black dwarf. Her face was white; her body was covered with scraggly black fur. She said to Efé, "I know you. Have you come here because you are dead?" He was frightened but boldly replied, "Not at all. I came here by chance while I was hunting." The hag sidled closer. "Spend the night with me, darling," she said to Efé. Revolted, he turned to leave. The sorceress jumped onto his back and wrapped her arms around his neck. "Now you will go to my house," she commanded.

Efé carried her through the forest, protesting vainly, "I am not dead! I do not have to go to your house!" When they arrived, she said, "Are you hungry?" He replied, "I am famished." The woman gave him bananas. After he ate them, she said, "Now you cannot escape, my dear Efé. Now you must stay." The hero sat in her house, helpless, while she went to fetch her husband. He was the ghost of a sorcerer. He looked like his wife except for his long white beard. "Behold, our Efé has arrived," that horrible woman said to her husband. "Are you dead?" he asked Efé. "You can see that I am alive. I traveled through the caves to your country," the Pygmy replied.

The sorcerer chief of the ghosts led Efé to the center of the underworld village where all of the ghosts assembled. They asked, "Is he dead?" Their chief explained, "He is not dead but he must stay here for a while." The chief sat Efé down on a stool that stuck to his posterior. Efé danced, stool and all, to entertain the ghosts. When the stool became fixed to the ground, Efé sang, played the harp and told stories. The ghosts wished that he could stay with them forever because he brought joy to their gloomy existence. Meanwhile, back at Efé's village, the people mourned him for dead and his wife pined away until she was scarcely bigger than a thumb. Efé had already spent three entire months in the kingdom of the dead. Finally, during the fourth month, he was permitted to leave.

The underworld chief gave Efé some goats. The Pygmy cut their throats, beheaded the goats and packed the meat. The ghosts gave him tools, ornaments and treasures of every kind. "What road do we take to return?" asked Efé. "We will take you back along the road by which you came," answered the ghosts. They formed a long train of porters, carried Efé's food and treasures through the caverns, set their burdens down on the ground near his village, told him to run home, and warned him not to come back. He rushed to his house while the ghosts disappeared into the mouth of the cavern. The people were overjoyed to see Efé, whom they had given up for dead. They fetched the treasures, which Efé gave to them, and made a banquet celebration with the food that he brought from the kingdom of the dead.

The hero's apparent death ensued when he hunted a giant black hog. Osiris' murderer Set sometimes transformed himself into a black hog. A wild boar that was really Ares, the cruel god of tempests and war, killed the beautiful Greek god Adonis while he was hunting on Mount Lebanon. Nin-Shach, the war-god "lord of the wild boar," slew the Sumerian-Babylonian god Tammuz. A wild boar killed the Phrygian god Attis and the Cretan Zeus. A gigantic boar of supernatural origin ravaged the Greek town of Calydon and killed several eminent heroes who participated in the famous Calydonian hunt. Meleager, the greatest javelin-thrower in Greece, slew the boar but died by magical means as a result of the hunt. The hero-god Diarmaid died after he killed the magic boar of Beann Ghulban in County Sligo, Ireland. The boar had once been Diarmaid's foster brother. Set, the demon who sometimes took the form of a black pig, was the younger brother of Osiris.

Set was portrayed in some Egyptian stories as the cause of every conceivable cataclysm, and in others as an amiable and even helpful fellow. The magic monsters of Pygmy theology are associated with Doru, the junior male of the hero's supernatural household. He launches the great disasters caused by Efé's wayward consort Matu. He collaborated with Matu in the forbidden fruit affair. In another story, he practices sorcery in order to steal the sacred fire that she tends in extremely negligent style. Their prime manifestations in the underworld are the ghostly sorcerer and sorceress. These characters have a hideous appearance but they are not devils in the ordinary sense of the word. They did not harm the hero when they detained him in the kingdom of the dead. They simply kept him there for a secret reason, and gave him all kinds of goodies when they let him return to the world of the living.

In this story Efé is armed with the three iron spears that he brought back from heaven. He goes hunting in the forest near the lunar mountains and travels through a cave into a ghostly kingdom whose entrance is traditionally located "somewhere in the Mountain of the Moon." In the myth of the savior, Efé's son emerged with three iron spears from a mother associated with the Mountain of the Moon. He was "born" after the giant monster demolished all the camps and swallowed a man whom Matu identified as the father of the hero. We previously assumed that this man was the father-incarnation of the savior. Now it appears that the man who led the exodus from the monster's belly was the savior's stepfather—Doru, the second husband of Matu.

The savior-son was installed as the chief of the country. A Pygmy chief or king is by definition the elder. No son could conceivably take precedence over his living father and govern a Pygmy community. Efé, the senior male, resumed command after he delivered himself from the womb of Matu by cutting a path through her foot. According to some Pygmy versions of this story, the son of Matu was born as a child and immediately turned into a man. He was always a man, according to others. At Muhekuva, where I was compared to the savior's monstrous adversary Lulu, I obtained the version which appeared in my book *Congo Kitabu:*

> Once, a long time ago, the *lulu* monster ate everyone in the world—except for one pregnant Pygmy woman. She escaped and hid herself away in the deepest part of the forest. Then, when her time came, the baby talked to her from the bottom of her belly; he told her he didn't want to come out from the usual place and not to be surprised at whatever happened. Then he was born—out of a little hole under his mother's big toe. That was really something! What's more, he was full-grown, smart, brave and knew how to handle a spear. He asked his mother right away where the rest of

the people were, and she told him how the *lulu* monster had killed all the Pygmies in the forest. "Then I will kill *him* to take revenge," her son said, and he went to look for the monster.

"*Lulu odi avié!*" he called, again and again—"Lulu, killer of man!"—but it took a long time for the monster to come. At first he couldn't believe his ears because he thought he had eaten everyone in the world. Then he rushed through the forest, roaring like a tornado, breaking down the big trees, and opened his mouth to swallow the Pygmy hero. That was his big mistake! The Pygmy hurled his spear into the blood-red hole, as big as a house, and killed him. Then he cut off the monster's head and opened up his belly with the spear blade—and all of the Pygmies crawled out through the hole and marched back into their forest. That happened a long time ago, but some people think that the *lulu* monster is still alive.

The hero is Evé or Efé, the Pygmy. He sets out to avenge the death of Avi or Afi, Man, who has been swallowed by the monster. The words for Pygmy and man are constantly interchanged. As a result, the monster alternately swallows Pygmies and men who are alternately resurrected in the local variants of this story. Efé invariably survives the monster's onslaught in the sheltering womb of Matu. Efé, the godly father or nation, is the senior male of the legend cycle. Man is the human form of the junior male, Doru, an anti-hero who is innately good but performs all sorts of destructive deeds.

Man is described in some Pygmy stories as "Efé's son, the tall white man." Lulu, the supernatural or geophysical destroyer, is a giant white ogre patterned after the human destroyer. Man is resurrected from the monster's bowels by his divine parent, Efé. The savior is represented as the son of Matu, the Mother of God. He achieves his miraculous birth, as a child or a full-grown man, by traveling from the lady's womb to her foot and opening a path which expedites his return into the light of day. Efé emerged through a tunnel whose entrance is located "somewhere in the Mountain of the Moon." The lunar mountain is itself a form of the great mother, Matu. Efé went into the mountain through a cave and apparently sojourned in the ghostly kingdom while the cataclysmic monster ravaged the world.

Arabic legends maintain that the lunar prophet Thoth-Hermes-Idrisi survived the Biblical deluge by retreating to the Mountain of the Moon:

It is said that in the days of Am Kaam, one of the Kings of Egypt, Idrisi was taken up to Heaven, and he prophesied the coming of the flood, so he remained on the other side of the equator and there built a palace on the slopes of Mount Gumr . . .

King Am Kaam, mentioned above, is Hermes I. The devils carried him to this mountain, which is called Gumr, and there he saw how the Nile flows out of the Black Sea and enters into the mountain of Gumr . . .

There is a difference of opinion as to the derivation of the word "Gumr." Some say it ought to be pronounced "Kamar," which means the moon, but the traveller, Ti Tarshi, says that it was called by that name because "the eye is dazzled by the great brightness." This mountain, the Gumr, extends eastward and westward into uninhabited territory on both sides. Indeed, this whole chain is uninhabited on the southern slope. This chain has peaks rising up into the air, and other peaks lower. Some have said that certain people have reached these mountains, and ascended them and looked over to the other side, where they saw a sea with troubled waters, dark as night, this sea being traversed by a white stream, bright as day which enters the mountains from the north, and passes by the grave of the Great Hermes, and Hermes is the prophet Idrisi.

It is said that Idrisi there built a dome. Some say that people have ascended the mountain, and one of them began to laugh and clap his hands, and threw himself down on the further side of the mountain. The others were afraid of being seized with the same fit, and so came back . . .

It is said that a certain king sent an expedition to discover the Nile sources, and they reached copper mountains, and when the sun rose, the rays reflected were so strong that they were burnt. Others say that these people arrived at bright mountains like crystal, and when the rays of the sun were reflected they burnt them. Others say that Mount Gumr is a mountain on an island which is called by this same name. Opposite to it is the land of Serendib, four months' journey in length and twenty days' journey in breadth, and that from this mountain comes the bird called gimre . . .

Some people have said that when they were there they saw

neither sun nor moon, but the only light was the light of the most merciful God like the light of the sun.

Other explorers have said that the four rivers, Gihon, Sihon, the Euphrates, and the Nile arise from one source—from a dome in the gold country, which is beyond the dark sea, and that that country is a part of the regions of Paradise, and that the dome is of jasper. They also say that Hyad, one of the children of Ees, prayed God to show him the extreme end of the Nile. God gave him power to do this, and he traversed the dark river, walking upon it with his feet over the water which did not stick to his feet until he entered that dome.[1]

Yima, the first man or first king of Zoroastrian legend, survived a "cataclysmic storm" by retreating to a cave or enclosure in the mountains. His treasure is still supposed to be hidden in the cave, somewhere in the Persian hills. Yima was "the god of light on earth" and the terrestrial twin of Mithra, the heavenly god of light or the sun. The lion-headed Mithra resembles Bes, the cat-headed Pygmy who was the "aged sun-god" of the Metternich Stele. The Zoroastrian apocalypse describes the principal events of the Pygmy savior story and an obviously volcanic cataclysm that the virtuous survive by unexplained means:

At last the great dragon is let loose and the worst time comes, but Mazda sends a man to slay it. Then the saviour Saoshyant is born of a virgin. The dead arise, the sheep and goats are divided, and there is lamentation on the earth. The mountains dissolve and flood the earth with molten metal, a devouring agent of destruction to the wicked, but from which the good take no hurt. The spiritual powers have now to fight it out. Mazda and Sraosha overcome Ahriman and the dragon, and "then age, decay, and death are done away, and in their place are everlasting growth and life."[2]

Surt, the volcanic fire-giant of the perilous southern paradise, flings fire over the world in the Germanic apocalypse of Ragnarok or Götterdämmerung. The white elves apparently survive in Odin's

---

[1] H. M. Stanley, *In Darkest Africa*, Vol. 2, pp. 304–9. Extracts from an Arabic manuscript (1686 A.D.) in the possession of H. E. Ali Pasha Moubarek, the present Minister of Public Instruction, Egypt.

[2] *A Dictionary of Non-Classical Mythology*, compiled by Marian Edwardes and Lewis Spence (London: J. M. Dent, n.d.), p. 198.

residence at Gimlé, which means "fire lee" or "fire shelter." The poem "Sibyl's Vision" describes the onset of Ragnarok, asks "How fare the elves?" and then tells of "dwarfs by their doorways of stone." Odin's hall of Valhalla has "more than six hundred and forty doors," whence a host of champions will come forth "advancing on the monster." They dine on the magic boar called Saehrimnir, which is "boiled every day, and comes alive every evening." Efé pursued the giant hog through a cavernous door in the mountain while he was hunting for meat. He apparently slew the beast, which then came to life and led him through the tunnels to the funereal kingdom whence he or his so-called son returned to the light of day and slew another manifestation of the monster.

An Etruscan wine jar from Tragliatella shows the sacred king and his tanist or heir traveling in "a sunwise procession" from the depths of a maze. The king is unarmed. "Seven men escort him, each armed with three javelins and a shield with a boar-device, the spear-armed tanist bringing up the rear . . . The scene takes place on the day of the king's ritual death, and the Moon-queen has come to meet him: a terrible robed figure with one arm threateningly akimbo. With the outstretched other arm she is offering him an apple, which is his passport to Paradise; and the three spears that each man carries spell death. Yet the king is being guided by a small female figure robed like the other—we may call her the princess Ariadne, who helped Theseus to escape from the death-maze at Cnossos."[3]

During her hectic career as the first woman, Matu brought death to mankind by distributing the fruit of the forbidden *tahu* tree. The lunar lady's sorceress ghost preserved Efé's life by feeding him fruit of an apparently different nature that detained him in the sepulchral kingdom whence he triumphantly returned. The flora of Eden included a forbidden "tree of the knowledge of good and evil" and another tree whose fruit conferred immortality on those who consumed it. The Etruscan scene takes place on the day of the sacred king's "ritual death." Everyone thought that Efé had died when he failed to return from the boar hunt. He and his son are traditionally equipped with three spears. Three javelins are

---

[3] Robert Graves, *The Greek Myths*, Vol. 1, p. 370.

carried by the members of the Etruscan cortege that leads the sacred king and his son out of the maze.

The Pygmy tunnels lead into a legendary kingdom of the dead that is situated inside a mountain. A maze of Pygmy-sized tunnels connect the chambers of an eerie Etruscan necropolis (city of the dead) that was discovered inside the Italian hill of Poggio Gajella:

> About three miles to the north-north-east of Chiusi is a hill called Poggio Gajella, the termination of the range on which the city stands. There is nothing remarkable in the appearance of this height; it is of the yellow arenaceous earth so common in this district; its crest is of the same conical form as most of the hills around, and it is covered with a light wood of oaks. There was no reason to suspect the existence of ancient sepulchres; for it was not a mere tumulus, but a hill, raised by nature, not by art . . .
>
> I know not what first induced Signor Pietro Bonci-Casuccini, the owner of the hill, to make excavations here; it may have been merely in pursuance of his long and systematic researches on his estate. But in the winter of 1839–40 the spade was applied, and very soon brought to light the marvels of the mound . . .
>
> The marvel and mystery of this curious hive of tombs are the dark passages, which have given rise to as much speculation as such obscurities are ever wont to excite, in works sepulchral or literary, ancient or modern, of Cheops or Coleridge. They are just large enough for a man to creep through on all fours. Here, traveller, if curious and enterprising, "you may thrust your arms up to the elbows in adventures." Enter one of the holes in the circular tomb, and take a taper, either between your teeth, or in your forepaw, to light you through your Nebuchadnezzar-like progress. You will find quite a labyrinth in the heart of the mound . . .
>
> What can these *cuniculi* mean? is a question everyone asks, but none can satisfactorily answer. Had they been beneath a city, we should find some analogy between them and those often existing on Etruscan sites, not forgetting the Capitol and Rock Tarpeian. Had they been beneath some temple, or oracular shrine, we might see in them the secret communications by which the machinery of jugglery was carried forward; but in tombs—among the mouldering ashes of the dead, what purpose could they have served? Some have thought them part of a regularly planned labyrinth, of which the circular tomb was the centre or nucleus, formed to preserve the remains and treasure there deposited from profana-

tion and pillage. But surely they would not then make so many superfluous means of access to the chamber, when it already had a regular entrance. Moreover, the smallness of the passages—never more than three feet in height, and two in width, as small, in truth, as could well be made by the hand of man, which renders it difficult to thread them on all fours; the irregularity of their level; and the fact that one has its opening just beneath the ceiling, destroying the beauty of the walls which were painted with dancing figures, and that another actually cuts through one of the rock-hewn couches—forbid us to suppose they were designed for regular communication, or were constructed throughout on any determined system. In truth, the latter facts would seem to show that in those cases, at least, they must be of subsequent construction to the tombs. Could they then have been formed either by the burrowings of some animal, or by former plunderers of the tombs in their search for treasures?

To the first it may be safely objected that these passages are too large, and in general too regular. In one of the tombs in the upper tier, however, are certain passages too small to admit a man, and therefore in all probability formed by some animal. I learned from the peasants who dwell at the foot of the hill, that badgers have been killed here. On the roofs of several of the chambers, which I was told had been found choked with earth, I observed the marks of that animal's claws. But it is impossible to believe that these labyrinthine passages have been made by that or any other quadruped.

It is more easy to believe that they have been formed in bygone researches for buried treasure. That the tombs have been opened in past ages is evident from the state in which they were discovered, from the broken pottery and urns, and from the pieces of a vase being found in separate chambers. Yet in general there is too much regularity about them, for the work of careless excavators. In one instance, indeed, in the second tier, there is a passage of very careful and curious formation, which gradually diminishes in size as it penetrates the hill, not regularly tapering, but in successive stages—*magna componere parvis*—like the tubes of an open telescope. From a careful examination of the *cuniculi* in this hill, all of which I penetrated, I cannot but regard them as generally evincing design; here and there are traces of accidental or random excavation, such as the openings into the tombs which spoil their symmetry; but these, I think, did not form part of the original construction; they must have been made by the riflers carrying on the passages which were left as *cul-de-sacs*.[4]

Ordinary men crawl on their hands and feet through the maze of Etruscan tunnels that are never more than thirty-six inches high. Stanley measured a full-grown, perfectly formed Pygmy woman who was thirty-three inches tall. The smallest Pygmy man on record was thirty-six and a half inches tall. The Pygmies maintain, in general, that their ancestors were even smaller than the present-day representatives of their race. Homer's Pygmies dwelled in caverns near the great lakes of the Nile, according to the Greek philosopher-scientist Aristotle. The well-known caves of Mount Hoyo and many other caverns are located in the mountains that border Lakes Edward and Albert on the eastern edge of Efé territory. The Pygmies do not dwell in caves, which they represent as the lairs of spooks and monsters. Efé instead travels through maze-like caves or tunnels to a funereal kingdom inside or under a mountain, and is resurrected when he returns by his original route.

Down into the nineteenth century British children embarked on a ritual trip through the turf-cut mazes called "Troy-town" to celebrate the resurrection holiday of Easter.

> A maze dance seems to have been brought to Britain from the eastern Mediterranean by neolithic agriculturalists of the third millennium B.C., since rough stone mazes, similar to the British turf-cut ones, occur in the "Beaker B" area of Scandinavia and Northeastern Russia; and ecclesiastic mazes, once used for penitential purposes, are found in Southeastern Europe. English turf-mazes are usually known as "Troy-town," and so are the Welsh: *Caer-droia*. The Romans probably named them atfer their own Troy Game, a labyrinthine dance performed by young aristocrats in honour of Augustus's ancestor Aeneas the Trojan; though, according to Pliny, it was also danced by children in the Italian countryside . . . Easter was the season when the Troy-town dances were performed in the turf-cut mazes of Britain, and Etruria too.[5]

The twelvefold Etruscan nation was modeled after the pattern of Troy. The Pygmy-sized maze and necropolis inside the Etruscan

---

[4] George Dennis, *The Cities and Cemeteries of Etruria*, Vol. 2, pp. 344–50.

[5] Robert Graves, *The Greek Myths*, Vol. 1, pp. 346 and 370.

hill near the city that the Romans called Clusium (Italian Chiusi) duplicates the original establishment inside the Mountain of the Moon. The western Pygmy ancestors came from the land of Kimi: Etruscan Kam, the legend printed on a coin of Clusium which has a wild boar inscribed on both sides. The boar emblem was prominently featured in the Etruscan resurrection scene that shows the sacred king emerging from the maze. Kamars was the Etruscan name of Clusium, the city of the maze. When first discovered, the diminutive labyrinth and three-tiered necropolis inside the hill of Clusium was thought to be the long-lost tomb of Lars Porsena, the legendary King of Clusium. Arabic legends locate the tomb of the fabulous Egyptian king Am Kaam or the lunar prophet Thoth-Hermes-Idrisi in the mountain of Kamar. Porsena's tomb consisted of Egyptian pyramids arranged in three tiers above the labyrinthine entrance:

> It is a notable fact that but one description of an Etruscan tomb is to be found in ancient writers; and that tomb was at Clusium—the mausoleum of Lars Porsena. It is thus described by Varro, as quoted by Pliny:
> "He was buried under the city of Clusium, in a spot where he has left a monument in rectangular masonry, each side whereof is three hundred feet wide, and fifty high, and within the square of the basement is an inextricable labyrinth, out of which no one who ventures in without a clue of thread, can ever find an exit. On that square basement stand five pyramids, four at the angles, and one in the centre, each being seventy-five feet wide at its base, and one hundred and fifty high, and all so terminating above, as to support a brazen circle and a *petasus*, from which are hung by chains certain bells, which, when stirred by the wind, resound afar off, as was formerly the case at Dodona. Upon this circle four other pyramids are based, each rising to the height of one hundred feet. And above these, from one floor, five more pyramids, the height whereof Varro was ashamed to mention. The Etruscan fables record that it was equal to that of the rest of the structure."
> This description is so extravagant, that it raised doubts even in the mind of the all-credulous Pliny, who would not commit himself by recording it, save in the very words of Varro. Can we wonder that the moderns should be inclined to reject it *in toto*? Niebuhr regarded it as a mere dream, "a building totally inconceivable,

except as the work of magic"—no more substantial than the palace of Aladdin.[6]

In Robert Graves's book *The Greek Myths* the Etruscan maze-scene on the Tragliatella vase was compared to the escape of the Athenian king Theseus from the "death-maze" at Knossos, the ancient capital of Crete. Theseus heroically dispatched a white sow named Phaea that ravaged Crommyon, a district in Corinth. Phaea, a child of Typhon, was sometimes represented as the mother of the boar that ravaged the Greek town of Calydon. She was also described as a boar and the Calydonian monster as a sow in these divergent stories of Efé's combat with the giant hog. The boar was sent to Calydon by Artemis, the mountain-dwelling goddess of the moon who apparently represents Matu as the lovely but sometimes lethal lady of the lunar mountains. Theseus and his friend Peirithous, the king of a Greek people called the Lapiths, participated in the Calydonian boar hunt. As the fourth of his famous labors, Theseus' cousin Heracles or Hercules hunted the Erymanthian boar that ravaged the country around Psophis in the Greek region called Arcadia. "Here Heracles is the child Horus and avenges the death of his father Osiris on his uncle Set who comes disguised as a boar," commented Robert Graves in *The Greek Myths*.

The Metternich Stele portrays Horus' father as Bes, the Pygmy harpist and Dancer of God who wore stylish cat-skin clothing. Theseus was famed for his skill as a lyre player and dancer. He customarily traveled about in a lion-skin garment, performing all sorts of difficult labors. His resemblance to Hercules was proverbial. These divergent forms of the Pygmy hero embarked on separate trips to the ghostly kingdom of Pygmy legend, where they met in a farcically confused version of Efé's apparent death and resurrection.

Theseus and his friend Peirithous descended to the abyss of Tartarus through a cave in the Taenarus promontory of southernmost Greece. When the intrepid heroes reached the palace of Hades and Persephone, the king and queen of the underworld, Hades suavely invited his guests to be seated. They sat down on Hades'

---

[6] George Dennis, *The Cities and Cemeteries of Etruria,* Vol. 2, pp. 338–39.

ingenious "Chair of Forgetfulness," which welded itself to their posteriors. Efé got stuck to the magic stool after he went, against his will, to the house in which the ghosts of Doru and Matu dwell. Efé had to sit on the stool for three months and part of a fourth month. For four whole years, Theseus was trapped on Hades' chair. Then he was rescued by Hercules, who used rather drastic means to free Hades' victims from a chair which had apparently become fixed to the ground, like the supernatural stool of the Pygmy legend: "Heracles thereupon grasped Theseus by both hands and heaved with gigantic strength until, with a rending noise, he was torn free; but a great part of his flesh remained sticking to the rock, which is why Theseus's Athenian descendants are all so absurdly small-buttocked. Next, he seized hold of Peirithous's hands, but the earth quaked warningly, and he desisted; Peirithous had, after all, been the leading spirit in this blasphemous enterprise."[7]

Theseus and Peirithous had traveled to Tartarus with the intention of kidnapping Zeus's daughter Persephone. She had previously been kidnapped by Zeus's brother Hades while she was gathering flowers in Sicily. When Hades took her downstairs, Persephone ate some pomegranates or pomegranate seeds. Because she consumed this food, Persephone was condemned to spend a third of each year in Tartarus. Efé ate the ghostly bananas and then had to dwell for three months and part of a fourth month in the kingdom of the dead. He does not embark on this excursion each year.

"Now you cannot escape, my dear Efé. Now you must stay," the sorceress ghost of Matu proclaimed after she fed the hero with her fruit. She is the Pygmy counterpart of Hecate, the Greek queen of witches and moon-goddess of Tartarus. Hecate was associated or identified with Persephone, the heroine who ate the underworld fruit. Like Matu, Hecate was a lady of very ambivalent character: "Hesiod's account of Hecate shows her to have been the original Triple-goddess, supreme in Heaven, on earth, and in Tartarus; but the Hellenes emphasized her destructive powers at the expense of her creative ones until, at last, she was invoked only in clandes-

---

[7] Robert Graves, *The Greek Myths*, Vol. 1, p. 364.

tine rites of black magic, especially at places where three roads meet."[8]

Persephone, the kidnapped lady who ate the funereal fruit, combines Matu and Efé. When during her girlhood years Matu was kidnapped, the Pygmies took up arms and set out on an expedition to recover their protean lady. She was abducted by the infernal powers, but she was not taken through the caverns to the kingdom of the dead. Before they descended to Tartarus and tried to abduct Zeus's daughter Persephone, Theseus and Peirithous kidnapped Zeus's daughter Helen from the temple of the moon-goddess at Sparta. Another pair of valiant Calydonian boar hunters, the Spartan heroes Castor and Pollux, assembled an army and marched on Athens to recover their sister Helen. They were born at the same time as Helen, who was only twelve years old when she was kidnapped from Sparta. The Spartan brothers nevertheless conducted such a successful campaign that they laid the Attic confederation waste in the Peloponnesian War.

Theseus and Peirithous sat with their posteriors glued to Hades' magic chair while Helen was brought back to Sparta. She married King Menelaus but was soon abducted by Paris, the erratic younger brother of the great Trojan hero Hector. The Greeks thereupon set out to recover Helen. They traveled to Mysia, a country in Asia Minor which they mistook for Troy and tried to attack. They were routed and left in confusion, since no one seemed to know the location of Troy. The Greek dramatist Euripides maintained that Helen was taken to Egypt rather than Troy: "Euripides, in his drama, *Helen*, holds that Helen never went to Troy at all; he says that there never was any Helen of Troy; she was confined by Proteus, king of Egypt, during the Trojan War, and Menelaus recovered her from Egypt after the war."[9]

Proteus' son Theoclymenes wanted to marry Helen, who stayed with him in Egypt while "an illusionary Helen" went with Paris to Troy. Helen's Athenian kidnapper, Theseus, lost part of

[8] *Ibid.*, Vol. 1, p. 124.

[9] J. E. Zimmerman, *Dictionary of Classical Mythology* (New York: Bantam Books, 1966), p. 119.

his illusionary posterior when Hercules finally arrived in Tartarus and pulled him off the illusionary chair. Hercules had been ordered, as his twelfth and most difficult labor, to capture and bring back alive the snaky-headed dog Cerberus that dwells on the shores of the underworld river Acheron or Styx. Efé was determined to catch the giant hog, who led him through the caverns to the sepulchral river and cataracts where the monster's lair is traditionally located. In another Pygmy legend, Efé escapes from the dog-dragon manifestation of the monster by riding across a river in a boat.

Hercules, the hero-villain who kidnapped the Pygmies, rode the ferryboat across the underworld river to reach the shore on which Cerberus dwells. He had descended to the kingdom of Hades through the cave at Taenarus, which was represented as a rear entrance or back door to Tartarus. The main entrance was located, like Homer's Pygmies, on the Great Stream or River of Ocean:

> When ghosts descend to Tartarus, the main entrance to which lies in a grove of black poplars beside the Ocean stream, each is supplied by pious relatives with a coin laid under the tongue of its corpse. They are thus able to pay Charon, the miser who ferries them in a crazy boat across the Styx. This hateful river bounds Tartarus on the western side, and has for its tributaries Acheron, Phlegethon, Cocytus, Aornis, and Lethe. Penniless ghosts must wait forever on the near bank; unless they have evaded Hermes, their conductor, and crept down by a back entrance, such as at Laconian Taenarus, or Thesprotian Aornum. A three-headed or, some say, fifty-headed dog named Cerberus, guards the opposite shore of Styx, ready to devour living intruders or ghostly fugitives.[10]

Hermes, the guide who escorts the ghosts, was identified with the Egyptian moon-god Thoth. The Arab geographers located Hermes' tomb in the Mountains of the Moon, beside a black sea "traversed by a white stream, bright as day, which enters the mountains from the north" and which probably represents a combination of the Pygmies' earthly and underworld rivers. Efé was greeted by the hideous ghost of Matu when he reached the shores of the infernal river. Hercules stepped off the ferryboat and

---

[10] Robert Graves, *The Greek Myths*, Vol. 1, p. 120.

promptly encountered the grim ghost of Medusa, the Gorgon, who had once been a beautiful lady. Her name, Medusa or "Cunning One," was a title of the moon-goddess. Thetis, another form of the goddess, turned into the Hydra during her wedding. Medusa was transformed into a snaky-haired monster when she went to bed with Zeus's brother Poseidon, the sea-god who was called Earth-Shaker because he made earthquakes.

Matu was a dear little girl until she married Efé's brother or son, Doru. His human form, Man, commits the sinful deeds that are said to cause cataclysms. His superhuman forms deliver the cataclysms. His underworld ghost, like man, is not a truly wicked character. Zeus's brothers Poseidon and Hades, the Earth-Shaker and the cruel king of Tartarus, are divergent and decadent forms of Doru. Zeus's son Hercules was involved, like Doru and Adam or "man," in the theft of the sacred fruit. As Efé, the divine father-son, Hercules brawled with the Erymanthian boar and other manifestations of the Pygmies' shape-changing monster.

Hercules met the ghost of Meleager, the hero who killed the Calydonian boar, on the shores of the River Styx. Meleager and Medusa, the lunar Gorgon, greeted Hercules while all of the other ghosts fled in terror at the mere sight of Zeus's mighty son. Meleager, the deceased adversary of the boar, may have associated with Medusa because of the apparently amorous proposition that Efé received from Matu when they met near the banks of the river. "Spend the night with me, darling," she said to the hero who had pursued a manifestation of *lulu*, the roaring ogre, to the monster's cavernous lair in the kingdom of the dead. Efé was appalled by this invitation, one which Matu advanced with an ulterior motive since she chastely delivered the Pygmy hero to the ruler of the infernal kingdom. The Danish and Babylonian heroes of this story took Matu's proposition seriously: "In Saxo's mythical history of Denmark, Frey as Frode is taken prisoner by a storm giant, Beli, 'the howler,' and is loved by his hag sister in the Teutonic Hades, as Tammuz is loved by Eresh-ki-gal, spouse of the storm god Nergal, in the Babylonian Hades. Frode returns to earth, like Tammuz, in due season."[11]

---

[11] Donald A. Mackenzie, *Myths of Babylonia and Assyria*, p. 95.

Frey was the king of Elf-Land, which the Eddas locate in the southern paradise of Germanic legend. Efé, the original elf, was the brother of Matu and her disastrous second husband Doru. Frey's twin sister, Freya, was accused of having love affairs with all of the elves and giants. Matu is the wife, sister, mother and/or daughter of all the male characters in the Pygmy legend cycle. Frey and Freya owned a magic boar that was made by the dwarfs or elves. The big black hog that Efé hunted is based on a real animal, the giant forest hog (*Hylochoerus meinertzhageni*) that the Pygmies still hunt with spears and call by the name *bari:* Anglo-Saxon *bar,* boar. French *porc,* hog, swine, pig, pork. Latin *porcus,* hog or pig. Greek *phorcys,* boar, the name of Medusa's father. English *boar.* Dutch *beer,* a wild boar or a bear.

Hercules freed the Athenian boar hunter, Theseus, whom he found sitting on Hades' chair near the mortuary palace. Then he slaughtered one of Hades' cattle in order to "gratify the ghosts with a gift of warm blood." The residents of the Efé underworld do not drink libations of blood like the vampirish ghosts of Greek theology. Efé slaughtered the underworld cattle by the quasi-kosher method of cutting their throats. The part-Pygmy Dorobo of Kenya and Tanzania still serve as the official cattle-slaughterers for the suspected Masai descendants of early Hebrews. As his tenth labor, Hercules had to bring a herd of cattle from the island of Erytheia that was situated somewhere "near the Ocean Stream." The cattle belonged to a monster named Geryon who was identified with the swallowing ogre Cronus. So Hercules brought the living cattle from the underworld home of the Pygmies' giant ogre while the ghosts carried Efé's butchered goats out of the Greek Tartarus.

As the grand climax of his twelfth labor, Hercules brought the dog-dragon Cerberus up from the depths of Tartarus. Efé cut a liana rope with the intention of hauling the carcass. Horus, the son of Osiris and/or the Pygmy god Bes, dragged Set's body with chains which the Pygmies call "metal ropes." Then Set turned into a serpent and hid in his hole. Hercules "dragged Cerberus, bound with adamantine chains, up a subterrene path which leads to the gloomy cave of Acone, near Mariandyne on the Black Sea." He alternately "half-dragged, half-carried Cerberus up the chasm near Troezen," a Troy-like town in Greece where the Athenian hero

Theseus spent his childhood years. "Still another account is that Heracles came back to the upper air through Taenarum, famous for its cave-like temple with an image of Poseidon standing before it; but if a road ever led thence to the Underworld, it has since been blocked up. Finally, some say that he emerged from the precinct of Laphystian Zeus, on Mount Laphystius, where stands an image of Bright-eyed Heracles."[12]

The Efé kingdom of the dead is reached through a hole, cave, or *kovu* in the mountain of paradise: English *cove*, hollow, cave, cavern, concave surface. Latin *cavum*, hole, hollow, cavity; *cavea*, cave, stall, cage, coop; *caverna*, cave, vault, cavern. Anglo-Saxon *cofa*, cave, den, chamber, ark, closet. The Efé word *kovu* has the very frequent variant *ovu*: Lettish *avuts*, Sanskrit *avata*, pit or well. Persian *var*, the underground enclosure that sheltered Yima during the cosmic cataclysms of legend.

Efé went to the cavernous kingdom of the dead and then had to stay for three months and part of a fourth month: "In his character as a long-lived patriarch, Tammuz, the King Daonus or Daos of Berosus, reigned in Babylonia for 36,000 years. When he died, he departed to Hades or the Abyss. Osiris, after reigning over the Egyptians, became Judge of the Dead."[13] Osiris' residence was traditionally located "in the mountain of Amentet." Ament was a title of the Egyptian mother-goddess. The Mountain of the Moon is a form of the Efé mother. The lunar angel Efé went to his apparent death in the mountain. "Osiris Moon" and "Thoth Moon" were forms of the same deity. The tomb of the lunar monarch Thoth-Hermes-Idrisi was located by the Arab geographers in the Mountain of the Moon. Thoth reigned on earth for about 3,200 years before he embarked on Efé's ascent to the heavens. The Babylonian patriarch reigned for 36,000 years before he set out on Efé's descent to the abyss. These gods or heroes are variant forms of Efé-Osiris.

Osiris' mother was called Nut in many Egyptian texts. "The goddess is usually represented in the form of a woman who bears upon her head a vase of water . . . sometimes she appears in the form which is usually identified as that of Hathor, that is as a

---

[12] Robert Graves, *The Greek Myths*, Vol. 2, p. 155.

[13] Donald A. Mackenzie, *Myths of Babylonia and Assyria*, p. 86.

The goddess Mut pouring out water from the sycamore tree over the
deceased and his soul

woman standing in a sycamore tree and pouring out water from a vase, for the souls of the dead who come to her. The 'sycamore tree of Nut' is mentioned in Chapter lix of *The Book of the Dead,* and in the vignette we see the goddess standing in it. On a mummy-case at Turin the goddess appears standing on the emblem of gold . . ."[14] The Mountain of the Moon stands in the Egyptians' "Land of Trees" or "Land of the Gods" and pours water down from the perpetual snowfields and glaciers that it carries on its head. The mountain stands on the gold country of Arabic legend, where gold has been mined during the twentieth century. The mountain stands in the land of the Pygmy.

At Thebes, the ancient capital of Upper Egypt, the mother-goddess Mut was known as the "lady of the southern sycamore." Efé Matu is equivalent to Mut, mother or the mother-goddess. In the illustration on page 206, we see Mut as a beautiful lady who stands in the branches of the tree and pours water down from her vase. Matu is associated with the lunar mountain in particular and mountains in general. The Egyptian mother-goddess "slew mankind on the mountain" by pouring fire out of herself like a volcano and causing a deluge. Then Efé returned from the lunar mountain where the legendary Egyptian king Am Kaam or Thoth-Hermes-Idrisi survived the great deluge of Arabic legend.

During his sojourn in the cavernous kingdom of the dead, Efé gave a musical performance that brought joy to the gloomy existence of the ghosts. The great bard Orpheus charmed all the residents of Tartarus with his music and temporarily suspended the tortures of the damned. Orpheus was a priest of Dionysus or Dionysus himself, the god whom the Greeks identified with that eminent Egyptian music lover Osiris. Orpheus played on the lyre he had received from his father Apollo, the god of musical arts and the sun. Efé played the harp of Bes, the Egyptians' Pygmy god of the musical arts. Bes was the "aged sun-god" of the Metternich Stele and father-incarnation of Horus the Child, and hence of the Greek god Apollo.

Zeus, the father of Apollo, was imprisoned in the cave of the giant man-dragon Typhon. Efé had to stay in the monster's under-

---

[14] Sir E. A. Wallis Budge, *The Gods of the Egyptians,* Vol. 2, pp. 103–4.

world home for three months and part of a fourth month. His son emerged from the cavernous mountain mother and fought with the monster. When the fourth day of his life dawned, Apollo sallied forth to fight the giant beast Python, who was identified with Typhon in Homer's "Hymn to Apollo." The solar musician was born on the floating island-mountain of Delos, which was raised from the sea to provide a refuge for Apollo's pregnant mother Leto. Python is said to have sprung from the stagnant waters that remained after the deluge sent by Zeus in the age of the Greek Noah, Deucalion. His ark has been described as a "moon-ship." Zeus's son Megarus survived the flood at the peak of Mount Gerania, which remained above water. This was the mountain of Geranos, the Greek "crane," which was the sacred bird of Hermes. When Typhon attacked Olympus, Hermes turned into an ibis, the very similar sacred bird of the Egyptian moon-god Thoth and the lunar angel Efé. So Zeus's son weathered the cataclysm at the lunar mountain of our old friend Efé-Thoth-Hermes-Osiris-Idrisi-Am Kaam.

Apollo's pregnant mother Leto fled from the monster in the style of the pregnant Pygmy lady. In Letopolis, the Upper Egyptian "city of Leto," the goddess Net or Athene was pictured as the lion-headed mother of the feline sun-god Ra, and accordingly, of the cat-headed Pygmy god Bes. Athena, the Virgin Mother of Heaven, stood alone when Typhon attacked Olympus and all of the gods fled in terror to Egypt. The gods' flight to Egypt has been interpreted as "a frightened exodus of priests and priestesses from the Aegean Archipelago, when a volcanic eruption engulfed half of the large island of Thera, shortly before 2000 B.C."[15] Archaeologists currently favor a theory that Thera was Plato's sunken island of Atlantis. The Olympian gods are thus supposed to have fled from their home in Atlantis, which was not their home according to Plato's dialogues *Timaeus* and *Critias*. Atlantis, the aggressor, was opposed by the godly city of Athens in a conflict that Plato dated at around 9600 B.C.

The legends of the lost paradise locate the home of the gods in the paradisaical Mountains of the Moon at the center of the earth and source of Okeanos-Nile, where the Virunga volcanoes erupted

---

[15] Robert Graves, *The Greek Myths*, Vol. 1, p. 135.

during the era of Plato's cataclysmic war. The last paragraph of his unfinished dialogue *Timaeus* explains that Zeus decided to punish the formerly virtuous but decadent people of Atlantis: "Zeus, the god of gods, who rules with law, and is able to see into such things, perceiving that an honorable race was in a most wretched state, and wanting to inflict punishment on them, that they might be chastened and improved, collected all the gods into his most holy habitation, which, being placed in the center of the world, sees all things that partake of generation. And when he had called them together he spake as follows . . ."

Odin and the white elves survive the volcanic eruption and deluge of Ragnarok in their holy habitation, Gimlé, the fire-shelter in the heavenly mountain of Asgard-Troy near the center of the world. Efé travels into the Troy-town maze of the lunar mountain and returns from the kingdom of the dead. A coin from Knossos in Crete shows a new moon set in the center of a maze. The Athenian king Theseus went into the legendary maze of Knossos, killed a monstrous bull-headed man known as the Minotaur, and returned by his route of entry. "The Cretans, however, refuse to admit that the Minotaur ever existed . . . They describe the Labyrinth as merely a well-guarded prison, where the Athenian youths and maidens were kept in readiness for Androgeus's funeral games."[16]

Theseus battled with the Minotaur in its dwelling at the center of the maze. The Minotaur was supposed to be the son of Minos, the king of Knossos. Minos' father, the elder Minos, was the chief judge who presided in the ghostly land of Tartarus. Theseus went through the maze that leads into the Efé kingdom of the dead and the lair of the shape-changing monster. When he came back from his apparent battle with the lulu monster, Theseus introduced the dance of the crane, which was performed to the accompaniment of harps: "The Delians still perform this dance, which Theseus introduced from Cnossus; Daedalus had built Ariadne a dancing floor there, marked with a maze pattern in white marble relief, copied from the Egyptian Labyrinth. When Theseus and his companions performed the Crane at Knossus,

---

[16] *Ibid.*, p. 340.

this was the first occasion on which men and women danced together. Old-fashioned people, especially sailors, keep up much the same dance in many different cities of Greece and Asia Minor; so do children in the Italian countryside, and it is the foundation of the Troy Games."[17]

Theseus, the Athenian king who was born in the town of Troezen, embarked on alternate trips to the fabulous death maze at Knossos and the sepulchral kingdom of Hades. He sat on the magic chair like Efé, the great Pygmy harpist and dancer. He hunted the magic boar of the lunar mountain. His attendants are equipped with boar emblems and the three spears of Efé on the Etruscan vase that shows him returning from the maze. His Troy-town dances were performed at Easter. He holds an Easter egg, the egg of the resurrection, in the Etruscan maze scene. It may be a symbol of the earth, an ovate spheroid into which the hero descends and is later hatched forth like a chick from the egg.

Efé, the divine hero or nation, made the original trip to the underworld. The men of Plato's paradisaical Athens "in a body sank into the earth." The gods were thus collected by Zeus into his most holy habitation, the mortuary mountain of Osiris or the tomb of the Arabic moon-king in the Mountain of the Moon. The aggressors from Atlantis were punished when their island "disappeared beneath the sea."

In the Germanic apocalypse the earth sinks into the sea and the sinful race of man is obliterated. But "hosts of the righteous" survive in Odin's elfin shelter in the lost paradise of Asgard-Troy. The cataclysms were sent by the Zoroastrian god Ahura Mazda to punish the "wickedness on earth." Yima and his elite survived in their cavernous shelter. In one of the most enigmatic Ituri Forest legends, Efé deliberately causes the deluge. Who do you think survives?

---

[17] *Ibid.*, p. 343.

The Great Stream of Ocean

Efé survives a cataclysmic deluge in the Ituri Forest legend of the ancient flood that "turned into a mighty river and went all around the world." The story, as told by some Pygmy narrators, has the specious air of a creation myth. According to Homer's account of the creation, "Some say that all gods and all living creatures originated in the stream of Okeanos which girdles the world." The third book of his *Iliad* places a legendary people called Oi Pygmaioi on the shores of "the streaming Ocean."

The mighty river alternately flows "all over the world" like the great deluge of Genesis and many similar legends. The Czechoslovakian missionary-anthropologist Schebesta recorded several versions of this story, which is intimately related to the Efé saga of the savior and the swallowing monster. The very archaic and

far-from-literal character of these stories is probably responsible
for Schebesta's statement that the deluge is "unknown" to the
Pygmies. I obtained the following narrative from Mwenua, the
elder of Ebuya in the southeast Ituri:

> A long time ago, men fought a terrible war. Efé escaped by
> climbing a tree which had a big hole in the trunk. He hid in the
> hole while the battle raged on earth and in heaven. Then our
> chameleon man, our angel and savior, came with his axe and cut
> the trunk of the tree. The flood gushed out of the trunk, turned
> into a mighty river, and went all over the world. Efé came out with
> the flood, but the water did not wet him.
>
> Efé thought he would be lonely, since he was the last man on
> earth. Then he met a beautiful woman who was white, like him-
> self. All of the Pygmies had very white skin and long hair back in
> the olden days. The woman said to Efé, "Beloved one, I knew you
> were hiding inside my tree. I told my father to cut the tree with
> his axe." The woman was much taller than Efé. He did not under-
> stand how this could be, since women are smaller than men.
>
> "How did you grow so tall?" he asked the woman. She said,
> "You are smaller. I am not taller. You went into the tree as a man
> and came out as a little boy." Efé replied, "I am a man." When he
> uttered these words, he turned into a virile adult and married the
> lady. All men are their children.

There was war on earth and in heaven. All earthly things,
institutions and events have heavenly counterparts and vice versa.
"They speak of a celestial world, analogous to the terrestrial
world, where the God of the sky has his hamlet, his forest, his
hunting ground and his game," Schebesta commented on this
aspect of Pygmy theology. All past and future events are said to
be parallel in the parallel kingdoms of earth and heaven. Efé is
the first man and last man.

The Egyptian gods fought with Set, the Satan-like adversary
whom Christ will conquer in the apocalyptic future. "Thy kingdom
come, thy will be done, on earth as it is in heaven," he taught his
disciples to pray. "I am Alpha and Omega, the beginning and the
end, the first and the last," he declared in the book of Revelations.
"I am Yesterday and I am Today, and I have the power to be born
a second time," said the slain and resurrected man-god Osiris.

Pygmies of the Avogbaya camp in the Ituri Forest of Zaïre. The Pygmies are nomadic hunter-gatherers who dwell in temporary camps rather than villages. For untold millennia they have lived in harmony with their shady forest. The Pygmies are above all free souls who manage to achieve an almost perfect adaptation to their natural environment without being burdened with unnecessary labor and worries.

Mandu, a young man of the Mamiki camp,
is framed by his bow and arrow.

LEFT: Ebuné, the elder of the Antigbetu camp.

RIGHT: Asina, a Pygmy woman of the Antikakésé camp. Thin lips and yellow-tan to red-brown skin are racial traits of the Pygmies. Some Pygmies have dark blue eyes, like the Berber people of northern Africa and the Nordic type of Europe. Some babies are almost blond. Prominent brow ridges, heavy beard growth and ample body hair are other physical traits that Pygmies share with white men.

Kamabu and Anne Kahindo, a Negro man and woman of the Nande tribe. Their people are tall black agriculturalists who invaded the Ituri Forest a few centuries ago, cleared plantations and gradually reduced the Pygmy hunter-gatherers to a state of feudal servitude. Both physically and culturally, the Pygmies differ profoundly from the Negro people of modern Black Africa.

TOP LEFT: Ngilise, a middle-aged man of the Anti'ina camp, has the typical proportions of an Ituri Forest Pygmy: short legs, long arms, a long torso and a large head. Men average four feet eight inches and weigh about eighty-five pounds; women are usually three inches shorter and weigh eighty pounds. TOP RIGHT: Mangubele, a woman of the Avogbaya camp, is about twenty-five years old. BOTTOM RIGHT: Mosi'ibi, a teen-aged Pygmy with a mustache and a wispy little beard.

Pygmy physiognomy, complexion and hair color vary greatly from one individual to the next. TOP LEFT: Munengu, a sixty-year-old patriarch of the Antimapi camp. His hair is reddish-gray; his skin is pale yellow-tan. TOP RIGHT: Maliabu'ana, a young man in his early twenties. Olive skin, dark hair and a heavy mustache give him the air of a diminutive Spaniard or Italian. BOTTOM: Yonasi and Mala, a pair of middle-aged Pygmies who look rather like Middle Eastern Semites.

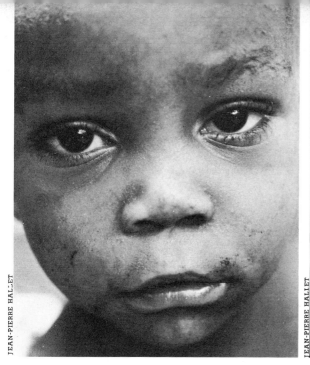

OPPOSITE: The youngest Pygmy ever to be photographed. This little boy is only a few hours old. He was born at the Antigbola camp in August 1968, while the author was visiting the camp.

TOP LEFT: Bobo, a little boy of the Antikakésé camp, came into this world in 1969. TOP RIGHT: Atosa, a baby boy of the Ngite area, was born in 1970. Pygmy children sometimes have light hair that gradually darkens to brown or auburn. BOTTOM LEFT: Kisangani, a twenty-year-old father, plays with his baby at the Antigbetu camp. BOTTOM RIGHT: Aluné plays with her infant son at the Antimapi camp. The monogamistic family life of many Pygmy bands has been disrupted by the invasion of polygamous Negro tribes who take Pygmy women for auxiliary wives.

JEAN-PIERRE HALLET

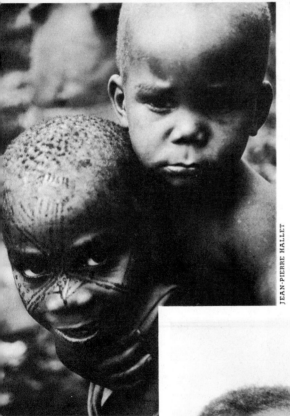

JEAN-PIERRE HALLET

JEAN-PIERRE HALLET

TOP: Pygmy women love to paint their faces. Streaks of black paint can be seen on the dignified countenance of Sa'u, a fifty-year-old grandmother.

CENTER: An elaborate design is painted on the face of Madeleni, a little girl of six. The piggyback rider is her blond two-year-old brother.

BOTTOM: Onaso, a painted Pygmy mother of the Antikakésé camp. She is nearly forty; her baby is about ten months old.

Mwenua, the elder of Ebuya. Pygmy elders practice and teach a lofty code of laws. They say that the laws were composed by "Our Father," which is a Pygmy epithet for God. The deity is represented in many legends as a tall, bearded white man.

JEAN-PIERRE HALLET

JEAN-PIERRE HALLET

TOP: Bové, a teen-aged hunter with his fur headdress.

BOTTOM LEFT: Kalingama stands in a tree. His legs are un-usually long; he is about twenty-five years old and dwells at the Antigbetu camp, near Mbau.

BOTTOM RIGHT: Ndzuzi, a thirty-year-old man of Anti'aputi, is the proud owner of a hunting dog. Dogs of the barkless Basenji type are indispensable for tracking down the game. During the hunt, these silent dogs wear wooden bells that signal their position.

JEAN-PIERRE HALLET

JEAN-PIERRE HALLET

JEAN-PIERRE HALLET

TOP LEFT: Archery is the favorite sport of Pygmy boys.

TOP RIGHT: Stilt-walking is another popular traditional game.

CENTER: Pygmy girls clap happily while they sing.

BOTTOM: A game of archery-ball. The ball (a *mukolé* fruit), transfixed by an arrow, can be seen in the fore-ground.

JEAN-PIERRE HALLET

JEAN-PIERRE HALLET

Pygmy housewives building a house. Women perform most of the manual labor of the camp. Huts are made from bent saplings thatched with leaves; the finished product looks like a shaggy green igloo.

LEFT: Otonu'é, an eight-year-old girl of the Antiba'oma camp.

RIGHT: A child's playhouse.

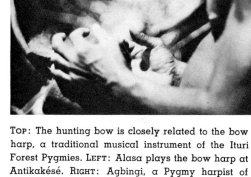

TOP: The hunting bow is closely related to the bow harp, a traditional musical instrument of the Ituri Forest Pygmies. LEFT: Alasa plays the bow harp at Antikakésé. RIGHT: Agbingi, a Pygmy harpist of Antigbola.

BOTTOM LEFT: Dolu plays a *luma* bamboo flute.

BOTTOM RIGHT: Ebuné, the elder of Antigbetu, leads a line of Pygmy dancers. Egyptian texts that date back to 3000 B.C. call the Pygmies "Dancers of God." Bes, the Egyptian god of the musical arts, was represented by pictures of a Pygmy.

TOP LEFT: Kakésé's fur bonnet is adorned with a bright blue feather. Men, not women, wear the fancy hats in Pygmy society.

TOP RIGHT: Isésé, a six-year-old boy.

BOTTOM RIGHT: Paso'u, a man of seventy.

BOTTOM LEFT: Butsè, the elder of the Anti-ubu camp, smokes hemp in his bamboo water pipe. Hemp is the same controversial plant called marijuana.

TOP LEFT: String figures are a popular diversion among Pygmy girls and women. This figure is called *Apadupa*, "The Butterfly." The lady is Aliona, a fifty-year-old grandmother of the Avogbaya camp; her husband, Pilikibi, is the elder of the camp.

TOP RIGHT: The delicate hands of Sénia, a teen-aged girl of Avogbaya, make the string figure called *Méli'utu*, "The Honeycomb." String figures are wholly alien to the culture of the surrounding Negro tribes. In the Western Hemisphere, where many ancient Pygmy fossils have been found, many Indian tribes traditionally make string figures. Some are identical to those of the Pygmies.

Pygmy women say that these knotted cords are "writing," but cannot explain how the system works. In Peru, the modern Indian tribes can no longer decipher the quipus or knotted cord writing of the Incas.

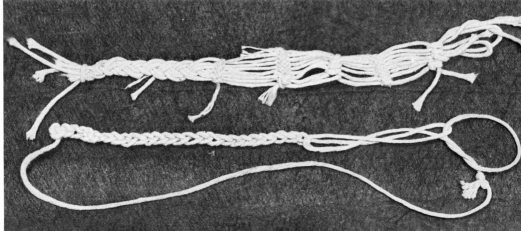

JEAN-PIERRE HALLET

JEAN-PIERRE HALLET

TOP: On the eastern edge of the Ituri Forest, there is a towering massif that the Pygmies call Baba Tiba, the Mountain of the Moon. Egyptian texts refer to the Pygmies as "the little men from the land of trees and spirits at the foot of the mountains of the moon." Greco-Roman legends call the little men Oi Pygmaioi, the Pygmies, and locate their residence at the source of the Nile in the land of Montes Lunae, the Mountain of the Moon. Arabic legends locate the Biblical Garden of Eden in the Central African neighborhood of Jebel Kamar, the Mountain of the Moon. Its modern name is Ruwenzori.

BOTTOM: Modern "civilization" comes to the Pygmy Garden of Eden. Apasuba'bili, a man of the Avogbaya camp, wears castoff Western clothing. The continuing invasion of the Ituri is destroying Pygmy culture; if it goes on unchecked, the Pygmies will soon be brought to the brink of extinction.

The Egyptians' "doubly hidden underworld" and the residence of Osiris were sometimes located in the sky. The Pygmy kingdom of heaven is duplicated by the kingdom of the dead, a parallel world within the kingdom of earth. Osiris was the god of the dead, of the moon and of the Nile. His residence in the "funeral mountain" of the underworld is the legendary Arabic tomb of the moon-king in the Ituri Forest Pygmies' Mountain of the Moon.

The Greek moon-goddess Artemis sent the magic boar that was really Ares, the god of tempests and war. Adonis met his apparent death when he encountered the boar on the slopes of Mount Lebanon. He had previously been born on a hill on the island of Cyprus. His mother, Myrrha, transformed herself into a myrrh tree. His father and grandfather in one, King Cinyras of Cyprus, cleaved the tree with a sword. Out tumbled the infant Adonis. His male parent was alternately described as King Theias the Assyrian or King Phoenix of the Phoenician city Byblos. Efé came out with the waters of the flood. So did Tammuz, the well-known Mesopotamian counterpart of Adonis, Osiris and many other pre-Christian versions of Christ:

> Whither went Tammuz? His destination has already been re-ferred to as "the bosom of the earth," and in the Assyrian version of the "Descent of Ishtar" he dwells in "the house of darkness" among the dead, "where dust is their nourishment and their food mud," and "the light is never seen"—the gloomy Babylonian Hades. In one of the Sumerian hymns, however, it is stated that Tammuz "upon the flood was cast out." The reference may be to the submarine "house of Ea," or the Blessed Island to which the Babylonian Noah was carried. In this Hades bloomed the nether "garden of Adonis" . . . Although Tammuz of the hymns was slain, he returned again from Hades. Apparently he came back as a child. He is wailed for as "child, Lord Gishzida," as well as "my hero Damu" . . . The ancient Greek god Eros (Cupid) was represented as a wanton boy or handsome youth . . . Apparently it was believed that the child god, Tammuz, returned from the earlier Sumerian Paradise of the Deep, and grew into full manhood in a compara-tively brief period, like Vyasa and other super-men of Indian my-thology.[1]

---

[1] Donald A. Mackenzie, *Myths of Babylonia and Assyria*, pp. 89–90.

Whither went Efé? In some versions of this story, he and his beautiful lady together emerge as "the first human couple" from the hole in the tree. Due to the Pygmies' penchant for collective nouns, a hole in the tree may also be a hole in the forest. Two human beings emerge from the World Tree, or a place called Hoddmimir's Wood, after the fratricidal wars and cosmic disasters of the Germanic apocalypse. There are plagues of darkness and a "great winter" which corresponds with numerous Pygmy legends of "the icy cold" or "the killer cold." The southern fire-giants erupt and earth sinks in the ocean. The world-age has ended. Every world-age ends and begins with the past and future couple who hide in the tree:

> Their names are given as Líf and Lífthrasir, and they are said to shelter in the World Tree and to be nourished by dew from its branches while the rest of the world suffered the great winter. Snorri, however, interprets this to mean that the two remained in the tree throughout the destruction of the world, and repeopled the earth after the time of terror was over. If indeed we are to view the whole series of events as a recurring cycle, as seems to be the case, then there must be a new creation after every destruction of the world. It is in accordance with the teaching concerning the World Tree that it should be from here that life once more emerges after the catastrophe.[2]

One cannot survive such events by retreating to a hole in a tree. The hole in the forest is the cavernous entrance to the kingdom of the dead. All-Father Odin, the god of the dead, is the proprietor of a much more substantial shelter. "I know where stands a hall brighter than sunlight, better than gold, in Lee-of-flame, Gimlé," declares the poem "Sibyl's Vision." "The white elves of Gimlé are fairer than the sun to look upon." Gold is the heraldic color of the sun, silver is the color of the moon. The fire-shelter of these moon-bright elves is the Pygmy necropolis in the Mountain of the Moon.

The world-age ends and begins when the good spirit, god or angel of the moon releases the waters of the deluge. Chameleon man or "the giant chameleon" is a supremely powerful manifesta-

---

[2] H. R. Ellis Davidson, *Gods and Myths of Northern Europe*, p. 202.

tion of the lunar deity. Ordinary chameleons are his observers, messengers and subsidiary angels. "The sacred animal of God, who plays the most important role in the history of the creation, is the chameleon," wrote Schebesta. "The chameleon is the sacred animal of the Efé. One should neither kill it, wound it, nor make it suffer in any other manner. When one encounters it on a path, one should carefully place it on the side. It is the animal of God, that climbs to the treetops to be close to the moon. It swings there in the wind. The chameleon is in rapport with the lightning and the storm: for, they say expressly, if you harm it, a storm comes and lightning strikes you dead."

The chameleon is not worshiped. He is not a totem animal and he is not taboo in the ordinary sense of the word. Pygmy children, and even adults, love to play with chameleons. The kiddies stroll about with these beautiful horned lizards perched upon their heads. When they engage in strenuous games, they carefully place their reptile playmates on branches, lianas or the sloping walls of the leaf-thatched Pygmy huts, which look rather like shaggy green igloos. The Efé housewives go about their tasks, unperturbed, while the sacred animal of God catches flies or moths for its dinner.

The Negro invaders of the Ituri Forest run in superstitious terror at the mere sight of a chameleon. In my book *Animal Kitabu* I talked about their attitude toward the Pygmies' corps of reptilian angels: "Bantu and Sudanese tribesmen of the Ituri call them 'sacred' but do not worship them—they fear and shun these utterly harmless and defenseless little lizards as omens and agents of black magic, possessed of the 'evil eye.' Everything about *kinyonga*, as they call him in Swahili, strikes the bush natives as weird and other-worldly. His color-changing, which so impresses Westerners, is only the smallest part of it: the Africans are far more troubled by his air of slow, profound deliberation as he moves from branch to branch, clamping and unclamping his four pincerlike feet, and the ominous all-seeing way he rolls his ball-turreted eyes. He is looking for men, they say, so that he can steal or possess their human souls."

A thousand miles to the west, the Pygmies of Gabon and Cameroon define chameleons as "the envoys of the Creator and the good spirits." The foremost representative of the good spirits is "the messenger of heaven" or angel of the moon. The Efé chameleon angels wear on their heads the horns of the crescent moon; the lunar angel of Efé theology is said to govern the world from twin command posts on the moon and the Mountain of the Moon. The Western Pygmy version of his giant chameleon manifestation guards the gates of Dan, the kingdom of the dead. "At the entrance to these caverns, according to a legend," reported Father Trilles, "dwells as the guardian a hideous monster, a sort of enormous lizard, completely covered with red and green scales and who carries upon his head a sort of long and strong horn. Revival of antediluvian monsters? Antique unicorn or rhinoceros?"

Trilles asked this question on page 185 of his book *The Soul of the African Pygmy*. He remarked on page 165: "The chameleon, singularly enough, is not only for the Pygmies but for some of the neighboring peoples a sacred animal. This is the case among their Fang neighbors. A Fang legend says that one day God pursued Bingo, his son. Bingo took refuge in a cavern. At the entrance stood a chameleon. God asked him if he had seen Bingo. Negative response. God, trusting the reply of the chameleon, continued on his way. Saved by the chameleon, Bingo recompensed him by giving him the power to change his color at will and thus to protect himself from danger."

This distorted account of "our chameleon man, our angel and savior" has undoubtedly been borrowed from the Western Pygmies. The Negro tribes of the Ituri Forest have accepted the chameleon's sacred status without in the least understanding the role that he plays in Pygmy religion. Efé, the human son of the lunar angel, was saved by the chameleon manifestation of his father. Efé alternately retreated to the hole in the tree or traveled through the hole in the forest to the ghostly kingdom where he was detained for three months and part of a fourth month. The Egyptian moon-god known as Khensu or Khensu-Thoth journeyed to the legendary land of Bekhten where he was compelled to stay for three years, four months, and five days.

Khensu was represented at the Egyptian city of Pa-Sebek as the son of the great god Sebek-Seb. Egyptian bas-reliefs show Sebek as a crocodile-headed man with one or two pairs of horns.

Seb, the father of Osiris, was a porter at the gates of paradise. "The doors of heaven are opened for me, the doors of earth are opened for me, the bars and bolts of Seb are opened for me," the deceased Egyptian soul declares in *The Book of the Dead* (Chapter LXVII, 2). At the city of Ombos, Sebek was likewise identified with Seb, the father of Osiris. As Sebek-Ra-Temu, he was called "the beautiful green disk which shineth ever, the creator of whatsoever is and of whatsoever shall be, who proceeded from Nu, and who possesses many colours and many forms." The Egyptians' Masai relatives define "the green days of the moon" as the time of the month when the lunar orb is "fat and perfectly round." When the moon changes from disk to crescent, it wears the horns of the colorful Efé chameleon.

Sebek, the chameleon-like crocodile, was the chief god of an Upper Egyptian town that the Greeks called Crocodilopolis, the city of crocodiles. Near this city, on the eastern side of Lake Moeris, the Egyptians built an enigmatic monument that is described in the *Britannica* article entitled "Labyrinth":

> According to Herodotus, the entire building, surrounded by a single wall, contained twelve courts and 3,000 chambers, 1,500 above and 1,500 below ground. The roofs were wholly of stone, and the walls covered with sculpture. On one side stood a pyramid 40 orgyiae, or about 243 ft. high. Herodotus himself went through the upper chambers, but was not permitted to visit those underground, which he was told contained the tombs of the kings who had built the labyrinth, and of the sacred crocodiles. Other ancient authorities considered that it was built as a place of meeting for the Egyptian nomes or political divisions; but it is more likely that it was intended for sepulchral purposes. It was the work of Amenemhē III, of the 12th dynasty, who lived about 2300 B.C. It was first located by the Egyptologist Lepsius to the north of Hawara in the Fayum, and (in 1888) Flinders Petrie discovered its foundation, the extent of which is about 1,000 ft. long by 800 ft. wide.[3]

On the Cretan labyrinth of Greek legend, the *Britannica* says, "It is doubtful whether it ever had any real existence." Daedalus, the first Athenian aviator, is supposed to have built the

---

[3] *Encyclopaedia Britannica*, 14th ed., Vol. 13, p. 561.

Cretan structure after the pattern of the Egyptian labyrinth. "He will never get off the ground," the spectators predict when Doru dons artificial wings and prepares to embark on the pioneering flight of Pygmy legend. The ghost of Doru seats Efé in the chair where the Athenian king Theseus lost part of his posterior. Theseus returns from Tartarus or the labyrinth marked with the name Truia or Troy on the Etruscan Tragliatella vase. "The maze pattern has been shown to represent 'Spiral Castle' or 'Troy Town,' where the sacred Sun-king goes after death and from which, if lucky, he returns," commented Robert Graves in his book *The White Goddess*.

According to the medieval British historian Giraldus Cambrensis a circular stone monument called Stonehenge was built with stones brought from Africa. The Greek goddess Athena was born in Africa. The Athenian king Theseus was born in the Troy-like town of Troezen and resurrected from a maze called "Troy" that was supposed to be patterned after the Egyptian maze at Crocodilopolis. A giant chameleon guards the entrance to the Western Pygmy kingdom of the dead. The giant ogre Ngoogounogounmbar, who sometimes turns into a crocodile, dwells in a gloomy cavern near the underworld river that flows through the Efé kingdom of the dead. The crocodile is not a form or symbol of the giant ogre Lulu. Crocodiles are regarded as cousins of the angelic chameleon.

Trilles defines the chameleon as a "sacred animal" that is "not at all totemistic." He describes as a "clan totem" the popular crocodile emblem of many Pygmy bands. The crocodile, he suggests, may have been the ancient "national totem" of the primordial Pygmy nation: "A legend of the Fang, their neighbors of Gabon and of the Congo [sic], seems to prove that at a very remote epoch, the Pygmies were a sole and single nation, since *they had a national totem, the crocodile, Omburé.* The dispersion of the tribes caused the disappearance of the national totem, after an indefinite period, but the legend remains as a living proof of the vanished past."

Plutarch's treatise on Isis and Osiris describes the crocodile as "the image of God." Osiris, the Egyptian Christ, was worshiped under the form of a crocodile at the city of Apis. Osiris' father Seb was identified with Sebek, the colorful crocodile-man who was the patron saint of the labyrinth at Crocodilopolis. Osiris' mother Nut was the wife of Sebek-Seb, the fatherly member of the holy trinity at the city of Pa-Sebek. Their son Khensu or Khensu-Thoth was worshiped at Thebes as the son of Amen-Ra and the motherly goddess Mut. Kensu, the divine physician of Thebes, stood in triumph on a pair of crocodiles. The pottery Pygmy of the resurrection figurines stands on the back of a wicked crocodile. He is the crocodile manifestation of the Egyptian fiend Set or the Western Pygmy monster Ngoogounogounmbar.

"The crocodile played a prominent part in Egyptian mythology, in which it appears both as the friend and foe of Osiris," wrote E. A. Wallis Budge. "One legend tells how the creature carried the dead body of Osiris upon its back safely to land, and another relates that Isis is obliged to make the little ark in which she placed her son Horus of papyrus plants, because only by this means could she protect her son from the attacks of the crocodile god Sebek." *The Book of the Dead* and the Pyramid Texts describe Sebek as the kindly companion who helped Osiris' son Horus to overthrow Set and take his rightful seat on the throne of Osiris. Sixth-dynasty texts place "the Pygmy" between the thighs of Osiris' mother Nut. The Pygmies identify the Mountain of the Moon with the throne and the mother. *Atsédu* is one of the several Efé words for a seat:

Egyptian *ast* or *auset*, seat, throne or "Isis." Old Norse *seta*, seat or sitting; *set-berg*, seat-shaped mountain or rock. Welsh *sedd*, seat or pew, Latin *sedes*, seat, chair, home or abode; *sedile*, seat or chair. Anglo-Saxon *setl*, seat, throne, residence. German *sitz*, seat or residence. Dutch *zitvlak*, seat or bottom of a person. English *seat*. Hebrew *sheth*, the buttocks, as in "seat of the pants."

Dante's *Inferno* identifies the devil's buttocks or seat with the center of the earth, which Dante and the ghost of the Roman poet Vergil visited during their famous trip to the kingdom of Hades. The devil is a corrupt version of Doru, the sorcerer chief of the ghosts. The kingdom of the dead is located underneath the lunar mountain of paradise. An Egyptian picture shows Isis, the earthly seat of Osiris, wearing the seat as her headdress while she stands beside the disk of the moon (see illustration on page 221).

Osiris, the god and judge of the dead, sits in the lunar angel's heavenly residence with his son Harpokrates or Horus the Child. Sebek, the god of the labyrinth where the sacred kings were entombed with their beloved crocodiles, carries Osiris' mummy on his back.

Isis was identified in some Egyptian texts with Nut, the mother of Isis and Osiris. In some versions of the deluge story Matu, the lady of many manifestations, is born with Efé. She emerges from the hole in the tree, which is really the hole in the forest or the entrance/exit to the ghostly kingdom in the Mountain of the Moon. In another version Efé emerges alone and meets the tall, tall lady. The mountain itself is a form of Matu. When Nut gave birth to Isis, she exclaimed *As!* or "Behold!" The child was therefore called Ast or Isis, according to a popular Egyptian tradition. Efé *Osi!* means "See!" as in Egyptian *As!* and English *See!*

Nut stood on the emblem of gold. An Egyptian traveler visits the land of the golden dragon in a story that scholars regard as one source of Plato's Atlantis legend:

> This is the famous "tale of the shipwrecked traveller" wherein an Egyptian relates how he was shipwrecked whilst sailing to Pharaoh's mines—presumably to Sina. His prudent precautions proved unavailing although he had selected a ship 120 cubits long and 40 cubits wide, in which "were the finest Egyptian sailors. They knew the sky, they knew the earth and their heart was stauncher than a lion's. They could foretell the tempest before it burst and bad weather before it broke." Notwithstanding, a dreadful storm blew up and a wave 8 cubits high, borne by the wind, shattered the ship and all were lost save our shipwrecked traveller who, clinging to a log, was cast up on an island. There, a wonderful dragon lived which was 30 cubits long and whose body was encased in gold; its beard, which was more than 2 cubits long and its eyebrows were of pure lapis lazuli. It snatched up the shipwrecked man in its jaws and bore him to its lair. However, it did him no harm and on hearing his tale informed him that he was "on an island of the sea and both its shores lie in the midst of the waves . . . This is an island of blissful beings where all the heart may desire can be found and its riches abound . . ." It continued

Osiris in the character of Menu, the "god of the uplifted arm," and Harpokrates as they sat in the disk of the moon, from the third day of the new moon until the fifteenth day. Below is the crocodile-god Sebek bearing the mummy of the god on his back. To the left stands Isis.

by telling him that its brothers with their children, in all 75 sublimely happy dragons, lived on the island but that once, when it was absent, a star fell which burnt them all up to a cinder. It then went on to prophesy that very shortly the Egyptian would be taken away by a ship belonging to his countrymen and that he would die happy with his family around him. It heaped him with gifts and revealed that it was the sovereign of Punt and that all perfumes and myrrh belonged to it. But, it added, "never more shall you see this island because it will be swallowed up by the waves." This tale of a supremely happy island with its contented people which later became submerged and vanished was, therefore, clearly familiar to the Egyptians. This is the tale the Saite priest confused with other traditional accounts concerning Atlantis because they contained similarities.[4]

The kindly dragon revealed that it was "the sovereign of Punt." The country called Punt has been dubiously identified with East African Somaliland. Punt was a traditional home of the Pygmy god Bes: "In the texts, especially those of the late period, Bes is sometimes mentioned in connexion with NETER TA, or the 'Divine Land,' or 'Land of the God,' i.e., Arabia, and as this name is also used in connexion with Punt, and is applied to the adjacent lands, attempts have been made to prove that the god is of Arabian origin."[5] Bes's earthly kinsmen dwelled in the far southern country of TA NETERU, the "Land of the Spirits" or "Land of the Gods." Net-Athena of Sais, the African mother of the Athenian state that warred with Atlantis, was described in *The Book of the Dead* as the mother of Sebek. She was called Sebek-Net. Her son was alternately portrayed as the divine crocodile-man Sebek and Horus the Child. His father was identified on the Metternich Stele with the Pygmy god Bes.

The divine dragon of Punt dwelled on "an island of the sea and both of its shores lie in the midst of the waves." An Egyptian inscription discovered in 1890 at Sâhal describes the super-sacred source of the Nile as "the Island of Elephantine whereon stood the first city that ever existed." The historic Island of Elephantine was located in Upper Egypt, near the modern Aswan High Dam. Arabic stories describe the Mountain of the Moon as "a mountain on an island which is called by this same name." The lunar mountain is located between Lakes Edward and Albert. To the south of the Virunga volcanoes lies the vast abyss of Lake Tanganyika which the Arabs called Bahari, the Sea.

The shipwrecked traveler was heaped with gifts by the generous dragon who dwells in the holy land of the Pygmy god Bes. Chameleon Man, or the lunar angel, is the secret governor of the sepulchral kingdom in the Mountain of the Moon. There his

---

[4] Sp. Marinatos, *Some Words About the Legend of Atlantis*, 2nd ed. (Athens, 1971), pp. 14–15.

[5] Sir E. A. Wallis Budge, *The Gods of the Egyptians*, Vol. 2, p. 287.

divine son Efé was detained and presented with all kinds of treasures. Sebek-Seb of the Egyptian city Pa-Sebek was the reptilian father of the lunar angel and divine physician Khensu or Khensu-Thoth. A stele discovered at Thebes, where Khensu was the junior member of the local trinity, describes his fabulous journey to "a remote country called Bekhten" where he was detained and given all kinds of treasures:

> As soon as he had been welcomed to the country by the Prince of Bekhten and his generals and nobles the god went to the place where the princess was, and he found that Ben-reshet was possessed of an evil spirit; but as soon as he had made use of his magical power the demon left her and she was healed straightway. Then that demon spoke to Khensu, and acknowledged his power, and having tendered to him his unqualified submission he offered to return to his own place; but he begged Khensu to ask the Prince of Bekhten to make a feast at which they both might be present, and he did so, and the god, and the demon, and the Prince spent a very happy day together. When the feast was concluded the demon returned to his own land, which he loved, according to his promise. As soon as the Prince recognized the power of Khensu he planned to keep him in Bekhten, and the god actually tarried there for three years, four months, and five days, but at length he departed from his shrine and returned to Egypt in the form of a hawk of gold. When the king saw what had happened he spoke to the priest, and declared to him his determination to send back to Egypt the chariot of Khensu, and when he had loaded him with gifts and offerings of every kind the Egyptians set out from Bekhten and made the journey back to Thebes in safety. On his return Khensu took all the gifts which had been given to him by the Prince of Bekhten, and carried them to the temple of Khensu Nefer-hetep, where he laid them at the feet of the god. Such is the story which the priests of Khensu under the New Empire were wont to relate concerning their god "who could perform mighty deeds and miracles, and vanquish the demons of darkness."[6]

The texts engraved on the moon-god's temple at Thebes describe the hero of this story as "the beautiful youth, who maketh himself young in Thebes in the form of Ra, the son of the god-

---

[6] *Ibid.*, Vol. 2, pp. 40–41.

dess Nubit, a child in the morning, an old man in the evening, a youth at the beginning of the year, who cometh as a child after he had become infirm, and who reneweth his births like the Disk." Khensu-Ra was the god of the moon and the sun. In "The Myth of Ra and Isis" the goddess Isis demands that Ra tell his name or reveal his identity. Ra declares: "I am he who, if he openeth his eyes, doth make the light, and, if he closeth them, darkness cometh into being. At his command the Nile riseth, and the gods know not his name. I have made the hours, I have created the days, I bring forward the festivals of the year, I create the Nile-flood. I make the fire of life, and I provide food in the houses. I am Khepera in the morning, I am Ra at noon, and I am Temu at even."

A female sphinx asked the residents of a Greek city called Thebes (about forty-four miles from Athens) to solve her famous riddle. She said: "In the morning it goes on four feet, at noon on two, and in the evening on three. Of all creatures living, it is the only one that changes the number of its feet, yet when it walks on the most feet, its speed and strength are at their lowest ebb." Oedipus, the son of the Theban king Laius, gave an ostensibly correct answer to the Riddle of the Sphinx. He said: "It is Man. In the morning of his life, when he is a weak and helpless child, he crawls on his two hands and two feet. At the noon of his life, he has grown strong and walks on his two feet, but when he is old and the evening of his life has come, he needs support and takes a staff for a third foot."

The female sphinx dwelled on the cliffs of Mount Phycium, near the Greek city of Thebes. She has been interpreted as a form of the Theban moon-goddess. She killed and devoured people who could not answer her riddle. She did not hurt Oedipus, the son of the Theban king. Hathor, the lady who slew mankind on the mountain, presided over the western cliffs at the Egyptian city of Thebes. She was identified in numerous texts with Mut, the Theban mother of the lunar angel Khensu. His father Amen-Ra was the Theban king of the gods. In the legend called "The Destruction of Mankind," Ra tells Hathor to punish his rebellious, blasphemous and wicked subjects. Hathor collaborates with Sekhet, the mother of the divine physician I-em-Hetep whom Ptah begat in the lunar image of Thoth. Nut-Hathor of Pa-Sebek was the mother of the lunar angel Khensu. His Theban mother, Mut, was identified in *The Book of the Dead* (Chapter CXLIV with Sekhet-Bast-Ra, the triune "mistress and lady of the tomb, Mother in the horizon of heaven, gracious one, beloved, destroyer of rebellion." Sekhet-Bast-Ra is pictured as a man-headed woman with lion's claws, wings attached to her arms, a man's phallus, and the heads of two vultures springing from her head or neck. The female sphinx had the head of a woman, eagle's wings, the body of a lion, and the tail of a snake.

The Egyptian picture shows Mut or Sekhet-Bast-Ra with two dwarfs. Each dwarf has two faces, one of a hawk and one of a man. "According to the Rubric, the deceased for whom pictures of the goddess and the two dwarfs were made would become like the immortals, and worms would not eat his body, and his soul would never be fettered, and he would drink water at the source of the river, and would have a homestead of his own in Sekhet-Aanre, and he would become a star of heaven, and he would fight and overcome the fiends Tar and Nekau."[7] The Efé Pygmies believe that the vital force or immortal constituent of the human personality "returns to heaven, where God transforms it into a star." Another constituent goes to the kingdom of the dead, where it dwells as a ghost. Efé traveled to this legendary kingdom through a maze of caverns in the Mountains of the Moon. The chameleon manifestation of the lunar angel resembles Sebek, the crocodilian god of the Egyptian labyrinth. Sebek-Seb of Pa-Sebek was the father of the lunar angel Khensu. His Theban father Amen-Ra was sometimes pictured as a crocodile-headed man. Other portraits show Amen-Ra as a man-hawk. Khensu himself was frequently pictured with the heads of a man and a hawk. The two dwarfs shown with Mut or Sekhet-Bast-Ra are probably her divine father-son.

The goddesses Mut and Net of Thebes were both wives of Amen-Ra and mothers of Khensu. Plato's dialogues describe Net or Athena as the mother-goddess of the paradisaical Athenian state. Plutarch's treatise on Isis and Osiris maintains that the

---

[7] *Ibid.,* Vol. 1, p. 520.

Egyptians frequently called Athena by the name Isis. Plutarch identifies Isis' father with the Greek god Hermes. Arabic legends locate the tomb of the Great Hermes, the prophet Idrisi, or the prehistoric Egyptian king Am Kaam in the Mountain of the Moon. Thoth-Hermes was the chief god of Khemennu or Hermopolis, the Upper Egyptian City of Hermes. "Khensu-Thoth, the twice great, the lord of Khemennu" was a form of the god. Hermes and his father Zeus were alternate fathers of Cupid-Eros, the erotic lunar angel who was hatched from the silver egg of the moon.

Eros' mother was usually described as Aphrodite, the goddess of love, whom the Greeks identified with Hathor. Egyptian texts identify Hathor with a vast troop of goddesses, including Net-Athena of Egypt and Athens. Khensu, the lunar son of the Theban Hathors, was the beautiful god of love and the healing arts. He was sent to a remote country by an Egyptian king of uncertain identity. King Laius of the Greek Thebes tried to murder his infant son Oedipus by locking him into a chest which was lowered into the sea from a ship. The chest drifted ashore at Sicyon, near the city of Corinth. Oedipus was adopted by King Polybus of Corinth. Greek legends describe another Polybus as the king who reigned at the Egyptian city of Thebes during the Trojan War.

Plutarch's Greco-Egyptian treatise on Isis and Osiris claims that Set and his confederates tricked Osiris into entering a beautifully ornamented chest which they nailed shut, sealed with molten lead, and threw into the Nile. The chest was conveyed to the sea through the mouth of the river. Isis wandered about, frantically searching for the chest:

> At length she receives more particular news of the chest, that it had been carried by the waves of the sea to the coast of Byblos, and there gently lodged in the branches of a bush of Tamarisk, which in a short time had shot up into a large and beautiful tree, growing round about the chest and enclosing it on every side, so that it was not to be seen; and farther that the king of the country, amazed at its unusual size, had cut the tree down, and made that part of the trunk, wherein the chest was concealed, a pillar to support the roof of his house . . . Now the name of the king, who reigned at this time at Byblos, was Melcarthus, as that of his queen

was Astarte, or according to others, *Saosis,* though some call her Nemanoun, which answers to the Greek name of *Athenais.*[8]

Isis finds the chest inside the tree where Efé hid and from which he emerged with the waters of the deluge. The conspirators packed Osiris into the chest "upon the 17th day of the month Athyr, when the sun was in Scorpio, in the 28th year of Osiris's reign; though there are others who tell us that he was no more than twenty-eight years old at the time." Noah entered the ark on "the seventeenth day of the month," according to Genesis 7:11. On that same day "were all the fountains of the great deep broken up, and the windows of heaven were opened." In the Pygmy legend of the dog-dragon, Efé is saved when he crosses a river in a boat. This story was probably combined with the legend of his sojourn in the tree trunk to produce Plutarch's account of Osiris' chest inside the tamarisk tree.

The waves carried Osiris' chest to the coast of Byblos. An Egyptian city called Byblos was located in the papyrus swamps of the Nile Delta. The ruins of Phoenician Byblos are about twenty miles north of Beirut, Lebanon. King Phoenix of Byblos was a reputed father of Adonis, the Greek god who encountered the magic boar while he was hunting on Mount Lebanon. His ghost descended to Hades or Tartarus, the kingdom of the dead. He had previously been born from the tree trunk on the island of Cyprus. The goddess Aphrodite concealed the infant Adonis in a chest. She gave the chest to Persephone, the underworld queen of the dead, and told her to stow it away in a dark place.

The Theban infant Oedipus meanwhile floated about in his chest. "This chest drifted ashore at Sicyon, where Periboea, Polybus's queen, happened to be on the beach, supervising her royal laundry women. She picked up Oedipus, retired to a thicket and pretended to have been overcome by the pangs of labour. Since the laundry-women were too busy to notice what she was about, she deceived them all into thinking that he had only just been born. But Periboea told the truth to Polybus who, also being childless, was pleased to rear Oedipus as his own son."[9]

---

[8] *Ibid.,* Vol. 2, pp. 189–90.

[9] Robert Graves, *The Greek Myths,* Vol. 2, p. 9.

Moses' mother meanwhile put her infant son in an ark made of bulrushes and hid the ark on the edge of the River Nile. Moses' sister watched from a distance to see what would happen:

> And the daughter of Pharaoh came down to wash herself at the river; and her maidens walked along by the river's side; and when she saw the ark among the flags, she sent her maid to fetch it.
>
> And when she had opened it, she saw the child: and, behold, the babe wept. And she had compassion on him, and said, This is one of the Hebrews' children.
>
> Then said his sister to Pharaoh's daughter, Shall I go and call to thee a nurse of the Hebrew women, that she may nurse the child for thee?
>
> And Pharaoh's daughter said to her, Go. And the maid went and called the child's mother.
>
> And Pharaoh's daughter said unto her, Take this child away, and nurse it for me, and I will give thee thy wages. And the woman took the child, and nursed it.
>
> And the child grew, and she brought him unto Pharaoh's daughter, and he became her son. And she called his name Moses: and she said, Because I drew him out of the water.[10]

Why did Moses' mother put her baby in the ark?

A cruel Pharaoh told two Hebrew midwives to kill all the male infants born to the Hebrew women. The midwives instead saved the men children. "And Pharaoh charged all his people, saying, Every son that is born ye shall cast into the river, and every daughter ye shall save alive," declares Exodus 1:22. Had any historic king of Egypt given such orders to all his people, he would have been led away to a padded cell. Had his people followed these instructions, the ensuing generation of exclusively female Egyptians would have experienced grave difficulties in producing another generation. Biblical commentators nevertheless identify the cruel king or so-called Pharaoh of the Oppression with Ramses II (1292–1225 B.C.) and other historic Egyptian kings who reigned during that relatively recent era.

King Laius of Thebes tried to murder his infant son Oedipus

---

[10] Exodus 2:5–10.

by dumping him into the sea. Laius alternately pierced the child's feet with a nail, tied them together, and exposed the mutilated baby on Mount Cithaeron. Yet according to the Greek legend "the Fates had ruled that his boy should reach a green old age. A Corinthian shepherd found him, named him Oedipus because his feet were deformed by the nail wound, and brought him to Corinth, where King Polybus was reigning at the time." The son pierces his mother's foot with a spear blade in the Efé myth of the savior. He is "born" from a mother who is identified with the Mountain of the Moon. The childlike size and legs of the Pygmies, combined with their story of the child-man hero who wounds his parent in the foot, are together responsible for many stories of "lame" kings, gods, smiths and/or dragon-fighters. The confusion of male and female characters is greatly expedited by the character of the original Pygmy language.

Efé is a wholly sexless or genderless language.* *Otu* means forefather, grandparent, or ancestor. Schebesta gave *odu* as the Efé word for grandfather and/or father-in-law, and *adu* as mother-in-law. These words are local variants of *otu*, which the Pygmies use as a polite title for parental personalities, including "Efé, the first man and father of all who came after."

Russian *otets*, Egyptian *atef*, father. Etruscan *ati*, mother. Gothic *aithea* and *atta*, mother and father. Sumerian *adda*, father. Hebrew *adam*, man or the first man. Egyptian *Atmu*, *Temu*, or *Tem*, the first man-god and father of the human race. He releases the waters of the great deep in a fragmentary deluge legend. Everyone drowns except his friends or family, who are saved in his boat. Andaman Pygmy Tomu, a title of God or the first man. He cut the tree that somehow supports the earth and thus made the world-destroying floods of the past. He will cut the tree again in the apocalyptic future. Then the living will change places with those who dwell in the kingdom of the dead. Western Pygmy Taum or Ntaum, a title of the first man. In one creation legend he and his lady emerge from a canoe that floats on a waste of waters.

---

* The Efé usually suffix the word *tobu*, "female," to designate a strictly feminine version of any entity. An example: *adalo*, nephew; *adalo'tobu*, female nephew, niece. The word *adalo* may be related to Greek *adelphos, adelphe, adelphide,* and *adelphideos:* brother, sister, niece, and nephew.

"I am Tem in rising; I am the only One; I came into being in Nu," Tem declared in *The Book of the Dead*. He emerged on the first day of his life from Nu, the watery abyss. He wiped out everyone but his elite when he turned loose the waters of the great deep. He was identified in *The Book of the Dead* with Thoth, the lunar author of these texts. "I am he who sendeth forth terror in the powers of rain and thunder," the deceased Egyptian declares in Chapter XCV. "I have made to flourish my knife along with the knife which is in the hand of Thoth in the powers of rain and thunder."

The superhuman form of the lunar angel annihilated everyone but his son Efé, the first and last man, when he cut the tree and released the deluge. Efé came out with the flood, but he was not wet by the water. Hyad, one of the children of Ees, prayed God to show him the extreme end of the Nile. "God gave him power to do this, and he traversed the dark river, walking upon it with his feet over the water which did not stick to his feet, until he entered that dome." Hyad walked on the water and went into the dome that the Arabs located in the equatorial Mountain of the Moon. Jesus went "into a mountain" and prayed. Then he walked on the Sea of Galilee. The waters apparently failed to wet Tammuz, the pre-Christian Christ of Mesopotamian legend, when he was cast out "upon the flood." Like Efé, Tammuz returned as a child or a man.

Whither went Tammuz?

Jesus was buried in a cavernous stone tomb whose entrance was sealed by a great stone. The chief priests and Pharisees went to Pontius Pilate, saying, "Sir, we remember that that deceiver said, while he was yet alive, After three days I will rise again. Command therefore that the sepulchre be made sure until the third day, lest his disciples come by night, and steal him away, and say unto the people, He is risen from the dead: so the last error shall be worse than the first." Pilate said, "Ye have a watch: go your way, make it as sure as ye can." So they went and made the sepulchre sure, "sealing the stone, and setting a watch."[11]

The conspirators sealed Osiris in a chest. King Laius of

---

[11] Matthew 27:63–66.

Thebes sealed his son Oedipus in a chest. Efé did not understand why he had to stay in the kingdom of the dead for three months and part of a fourth. The members of his family do many things that Efé does not understand. They made Efé go through the hole in the forest or hole in the tree to the ghostly kingdom inside the mountain. He returned by his route of entry. Jesus was resurrected from the tomb in the orchard or garden of Gethsemane, which is a part of the Mount of Olives. Adonis came out of the tree on a hill on the island of Cyprus. Tammuz was born at the sacred cedar. Khensu, the lunar son of the southern sycamore lady, is compared to Tammuz in Mackenzie's study *The Myths of Babylonia and Assyria*. Mackenzie remarked that "traces of the Tammuz-Osiris story in various forms" are found from Sumeria to the British Isles.

A beautiful being called Líf or "Life" comes out of the Germanic World Ash Tree or Hoddmimir's Wood. He is resurrected from the Troy-town maze of the Easter festival. He survives at Odin's hall or shelter in the mountain of heaven. Kimi is a Pygmy name for the land of paradise: Egyptian Khemennu, the holy city of the moon-god; Old Norse Himinn, heaven or the sky; Himinbjörg, the heaven-mountain at the southern end of heaven.

An angel rolled away the great stone that sealed Jesus' tomb in the garden. When he was an infant, an angel came in a dream and warned that "Herod will seek out the young child to destroy him." King Herod's minions supposedly "slew all the children that were in Bethlehem, and in all the coasts thereof, from two years old and under." The mythical Pharaoh of the Oppression gave orders to kill all the men children. Jesus has been called "the resurrected Moses." The legends of Jesus are older than the man who may have reenacted the ritual death of the divine king in first-century Jerusalem.

An Assyrian general became king of his country in 722 B.C. He took the name of a king who had reigned two thousand years prior to his time. "I am Sargon, the mighty King of Akkad. My mother was a vestal, my father an alien, whose brother inhabited the mountain," he proclaimed. "When my mother had conceived me, she bare me in a hidden place. She laid me in a vessel of rushes, stopped the door thereof with pitch, and cast me adrift on the river . . . The river floated me to Akki, the water drawer, who, in drawing water, drew me forth. Akki, the water drawer, educated me as his son, and made me his gardener. As a gardener, I was beloved by the goddess Ishtar."[12]

Ishtar, the Queen of Heaven, mourned the death of the beautiful youth who was called "Tammuz of the Abyss." The Babylonian historian Berosus identified Tammuz with a mythical king called Daonus or Daos who reigned in Babylon for 36,000 years and then departed to Hades or the Abyss. Efé took refuge in a hole, cave or *kovu:* English *cove* and *cave.* Anglo-Saxon *cofa,* cave or ark. British stories tell of a child who comes out of the water with the treasures of Efé and returns to the flood with his treasures as an old man:

> The legend runs that one day a boat was seen approaching the shore; it was not propelled by oars or sail. In it lay a child fast asleep, his head pillowed upon a sheaf of grain. He was surrounded by armour, treasure, and various implements, including the fire-borer. The child was reared by the people who found him, and he became a great instructor and warrior and ruled over the tribe as king. In *Beowulf* Scyld is the father of the elder Beowulf, whose grandson Hrothgar built the famous Hall. The poem opens with a reference to the patriarch 'Scyld of the Sheaf.' When he died, his body, according to the request he had made, was laid in a ship which was set adrift:
>
> "Upon his breast lay many treasures which were to travel with him into the power of the flood. Certainly they (the mourners) furnished him with no less of gifts, of tribal treasures, than those who had done who, in his early days, started him over the sea alone, child as he was. Moreover, they set besides a gold-embroidered standard high above his head, and let the flood bear him— gave him to the sea. Their soul was sad, their spirit sorrowful. Who received that load, men, chiefs of council, heroes under heaven, cannot for certain tell."[13]

Whither went Tammuz?

Hera, the sister-wife of Zeus, threw her infant son Hephaes-

---

[12] Donald A. Mackenzie, *Myths of Babylonia and Assyria,* p. 91.

[13] *Ibid.,* pp. 92–93.

tus into the sea from the heights of Olympus. The divine smith was rescued by two nymphs, who reared the founding father of Plato's paradisaical Athens in their submarine grotto. Aphrodite put Adonis in a little chest and told the underworld moon-goddess Persephone-Hecate to stow it away in a dark place. Adonis spent his childhood years in the underworld palace of Hades and Persephone. Adonis' father and grandfather, the king, tried to kill Adonis' mother Myrrha or Smyrna because she tricked him into committing incest with her. Pygmy laws and marriage customs forbid incestuous relationships. The symbolic characters of the Pygmy legend cycle engage in all kinds of apparently incestuous marriages. Their miraculous "births" reveal the nonsexual character of these relationships. Schebesta reported the popular Pygmy opinion that "carnal commerce" or sexual intercourse was unknown to the people of paradise.

"You will kill your father and marry your mother!" the Delphic Oracle predicted to Oedipus. "The Freudian theory that the 'Oedipus complex' is an instinct common to all men was suggested by this perverted anecdote," Robert Graves commented in *The Greek Myths*, "and while Plutarch records (*On Isis and Osiris* 32) that the hippopotamus 'murdered his sire and forced his dam,' he would never have suggested that every man has a hippopotamus complex."

King Laius of the Greek Thebes locked his son Oedipus into a chest, which was lowered into the sea from a ship. The chest came ashore in the land of King Polybus. Was Oedipus reared by Polybus of Corinth or Polybus of the Egyptian Thebes? The queen happened to be on the beach with her royal laundry women. She rescued little Oedipus. Pharaoh's daughter retrieved Moses from the bulrush ark that was sealed with pitch. "This is one of the Hebrews' children," she declared. In his book *Moses and Monotheism*, Sigmund Freud identified Moses with the eighteenth-dynasty Pharaoh Akhnaton. In his book *Oedipus and Akhnaton*, Abraham Velikovsky identified Oedipus with the same Egyptian monarch.

Osiris went into the chest on the same day that Noah entered his animal-laden ark. Yima stocked his Zoroastrian cave with the seed of all species against the wrath to come in cata-

clysmic storm. The wise old Arabic moon-king survived the deluge
by retreating to the Central African mountain of Osiris, Thoth
and Horus. Young Thoth or Khensu went to a country called
Bekhten and returned to Thebes with the treasures of Efé. Sir
E. A. Wallis Budge suggested that Ramses II was the Egyptian
king who sent Khensu to Bekhten. Ramses II has been identified
with the oppressive Pharaoh of Exodus, who told all of his people to throw the male babies into the sea. The sole survivor of
the cataclysmic storm came out of the sea and was heaped with
treasures by the godly dragon-king of Punt. Efé came out with
the flood and received the treasures in the kingdom of the dead.

Osiris' richly ornamented chest drifted ashore at the Egyptian or Phoenician city of Byblos. The chest was found inside a
tree. Efé apparently hid in a tree trunk. "Beloved one, I knew
you were hiding inside my tree. I told my father to cut my tree
with his axe," said Matu, the Mother of God. The Egyptian
mother of the divine child was called by the title "lady of the
southern sycamore." King Phoenix of Byblos was a reputed father
of Adonis, the Greek god whose mother turned into a tree and
was then cleaved with a sword to accomplish the birth of Adonis.
The Arabic phoenix sometimes took the form of a salamander.
According to a very ancient legend, this lizard-like amphibian
cannot be burned by fire. Efé, the nation of the chameleon, dwells
in the near vicinity of the fiery Virunga volcanoes. The Germanic
fire-giants of the southern continent erupt and the deluge of
Ragnarok follows. "The best place to be in at that time will be
Gimlé in heaven," declares the Prose Edda. Efé goes into Gimlé,
the "fire-shelter" of paradise. Efé survives like the salamander in
the midst of the flames. Chameleon Man makes the deluge.

Sebek, the chameleon-like crocodile who possessed "many colours and forms" came out of Nu, the watery abyss. Sebek-Net
was a title of Athena, the heavenly mother of Plato's prediluvian
Athens. Amen-Ra, her husband at the Egyptian Thebes, was sometimes pictured as a crocodile-headed man. The crocodile was the
great pet or mascot of Thebes and Crocodilopolis, the site of the
Egyptian labyrinth: "At Thebes and near Lake Moeris they were
held to be sacred, and when tame the people put crystal and gold

earrings into their ears, and bracelets on their forepaws, and they fed them regularly with good food; after death their bodies were embalmed and then buried in sacred vaults."[14]

Oedipus, the aged king of the Greek Thebes, was buried by the Athenian king Theseus in "the precinct of the Solemn Ones at Athens." The grave has never been found. Was he buried in the Greek Athens or the paradisaical Athens? Theseus went into a mythical Troy-town maze on the island of Crete and came out by his route of entry. Mother Earth hid the infant Zeus in the cave of Dicte on the Aegean hill of Crete. Zeus's son Apollo was born on the floating island mountain of Delos. Krishna saved his Hindu friends from the deluge by holding a sacred mountain above the waters of the flood. "I am the Mountain," said Krishna. Meanwhile, at the Aegean hill of Crete, the nymphs of the World Ash Tree fed Zeus with a diet of honey and goat's milk. Efé *méli* is honey, *upoyi* is milk: Greek *meli*, honey. Sanskrit *payas*, milk; *piyusa*, "beast milk." The Efé word *méli* is sometimes used to describe the sweet sap or milk of trees: Dutch *melk*, German *milch*, English "milk." Gothic *miluks* and *milith*, milk and honey. *Méli* is also the Efé name of the equatorial forest; in the Sua dialect, *méli* means tree: Greek *mélia*, the World Ash Tree. The Germanic survivors of Ragnarok are nourished by the honeydew that drips from the World Ash Tree at the center of the earth. Efé *mélida* is nectar or liquid honey. Anglo-Saxon *meledeaw*, nectar, honeydew, "mildew."

An English poet named John Milton wrote in *Paradise Lost* of a place that some people have believed to be the "true paradise." It is the land of Mount Amara "under the Ethiop line by Nilus' head, enclosed with shining rock, a whole day's journey high." An English poet named Samuel Taylor Coleridge dreamed that he fed on honeydew and drank the milk of an Abyssinian paradise located in the neighborhood of Mount Abora. His poem describes the Pygmies' kingdom of the dead. Coleridge said that he dreamed the poem while he was under the influence of an opiate. He called it "Kubla Khan, Or, A Vision in a Dream":

---

[14] Sir E. A. Wallis Budge, *The Gods of the Egyptians*, Vol. 2, p. 354.

In Xanadu did Kubla Khan
A stately pleasure-dome decree:
Where Alph, the sacred river, ran
Through caverns measureless to man
    Down to a sunless sea.
So twice five miles of fertile ground
With walls and towers were girdled round:
And there were gardens bright with sinuous rills,
Where blossomed many an incense-bearing tree;
And here were forests ancient as the hills,
Enfolding sunny spots of greenery.

But oh! that deep romantic chasm which slanted
Down the green hill athwart a cedarn cover!
A savage place! as holy and enchanted
As e'er beneath a waning moon was haunted
By woman wailing for her demon-lover!
And from this chasm, with ceaseless turmoil seething,
As if this earth in fast thick pants were breathing,
A mighty fountain momently was forced:
Amid whose swift half-intermitted burst
Huge fragments vaulted like rebounding hail,
Or chaffy grain beneath the thresher's flail:
And 'mid these dancing rocks at once and ever
It flung up momently the sacred river.
Five miles meandering with a mazy motion
Through wood and dale the sacred river ran,
Then reached the caverns measureless to man,
And sank in tumult to a lifeless ocean:
And 'mid this tumult Kubla heard from far
Ancestral voices prophesying war!
    The shadow of the dome of pleasure
    Floated midway on the waves;
    Where was heard the mingled measure
    From the fountain and the caves.
It was a miracle of rare device,
A sunny pleasure-dome with caves of ice!
    A damsel with a dulcimer
    In a vision once I saw:
    It was an Abyssinian maid,
    And on her dulcimer she played,

Singing of Mount Abora.
Could I revive within me
Her symphony and song,
 To such a deep delight 'twould win me,
That with music loud and long,
I would build that dome in air,
That sunny dome! those caves of ice!
And all who heard should see them there,
And all should cry, Beware! Beware!
His flashing eyes, his floating hair!
Weave a circle round him thrice,
And close your eyes with holy dread,
For he on honey-dew hath fed,
And drunk the milk of Paradise.[15]

Samuel Taylor Coleridge was born at Ottery in 1772 and died at Highgate in 1834. The Efé Pygmies would call his composition an *oda,* a story, legend or poem: Russian *oda,* Greek *ode,* Welsh *odl,* poem or song. English *ode.* Old Norse *óthr,* poetry, song or a god who has been defined as "the strange double of Odin." He was the husband of Freya, the Queen of Elf-Land. She mourned for him when he mysteriously departed. Efé is the *otu* or ancestor. *Olu* is every or all. *Afa* is father. Old Norse Othinn, Odin, was the god of poetry. He was called *all-fothr,* the father of everybody.

In his book *The Soul of the African Pygmy,* Father Trilles said that one needs "the soul of a missionary" to understand the Pygmies. I prefer "the soul of a poet." God the Father was represented on the Egyptian Metternich Stele by a picture of Bes, the Pygmy god of the musical arts. Bes's son Horus the Child is Apollo, the god of poetry, music and art. Apollo's wife Calliope was the Muse of epic poetry. Orpheus, the son of Apollo and Calliope, was a priest of Dionysus or Dionysus-Osiris. Orpheus played his lyre, Efé played his harp, and an Abyssinian maid played her dulcimer in the land where Alph, the sacred river, ran through caverns measureless to man.

The river that flows through the Pygmies' ghostly kingdom may be the Krypto-Nile or "hidden Nile." Geologists recently dis-

---

[15] *Poetical Works,* edited by Ernest Hartley Coleridge, (London: Oxford University Press, 1970), pp. 297–98.

covered this phenomenal stream, which flows under the earth of Africa and delivers about one hundred times the amount of water produced by the overland Nile. The sacred Spring of Destiny flows under the paradisaical root of the Germanic World Ash Tree. The Egyptian text inscribed on a rock at Sâhal says that the ultimate source of the Nile is a "double cavern" on the island of Elephantine whereon stood the first city that ever existed. The *Prose Edda* calls the city Asgard or Troy. It is the home of the poet Pygmies on the Great Stream of Ocean.

The Children of Efé

Nu-mohk-muck-a-nah, the first or only man, was the sole survivor of "the sad catastrophe which had happened on the earth's surface by the overflowing of the waters." His people, the Mandan Indians, were a branch of the great Sioux nation. They have been called "white Indians" because of their fair complexion and sometimes blue eyes. The ancestors of the Sioux nation survived the sad catastrophe by retreating to a vast cavern where they dwelled in a village near a subterranean lake. The Choctaw ancestors escaped the Deluge in the cave of a towering mountain called Nunne Chaha. The Blackfoot ancestors fled to the cave of Nina Stahu. When the waters of the flood receded, the great god Esaugetuh Emisee took up his residence on Nunne Chaha and modeled the Creek Indian ancestors out of clay. The Shoshone ancestors repeopled the world when they returned from the cavern. The Pawnee ancestors brought the pipe, drum, fire, corn and pumpkin seeds back from the cave where they took shelter during the Deluge.

The ancestors of the Ipurinas and Yurakares tribes, who dwell in Bolivia and northwestern Brazil, sought refuge in an enormous cave. After the great flood that followed the burning of the world, the ancestors found that the entrance to the cave was blocked; with considerable effort they were able to escape. Poshaiyankaya, the founding father of the Zuni and other Pueblo Indian tribes, cut an exit from the cave after the Deluge had subsided. Apocatequil, the chief priest of the moon-god, cut the opening that enabled the Inca ancestors to emerge from Pacari, the Cave of Refuge. He was the son of Guamansura, the first mortal to descend to earth.

The son of Efé cut a hole or path through the foot of the Mountain Mother after the *lulu* monster extirpated the men and cities of the ancient world. The lunar angel form of Efé made the trip to earth and modeled his earthly incarnation out of soil. Efé, the first man and last man on earth, came back from the cavernous kingdom of the dead and survived the Deluge. All men are his children.

Itzamna or Kabul, the Mayan god of the moon, was the father of gods and men. Archaeologist J. E. S. Thompson described "Our Mother," the Mayan moon-goddess, as "a lady of lax morals." Matu, the lady of the lunar mountains, cannot be judged by human standards. The Quiche Indian branch of the Maya nation say that their ancestors returned from the Seven Caves of Tulan-Zuiva after the rest of mankind were annihilated by fire and flood. The Aztec ancestors survived the disaster in a shelter called Chicomoztoc, the Cavern of the Seven Chambers. It has been identified with Mictlan, the Aztec Hades or kingdom of the dead.

In the saga of the hero's trip to Hades, Efé came back from the cave-world; in the legend of the deluge, he climbed a tree. In Brazil, the Tupi-Guarani tribes say that their ancestors survived the deluge by hiding in caves and climbing trees. In the Guianas, the Arawak Indians tell the story of Sigu, the king of the forest, who caused and survived the Deluge: "In the forest was a tree of knowledge which Sigu cut down in order to plant its seeds all over the earth. From the stump, however, water began to gush forth and soon turned into a great deluge. The birds and climbing animals took refuge on the tree-tops while the others were led by Sigu into a cave where they remained in safety until the disaster was over . . . When the Deluge came he placed those animals which could not climb in a cave, the entrance of which he sealed. He himself climbed into the branches of a high tree where he remained until the flood was over."[1]

The Amerindian tribes have been repeatedly accused of "borrowing" their deluge legends and other quasi-Biblical stories from Christian missionaries. The Arawak flood gushed from the ruptured tree of the Pygmy legend. Pygmy fossils have been found in the Guianas, New Mexico, Guatemala, Peru, Chile and other American localities. The many pygmoid tribes of the New World include the Lacandones Indians, a Mayan people who dwell in the forests of Yucatan and Guatemala. The Christian missionaries who came to this region were greatly disconcerted by the quasi-Christian customs and theology of the Mayas: "The number of similarities between the two faiths led them to believe that St. Thomas had preached the gospel in these parts and that after some fifteen hundred years of degeneration Christian practices remained. However, there is no reason to believe that Christianity reached the New World before the arrival of Columbus."[2]

Twelve Christian missionaries sailed with Columbus on his second voyage to the Americas. Five shiploads of Carib Indians were sent to Seville on June 24, 1495, to be sold as slaves. Heavy tributes were imposed on the West Indian tribes. There are no more Carib Indians. They somehow "became extinct." The Pygmies discovered America long before Columbus and his missionaries brought their brand of civilization to the New World. Where did the Pygmies come from?

On August 15, 1971, the Belgian newspaper *Le Soir* re-

[1] Egerton Sykes, *Everyman's Dictionary of Non-Classical Mythology*, pp. 16 and 194.

[2] J. Eric S. Thompson, *The Civilization of the Mayas* (Chicago: Chicago Natural History Museum, 1958), p. 66.

ported: "Forty-two skeletons of Pygmies who inhabited Venezuela during the Neolithic period have been discovered in a street of the town of Quíbor, in the State of Lara, in the west of the country. This discovery has been qualified as sensational by the director of the Anthropology Center of the State of Lara, Professor Adrián Lucena, who, thanks to carbon 14, was able to establish the antiquity of the remains. According to Professor Lucena's first hypothesis, the skeletons, whose average height is one meter fifty centimeters, are those of a tribe of Ayamanes Pygmies, who, originally from Africa, arrived in America by unknown means during the Paleolithic period."*

Where do the Amerindian tribes locate the land of their ancestors?

"All the tribes of the Indians were formerly one, and all dwelt together on an island or at least across a large water towards the East or sunrise," say members of the Iowa Indian branch of the Sioux nation. The Lenni-Lenapi or Delaware Indian representatives of the Algonquian nation described their original home as "the first land, Netamaki, beyond the great ocean Kitahikau." The Quiche-Maya book of *Popul Vuh* situates the Indians' ancestral paradise in "the East, on the shores of the sea whence their fathers had come." In his book *Atlantis: the Antediluvian World*, Ignatius Donnelly interpreted these and many similar legends as evidence that the Amerindian ancestors dwelled on Plato's sunken island in the Atlantic Ocean. The Island of Mogreb is an Arabic epithet for the continent of Africa.

Did the Amerindian ancestors dwell in the African paradise where Alph, the sacred river, ran through caverns measureless to man?

* The discovery was originally revealed at the XXXIX Congreso Internacional de Americanistas, Lima, Peru. Since then, I have been corresponding regularly with Professor Adrián Lucena Goyo who is Director at the Scientific Center of Anthropology and Paleontology of the State of Lara, Venezuela. In a personal letter, he informed me, on June 22, 1972, of the subsequent discovery of SIX other "Pygmy" cemeteries in the vicinity of Quíbor. He also mentioned that Doctor José Alcina Franch has published a treatise supporting the theory of a prehistoric African Pygmy migration to the Americas.

This study, entitled "Origen Transatlántico de la Cultura Indígena de América," appeared in *Revista Española de Antropología Americana,* Vol. IV (Madrid, 1969), pp. 9–64.

The Quiche-Maya book of *Popul Vuh* tells the story of two heroes who went to Xibalba, the cavern world and Hades-like land of the dead. They crossed a river of blood and traveled to a palace where they saw a pair of seated figures, the rulers of Xibalba. Invited to sit down, the heroes sat on a stone that proved to be red hot. The Athenian king Theseus and his friend Peirithous went to the palace of Hades and Persephone in the cavernous land where the underworld river flows through the Greek kingdom of the dead. According to some versions of this story, Theseus was seated in "a fiery chair." He was tortured by the Furies and mauled by the dog-dragon Cerberus while he sat in the "cruel chair" of Hades. Efé was compelled to sit on the magic stool, but he was not harmed or tortured during his trip to the cavernous land where the underworld river flows through the Pygmy kingdom of the dead.

Odin's son Balder sat on "a chair of honor" during his famous sojourn in the Germanic land of the dead. There he met the goddess Hel or "Hell," a lady who corresponds with the grim-looking ghost of Matu:

> She lived underground, in the land of shades, which in many ways was like the Orcus of the Ancients, but it must not be thought of as a place of torture and punishment like the Christian hell . . . She looked rather strange, for half of her face was normal and the other half was entirely black. But, even though she could look terrifying, the palace where she lived resembled the palace of the gods; she allocated a place to each newcomer, and the dead led a communal life which seemed very peaceful. When Balder, the god who was murdered, made his appearance, he was received with due honour, in a huge hall decorated in gold, where serving women hastily prepared a banquet. When the question arose of whether or not Balder would return to earth, Hel was neither cruel nor unjust. But the fact remains that this goddess, who does not seem to have had her own cult, must have been created by poets; the way in which she is portrayed reminds one of a queen of the shades.[3]

Odin's son Hermod traveled to the infernal kingdom with the intention of ransoming his brother Balder. Hermod rode for

---

[3] *Larousse World Mythology*, p. 389.

nine days on Odin's horse Sleipnir until he finally reached the river that borders the land of the dead. He passed the guardian of the bridge and arrived at the iron gate that bars the way to Hel's kingdom. Sleipnir leaped over the gate and carried Hermod into her shadowy domain. There he saw Balder, sitting on his honorable seat in the enormous hall. "If everything in the world, living and dead, mourns him, he shall return to the Aesir; but he shall stay with Hel if anyone refuses and will not weep," said the lady called Hel.

Everyone wept for Balder except his murderer, Loki, who disguised himself as a giant witch and hid in a cave. The sorcerer ghost of Doru collaborated with the ghost of Matu to detain Efé in the cavernous kingdom of the dead. People wept for Efé, the kindly and generous hero who returned from the dead. Balder is resurrected after the great deluge of Ragnarok washes every iniquity off the face of the earth. Efé sires children to people the postdiluvian world. Heimdall, the guardian of the Heaven-Mountain, performs this task in some Germanic legends. Balder and Heimdall have both been compared to Christ, Tammuz and the other divine heroes who returned from the kingdom of the dead.

The Athenian king Theseus alternately emerged from Tartarus or the tunnels of a legendary "death-maze." The New World offers some rather revealing evidence as to the racial affiliations of the original labyrinth builders:

> Archeologists have long been puzzled by the maze of undersized tunnels and stairways which were found in the pre-Inca ruins of Sachuaman and other South American dawn cities. Tunnels so tiny that children have difficulty negotiating their sharp turns; doorways so small that their use would have been restricted to what we call midgets. Yet, both the tunnels and the doorways bear evidence of use, a great deal of it, for the hard stone from which the passageways were made is deeply worn.
>
> Who were these little people?
>
> Where did they come from?
>
> What happened to them?
>
> At this late date it is unlikely that we shall ever have the answers to those questions, barring some near-miracle discovery of evidence which could provide the clues we need. All that remain

are the miles of narrow tunnels cut through solid rock and deeply worn by tiny feet . . .[4]

A maze of Pygmy-sized tunnels connect the chambers of the Etruscan necropolis inside the Italian hill of Poggio Gajella. This monument was apparently patterned after the Pygmies' legendary kingdom in the Mountain of the Moon. Arabic legends describe the lunar mountain as the source of the four rivers that flowed out of Eden. The four rivers flow from a legendary mountain, Kun-lun, that was the earthly capital of the Chinese deity called "the Lord of the Sky:"

> This mountain was in the west of the world . . . The approach to it was protected by mysterious thin water, where nothing, not even a goose-feather, could float, or else by red water (vermilion), which encircled the mountain three times before returning to its source. Anyone who drank of it obtained immortality. According to concurrent traditions, the Kun-lun was either the source of the Yellow River or the source of four great rivers, including the Yellow River, which flowed in four directions (excluding north). This detail regarding the four rivers is important, for it is the firmest in favour of a comparison between the Kun-lun and the Sumeru of Indian mythology. The mountain itself towered up in nine superimposed steps or storeys like the sky. In its sides or summit were doors—four, nine or four hundred and forty in number according to various authors—and through them emerged the winds.[5]

"Sumeru" and "Meru" were both titles of the Hindu Olympus at the center of the earth. The Germanic Heaven-Mountain, World Ash Tree and city of Asgard-Troy were all located at the center of the earth. Etymologists have suggested that "hill or rock with an opening" is the meaning of Hlithskjálf, the name of Odin's high seat or throne. Odin's hall of Valhalla had "more than six hundred and forty doors." Thor's residence, Bilskirnir, was an enormous house of "winding ways" with "more than six hundred and forty floors." The tunnels of the original Troy-town maze wind their way into the mountainous house of the gods.

[4] Frank Edwards, *Stranger than Science* (New York: Bantam Books, 1967), pp. 80–81.

[5] *Larousse World Mythology*, pp. 283–84.

Brutus the Trojan led a legendary party of refugees to the British Isles where he built the city of Trojanova—New Troy—which is now called London. Spiral Castle or the Castle of Arianrhod was another British version of the Troy-town maze. Efé went through the maze and was then imprisoned for three months and part of a fourth month in the kingdom of the dead. "I have been three periods in the prison of Arianrhod," Little Gwion declared in the Welsh riddle-poem of Hanes Taliesin. He was a magic child who turned into the god-poet Taliesin. "Primary chief bard am I to Elphin and my original country is the region of the southern stars," said Little Gwion. "Idno and Heinon called me Merddin, at length every king will call me Taliesin." Efé is miraculously transformed from a child to a man in several Pygmy legends of his return or resurrection. His skill as a bard was shared by Bes, the Pygmy god of the Egyptian musical arts. His ultimate homeland is the celestial paradise "somewhere in the stars." The southern stars twinkle over his earthly residence in the Egyptian-styled "Land of the Gods."

Gwion-Taliesin identified himself with Merddin or Merlin, the Druidic bard who was King Arthur's chief counselor. To build a sepulcher for Arthur's father, Pendragon, Merlin magically transported the enormous stones of Stonehenge from Ireland to England. The British tradition that the stones were previously brought from Africa probably meant, originally, that the labyrinthine tomb of the resurrection is located in the land of the poet Milton's paradisaical mountain "under the Ethiop line by Nilus' head, enclosed with shining rock, a whole day's journey high."

Efé traveled through the mountain to the kingdom of the dead. The Germanic "Hell" was alternately described as a land of ice and darkness under the land of paradise, or the dark frozen continent of the north. The "spirits of cold" and "spirits of night" dwell in the underworld kingdom of Western Pygmy theology. Their original home is described as "the very far countries where it is always very cold, so that they are always frozen." We have already met the giant ogre Ngoogounogounmbar, who dwells in a somber cavern near the underworld river. His confederate,

Ogrigrigwabibikwa, sometimes comes out of the mortuary kingdom to work mischief in the land of the living:

> Ogrigrigwabibikwa is a hideous dwarf from whom one must
> guard oneself with the greatest care. Like his confrere, the giant,
> he has a long beard which is his only clothing, but his beard is
> black. He possesses also enormous ears, which he folds over his
> eyes in order to sleep. He is completely hairy from head to
> foot, and when he touches someone he gives that person the itch.
> As he is very mischievous, he likes to touch people while they are
> sleeping in order to see them scratch with frenzy. Then he dances
> with joy! His hands and his feet are enormous, as big as those of
> an elephant. He frequently hides near villages, preferably in the
> trunk of a tree. From there he bounds out at stragglers, installs
> himself on their backs, and forces them to carry him all through
> the night . . .
>
> Ogrigri also likes to disguise himself as an animal, above all
> a snake. He prefers dead flesh to living flesh, but does not disdain
> the latter. The best thing is to avoid him—sage and prudent ad-
> vice that we share entirely.
>
> Despite these wicked phantoms and spirits of the night, it is
> curious that the Pygmies are not at all afraid of nocturnal strolls
> and even like to hunt at night. The night to them is friendly and
> propitious.[6]

Ogrigri is a caricature of the shaggy dwarfs who make their
home in the Efé kingdom of the dead. They have white faces,
long beards, and scraggly black fur or black bodies covered with
white fur. They sometimes travel about in the forest performing
various errands. The black dwarfs of the Germanic underworld
had pale faces and long beards. The hairy dwarfs called "wood-
men" and "women of the woods" traditionally dwelled in the
forests of northern Europe. The folklore of Brittany tells of
dwarfs called korrigans who jump or ride on people's backs. The
ghost of Matu, in the guise of a lady dwarf, jumped on Efé's
back and drove him to her house in the kingdom of the dead. The
black and white lady of Hell made Balder stay in her palace. He
sat on his chair of honor while the Ragnarok cataclysms de-

---

[6] Henri Trilles, *The Soul of the African Pygmy*, p. 169.

stroyed and re-created the world. He is resurrected in the beginning or springtime of every world-age, not in the spring of each year when Tammuz and many similar god-hero-kings were said to return from Hades or the Abyss.

The American Indian ancestors came back from the caveworld after the cataclysms subsided. They do not make this trip every year. Some critics explain that Yima and his elect retreated to the Zoroastrian cave to escape "a cataclysm which takes its pattern from the icy winters and torrential thaws of central Asia."[7] Winter never comes to the equatorial forest in which the Pygmies tell numerous legends of "the terrible cold, the killer cold" that ravaged the ancient world.

"The men had left the great village. Where were they? Everywhere! But they were not happy, they were hungry, they were thirsty, they were cold. They were cold, and that, that was the worst of all," according to a Western Pygmy story. The giant ogre Ngoogounogounmbar is a "spirit of cold" and "spirit of night" who came from the icy countries of legend. In the Efé myth of the savior the giant ogre Lulu swallows mankind and destroys the cities of antiquity. The giant ogre Grendel swallowed men, prowled at night and preyed for "twelve long winters" on the residents of a hall that was eventually destroyed in a fiery cataclysm; these events are described in the Anglo-Saxon poem *Beowulf*. Fimbulvetr, the Great Winter or Terrible Winter, launches the epic disasters of Ragnarok:

> The real point of interest in this is that the tale goes back to the onset of the last great ice age which ended soon after 10,000 B.C., and must date back at least twenty thousand years before then. This does not imply that the Scandinavian races had spent the intervening period in northern Europe but rather that they had always dwelt in the most northerly latitudes and that when the ice age set in they had been obliged to retreat southwards in order to survive. And, later, as the ice glaciers receded, the ancestors of the Norsemen moved northwards and occupied the lands vacated by the ice-fields. The ensuing disaster, Ragnarok, completes the destruction of the first Nordic culture.[8]

---

[7] *Larousse World Mythology,* p. 200.

[8] Egerton Sykes, *A Dictionary of Non-Classical Mythology,* p. 250.

In the most revealing Efé legend of the stolen fire, the sacred fire of God is extinguished, the Mother of God freezes to death, and the fire brings death to mankind. Like most Efé stories, this is a deeply symbolic rather than literal chapter in the history of the world. I recorded the following text in the Kisiki region of the northeast Ituri. It agrees in most details with a version obtained by Schebesta.[9]

In the beginning, God gave man everything but fire. Life was wonderfully pleasant in the blessed land of paradise. People shivered, however, in the chilly evenings. They had no cheerful hearths in their huts to warm them while they slept. They had no cooking fires outside the huts, as the Efé have today. They had to eat all of their food raw. Then, one day, a man who was lost in the forest found the fire of God. It was warm, bright and beautiful!

He watched the flickering flames from hiding, since the Mother of God was sitting near the fire. From time to time, the old lady put on another piece of wood. Finally, she fell asleep. As soon as she started snoring, the man came out of the bush and tiptoed across the clearing. By now, the fire had burned down to a single piece of wood. He took the burning brand and sneaked away, heading toward camp. No one had seen him. He felt confident that God would never catch him.

Matu, the Mother of God, was meanwhile awakened by the cold. "The fire!" she cried. "Someone has stolen the fire!" God heard her screaming and rushed to her aid. He came swinging through the forest on a long, long liana. It was so long that he could swing across all the streams and rivers of our forest. "Mother, why are you crying?" he asked. "Our fire has been stolen," she replied. "Someone came and stole it while I was sleeping." He gave her a big hug. "Do not worry," he consoled her. "I shall catch the thief."

God swung through the forest, looking for the gleam of the stolen fire. He spotted the thief, who was still miles away from his camp. The man tried to run away. Then he tried to hide. God caught him easily and took away the burning brand. He said to the shamefaced thief, "Didn't I tell you that fire is forbidden? If I catch you again, I shall have to punish you!"

The thief returned to camp. He was still shaking with fear.

---

[9] P. Schebesta, *Les Pygmées du Congo Belge*, p. 160.

He told the story of his misadventure to his brother. "You can be sure that I'll never go near the fire again," he concluded. "Why don't I try?" the brother suggested. "He hasn't given me any warning. So, if I fail, he won't punish me. If I succeed, we'll have the fire." The first brother said, "How can you hope to succeed? When he seized me, I was like a piglet in the paws of a leopard." His brother smiled. "I am smarter and stronger than you. Just wait and see."

The second thief set out through the forest. He found the fire and waited until Matu fell asleep. Then he stole the fire and ran away at full speed. The old lady woke up and started screaming. God came immediately. He leaped onto his liana, swung in a great arc, caught the thief, took away the fire, and told the man to behave himself. The man waited until his heart stopped thumping with fear. Then he returned to his home. "I nearly did it," he bragged to his brother. "No man ever fought more courageously than I. You should have seen me! But it is hopeless. Who can defeat God?"

"I can," said a man named Doru. He was a great magician. He wielded powers unknown to other men. To steal the fire, Doru first stole the feathers of the sacred *tawa* bird. He may have stolen its shape or turned himself into the bird. Most of the elders say that he cut off the bird's wings and pasted them onto his shoulders. Then Doru ran back and forth on the ground, flapping his wings to test them. People smiled behind their hands. "He will never get off the ground," they predicted. Doru leaped into the air. "He will soon fall," said the two envious thieves. Doru soared upward and flew through the sky, just like a real bird or the white man's war-birds [airplanes] that fly over our forest. He sped to the farthest horizons, practicing all the maneuvers of flight. Then he swooped down from the sky and snatched up the fire of God.

Matu was soon awakened by the cold. "Someone has stolen the fire!" she screamed. God saw a flaming streak in the sky. It was Doru, the magic bird-man, flying off with the fire. God swung to the heights of heaven. Doru swooped downward. God swung to the deepest abysses. Doru soared, swooped and soared again. No matter how hard he tried, God could not catch Doru. Breathless, exhausted, he cried, "Doru, you are my brother! Doru, we were born of the same mother! Doru, why have you done this thing?"

Doru flew away without answering. God clung to a tall tree. "Matu!" he cried. "O Matu, help me!" There was no answer. After a while he went home. When he arrived, he saw the most terrible sight in the world. Matu lay stiff and lifeless beside the extinguished hearth. She had frozen to death when Doru stole the fire. "For this man will die," said God. "He has killed our mother."

Doru descended from heaven with the stolen fire. He lighted burning brands from the sacred fire of God. He gave them to the people. Each man gave him a daughter in return. They thought he had brought them the greatest possible blessing. Then the men started to die, one after the other. Since that time, men have always had fire . . . and death.

Doru stole the shape or wings of the sacred ibis. Then the false *tawa* bird flew to the forest and assaulted the earthly household of God. In the third book of Homer's *Iliad* a flock of ibis-like cranes fly to the land of paradise and attack the Pygmies. The cranes are compared to the Trojan warriors who fought with the Greeks:

> Now when the men of both sides were set in order by
> their leaders,
> the Trojans came on with clamour and shouting, like wildfowl,
> as when the clamour of cranes goes high to the heavens,
> when the cranes escape the winter time and the rains unceasing
> and clamorously wing their way to the streaming Ocean,
> bringing to the Pygmaian men bloodshed and destruction:
> at daybreak they bring on the baleful battle against them.[10]

Io, a Greek priestess or a form of the moon-goddess, visited "the sources of the Nile, where the Pygmies make perpetual war with the cranes." The Pygmies do not war with birds of any variety. "God loves the birds because they sing like the Pygmies," say the Efé. They rarely hunt or eat birds. Cranes, and birds in general, do not behave like the feathered fiends who attacked and killed people in Alfred Hitchcock's film *The Birds*. The crowned crane of the White Nile and Great Lakes region is an elegant little bird who wears a crest of golden feathers, strolls about unconfined in American zoos, and is no more capable of warring with Pygmies than a canary or parakeet.

Trilles suggested that Homer's Pygmies fought with ostriches,

---

[10] *The Iliad of Homer,* translated by Richmond Lattimore (Chicago: The University of Chicago Press, 1961), Book III, lines 1–7, p. 100.

apparently because the Kalahari Bushmen hunt ostriches. These immense flightless birds are indeed capable, if provoked, of killing small or tall people. They are not, however, capable of flying south to attack "Pygmaian men" on the shores of the "streaming Ocean." In the Greek legend of her African adventures the priestess or goddess Io assumes the shape of a cow. She was not a real or ordinary cow. Homer's brief account of the "War between the Pygmies and Cranes" is a symbolic, not a literal, story.

The Roman scholar Pomponius Mela (c. 40 A.D.) described the Pygmies as a diminutive race who were totally annihilated when they tried to save their fruit from the attacking cranes. Doru, the thief of the fruit, flew to the forest in the shape of a bird and stole the sacred fire from the lady custodian. In another story Matu is kidnapped by an underworld power associated with the cold and icy countries of legend. A Norse giant named Thjazi flew in the form of an eagle to the woods outside the paradisaical city of Asgard-Troy. He swooped down and snatched up the lady custodian of the sacred fruit, Idun, who carried her golden apples in a box or a bowl. He took the goddess and her fruit to his remote northern residence in Thrynheim or Storm-Home. The cranes came from the land of "the winter time and the rains unceasing."

Idun was the wife of Bragi, a god of poetry who was identified in numerous ways with Odin, the god of poetry and fatherly head of the Germanic pantheon. Odin and the Aesir or Elder Gods were very intimately associated with the Pygmy-like elves or dwarfs of the Eddas. On the Germanic names assigned to the little people, scholars note that "certain of these names are also names of Odin, thereby showing the close relationship between the Aesir and the dwarfs."[11]

Before Doru stole the fire, people had to eat all of their food raw. Before Thjazi stole the fruit, three Germanic gods vainly tried to roast an ox on a fire that would not cook their meat. Odin and his two companions were traveling somewhere outside the city limits of Asgard-Troy when they had this disconcerting experience. "Let them eat their flesh raw!" decreed Zeus, who withheld fire from man. As Roman Jupiter or the Sanskrit-styled

---

[11] Egerton Sykes, *Everyman's Dictionary of Non-Classical Mythology*, p. 62.

Dyaus Pitar, he is the "Heaven Father" of the Olympian paradise at the center of the earth. All-Father Odin, the corresponding head of the Germanic pantheon, could not cook his dinner in the tragi-comic saga of the giant bird-man who flew from the north and stole the golden apples from the forest of Olympus-Asgard-Troy.

Atlas, a man or a giant, took the golden apples from the Greco-Roman Garden of Hesperides. He was associated with a northern region known as "Mount Atlas in the Land of the Hyper-boreans." Atlas' aggressive empire, Atlantis, warred with the para-disaical Athens that was founded by the goddess Athena and Hephaestus, the "lame" god of fire and smithcraft. Atlas' brother Prometheus stole the first fire from the Olympian smithy of He-phaestus, according to some accounts of his paradoxical crime.

Prometheus, the mentor of man, had previously taught his human protégés smithcraft, mathematics, astronomy, navigation and other sophisticated sciences that he himself learned from the goddess Athena. Prometheus, and people in general, were osten-sibly incapable of making a fire or even preserving a fire of natu-ral origin. Zeus supposedly envied man's impressive accomplish-ments. He was determined to extirpate "the whole race of man." Prometheus urged clemency. Then this enigmatic demigod who "surpassed all in cunning and fraud" stole the forbidden fire and gave it to man.

Prometheus must have known that this deed would bring destruction to the people whom he allegedly protected from the wrath of Zeus. His accomplice was far from naïve. Who was this accomplice? Prometheus went to Athena "with a plea for a back-stairs admittance to Olympus." She let him enter the precincts of paradise. By this act, she apaprently betrayed Hephaestus, the gen-tleman founder of Plato's paradisaical Athens. Man, not Hephaes-tus, was smitten by every misery and the sudden advent of death soon after Prometheus' theft of the fire.

Matu tended the sacred fire of the Pygmy legend in remark-ably negligent style. If she had been more alert and conscien-tious, she might have prevented the crime. Two thieves successively snatched and ran away with burning brands, like participants in the torch race at the Greek Hephaesteia or Festi-val of Hephaestus. Then the master-magician Doru assaulted a sacred bird, embarked on his pioneering flight, and stole the forbidden fire. An ingenious smith, artificer and aviator named Daedalus murdered a smith who was sometimes called Perdix or "partridge" and represented as the father of Hephaestus. Daedalus learned his craft from Athena, the instructress of Prometheus. His parentage was unknown or disputed, but it was generally agreed that Daedalus was a junior member of the Erechtheids or royal family of Athens. Their ancestor Erichthonius was the son of Hephaestus and Athena, or Hephaestus and Mother Earth.

After he murdered the partridge-smith, Daedalus was banished or fled to the island of Crete. Zeus's son Minos, the king of Crete, locked the fugitive smith in the labyrinth that Daedalus had supposedly built after the pattern of the Egyptian maze at Crocodilopolis. Pasiphaë, the queen of Crete, freed the murderer and his son Icarus, who had been incarcerated with Daedalus in the depths of the maze. Pasiphaë was identified by the Greek scholar Pausanius with the moon and the goddess Athena. Ariadne, the daughter of Pasiphaë or a youthful form of the goddess, helped the Athenian king Theseus to enter and escape from the maze. Theseus is a form of Efé, the angelic hero who returned from the kingdom of the dead. Daedalus is a form of Doru, the junior male who commits many destructive deeds. The ghost and monstrous manifestations or confederates of Doru dwell in the kingdom of the dead. The lunar angel controls the labyrinthine entrance.

After the moon-goddess or the queen freed Daedalus from the labyrinth, the murdering master smith made artificial wings out of feathers threaded together and secured with wax. He and Icarus slipped their arms into the wings and soared away from the island of Crete. Völund the Smith was imprisoned in the original city of the Troy-town maze. According to the *Poetic Edda* King Nithud of Troy kept Völund as his prisoner. Völund murdered two dwarfs or two sons of King Nithud. He was called Wayland the Smith in the British Isles, where his forge was traditionally located in a cave of the Berkshire Hills. Aided by his brother Egil, Völund the "Wise Elf" made the first artificial wings or flying machine. According to Pygmy legend Doru possessed powers or knowledge unknown to other men. He flew like a bird or an airplane. "He will never get off the ground," said the dubious spectators when Doru prepared to take off. Similar comments were probably made at Kittyhawk, North Carolina, while the Wright brothers were preparing to make their successful flight.

Daedalus' son Icarus flew too near the sun. The heat melted the wax that secured his feathers. He plummeted downward and drowned in the sea. Two sons of Garuda, the giant Hindu eagle-man, set out on a similar flight. One of the brothers was killed by Ravana, the demon king of Ccylon. Rama, the great hero of the Sanskrit epic *Ramayana,* found the other bird-man in a disabled condition. He told Rama, "Once upon a time we two (brothers), with the desire of outstripping each other, flew towards the sun. My wings were burnt but those of my brother were not . . . I fell down on top of this great mountain where I still am." Garuda himself flew to the Olympian paradise of Mount Meru and stole the nectar of the gods. The Germanic eagle-giant Thjazi flew to the land of the Heaven-Mountain and stole the fruit of the gods.

Doru, the thief of the fruit, took the wings or shape of a bird when he stole the fire. The angelic savior of the Pygmy nation released the waters of the Deluge. The Tuleyone Indians of California say that the falcon Wekwek stole the fire and carelessly dropped it on the world, which was set ablaze. Then Olle, the Savior, released a great flood that submerged the entire world except for one mountaintop on which the survivors gathered. The world conflagration precedes the deluge in most Amerindian stories of the so-called creation. The fire is stolen by a bird—the fire-bird—in many, if not most, of the globally distributed legends concerning the theft of fire. Schebesta rather simplistically remarked in his book *Les Pygmées* that stories concerning the burning of the world and the deluge are both "unknown" to the Ituri Forest Pygmies.

Sanskrit hymns praise the eagle-giant Garuda as the "destroyer of all, creator of all" who burns all things and all creatures. Garuda has been compared with the Mesopotamian "Etana Eagle" that carried the hero Etana toward the celestial paradise of the mother-goddess Ishtar. The infant Gilgamesh was thrown down from the citadel of Babylon and rescued by this very remarkable bird: " 'A keen-eyed eagle saw the child falling, and before it touched the ground the bird flew under it and received it on its back, and carried it away to a garden and laid it down gently.' Here we have, it would appear, Tammuz among the flowers, and Sargon, the gardener, in the 'Garden of Adonis.' "[12]

Doru, the magic bird-man, brought death to mankind when he stole the sacred fire. The ghost of Doru helped rather than hurt Efé when the hero embarked on his trip to the kingdom of the dead. The banana groves and forests that Efé viewed when he reached the shores of the underworld river are the "Nether Garden of Adonis." The eagle and Etana fell to earth when they flew toward the celestial paradise of Pygmy legend. Doru's flight ended in catastrophe. The infant Gilgamesh was saved by the eagle. The adult Gilgamesh traveled through the labyrinthine caves or tunnels in the Pygmies' holy mountain:

> Gilgamesh set out on his journey and in time reached a mountain chasm. Gazing on the rugged heights, he beheld fierce lions and his heart trembled. Then he cried upon the moon god, who took pity upon him, and under divine protection the hero pressed onward. He crossed the rocky range and then found himself confronted by the tremendous mountain of Mashi—"Sunset hill," which divided the land of the living from the western land of the dead. The mountain peak rose to heaven, and its foundations were in Aralu, the Underworld. A dark tunnel pierced it and could be entered through a door, but the door was shut and on either side were two monsters of horrible aspect—the gigantic "scorpion man" and his wife, whose heads reached to the clouds. When Gilgamesh beheld them he swooned with terror. But they did him no harm, perceiving that he was a son of a god and had a body like a god.
>
> When Gilgamesh revived, he realized that the monsters regarded him with eyes of sympathy. Addressing the scorpion giant, he told that he desired to visit his ancestor, Pir-Napishtim, who sat in the council of the gods and had divine attributes. The giant warned him of the dangers which he would encounter, saying that the mountain passage was twelve miles long and beamless and black. Gilgamesh, however, resolved to encounter any peril, for he

---

[12] Donald A. Mackenzie, *Myths of Babylonia and Assyria*, p. 171.

was no longer afraid, and he was allowed to go forward. So he entered through the monster-guarded mountain door and plunged into thick unbroken darkness. For twice twelve hours he groped blindly onward, until he saw a ray of light. Quickening his steps, he then escaped from the dreadful tunnel and once more rejoiced in the rays of the sun. He found himself in an enchanted garden, and in the midst of it he saw a divine and beautiful tree towards which he hastened. On its gleaming branches hung clusters of precious stones and its leaves were of lapis lazuli. His eyes were dazzled, but he did not linger there. Passing many other wonderful trees, he came to a shoreland, and he knew that he was drawing nigh to the Sea of Death. The country which he entered was ruled over by the sea lady whose name was Sabitu. When she saw the pilgrim drawing nigh, she entered her palace and shut the door.[13]

Efé met the ghost of Matu in the "Nether Garden of Adonis" near the shores of the underworld river. She kidnapped the hero or forced him to go to her house. "I am not dead! I do not have to go to your house!" he protested. The ghost of Doru helped to keep Efé, the first man and last man, imprisoned in the kingdom of the dead. Enkidu, the Sumerian man of clay, dreamed that he was kidnapped by the magic bird-man form of Doru and taken to the house of the underworld lady. He told his dream to his friend or brother Gilgamesh in the Sumerian *Epic of Gilgamesh*:

> Last night I dreamed again, my friend. The heavens moaned and the earth replied; I stood alone before an awful being; his face was sombre like the black bird of the storm. He fell upon me with the talons of an eagle and he held me fast, pinioned with his claw, till I smothered; then he transformed me so that my arms became wings covered with feathers. He turned his stare towards me, and he led me away to the palace of Irkalla, the Queen of Darkness, to the house from which none who enters ever returns, down the road from which there is no coming back.
>
> There is the house whose people sit in darkness; dust is their food and clay their meat. They are clothed like birds with wings for covering, they see no light, they sit in darkness. I entered the house of dust and I saw the kings of the earth, their crowns put away for ever; rulers and princes, all those who once wore kingly

---

[13] *Ibid.*, pp. 177–81.

crowns and ruled the world in the days of old. They who had stood
in the place of the gods, like Anu and Enlil, stood now like servants
to fetch baked meats in the house of dust, to carry cooked meat
and cold water from the water-skin. In the house of dust which I
entered were high-priests and acolytes, priests of the incantation
and of ecstasy; there were servers of the temple, and there was
Etana, that king of Kish whom the eagle carried to heaven in the
days of old. I saw also Samuqan, god of cattle, and there was
Ereshkigal the Queen of the Underworld; and Belit-Sheri squatted
in front of her, she who is recorder of the gods and keeps the
book of death. She held a tablet from which she read. She raised
her head, she saw me and spoke: "Who has brought this one here?"
Then I awoke like a man drained of blood who wanders alone in
a waste of rushes; like one whom the bailiff has seized and his
heart pounds with terror.[14]

Enkidu died soon after his dream. Gilgamesh, mourning the
death of his friend or brother, went on his trip through the tunnels of Mount Mashu to visit his ancestor Utnapishtim or Pir-
Napishtim. The old man told Gilgamesh how he had survived the
Deluge in a boat loaded with his kinsmen, animals tame and
wild, smiths, and golden treasure. The boat grounded on the
mountain of Nisir. "Thus it was that the gods took me and placed
me here to live in the distance, at the mouth of the rivers," said
the Sumerian Noah. He is El, the Semitic moon-god who dwells
"near the sea-shore at the point where rivers flow into the ocean."

The Arab geographers located the Garden of Allah, the gold
country, the four rivers of Eden, and "the fountain which is the
first of all fountains" in or around the Central African Mountain
of the Moon. They claimed that the lunar god-king prophesied
the Deluge and retreated to the Mountain of the Moon. Yima, the
first man or first king, survived the catastrophe in a mountain
cave. Adventurers still hunt for Yima's treasure in the Persian
mountains. Yima's elect, or virtuous Zoroastrians, are supposed
to survive the past and future cataclysms that freeze, sizzle and
drown the rest of mankind. Yima's name means "twin." He was
the god of light on earth. His twin, Mithra, was the celestial god
of light or the sun. Persian pictures show Mithra as a lion-headed

---

[14] *The Epic of Gilgamesh*, pp. 89–90.

man. Bes, the cat-headed "sun-god" of the Metternich Stele, was the heavenly representative of the Pygmies.

In the Pygmy religion, the sun is the celestial fire of God. Doru stole the sacred fire of the Pygmy smiths from the earthly establishment of God. Prometheus stole the fire from the sun or the Olympian smithy of Hephaestus. Before he filched the fire, Doru attacked the lunar angel's sacred ibis. Set, the Egyptian "thief of light," stole the light of the sun and the moon. Thoth, the god of the moon, was sometimes pictured as an ibis-headed man. Doru and Prometheus brought the fire to man. Lucifer, the Light-Bringer, is an epithet of Satan. Down in the ninth and deepest circle of Dante's *Inferno,* a winged demon called Lucifer or Dis (the Roman Hades) stands breast-high in the ice. He is imprisoned in the dark and frigid Germanic abyss of "Niflhel that is down in the ninth world." The land of hell was alternately located beneath the land of paradise and in the frigid northern continent, Niflheim, that corresponds with Ice-Age Europe. The Pygmy "spirits of cold" dwell in the underworld and the frozen countries of legend.

To the best of my knowledge, no anthropologist has bothered to ask how the Central African Pygmies came to possess legends that seem more appropriate to Eskimos. The missionary-anthropologists think in almost exclusively Biblical terms. The secular anthropologists are justifiably repelled by their attitude. Georg Schweinfurth reached the Ituri Forest and rediscovered Homer's Pygmies in 1871. He remarked that the ultimate meaning of Homer's story concerning the Pygmies and the cranes "matters little to us." The important thing, said Schweinfurth, is that Homer and Aristotle somehow knew about the little people who dwell at the source of the Nile hundreds of years before the Christian era. The ancient Greeks' knowledge of the Pygmies is indeed significant. The meaning of Homer's story matters a great deal more than Schweinfurth thought.

A winged man-dragon named Typhon attacked the Olympian paradise of the Greek ancestor-gods at the center of the earth and the source of the Nile. He is intimately related to Satan and Set. He dragged Zeus into his cave. Zeus was imprisoned in the cave until his son Hermes—the Egyptian moon-god Thoth—came to

his rescue. The greatest gods, heroes, kings and ancestors of the
Old and New Worlds were resurrected from the cave, death-
maze or kingdom of the dead. The rest of the human species
perished.

The winged destroyer of the Pygmy legend was a false, not
a real fowl. Zeus's son Hercules battled with the avian monsters
known as the Stymphalian birds:

> Heracles's Sixth Labour was to remove the countless brazen-
> beaked, brazen-clawed, brazen-winged, man-eating birds, sacred to
> Ares which, frightened by the wolves of Wolves' Ravine on the
> Orchomenan Road, had flocked to the Stymphalian Marsh. Here
> they bred and waded beside the river of the same name, occasion-
> ally taking to the air in great flocks, to kill men and beasts by
> discharging a shower of brazen feathers and at the same time
> muting a poisonous excrement, which blighted the crops . . .
> Stymphalian birds are the size of cranes and closely resemble
> ibises, except that their beaks can pierce a metal breast-plate, and
> are not hooked. They also breed in the Arabian Desert, and there
> cause more trouble even than lions or leopards by flying at travel-
> lers' breasts and transfixing them. Arabian hunters have learned
> to wear protective cuirasses of plaited bark, which entangle those
> deadly beaks and enable them to seize and wring the necks of their
> assailants. It may be that a flock of these birds migrated from
> Arabia to Stymphalus, and gave their name to the whole breed.
> According to some accounts, the so-called Stymphalian birds
> were women: daughters of Stymphalus and Ornis, whom Heracles
> killed because they refused him hospitality. At Stymphalus, in the
> ancient temple of Stymphalian Artemis, images of these birds are
> hung from the roof, and behind the building stand statues of maid-
> ens with birds' legs. Here also Temenus, a son of Pelasgus, founded
> three shrines in Hera's honour: in the first she was worshipped as
> Child, because Temenus had reared her; in the second as Bride,
> because she had married Zeus; in the third as Widow, because she
> had repudiated Zeus and retired to Stymphalus.[15]

The phony crane or ibis was sacred to Ares, the god of
tempests and war. These brutal birds ate people in the predatory

---

[15] Robert Graves, *The Greek Myths*, Vol. 2, pp. 119–20.

style of the winged female sphinx and the swallowing-monster manifestations of the Pygmies' geophysical destroyer. The female sphinx has been interpreted as a form of the winged Theban moon-goddess. Images of the phony cranes decorated the Stymphalian temple of Artemis, the lunar lady whose magic boar dispatched so many Greek heroes to the land of Hades. The female sphinx did not gobble up the Theban prince Oedipus. Mut or Sekhet-Bast-Ra, the winged "lady of flame" and "destroyer of rebellion," did not incinerate her beloved son Khensu of the Egyptian Thebes.

The phony cranes were fiercer than leopards or lions. They bombed people with brazen feathers and showered them with poisonous excrement. They attacked Arabian hunters, who are much larger and stronger than Pygmies. According to the Arabic tale of Sinbad's fifth voyage the giant birds or eagles called Rocs bombarded ships with enormous rocks. When his vessel sank, Sinbad was marooned on an island and kidnapped by a small but powerful demon:

> I had penetrated some distance into the island when I saw an old man bent and feeble sitting upon the river bank, and at first I took him to be some shipwrecked mariner like myself. Going up to him I greeted him in a friendly way, but he only nodded his head at me in reply. I then asked what he did there, and he made signs to me that he wished to get across the river to gather some fruit, and seemed to beg me to carry him on my back. Pitying his age and feebleness, I took him up, and wading across the stream I bent down that he might more easily reach the bank, and bade him get down. But instead of allowing himself to be set upon his feet (even now it makes me laugh to think of it!), this creature who had seemed to me so decrepit leaped nimbly upon my shoulders, and hooking his legs round my neck gripped me so tightly that I was well-nigh choked, and so overcome with terror that I fell insensible to the ground. When I recovered my enemy was still in his place, though he had released his hold enough to allow me breathing space, and seeing me revive he prodded me adroitly first with one foot and then with the other, until I was forced to get up and stagger about with him under the trees while he gathered and ate the choicest fruits. This went on all day, and even

at night, when I threw myself down half dead with weariness, the terrible old man held on tight to my neck, nor did he fail to greet the first glimmer of morning light by drumming upon me with his heels, until I perforce awoke and resumed my dreary march with rage and bitterness in my heart.[16]

"You fell into the hands of the Old Man of the Sea," said the mariners who eventually rescued Sinbad the Sailor. Ogrigri, the monstrous dwarf of the Western Pygmy underworld, rides on people's backs all through the night. "Spend the night with me, darling," Matu said to Efé when they met in the orchard forest near the underworld river. She fed him the fruit that Sinbad's captor plucked for himself. Then the dwarf "ghost of a sorceress" jumped on Efé's back and led him away to her house. He stayed in the kingdom of the dead during "the long dark night" of Pygmy theology. It is the night of the great disasters and the killer cold, not the ordinary night which the Pygmies find so friendly and propitious. Balder, the Norse god of light, is imprisoned in the kingdom of hell during all the world-destroying cataclysms of Ragnarok. Gilgamesh traveled to the infernal orchard and river-bank through the long, long tunnel in Mount Mashu. When he arrived he met the Sea Lady and the Mesopotamian Noah or Old Man of the Sea.

Deucalion, the Greek Noah, descended from Mount Parnassus after the flood and took up residence in a cave. His ark grounded on Apollo's sacred mountain at the center of the earth after Zeus "broke up all the fountains of the deep, and opened the well springs of heaven, and it rained for forty days and forty nights continually." Noah's Ark supposedly grounded on Mount Ararat in Armenia. Deucalion descended to the cave where Gilgamesh met the Mesopotamian Noah after traveling through the Pygmies' legendary tunnels in the Mountain of the Moon.

After the Deluge, the ancestors of the Toltec people who founded the Aztec civilization of Mexico built a very high *zacuali* or tower "in order to take refuge in it should the second world be

[16] *Arabian Literature*, Ephiphanius Wilson, ed. (New York, The Colonial Press, 1900), pp. 121–22.

destroyed." According to the Arabic scholar Abou Balkhi enormous pyramids were built as shelters before the disaster:

> The wise men, previous to the Flood, foreseeing an impending judgment from heaven, either by submersion or fire, which would destroy every created thing, built upon the tops of the mountains in Upper Egypt many pyramids of stone, in order to have some refuge against the approaching calamity. Two of these buildings exceeded the rest in height, being four hundred cubits high and as many broad and as many long. They were built with large blocks of marble, and they were so well put together that the joints were scarcely perceptible. Upon the exterior of the building every charm and wonder of physic was inscribed.

These fabulous mountaintop pyramids are about twice as high as the Great Pyramid of Gizeh. Their ruins have never been discovered. The legendary Etruscan king Lars Porsena was buried in a titanic tomb that consisted of pyramids, arranged in three tiers, with a labyrinth in the basement. Pygmy-sized tunnels connect the three tiers of chambers inside a hill on the outskirts of Porsena's Italian city. Pygmy-sized tunnels and doorways were found in the ruins of pre-Inca cities. The pyramids of the Old and New World may have originated as shelters. They may also be replicas of the deity's sacred mountain whence the ancestors emerge at the beginning of every world-age.

The Pygmies will not divulge any frank or realistic information about the caverns that lead to the legendary land of the dead. "The mountain is a very dangerous place," they warn politely. "People die, disappear or go mad if they fool around on our mountain. Even we stay away from the mountain." Then they change the subject.

Efé was told not to return by the ghosts who carried his treasures through the tunnels. He was lured into the mountain and imprisoned in the kingdom of the dead. Doru and the other ghosts gave him all kinds of treasures. Doru, the magic bird-man, brought death to the world of the living. Someday it will all happen again, the elders darkly prophesy.

The Roman scholar Pomponius Mela claimed that the Pygmies were totally exterminated in their war with the cranes. The Pygmies are still around. The phony cranes, ibises or Stymphalian bird-women attacked and slaughtered people in general. They resembled the predatory bird-women called harpies. These creatures had the faces of women and bodies of vultures. They stank, defiled the food of their victims, carried away the souls of the dead, punished criminals and served in general as ministers of divine vengeance. The harpies dwelled in a cave on the island of Crete. They have been interpreted as personifications of the Cretan death-goddess in the form of a whirlwind or the triple-goddess Athena in her capacity of sudden destroyer. She helped the flying smith Daedalus to escape from the Cretan labyrinth. She let Prometheus steal the forbidden fire.

To avenge this crime, Zeus ordered his son Hephaestus to model a clay woman. When she opened her jar or box, a great cloud of miseries flew out, stung Pandora in every part of her body, and then attacked the race of mortals. When Psyche opened her underworld box, she was stupefied by noxious vapors and lay "like a sleeping corpse." Matu froze to death when her son Doru stole the sacred fire. Like many mountain mothers, Matu is a form of Mother Earth. Psyche was eventually revived by Cupid or Eros, "the god of all fire." He and Hephaestus, the god of smith-craft and fire, are forms of the same god. He was offended when Psyche stole a forbidden glimpse of his person. The first woman of Kango Pygmy legend peeked at the god who dwelled in the smithy and brought death to mankind.

The thief of fire fought with the divinely innocent, kindly and generous god of the forest or earth. "Doru, you are my brother! Doru, we were born of the same mother! Doru, why have you done this thing?" asked Toré or God. Doru flew away without answering. His enigmatic deeds left the earth-mother frozen and lifeless. "For this man will die," said God. "He has killed our mother."

Why did Doru destroy the world?

The legends of Efé and the stories told by his children can supply the answer to that question. All men are his children, say the Pygmies. The Mandan Indians called him Nu-mohk-muck-a-nah, the first or only man.

The Twilight of the Gods

The cranes launched an unprovoked attack on Homer's Pygmies. The ferocious birds called harpies assaulted King Senapis of Abyssinia after he led an aggressive expedition to the land of Homer's Pygmies. "It was said this punishment was inflicted upon the king because when young, and filled with pride and presumption, he had attempted to invade with an army the terrestrial paradise, which is situated on the top of a mountain whence the Nile draws its source"; at the foot of this mountain, there is "a cavern, which is thought to be the mouth of the infernal abodes."[1]

Dante's *Inferno* describes a literary trip through the under-

---

[1] "The Legends of Charlemagne," *Bulfinch's Mythology* (Feltham: The Hamlyn Publishing Group Ltd., 1968), pp. 607–8.

world caverns to the terrestrial paradise atop the mountain-island of purgatory in the southern hemisphere. Guided by the sound of a river, Dante and the ghost of the Roman poet Vergil emerged "through a circular opening in the cave." On the summit of the mountain, Dante saw the fatal tree of Eden: "With one voice all murmur'd 'Adam'; circling next a plant despoiled of flowers and leaf, on every bough. Its tresses, spreading more as more they rose, were such, as 'midst their forest wilds, for height, the Indians might have gazed at." The tree, or a branch of the tree, is described as a chariot pole. "The chariot-pole is the Cross, which, according to legend, was made from the tree of Eden," commented Edmund G. Gardner in his edition of Dante's *Divine Comedy*.[2]

A supernatural bird plummets downward like a dive bomber and strikes the tree, cross or chariot pole:

Never fire, with so swift motion, forth a stormy cloud leap'd downward from the welkin's farthest bound, as I beheld the bird of Jove descend down through the tree; and, as he rush'd, the rind disparting crush beneath him; buds much more, and leaflets. On the car, with all his might he struck; whence, staggering, like a ship it reel'd . . . Then it seem'd that the earth open'd, between either wheel; and I beheld a dragon issue thence, that through the chariot fix'd his forked train; and like a wasp, that draggeth back the sting, so drawing forth his baleful train, he dragg'd part of the bottom forth; and went his way, exulting . . . Thus transform'd, the holy structure, through its several parts, did put forth heads; three on the beam, and one on every side; the first like oxen horn'd; but with a single horn upon their front, the four. Like monster, sight hath never seen. O'er it methought there sat, secure as rock on mountain's lofty top, a shameless whore, whose ken roved loosely round her.[3]

The monster has seven heads and ten horns. "The seven heads are seven mountains on which the woman sitteth," declares the New Testament book of Revelation. "And the beast that was, and is not,

---

[2] *The Vision of Dante Alighieri*, translated by the Reverend H. F. Cary, introduction by Edmund G. Gardner (London: J. M. Dent, 1928), "Purgatory," Canto XXXII, pp. 283–84.

[3] *Ibid.*, pp. 286–87.

even he is the eighth, and is of the seven, and goeth into perdition
. . . And the ten horns which thou sawest upon the beast, these
shall hate the whore, and shall make her desolate and naked, and
shall eat her flesh, and burn her with fire." The heads of the great
dragon, that old serpent called the Devil and Satan, correspond
with the eight giant Virunga volcanoes at the source of the Nile.
The Egyptian man-dragon Set was the brother of Osiris and of
Horus the Elder, the great god of goodness and light. The picture
of Horus as the god comprehending all gods (page 102) shows eight
snake heads proceeding from the head of Horus.

Set alternately helped and opposed the "good" Egyptian gods.
Doru is the equally ambivalent brother-son of Efé and/or God. As
a cosmic power, Doru represents the destructive forces of nature
or God. He defeated a creative form of the deity in the story of the
magic bird-man. Garuda, the eagle-giant "destroyer of all, creator of
all," raided the Hindu Olympus. The thieving eagle-giant Thjazi
flew to the Germanic Olympus from his residence in the northern
mountains of Thrymheim or Storm-Home. An eagle-giant named
Hraesvelgr or "Corpse-Swallower" sits at the northern end of the
Germanic sky and flaps out the winds of the world.

Boreas, the winged North Wind, traveled to the Greek
Olympus in the Pelasgian story of the creation. The winged man-
monster Typhon attacked Olympus in a story of destruction. The
Greek winds were traditionally portrayed with feet or legs that
consisted of serpents. Typhon's thighs terminated in snaky coils.
He was identified with Python, the serpentine spirit of the North
Wind. He fathered Hydra, a giant water snake that was equipped
with eight mortal heads and was sometimes pictured with seven.
Dante's winged destroyer flew to the mountain of paradise and
caused the advent of a seven-headed monster. Revelation explicitly
identifies the heads of the scarlet dragon with a group of volcanic
mountains.

Dante described the ornithological attacker as an eagle, the
bird of Jove or Jupiter. Typhon dragged Zeus-Jupiter into his cave,
where the god was imprisoned. After an interlude in the cave, the
god returned like many resurrected heroes and subdued the geophysical destroyer. The windy eagle-giants of the Eddas made their
home in the north. Surt and his crew of volcanic fire-giants were

located on the southern continent. Typhon came like a storm-bird to Olympus and spat flaming rocks out of his mouth in the style of an erupting volcano. His serpentine offspring, the Hydra, rather closely resembles the many-headed dragon of Revelation.

The bird-demons of the north are associated or collaborate with the volcanic monster at the source of the Nile. The northern continent of the Eddas was a frozen wasteland. So was Europe during the Pleistocene period or Great Ice Age that is supposed to have ended around 10,000 B.C. Geological theories alternately describe massive outbursts of volcanism as a paramount cause and an effect of the ice ages. Professor Charles Hapgood's book *Earth's Shifting Crust* favors the theory that eccentrically balanced icecaps exert centrifugal force that causes crustal fractures, earthquakes, volcanic eruptions and polar shifts. Perturbations of the earth's axis are indicated in other theories of the Pleistocene. Many scientists maintain that the present or so-called Recent period is an interglacial lull in the catastrophic Pleistocene. They predict imminent polar shifts, the return of the North American and European icecaps, a sharp increase in mutation rates caused by changes in the earth's magnetic field, mass extinctions, and the destruction of urban civilization.

The Great Winter of Ragnarok or Götterdämmerung, the Twilight of the Gods, has rightly been compared to the onset of an ice age. The recurrent cycles or world-ages of Germanic theology correspond with the periodic glaciations of the Pleistocene. The end of the cultural epoch known as the Paleolithic period or Old Stone Age is traditionally dated, like the end of the Pleistocene, at around 10,000 B.C. African Pygmies traveled to the Americas "by unknown means" during the Paleolithic-Pleistocene, according to Professor Adrian Lucena's report on the forty-two skeletons of Venezuelan Pygmies that were unearthed in 1971. In his book *Men Out of Asia* (1947) Harold S. Gladwin suggested that the Pygmies may have migrated from Siberia to Alaska prior to 25,000 B.C., when Australoid or archaic Caucasoid people made a theoretical trek across the Bering Strait land bridge that connected Asia and North America during ice-age times.

"Pygmies Before Australoids in the New World?" asks Macgowan and Hester's study *Early Man in the New World*. The authors discuss the much-disputed identity of the earliest Americans:

> Both Imbelloni and Gladwin begin with a suggestion that Pygmies deserve consideration. These primordial migrants trod their tiny paces from some unknown fatherland to the forests of the Congo and the jungles of New Guinea, to islands like the Andamans and possibly to Tasmania. The presence of five-foot Yahgan in Tierra del Fuego suggests to both Imbelloni and Gladwin that Pygmies may have preceded the Australoids to the New World. The advent of Pygmies in Tierra del Fuego as well as in Tasmania may be open to question; for in both places the natives, though short, exceeded the average of Pygmy height by a few inches, and their heads, instead of being round like those of the Pygmies, are recorded as of medium cephalic index . . .
>
> Gladwin begins with what might be called a Pygmoid visitation. He does not dignify it with the word "migration." He is careful to say that there are only "rather vague indications." There is "just enough to make one wonder if there may not have been a few Pygmy groups who strayed over here long, long ago and were pushed off to the edges and the ends when the Australoid tide flowed in."
>
> If a scientific study is ever made in the Guayana highlands of Venezuela, some support may be given to the theory of an early Pygmy migration. Carl Sauer on a visit to Venezuela in 1946 saw photographs of a Pygmy-like people taken by a Venezuelan army officer who had paddled and packed the Guayana River for some years.[4]

There have been many unconfirmed reports of Pygmy tribes that survive in the South African bush. There have been many finds of Pygmy fossils in North, Central and South America, including the very spectacular discovery in western Venezuela. The pygmoid or part-Pygmy peoples of Africa are a few inches taller than the Pygmies, like the Yahgan and other pygmoid tribes of the Americas. Macgowan and Hester remark that the heads of the pygmoid Americans "instead of being round like those of the Pygmies, are recorded as of medium cephalic index." Statistics

---

[4] Kenneth Macgowan and Joseph A. Hester, Jr., *Early Man in the New World* (New York: Anchor Books, 1962), pp. 225–27.

reported by Schebesta prove that 66.3 percent of the Ituri Forest Pygmies are equipped with mesocephalic crania or heads of medium cephalic index. Round-headed or brachycephalic Pygmies account for 26.5 percent of the population. Only 7.2 percent are dolichocephalic or long-headed.[5] The predominantly long-headed Negro tribes very commonly call the Pygmies by the derogatory epithet "big-heads." The Pygmies sometimes reply with an apt proverb, "The bigger the calabash, the more there is inside." Since the Pygmy skull contrasts so strikingly with the Negro cranium, the Pygmies are often described as round-headed people.

African Pygmy and American Indian skin color typically ranges through shades of yellow-tan, bronze, copper and red-brown. Many Caucasoids of the Mediterranean stock or "brown race" have similar coloring. Some Pygmies and some American Indians have the gray or blue eyes of the European Nordics. Ituri Forest legends describe the ancient Pygmies as long-haired people with very white skin. The Pygmies' presently frizzly or kinky hair is usually described as a Negroid trait. Hair of the same texture is sometimes seen in remote Norwegian villages. Anthropologists explain that the kinky-haired Scandinavians are products of "spontaneous mutation." The Ituri Forest Pygmies alternately portray God or Efé as a tall, bearded patriarch and a Pygmy of similar appearance. He is Odin, the tall old gent or the elf. The many bearded white gods of the Americas include Quetzalcoatl, the benevolent civilizing hero who taught the Aztecs smithcraft in the lost paradise of legend.

The Pygmy fossils of the New World are described by most anthropologists as the remains of Negritos. The Negritos or Asiatic Pygmies are very dark-skinned people. The blue-black Andaman Islanders have been called "the blackest people in the world." They portray God or the first man as a tall bearded black patriarch. The pygmoid folk or aboriginal tribes of southern Asia are extremely swarthy. The anthropological theory that the Caucasoid stock arose in Africa locates the original home of the European Caucasians and the archaic Caucasoid or Australoid fossils of the Americas in the land of the comparatively pallid African Pygmies. The Pyg-

---

[5] P. Schebesta, *Les Pygmées du Congo Belge*, p. 62.

mies and the Australoids have both been credited with ice-age trips across the Bering Strait land bridge. *Early Man in the New World* comments on the chronology and difficulties of this journey:

> During the past 100,000 years, glacialists believe that there were three periods when the inland ice melted sufficiently to allow the southward passage of both animals and man. The first was more than 75,000 years ago in the Sangamon Interglacial period before the time when the last, or Wisconsin, glaciation had covered the plains of Canada . . . During the Wisconsin, a corridor probably opened about 50,000 years ago along the eastern foothills of the Rockies, and another, perhaps a little later, down the plateau between the northern Rockies and the Coast Range. The third opportunity for man to penetrate from the north came around 11,000 years ago, when the final retreat of the ice-sheets began in those same regions. Perhaps the land-bridge was still usable up to 10,000 years ago, but certainly later migrants had to cross Bering Strait by water or winter ice . . .
>
> The great glaciations presented early man with an opportunity and a difficulty; they threw a land-bridge across Bering Strait, but, for long periods of time, they also laid a barrier of ice and snow across his path to the south . . . about 65,000 years ago the barrier covered the whole depth of Canada. This would have meant a trip of some 2,000 miles across ice. For a time, as we have explained earlier, a corridor opened up for his passage. By 18,000 years ago, however, it had closed again. To be sure, there was a tongue of ice-free land that ran southward across part of Canada and shortened the journey over snow and ice to a thousand miles; but the invader would have had to be extremely lucky to hit the upper end of the open country. Far more important, none of the animals that he hunted, and that therefore led him on his southward journey, would have taken that thousand-mile trek across a frozen, foodless waste.[6]

According to *Men Out of Asia* the Eskimos or first Mongoloids reached the Americas around 500 B.C. They were equipped with boats such as the Arctic folk still use in their journeys among the Kurile and Aleutian Islands. They came long after the era of the Bering Strait land bridge, the North American icecap, and early

---

[6] Macgowan and Hester, *Early Man in the New World*, pp. 24 and 29.

man's miraculous march across the frozen, foodless waste. The Australoids accomplished this heroic journey around twenty-five thousand years ago, estimates *Men Out of Asia*. The Pygmies may have previously "strayed" across the Bering Strait bridge and crossed or skirted the barren fields of ice and snow that covered half of North America.

The Pygmies complain about the chilly nights in the Ituri Forest, which is located about two degrees north of the equator. These otherwise hardy little people are extremely sensitive to cold, raw weather. Bronchitis and pneumonia are the chief cause of death. Every surviving group of African and Asiatic Pygmies dwell in a tropical habitat. Pygmy-sized folk have been glimpsed in the Amazon basin, the Venezuelan bush and other warm American localities. Why would the Pygmies, of all people, migrate to Siberia and the North American ice fields? Why would any people move toward, rather than away from, death by freezing and starvation?

The early men of the Bering Strait theories are not real people. They are pawns that the scientists move like pieces on a global chessboard. The Life Nature Library publication *Early Man* estimates that 3,340,000 people inhabited the world of 25,000 B.C. The entire earth supposedly harbored fewer residents than the American state of Washington (according to the 1970 census, 3,352, 892). The Pygmies could have dwelled very comfortably in Zaïre (the Congo), which is about a dozen times larger than the state of Washington. There was ample room in Kenya and Tanzania for the fossil Caucasoids of Naivasha, Olduvai Gorge and Gamble's Cave. The Pygmy-Caucasoid population of equatorial Africa was even smaller in 50,000 B.C., when an ice-free corridor may have opened up to expedite the Pygmy-Caucasoid journey through western Canada. To reach the corridor, according to some theories, the first Americans paddled in small boats from Siberia to Alaska. Alternately, they might have marched across the Bering Strait land bridge or "freeway to the New World." The freeway led to five million square miles of ice that covered North America during the height of the glaciations. The population of the earth at that time was minuscule, according to conventional estimates. The Pygmies could not have been compelled by population pressure to migrate from the tropical regions of the Old World to the

Pleistocene Arctic. Their subsequent trek to the tropical countries of the New World is contingent on the prior migration toward the frozen, foodless waste.

The anthropological myth of early man's safari to the icecap is opposed by numerous American Indian legends of early man's impressive ocean voyages. In his *History of the Dakotas*, Major J. Lynd recorded Sioux accounts of "huge skiffs in which their ancestors floated for weeks, finally gaining dry land." The Iowa branch of the Sioux maintained that all of the tribes were formerly one and dwelled "on an island or at least across a large water towards the East or sunrise." The Algonquian ancestors "were always boating and navigating," according to the Delaware Indian traditions reported in C. S. Rafinesque's book *The American Nations*. The Delaware "Song of the Flood" mentions Tula and Tula-pin as places located in the first land, beyond the great ocean. Tulán and Tula-pan are names of the Maya homeland. "We are going to the East, there whence came our fathers," three Indian princes declare in the Quiche-Maya book of *Popul Vuh*. Then they went "to the other side of the sea to receive the paintings of Tulán, the paintings, as these were called, in which they wrote their histories."[7]

The Maya ancestors survived the cosmic cataclysms in the Cave of Tulán or the Seven Caves of Tulán-Zuiva. "Although it has not been possible to locate exactly the site of ancient Tulán of the caves or ravines, the common tradition preserved in Mexico and Guatemala gives all the people of this vast region an origin which, although purely legendary, marks the beginning of their historical evolution," translators Goetz and Morley commented in their edition of the *Popul Vuh*. The Mayan tribes named local places after Tulán or Tulapan, the legendary "cradle of the human race." The Delaware Indian legends of Tula or Tula-pin rather strikingly demonstrate that the ancestral paradise was not located in Mexico or Guatemala. The pan-Indian stories of the ancestors' sojourn in the mountain cave, cave-world or kingdom of the dead echo the legends of the African Pygmies who somehow reached the Amer-

---

[7] *Popul Vuh: The Sacred Book of the Ancient Quiche Maya*, English version by Delia Goetz and Sylvanus G. Morley, from the translation of Adrián Recinos (Norman: University of Oklahoma Press, 1969), pp. 206–9.

icas from their home in the Lost Indian Paradise Across the Great Water in the Land of the East. Numerous European legends locate the entrance to Hades or the cave-world at the foot of the Pygmies' Olympian mountain in the Lost Aryan Paradise at the Center of the Earth and the Source of the Nile.

Like the American Indians, the Europeans have many local versions of the Pygmies' resurrection cave in the mountain. Efé came back to his people by this route in the Pygmy legend of the hero's trip to Hades. European gods, heroes and kings of every era will someday return to their people in the same remarkable manner. Odin, Siegfried, Dietrich, Frederick Barbarossa, Charlemagne and Otto the Great will come back from caves in the mountains of Germany. Good King Wenceslaus and the Slavonic knight Stoymir will emerge from their caves in the mountains of Bohemia. Prince Marko will return from his cave in the mountains of Serbia. The Cid and the Moorish hero Alfatin will ride out of their caves in the mountains of Spain. King Arthur will be resurrected from his cave in the mountains of Wales.

Sir John Rhys commented in his study *Celtic Folklore* that "Arthur has taken the place of some ancient divinity" and that the British stories are connected with "the beliefs of the Latter-day Saints as to the coming of Christ to reign on earth." During the course of his fabulous career, King Arthur slew a giant cannibal ogre named Dinabuc. Efé or his miraculous son beheaded the giant swallowing ogre Lulu. King David beheaded the giant Philistine ogre Goliath. His divine descendant, the Messiah, is the future king of the Jews. The Pygmy god Bes conquered all the Typhonian beasts of the Egyptian Metternich Stele. His son Horus beheaded the man-monster Set and was thereupon hailed as the divine king of the earth. Efé's son is himself, the immortal hero of the past and the apocalyptic future. Arthur, the once and future king, is said to be buried in the abbey that Joseph of Arimathaea built in the English town of Glastonbury. Joseph of Arimathaea buried the Christian Messiah in a cave-tomb at the Mount of Olives.

The so-called European pagans recognized their own legends in the Biblical tales and identified their beloved ancestor-gods with the Judeo-Christian heroes. Even to discuss the Biblical traditions in connection with "pagans" or "savages" of any variety is heresy both against the modern churches and the university cliques who dominate the so-called science of anthropology. Robert Graves commented on the cautious tactics of Sir J. G. Frazer, the pioneering author of *The Golden Bough* and other studies in comparative religion: "Sir James Frazer was able to keep his beautiful rooms at Trinity College, Cambridge, until his death by carefully and methodically sailing all around his dangerous subject, as if charting the coastline of a forbidden island without actually committing himself to a declaration that it existed. What he was saying-not-saying was that Christian legend, dogma and ritual are the refinement of a great body of primitive and even barbarous beliefs, and that almost the only original element in Christianity is the personality of Jesus."[8]

If Jesus differed in any radical respect from the "pagan" concept of the divine hero, Christianity would never have been accepted on a global scale. The medieval romances combine "pagan" and "Christian" variants of the same age-old stories. The legends of Charlemagne describe Saint John, the patriarch Enoch, and the prophet Elijah as the "three holy inhabitants" of the earthly paradise on the summit of the Olympian mountain at the source of the Nile. Saint John, the beloved disciple of Jesus, is the traditional author of Revelation. This compilation of mystical traditions identifies the heads of the giant dragon with a group of volcanic mountains that match the Virunga volcanoes to the south of the Pygmies' lunar Olympus. Henry Morton Stanley, the nineteenth-century explorer who rediscovered the Mountains of the Moon, identified the patriarch Enoch with the Arabic prophet Idrisi, alias the Great Hermes or the Egyptian moon-god Thoth. The Old Testament prophet Elijah survived a cataclysmic windstorm, earthquake and conflagration in a cave of Horeb or Sinai, the Hebrew mountain of the law that was named after the Babylonian moon-god Sin.

Elijah and Enoch are associated in many apocryphal texts. "I was instructor to Eli and Enoch," Little Gwion/Merlin/Taliesin declared in the Welsh riddle-poem of Hanes Taliesin. "I was in Africa before the building of Rome, I am come now here to the remnants of Troia." The Celtic poet-god was "imprisoned" like Efé

---

[8] Robert Graves, *The White Goddess*, p. 242.

in the Troy-town maze, Spiral Castle, or resurrection cave in the mountain. Enoch has an Arabic tomb in the Mountain of the Moon. According to the legends of Charlemagne, to reach Merlin's tomb one travels to a towering mountain in the center of a forest. A cleft in the side of the mountain widens into a spacious cavern below. A door opens into a second cavern that resembles a subterranean temple. Another small door leads to the tomb. Little Gwion/Merlin/Taliesin dwelled in the original African Troy before he traveled to the British Isles. Remnants of the legendary Trojan nation migrated to Great Britain, built replica Troy-town mazes, and founded the city of New Troy or London.

Merlin, the great bard-magician, was credited with the invention of the magic mirror. Efé, the ancestral poet-harpist-singer-dancer, taught the art of "white magic" or "creative magic," as Schebesta called it. Malicious sorcery or "black magic" is sinful, criminal and absolutely forbidden by the Pygmy laws and commandments. The magic mirror may only be used to help the virtuous. The healing arts are a branch of the Pygmies' creative magic. Efé is Thoth, the good physician and magician, lawgiver and omniscient civilizing hero of Egyptian theology. King Gwydion, the great Welsh magician, bard and civilizing hero has been interpreted as an older version of King Arthur. He has also been likened to All-Father Odin, the great Germanic shaman or medicine man and omniscient god of poetry. Odin will someday return from a cave in the mountains of Germany. Odin and his elfin Elder Gods dwell in the Heaven-Mountain of the lost Germanic paradise that was called Asgard and identified with Troy.

King Arthur was represented as Merlin's protégé in the Arthurian romances. The once and future king will return from his cave in the Welsh mountains or from Fairyland, where he currently reigns. His sister Morgana the Fairy dwells in Avalon, the magic island of apples "far in the navel of the deep." Charlemagne's Danish knight Ogier was shipwrecked on Morgana's mountain-island, wandered about in her garden, met her on the bank of a stream, and stayed in Fairyland for more than a hundred years. Efé traveled through the mountain caves to the orchard-forest where he was kidnapped near the shores of the Stygian river by the hag-like ghost of that lovely lady Matu. Morgana's apple island in the navel of the deep is the Nether Garden of Tammuz-Adonis. Vergil's *Aeneid* locates a subterranean paradise called Elysium or "apple-land" in the abyss of Tartarus, the land where the funereal river flows through the Greco-Roman kingdom of the dead.

The souls of Japanese Buddhists embark on a traditional journey to Shide-no-Yama, the Mountain of Death. They grope their way over the mountain and cross the river by means of bridges. Mortal sinners are confronted on the opposite shore by a horrible old crone, the local version of Matu the Hag. Some critics have interpreted the Mayan legends of the mortuary cave-world as evidence that the Amerindian ancestors brought Japanese Buddhist legends to the New World via the Bering Strait. Buddhism originated in India during the sixth century B.C. The Indo-European people of India were close relatives of the Greeks and Romans. The Efé descendants of Homer's Pygmies dwell beside the main entrance to Tartarus at the foot of the original Olympus. African Pygmies reached the New World many millennia before the advent of Buddhism. Their Amerindian descendants tell stories derived from the legends of the Pygmies.

Efé or God the Father taught smithcraft and other useful arts to his ancient congregation. During his residence on earth, the divine Quetzalcoatl instructed the natives in the use of metal, agriculture, the science of government and so forth. He was the god-king of Tulán or the "God of the East." His people, the Tultecas or Toltecs, were the legendary founders of Mexican civilization. Efé will someday return like the Messiah. The Aztecs confidently awaited the return of Quetzalcoatl. Like the Great White Father form of Efé or God, he was represented as a tall white patriarch with a flowing beard. When Hernando Cortés and his Spanish conquistadors came to Mexico, the Aztecs thought that the benevolent Quetzalcoatl might have returned in the person of Cortés. The invaders subjugated and exploited the Mexican people. The fanatical friars made bonfires out of the Aztec and Mayan manuscripts. Some of the friars said that the devil had given the Indians a bogus version of Christianity. Others explained that one of Jesus' apostles, Saint Thomas, had made an evangelical journey to the Americas.

Efé, the godly hero, reunites Jesus with the Amerindian ancestors who came back from the resurrection cave in the mountain. The Sumerian stories of Gilgamesh-Tammuz' trip through the mountain caves date back to the fourth millennium B.C. The Bible stories of Elijah's sojourn in the cave of Mount Sinai or Jesus' resurrection from the cave in the Mount of Olives are neologistic versions of immensely older legends. Lord Raglan's study *The Hero* compares the miraculous careers of Elijah, King Arthur, Moses, Oedipus, Romulus, Hercules, Zeus, Dionysus, Apollo, Siegfried, Robin Hood, the Athenian king Theseus and many other legendary or pseudohistorical characters. Lord Raglan said about the Old World legends of the hero who returns from the cave in the mountain: "Two things are clear; the first is that these stories cannot have any basis in historical fact, and the second is that since the versions told in the various countries are almost word for word the same, they cannot possibly have arisen in the places where they are now told, but must be derived from a common source."

The American Indian versions of the story comprise the most important New World legend. In his study *The Native Races of America* historian H. H. Bancroft wrote: "It is now a recognized principle of philosophy that no religious belief, however crude, nor any historical tradition, however absurd, can be held by the majority of a people for any considerable time as true, without having had in the beginning some foundation in fact." What is the common source of the Old and New World resurrection legends?

"I was in Africa before the building of Rome," averred the Welsh god-poet. As Merlin, he built Stonehenge with stones that originated in Africa. As Arthur, the once and future king, he will someday return from the cave in the mountain or the land of the elves. As Efé, the original elf, he composed the African Pygmy legend of the resurrection cave in the mountain. A Roman author named Pliny the Elder (23–79 A.D.) declared in his *Historiae Naturalis* that the Pygmies embark every spring on a three-month expedition from the mountains to the seashore in order to wage war with the cranes. Efé traveled through the mountain caves to the shores of the funereal river and was then compelled to spend three months and part of a fourth month in the kingdom of the dead. In a chapter called "The Cave," the Koran maintains that a party of virtuous youths were divinely detained and slumbered for "three hundred years and nine days over" in the cave of a mountain or valley called El Rakim. Efé was given all kinds of treasures when he journeyed to the ghostly kingdom. Quetzalcoatl was heaped with gifts when he left Tulán, for uncertain reasons, and traveled to the fabled land of Tlapallan. He stayed for "almost thirty years" and eventually died in Tlapallan.

Everyone thought Efé was dead. Then the immortal hero or nation returned. It happened in the past and it may happen again in the future. Balder dies at the end of every Germanic world-age. He comes back from the cavernous kingdom of hell at the beginning of every world-age, after the cataclysms of Ragnarok have purged and purified the earth. Yima and his elite returned from the cave in the mountain after the cosmic cataclysms of Zoroastrian legend. The American Indian ancestors came out of the resurrection cave in the mountain after the great cataclysms that terminate the world-ages of Indian theology.

The legend originated as a super-historical saga of the Pleistocene disasters. In this form, it has a very real foundation in fact. The legend has withered with the passage of time. It has been corrupted by organized religions that have grappled for power, prestige and revenues. Efé's status as the divinely ordained ruler of the earth is the basis of kingship. The mystique of the divine king is responsible for the pseudohistorical tales that credit historical characters like Charlemagne with the attributes and exploits of the godly hero. The local versions of the Pygmy legends have been organized into national "histories" and equipped with conjectural chronologies. The Old Testament tales of the Israelites offer a particularly blatant example. These pseudohistorical chronicles cannot be resolved with the known history of dynastic Egypt. Sir Isaac Newton composed an opus called *The Chronology of Ancient Kingdoms Revised.* His subject matter consisted in large part of pseudohistory or rationalized legend.

Efé, the Pygmy, is a super-historical hero of inconceivably ancient vintage. In his book *The Twilight of Man,* anthropologist Earnest Hooton affirmed that the Pygmies "undoubtedly" preceded the Australoids in the continent of Australia. The first Australians were the Pygmies. The first Americans were the Pygmies, who preceded the Australoid or archaic Caucasoids of the New World. Pygmy fossils found in Switzerland, India and other Eurasian localities affirm that the Pygmies were the first Europeans and the first Asiatics. Nobody can compete with the Pygmies for the title of the first Africans.

The first Americans are supposed to have pursued herds of mammoths and other big-game animals across the frigid Bering Strait freeway from Siberia to Alaska. J. D. Dana's *Manual of Geology* describes the quick deaths of the now-extinct Siberian mammoths: "The encasing in ice of huge elephants, and the perfect preservation of the flesh, shows that the cold finally became suddenly extreme, as of a single winter's night, and knew no relenting afterward." In Alaska, sudden death came to mammoths, mastodons, horses, bisons and lions. "The most puzzling of all the fossils of extinct animals are those in the deep Alaska muck beds. Their numbers are appalling. They lie frozen in tangled masses, interspersed with uprooted trees. They seem to have been torn apart and dismembered and then consolidated under catastrophic conditions," Macgowan and Hester remark in their study *Early Man in the New World* (page 203).

Mammoth and hippopotamus remains have been found in the Thames Valley, Yorkshire, Somerset, Wales and other British localities. Two and a half million square miles of ice blanketed the British Isles and northwestern Europe during the height of the Pleistocene glaciations. The African Pygmies tell legends of the faraway frozen countries and the sudden coming of the killer cold. According to well-informed opinions, the Germanic legends of the frozen northern continent and the "Great Winters" of the Ragnarok cycles may have originated in the era of 30,000 B.C. Immanuel Velikovsky's book *Worlds in Collision* suggests that the mammoth herds may have been annihilated "in the days of the Exodus." He dated the Israelites' fabulous departure from Egypt to the era of 1500 B.C.[9]

The Israelites walked through the waters to the Sinai mountain of the moon-god Sin. Hyad walked on the waters of the Nile

---

[9] Immanuel Velikovsky, *Worlds in Collision* (New York: Dell Books, 1967), p. 332.

and went into the Central African Mountain of the Moon, according to Arabic legends. Jesus went into a mountain and walked on the waters. Moses ascended Mount Sinai after he walked through the waters. Elijah hid in a cave of Mount Sinai. Jesus was resurrected from a cave in the Mount of Olives. Efé returned to his people through the caverns of the lunar mountain. Efé was not wet by the waters of the deluge. Efé was the sole survivor of the Deluge. The Israelites escaped and the sinful "Egyptians" drowned in the troubled waters of Exodus. Noah and his virtuous family were saved from the great deluge of Genesis. Everyone else perished.

Efé resurrected the defunct people or Pygmies by slicing open the belly of the giant swallowing monster. Hercules slit the belly of a gigantic water snake, the Hydra, that had eight mortal heads and a ninth or immortal head. A nameless Masai warrior accomplished the resurrection when he carved up the nine-headed devil. Jehovah resurrected Jonah from the belly of the whale. According to Robert Graves' study *The Greek Myths* the Pelasgian Greeks were born from the great serpent Ophion. Marduk split the body of Tiamat, the Babylonian dragon of the deep, to accomplish the creation. "From China to Ireland rivers are dragons," comments Donald Mackenzie in his book *Myths of Babylonia and Assyria*. A divine power parted the waters for the Tswa Pygmy "Children of Djakoba," who dwell in Zaïre. In the first chapter of Genesis the Biblical deity achieved the creation by dividing the waters. To accomplish the Exodus, he supposedly parted the waters of the Red Sea for the Children of Jacob or Israel. The tribes "crossed the sea, the waters having parted when they passed," according to an equally fantastic Maya story of the ancestors' exodus from the land of Tulán.[10]

Efé emerged, unwet, after an angelic power cut a tree and released the waters of the Deluge. Andaman Pygmy legends maintain that the Deluge comes when God cuts the tree. Then the earth turns over. There are volcanic outbursts, cyclonic windstorms, torrential rains and all-engulfing inundations of the ocean. "On the

[10] Delia Goetz and Sylvanus G. Morley, *Popul Vuh: The Sacred Book of the Ancient Quiche Maya*, p. 183.

Andaman Islands the natives are afraid that a natural catastrophe will cause the earth to turn over," Velikovsky remarks. He comments that "the versions of the tribes and peoples of all five continents include the same elements, familiar to us from the Book of Exodus: lightning and 'the bursting of heaven,' which caused the earth to be turned 'upside down,' or 'heaven and earth to change places.'"[11] The Pygmies left their bones on all five continents during the geological era known as the Great Ice Age. According to some theories of the shifting poles and recurring glaciations of the Pleistocene, the earth periodically turns over or careens on its axis. Other scientists maintain that the crust of the earth slides over the mantle layer when a polar icecap attains critical mass, so to speak, and exerts sufficient pressure to precipitate a polar shift.

The Andaman Pygmy legend of the broken tree and turning earth describes past events that are predicted for the apocalyptic future. The Malayan and Philippine Pygmies tell similar stories of the cosmic disasters that occur when the earth "turns over." To prevent this denouement, they confess their sins to the deity and perform acts of atonement. Andamanese legends represent the tree as a titanic palm that stands in the center of a subterranean forest and supports the earth from beneath. The spirits of the dead dwell in the underworld kingdom and await "the day of the resurrection." This event will be accomplished when God breaks or cuts the tree and the ensuing cataclysms annihilate the present population of the earth. Anthropologist Schebesta compared the infernal kingdom of Andamanese legend to "the Greek Hades."[12] European legends locate the main entrance to Hades in the African Pygmies' labyrinthine Mountain of the Moon. Efé, the godly hero, was resurrected from the Ituri Forest kingdom of the dead in the past and may repeat this experience in the future.

The Semang, or Pygmies of the Malayan forests, gave Schebesta a very fascinating account of the cosmic mountain. The Batu Ribn, as they call it, is a towering limestone rock that stands on the shores of a river "at the center of the world." The rock is pierced

---

[11] Immanuel Velikovsky, *Worlds in Collision*, pp. 131–32.

[12] P. Schebesta, *Les Pygmées*, p. 166.

with great caves or grottos. In the past a titanic tree trunk reached toward the sky from the summit of the rock. The tree trunk is no longer visible. Underneath the Batu Ribn there is a vast abyss called Telaidn-Sapegn. The abyss contains a lake of blood that has accumulated from blood offerings made as acts of expiation. For this reason the Batu Ribn is called the Rock of Expiation or the Rock of Sin. The Semang identify the Batu Ribn with a local crag in the Malayan forest. For this reason Schebesta remarked that he "discovered" in the forest the Batu Ribn which is "surrounded by many legends and myths and known even to the Semang who have never approached it."[13]

Mount Olympus in Greece and Mount Zion in Jerusalem were both said to be situated like the Batu Ribn at the center of the world or earth. The Himalayas are associated with the Hindu Olympus at the center of the earth. The more archaic Germanic Olympus at the center of the earth was located in the southern continent of the white elves. The Efé Pygmies' Ituri Forest Olympus is the parent version of the Asiatic Pygmy Olympus that has a local surrogate at the center of the earth in the forested peninsula of Malacca.

The Mountain of the Moon and the Batu Ribn are reportedly riddled with tunnels or caverns. The ancestral heroes of the "resurrection cave in the mountain" story emerge from surrogate hills in Germany, Mexico, Wales, Bohemia, Spain and so forth. The prophet Elijah sojourned in the cavernous mountain of Sinai. Jebel Musa, the Arab-styled "Mountain of Moses" in the Sinai Peninsula, and Mount Zion at the Jerusalem center of the earth are local surrogates of the paradisaical mountain. The Batu Ribn stands on the shores of a river at the center of the earth. The Mountain of the Moon is the original Olympus at the source of the Nile and the center of the earth.

In the past, a titanic tree trunk reached toward the sky from the summit of Batu Ribn or the Rock of Expiation. An equally tall tree, cross or chariot pole stood in Dante's earthly paradise on the summit of a southern pinnacle called the Mountain of Purgatory. A lake of blood offerings made as acts of expiation have accumu-

---

[13] *Ibid.*, p. 156.

lated in the profound abyss underneath the Batu Ribn. Visitors to Xibalba, the Mayan kingdom of the dead, descend a flight of stairs and then cross several streams, a river of corruption and a river of blood.

The Malayan and Philippine Pygmies make blood offerings and confess their sins during thunderstorms. A sinner gashes his own legs, catches the blood in his cupped hands, and flings it up toward the sky. Self-flagellation and similar acts of expiation have been performed by the zealots of many comparatively modern religions, Christianity included. The Malay-Philippine Pygmy ritual is said to dissuade the angry deity from once again causing the earth to "turn over" and thereby destroy the world. The Andaman Pygmies, in very striking contrast, describe the global catastrophe in their legends and probably practice the least superstitious religion in the world. "The Andamans are not acquainted with any cult of God, no prayer, no sacrifice, no solicitation, no action of grace. Only the fear of God obliges them to obey his commandments," wrote Schebesta.[14]

I previously remarked that the commandments comprise the real "religion" of the Pygmies. The prayers of the Ituri Forest Pygmies are one of their more superstitious practices. "Toré! Stop the rain! Stop the wind! The big trees will crush your frightened children below! Toré, tell the wind to go home!" my Efé friend Mwenua prayed during a thunderstorm. Four or five men prayed aloud with Mwenua, the elder of Ebuya. "Toré must have heard all of them," I commented in my book Congo Kitabu, "since the storm stopped with dramatic abruptness a few minutes later (as storms very frequently do)."

The missionary-anthropologist Father Van Overberg was greatly impressed by the Philippine Pygmies' solemn "nights of prayer." They chant lengthy prayers in a liturgical language that they no longer understand. Father Van Overberg reported that they also pray every night, before they go to sleep, "Have pity on us. Give us life. Protect our children. Guard them from all sickness. To you, thanks." The missionary-anthropologist Father Trilles reproduced this prayer in his book The Soul of the African Pygmy

---

[14] Ibid., p. 163.

and remarked, "How many baptized children of God could learn a useful lesson from this humble child of the woods!"

The Pygmy version of "Now I lay me down to sleep" is indeed touching. A much more useful lesson can, however, be learned from the Pygmy legends of the Pleistocene disasters. Claude Levi-Strauss' study *The Savage Mind* avers that early historical man was "the heir of a long scientific tradition." The text comments on the Philippine Pygmies: "Another characteristic of Negrito life, a characteristic which strikingly demarcates them from the surrounding Christian lowlanders, is their inexhaustible knowledge of the plant and animal kingdoms. This lore includes not only a specific recognition of a phenomenal number of plants, birds, animals, and insects, but also includes a knowledge of the habits and behavior of each." Most of the Philippine Pygmies, the text points out, know the names of four hundred and fifty plants, seventy-five birds, twenty species of ants, forty-five types of mushrooms and fungi, and "most of the snakes, fish, insects, and animals. The botanical expertise of their herb doctors is truly astounding."

Anthropologist William Allan Reed described a rather astounding Philippine Pygmy pastime. The game of *sa'ro* is played with two little wooden cubes. Reed examined a pair of *sa'ro* cubes that had the symbols I, II, III, X, +, and # carved on their six faces. The cubes are thrown like dice. If the player fails to make a pair in five throws, he loses his bet. The Pygmies say that their ancestors invented this game. The taller tribes of Luzon agree that the Pygmies have "always" played the game of *sa'ro*. Reed likened the Pygmy gambler to "a Negro crap shooter." He made no other comparisons.[15]

Dice of an essentially modern type have been found in the tombs of ancient Egypt, Etruria, Greece, Rome and the Orient. In his *Germania* the Roman historian Tacitus reported that the "barbarians" or Germans were equally dedicated to gambling with dice. The Greek historian Herodotus ascribed the invention of dice to the residents of Lydia, in Asia Minor, from which the Etruscans made a theoretical migration. Etruscan dice from the tombs of

---

[15] William Allan Reed, *The Negritos of Zambales* (Manila: Dept. of Interior Ethnological Survey Publications, 1904), p. 48.

Italy were sometimes marked with the names of the numerals:
"The numerals 1–6 are *mach, ci, thu, huth, sa, zal;* they are written on the six sides of dice, so that it is impossible to say which
is 'one' and which is 'six.' Since other dice, which are marked
with dots, instead of words, shew an invariable arrangement, certain numbers being invariably opposite certain other numbers, we
have something of a clue, but not quite enough."[16]

The Pygmy dice are marked with symbols that resemble
Roman numerals and the related letters of the alphabet. The un-
familiar-looking symbols + and # were both used in ancient
European and Semitic versions of the alphabet. Scholar Robert
Graves commented on the classical legends concerning the origins
of dice and the alphabet: "Mercury was not only patron of dice-
players but prophesied from dice. He used five dice with four
markings on each, in honour of his Mother, precisely like those
given an Indian King at his coronation in honour of the Mother;
and if, as I suppose, he used them for alphabetic divination he
had his own alphabet of fifteen consonants and five vowels. The
game of hucklebones is still played in Great Britain with the
traditional set of five. In the case of six-sided dice, however, three
made a set in ancient times; these would provide the diviner with
eighteen letters of the alphabet, as in the thirteen-consonant Beth-
Luis-Nion [a Celtic version of the alphabet]."[17]

Thoth-Hermes-Mercury was credited in many stories with
the invention of dice and written symbols. Arabic legends describe
his ancient establishment in the Central African Mountain of the
Moon. In this neighborhood, the Ituri Forest Pygmies play a little
game called *bili.* Like many Pygmy customs, the game survives in
territories that have not been culturally annihilated by the Bantu-
Sudanese invasion. A heated arrowhead is used to mark symbols
on the opposing sides of two little wooden tablets that are shaped
like dominos. One of the tablets is sometimes marked with I and
IIII, the other with II and III. Some of the *bili* or gaming tablets
are inscribed with V and X. A player tries to predict which sym-

[16] George Dennis, *The Cities and Cemeteries of Etruria,* p. viii.

[17] Robert Graves, *The White Goddess,* pp. 331–32.

bols will be exposed when he tosses a pair of *bili* tablets into the air and they fall to the ground. If he guesses right, he wins a pebble. Each player is equipped with a pile of pebbles that are used like poker chips. When a player loses all of his pebbles, he is kaput.

Some of the surrounding Negro tribes recently acquired dice of the modern type from vendors of imported trade goods. The Pygmy game of *bili* has no parallel among the Negroes. It has not been borrowed from any outside source. Like the Philippine Pygmy dice, the tablets are marked with symbols that resemble Roman numerals and/or letters of the alphabet. The symbols are combined in standardized patterns on arrow shafts that the Pygmies use for sending messages. The Efé call this artifact *adani*, a message. One of the patterns represents a proposal of marriage. Another pattern warns that aggressive actions may lead to reprisals. Pygmy messengers frequently deliver this type of *adani* to the Bantu and Sudanese chieftains of their area. The Negroes "get the message," so to speak. The Pygmy *adani* system is, however, alien to the Negroes' traditional culture.

Pygmy men engrave special designs, their individual signatures, on the blunt ends of their arrows. Arguments as to who shot the antelope are thereby eliminated. The present-day Pygmies demonstrate in several ways that they are acquainted with the concept and uses of writing. The ancient Pygmies may have used an alphabetic system of writing whose vestiges are preserved in pseudoprimitive artifacts like the Ituri Forest tablets and Philippine Pygmy dice. During ancient times, dice were sometimes used for divining purposes. The related art of belomancy, as the Greeks called it, consisted of divining with arrows that were marked with names or symbols.

Pygmy women and children are said to "write" by making designs and pictures out of raffia string. Schebesta comments on this Ituri Forest art: "One must mention the women's string games, as numerous as they are complicated, which are played with the fingers and toes. Each figure, animal or object represented in the string game has its own particular name."[18] The photo-insert sec-

---

[18] P. Schebesta, *Les Pygmées du Congo Belge*, p. 190.

tion shows the "butterfly" and "honeycomb" designs. Two people sometimes collaborate to form figures with a piece of string, as in the game of cat's cradle. This Pygmy pastime is unparalleled, as usual, among the surrounding Negro tribes. The Philippine and Andaman Island Pygmies instead make string figures on their remote archipelagos. The globally distributed peoples who have versions of this Pygmy art or game include the Eskimos, American Indians, Polynesians, Chinese, Japanese, Europeans and Australian aborigines.

A thousand miles from the Ituri Forest, the pygmoid Twa make string figures in the Kasai River region of Zaïre. Back in 1904, when almost nothing was known of Pygmy culture, a band of Twa were exhibited as "cannibal Pygmies" at the St. Louis Exposition. There, in the American state of Missouri, Djakoba's gentle-mannered children taught an astonished American lady how to make a traditional string design that ethnologists call by the name of "Pygmy Diamonds." Caroline Jayne reported in her book *String Figures,* which was originally published in 1906:

> Among the African Batwa Pygmies from the Congo Kasai Valley, at the St. Louis Exposition, was a bright little man, "Ottobang," who taught me this figure . . . So far as I know, this figure is the first African string game that has ever been described. The nature of the Batwas and their isolation in the heart of Africa would not lead us to expect to find among them a relatively complicated figure, and make any resemblances which this figure may bear to other figures doubly interesting. We see at a glance that it has much in common with the "Caroline Islands Diamonds" and the "Turtle." The finished pattern is identical with the pattern formed after the *Sixth* movement of the Eskimo "Mouth"; hence you can go on and finish the "Mouth" from the finished pattern of the "Pygmy Diamonds." This is the only case, in my experience, where the finished pattern of one figure occurs as a stage in the development of another entirely different figure.[19]

A troop of Philippine Pygmies or Negritos attended the St. Louis Exposition. Their string figure repertoire, and that of the pygmoid Twa, includes an Ituri Forest design that the Efé call

---

[19] Caroline Furness Jayne, *String Figures and How to Make Them: A Study of Cat's-Cradle in Many Lands* (New York: Dover, 1962), pp. 276–82.

musésé, the little mouse. Caroline Jayne commented on "The Mouse" in her book *String Figures:*

> This figure is probably the most widely distributed of all the string figures. I have seen it done by the African Batwa Pygmies, the Philippine Negritos and Linao Moros, and American Indians of the Chippewa, Osage, Navaho and Apache tribes. Dr. Haddon gives it as an Omaha string trick and says it is known to the Japanese. I have been told that it is well known in Ireland. Dr. Haddon also met with it in Torres Straits; in Murray Island it is known as Kobe Mokeis = the Mouse; quite recently it has been reported from the Wajiji in British East Africa, and from the Alaskan Eskimos.[20]

The Jiji probably acquired their string figures from the pygmoid Twa folk of the Lake Tanganyika region. The Pygmies are the only people on the African continent who traditionally make cat's-cradle pictures and designs. Maori string figures are known in far-away New Zealand as "the game of Maui." Many pictures illustrate the adventures of Maui, the great ancestral hero of the Polynesian people. "Maui, the Adam of New Zealand, left this amusement to them as an inheritance," reported a nineteenth-century traveler.[21] Maui's career came to an apparently tragic end when he descended to Po, the subterranean land of the dead. There the traditional inventor of Polynesian string pictures was murdered by his suspected ancestress, Hina-Nui-Te-Po, the goddess of death.

People thought Efé was dead when Matu the Hag detained the hero in the kingdom of the dead. Efé traveled to her infernal abode through a hole in the foot of Matu the Mountain Mother and returned by the same route. In the myth of the savior, Efé was "born" by unorthodox means as the son of Matu. Maui died when he went between the legs and entered the gigantic body of his ancestress, the goddess of death. Maui's mother gave birth, before her time, to her miraculous son. Maui is a Polynesian version of Efé, the Pygmy inventor of string pictures (and everything else).

---

[20] *Ibid.,* pp. 340–41.

[21] Ernest Dieffenbach, *Travels in New Zealand* (London, 1843), Vol. 2, p. 32.

In Australia, where the Pygmies preceded the Australoids, some of the present-day tribes define their cat's-cradle figures as letters, words or writing. The Ituri Forest methods of string-writing include braided, knotted and tasseled cords that resemble macramé. The photo-insert section shows the macramé writing of a young lady named Senia, aged seventeen, and the rudimentary efforts of a nine-year-old girl. The Pygmy men, who never make cat's-cradle pictures, sometimes turn out very impressive-looking pieces of macramé writing. These cords are said to represent sentences or messages. I have yet to find a Pygmy who can explain how the system works. Like the arrow messages, the macramé writing probably represents a cultural fossil that has been inherited from the ancient Pygmy folk of remote prehistoric times.

In the Americas, where numerous Pygmy remains have been discovered, Inca writing and arithmetic were accomplished with the braided, twisted and fringed cords known as quipus. "The art of interpretation of *quipus* is lost, so that it is impossible to ascertain how far the knots were merely a mnemonic for the messenger, and how far they were intelligible without explanation to a stranger," comments the *Britannica*. "Recent examination of a series of complete *quipus* suggests knowledge of an astronomical nature, similar to that of the Mayas, and the use of these devices for magical purposes. Similar mnemonics were used among the Chinese, the Tibetans and other peoples of the Old World."[22]

Further investigations made during the past couple of years have led to the present theory that the quipus represent an ancient writing system. "The Eskimo evidence proves that cat's-cradle may, in part, have a magical significance and suggests a line for future inquiry, for we know that all over the world strings, cords, and knots enter largely into magical practices," Dr. Alfred C. Haddon wrote in his ethnological introduction to Caroline Jayne's treatise on string figures. The Pygmies' dice symbols, arrow messages, quipus-like cords and string figures suggest the additional possibility that a literate civilization was anciently demolished by the cosmic cataclysms of legend.

The Inca quipus have been associated with "knowledge of an

---

[22] "Quipus," *Encyclopaedia Britannica*, 14th ed., Vol. 18, p. 856.

astronomical nature." Father Trilles remarked that the Pygmies of Gabon and Cameroon possess considerable knowledge of the constellations. A sample of Ituri Forest astronomy: the Efé Pygmies traditionally define the planet Saturn as "the star of nine moons." In 1899, the American astronomer W. H. Pickering discovered Phoebe, the ninth moon of Saturn. The English satirist Jonathan Swift (1667–1745) described the two moons of Mars before they were discovered by astronomers. Some critics say that Swift may have had access to "ancient documents." If the ancients were acquainted with the Martian satellites, they must have used telescopes and other astronomical instruments. A Greek lady named Athena taught astronomy, mathematics, navigation and other advanced sciences during the paradisaical epoch that preceded Prometheus' disastrous theft of the fire.

The African-born mother of Athens was credited with the invention of the flute and trumpet. Hermes, the Greek Thoth, invented Apollo's seven-stringed lyre. The strings of the lyre were identified with the vowels of the Greek alphabet. Apollo and the Pygmy harpist Bes were the Greek and Egyptian gods of the musical arts. The Ituri Forest Pygmies' musical instruments include flutes of several types, large and small trumpets, the seven-stringed *alogu* or board zither, the five-stringed *ndomu* or bow harp, and the *rumu* or musical bow. The stringed instruments and the art of string-writing are dependent on the vegetable-fiber string that the Pygmies draw from raffia palms and other plants. The women weave and wear string-belts of incredible complexity. Athena invented spinning and weaving, according to the Greeks. Our Mother, the Mayan moon-goddess, invented the corresponding American Indian arts.

String is an essential ingredient of the bow harp, the musical bow and the intimately related hunting bow of the Ituri Forest Pygmies. The Pygmies of Gabon and Cameroon are equipped with hunting bows and musical bows. The Andaman Pygmies use their bows for shooting game and fish. The traditional Malayan Pygmy hunting bow is five and a half feet long. It is taller than a Pygmy, and in dense bush it is much more difficult to handle than the two and a half to three foot Efé hunting bow. The Philippine Pygmy archers shoot more than fifty types of arrows with their hunting bows. In his study *The American Aborigines* anthropologist Clark Wissler commented on the hunting bow: "This implement is widely distributed throughout the world and differs in form and efficiency from region to region; yet it is generally believed that all its forms are based upon a single invention which originated in one tribe."

The fossil Pygmies of the New World resolve the endlessly debated anthropological mystery of how the bow reached the Americas. The bow or "first civilized invention" has been attributed in some theories to comparatively recent and geographically limited people like the Babylonians and Egyptians. Numerous Egyptian pictures show Horus gods with "dwarf's legs" and hunting bows. Father Wilhelm Schmidt suggested that the Pygmies may have invented the hunting bow. "Since this is a complicated weapon, one hesitates to attribute its invention to a people so primitive," Schebesta commented on the Pygmies' hunting bows. The present-day material culture of the Pygmies is simple rather than primitive. Young boys use the musical bow to play "a sort of Twenty Questions," as Trilles reported. The questioners have to interpret answers that are given in the form of melodies. This, believe it or not, is a game played by Pygmy children.[23]

Many anthropologists maintain that the fire bow was the technological ancestor of the hunting bow. Efé religion bans the use of artificial fire-making apparatus. The Andaman Pygmies possessed no such apparatus when the British arrived at the turn of the eighteenth century, but the Andamanese cultural equipment included hunting bows, harpoons, canoes and pottery. The Efé and the Andamanese have repeatedly been described as people who are so stupid that they cannot make a fire by rubbing two sticks together. Charles Darwin libeled "the low and degraded inhabitants of the Andaman Islands" in his book *The Descent of Man*. The Ituri Forest Pygmies have been compared to "lower organisms."

The Pygmies make and use artifacts that are far more complicated than friction firesticks. This is a fact that their stupid or bigoted critics somehow fail to realize. They preserve "perpetual

[23] Henri Trilles, *Les Pygmées de la Forêt Equatoriale* (Paris: Librairie Bloud & Gay, 1932), p. 392.

fire" for religious reasons. Egyptians, Norsemen, American Indians, Greeks, Hindus, Persians, Hebrews, Christians and many other peoples have zealously maintained perpetual altar fires, lamps and candles. The Pygmies traditionally carry burning brands from one campsite to the next. The Greeks of early historic times brought fire to each new colony in identical style. The Pygmies supposedly marched through the blizzards of ice-age Siberia, Alaska and Canada to accomplish their "Pygmoid visitation" to the Americas. This very chilly journey has been attributed to people who possessed no means of making artificial fire.

A tall European fossil called Cro-Magnon man lacked the bow and arrow. He made spearheads, harpoon heads, axes, scrapers, and other implements out of stone or bone. If he had used the bow, he would have left arrowheads made from the same materials. His remains date back to at least 35,000 B.C. He became extinct around 10,000 B.C. He is generally regarded as the prototype of modern European man. He frequently exceeded six feet in stature and was taller, on the average, than the modern European. His supposed descendants of northwestern Europe consistently identified their ancestors with the dwarfs, elves or fairies.

"The 'little people' of the popular fairy lore of Christian Ireland are reductions of the earlier pagan divinities, the Tuatha De Danaan," Scholar Joseph Campbell commented on the diminutive ancestor-gods of Great Britain.[24] The Tuatha De Danaan, or people of Dana, had a hero named Lleu. He was a wonderful archer, harpist, smith, carpenter, historian and magician. His father, King Gwydion, was the paternal bard, magician and omniscient civilizing hero of the Celts. Gwydion's sister-wife Arianrhod was the mother of Lleu and the lady of Spiral Castle or the Troy-town maze.

Gwydion and Lleu are Efé, the elfin father-son who invented all of the arts and composed all of the legends or super-history of the world. The sister, wife, mother and/or daughter of Efé is Matu, the Mother of God. She detained Efé when he traveled through the original Troy-town maze in the Mountain of the Moon. Arianrhod incarcerated the Welsh god-poet in the Spiral Castle. "I was in

---

[24] Joseph Campbell, *The Hero with a Thousand Faces* (New York: Meridian Books, 1956), p. 330.

Africa before the building of Rome, I am come now here to the remnants of Troia," the great harpist Little Gwion/Merlin/Taliesin proclaimed in the poem of Hanes Taliesin.

The Greeks' pseudohistorical "Tale of Troy" was composed by a pseudohistorical author, according to Lord Raglan's study *The Hero:* "Homer, so Professor J. A. K. Thomson tells us, was the title given to the victor in the conquest of minstrelsy held at the festival of Apollo at Delos. He was the eponymous ancestor of the hymn-singers and sacred dancers, and was originally identified with the Delian Apollo. 'The hymn,' Professor Thomson continues, 'has given birth to the heroic epos. For these "men and women" are the old local Daimones—Achilles, Helen, and the rest. Their legends have been combined to form one great legend recited at the Delian festival in honour of Apollo the Father god of all the Ionians . . . The hymn gradually added to itself more and more of the inherited or borrowed legends of the Ionian race until it grew into the proportions of all "Homer." And as Homer was the traditional author of the original hymn, so he remained the traditional author of all the rest.' "[25]

The Egyptian god of the musical arts was the father-god of the Metternich Stele. He was Bes, the Pygmy harpist and Dancer of God. He and his son Horus, the Egyptian Apollo, are forms of the same god. Efé, the Pygmy, is the original Bes, Horus, Apollo and Homer. He is the eponymous ancestor of the Efé musicians, the first Dancer of God, and the traditional author of the Pygmy legends. The *Iliad* and the *Odyssey* are pseudohistorical versions of these stories.

Efé the Great Hunter of Heaven is a celestial form of the divine ancestor. God the Great Hunter of Heaven carries the Western Pygmy rainbow in his hand. The rainbow is the Irish bow of Lleu. His harp is a symbol of the Irish nation. Lleu, Gwydion, King Arthur, Odin and the other ancestral heroes of northwestern Europe were the little people, elves, dwarfs or fairies. Egyptian traditions confirm the ancestral character of the Pygmies, their hunting bows and their related stringed instruments.

The tall Cro-Magnon fossils have been "variously credited with

[25] Lord Raglan, *The Hero* (London: Watts and Company, 1949), p. 167.

producing the modern European man, the Eskimo, and even the Indian of America," Macgowan and Hester remarked in their study *Early Man in the New World*. The Europeans, Eskimos, and American Indians traditionally use the hunting bow. Cro-Magnon man did not. He cannot conceivably be interpreted as the father of the American Pygmy fossils who accomplished a theoretical safari from Siberia to North America. According to an equally dubious theory a Cro-Magnon type called Magdalenian Man walked across the icy wilderness from Europe to North America: "M. R. Harrington has mentioned the possibility that Magdalenian man of Glacial or Postglacial Europe may have crossed from Europe to Canada by way of Iceland and Greenland and various ice- and land-bridges to father the Eskimo."[26]

The Alaskan Eskimos tell many legends of a great hunter, the Man in the Moon or Spirit of the Moon. He observes human behavior and directs the powers of nature. He controls the supply of game, "the whale, the white whale, walrus, caribou, every animal in the world." The souls of virtuous Eskimos ascend to the paradisaical Land of the Moon. They live a life of "hunting and endless sport" while they wait for the Spirit of the Moon to effect their earthly reincarnation. When hunting is bad, the Alaskan shaman or priestly magician embarks on a spiritual ascent to the moon. The first shaman is said to have made this journey. That masterful hunter, the Man in the Moon, is said to be a personage of human origin.

Efé is the Great Hunter of Heaven and ever-vigilant Angel of the Moon who directs or controls all the powers of nature. Efé, the inventor of "white magic," made the ascent to the heavens long before Thoth, Osiris, Elijah, Jesus and other religious heroes who ascended to the sky. The Sua Pygmies of the southern Ituri say that the life force or immortal constituent of every creature returns to Songé, the good spirit, god or angel of the moon. Songé has "game preserves" in the forests of the moon. Virtuous Eskimos go to the happy hunting grounds in the Land of the Moon. There the Alaskan Spirit of the Moon has an enormous pool for the sea mam-

[26] Kenneth Macgowan and Joseph A. Hester, Jr., *Early Man in the New World*, p. 25.

mals and pigeonholes for filing away the souls of terrestrial animals. The reincarnation of the lunar Eskimos is accomplished when Songé, the lunar angel of the southern Ituri, makes new earthly creatures from his stock of life force.

Aré'bati, as the Efé sometimes call the lunar angel, created the animals or "goats of God" by sending a goat down to earth. The goat gave birth to the animals and returned to Are'bati. The Tutsi or "Watusi" people who dwell in the Rwanda and Burundi Land of the Moon say that the first cattle and the divine ancestors walked or fell to earth through a hole in the floor of the sky. Efé descended by means of a long, long liana through the Pygmies' hole in the vault of heaven. The Masai say in their legend called "Beginner of the Earth" that the first cattle walked down to earth on a long strip of cowhide. Before this event, the first man or Dorobo obtained a cow by unexplained means. God took the cattle away from the Dorobo or part-Pygmy people of East Africa and gave them to the Masai by sending the cattle down the cowhide strip that connected heaven and earth. The connection was broken when the diminutive first man shot the strip with his bow and arrow. The Pygmy thus wields the Pygmy hunting bow as the first man in the Masai legend "Beginner of the Earth."

Efé, the original Pygmy archer, uses three spears in the Ituri Forest stories of his combats with giant monsters. As the miraculous son of Matu, the Mother of God, he was "born" with a spear in his hand. Four spears were the symbol of Mexitli, the miraculous son of a devout widow named Coatlicue. He was born with a spear in his right hand, a shield in his left, and a tall feathered headdress. The ancestors of the Aztecs were led to present-day "Mexico" by Mexitli or Huitzilopochtli, the head of the Aztec pantheon. Efé the miraculous son was installed as the chief after his spear fight with the giant swallowing monster. Horus, the miraculous son of the Egyptian mother-goddess, became the divinely ordained god of the earth after he speared Set-Typhon, a character whom the Greeks defined as "the largest monster ever born." Horus' Pygmy father Bes was sometimes pictured as a warrior, with a short sword in his right hand and a shield in his left. Bes wears a tall feathered headdress in many Egyptian pictures of the heroic Pygmy musician. Mexitli was equipped with similar accouterments. His spears were symbols of the "divine war spear." He was the god of war, like many conquerors of the Pygmies' giant monsters.

Historian W. H. Prescott commented on the Aztec story of Mexitli-Huitzilopochtli and his mother: "A similar notion in respect to the incarnation of their principal deity existed among the people of India beyond the Ganges, of China, and of Thibet. 'Budh,' says Milman in his learned and luminous work on the History of Christianity, 'according to a tradition known in the West, was born of a virgin. So were the Fohi of China, and the Schaka of Thibet, no doubt the same, whether a mythic or a real personage. The Jesuits in China, says Barrow, were appalled at finding in the mythology of that country the counterpart of the Virgo Deipara.' "[27]

Christian zealots represent the Virgo Deipara or "God-bearing Virgin" as a real woman of historic vintage. Mexitli's mother was a chaste widow. Matu, the Mother of God, was widowed by the giant swallowing monster that destroyed mankind and demolished the cities of the ancient world. A lady named Leto gave birth to the heroic Greek musician Apollo on an island mountain that was raised above the waters of the Deluge. The Mountain Mother is a form of Matu. Her musically gifted son, husband, brother and/or father is Efé, the Pygmy. The Mountain of the Moon is also represented as the "great throne of God." A lady named Isis was the Egyptian throne or seat of her son, husband, brother and/or father, Osiris. The senior and junior forms of Isis' consort are represented as Bes and Horus on the Metternich Stele. Sir E. A. Wallis Budge tactfully refrains from mentioning Bes's earthly kinsmen, the Pygmies, when he discusses the Metternich texts: "Several of the incidents of the wanderings of the Virgin with the Child in Egypt as recorded in the Apocryphal Gospels reflect scenes in the life of Isis as described in the texts found on the Metternich Stele, and many of the attributes of Isis, the God-mother, the mother of Horus, and of Neith, the goddess of Sais, are identical with those of Mary the Mother of Christ."[28]

Isis and the goddess Neith or Net of Sais were both identified

---

[27] W. H. Prescott, *The Conquest of Mexico* (London: J. M. Dent, 1948), Vol. 1, p. 42.

[28] Sir E. A. Wallis Budge, *The Gods of the Egyptians*, Vol. 2, p. 220.

by the Greeks with Athena, the Virgin Mother of Heaven. The priests of Sais are supposed to have told Solon of Athens the story of the Athenian war with Atlantis, the earthquakes and the Deluge. Revelation describes the divine mother's encounter with the geophysical dragon that tried to swallow her child. Matu, the Mother of God, plays a very important role in the Ituri Forest legends of doomsday. Matu has an Asiatic Pygmy counterpart, Mité, the Andamanese Mother of God the Son. The Latin and Greek mothers are *mater* and *mitera*. Philologists maintain that the Andamanese dialects are not related to any other form of human speech. The Andamanese, Malayan and Philippine contingents of dark-skinned Asiatic Pygmies are unquestionably related to the paler African Pygmies. These peoples have been separated for an incalculable period of time. Their echoing doomsday legends are concerned with the great disasters of the Pleistocene. The miraculous "birth" or resurrection from the superhuman mother is part of this story.

Matu as the ghostly hag has a house in the Pygmy kingdom of the dead. To this abode goes the ghostly constituent of the human personality. The ghosts are alternately represented as shadow people or shaggy dwarfs about half the size of Pygmies. Efé traveled to their residence through a cave or hole. Then Matu the Hag and her spouse, the ghost of Doru, incarcerated the hero. Efé brought meat to his people when he returned from the land where the Stygian River flows through the African Pygmies' kingdom of the dead. The legends of Greenland and Canada maintain that the first Eskimo shaman traveled to the subterranean purgatory where a hideous woman named Sedna has a stone dwelling at the bottom of the sea:

> It was a period of hunger that brought about the emergence of the first angekkok. To save starving humanity, a man decided to go to the mother of sea-creatures, so he "dived" through the ground and made his way to the "abode of sustenance" and brought back game to feed mankind. Now, whenever famine threatens, angekkoks (Eskimo conjurers) follow the same course. There are many obstacles. On the sea-bed are moving boulders. The more famous the shaman, the easier his path. At the goddess's gate a Cerberus— sometimes her dog-husband—mounts guard, then farther on Sedna's father tries to get to grips with the intruder . . . Sedna's

kingdom, which goes by the name of Adlivun, is also used as a sojourn, at least of a temporary kind, for the souls of the dead, a sort of purgatory where the deceased stop to be purified before they go on to a more pleasant spot, the Land of the Moon, for instance, to which only a few privileged people and those who die a violent death accede immediately.[29]

The Eskimo dog-monster is the Pygmies' dog-dragon or the snaky-headed hound, Cerberus, that dwells on the shores of the River Styx in the Greek kingdom of Hades. Sedna is Matu the Hag. Matu and Medusa, the lunar Gorgon, greeted Efé and Hercules on the shores of the river. Efé slaughtered the goats and brought back the meat. In the Greek stories of his exploits Hercules slaughtered one of Hades' cattle, brought cattle out of the cave-world, and hauled Cerberus up to the surface. The Eskimo shaman obtains the game by capturing Sedna with a hook and bringing her up to the surface. Efé procured a long liana with the intention of hauling the giant black hog out of the caverns. The beast meanwhile returned to the infernal kingdom. Even Efé, the elfin smith, could not lift or carry that beast.

Thor, the thundering smith-god, tried in vain to lift a big gray cat that was really the Midgard Serpent in disguise. Thorinn, Throrinn and Thror are mentioned in the *Prose Edda* as names of elves or dwarfs. Thror was a title of Thor's son or father, Odin. Thor encountered the cat form of the beast when he traveled from Asgard-Troy to a place called Utgard. His chariot was drawn by two goats. He stopped at a farmer's house where he slaughtered the goats, skinned them and cooked them in a cauldron. He shared the supper with the farmer, the farmer's wife and their children. Then he brought the goats back to life.

Game animals are the Pygmies' "goats of God." Efé slaughtered goats in the kingdom of the dead. The ghosts carried the meat and other treasures through the caverns in the Mountain of the Moon. Efé, the Pygmy, still dwells at the foot of the lunar mountain. Matu the Mountain Mother gave birth to Efé when he cut a hole or tunnel through the big toe of her right foot. A Masai warrior and all of the animals were resurrected through the stump

---

[29] *Larousse World Mythology*, p. 443.

of the devil's big toe. People and animals emerged when the Taveta savior cut off the demon's thumb and fingers. The sea mammals were produced when Sedna's father cut off her fingers. Then Sedna went to the Eskimo purgatory where she reigns like Hel, that sinister-looking but very just lady who presides in the Germanic land of hell.

Sedna has a pool for sea mammals in her purgatorial abode. The Man in the Moon has an identical pool in the celestial paradise. The Eskimo shamans of Greenland and Canada obtain game by a mystical repetition of Efé's trip to the infernal kingdom. The Eskimo shamans of Alaska embark on Efé's ascent to the moon. The medieval legends of Charlemagne describe a trip to the lunar paradise. Saint John drives the chariot in which he was "accustomed to make excursions among the stars, the same which was employed long ago to convey Elijah up from earth." According to the theories expressed in Barry H. Downing's book *The Bible and Flying Saucers* Elijah and Jesus ascended to heaven in "some kind of UFO." Saint John took Charlemagne's English knight Astolpho to "the great continent of the Moon."

Astolpho was thrilled by the lunar rivers, lakes, plains, hills, valleys, cities and castles. He saw vast forests where "the nymphs were following the chase." Artemis or Diana was the Greco-Roman goddess of hunting and the moon. Efé, the Great Hunter of Heaven and Angel of the Moon, is a much more suitable patron saint for manly hunters who bring home the bacon to their wives and children. Efé is that great Eskimo hunting expert, the Man in the Moon. Efé receives the South African prayers that the Bushman hunters address to the moon. Efé is a much more ancient character than Jacob or Israel, the Hebrew patriarch who made the Talmudic trip to the moon. Efé the godly hero or nation is the ancestor of Israel, the hero or nation whose Biblical tales were derived like the Homeric poems from the ageless Pygmy legends. Efé is the omniscient bard who composed the Pygmy legends and gave the Pygmy laws to mankind. He is Everyman's Homer, Thoth and Moses. His people dwell in Moses' land of Eden at the source of Gihon-Nile.

Saint John and Charlemagne's fabulous knight Astolpho traveled to the moon from the earthly paradise on the summit of the Pygmies' lunar mountain at the source of the Nile. Astolpho visited the cavernous mouth of hell at the foot of the mountain. The Egyptians' wonderful "little men from the land of trees and spirits at the foot of the mountains of the moon" tell legends that have no parallel among the modern Negro invaders of the Ituri. Globally distributed stories instead echo the ancestral legends of the Pygmies.

Mweiya, the Pygmy Moses of East Africa, descended from heaven to the summit of a mountain. The Masai presently identify this pinnacle with Mount Ngong near Nairobi. "Do not move from this spot," Mweiya told his children. For this reason, the members of Mweiya's elite Aesir clan "do not go far from their mountain." In the story of the hero's trip to Hades Efé traveled through the caverns of the original Pygmy mountain. The Lumbwa tribes of the Masai nation journey through the caverns of Donyo Sabuk, the Fat Mountain, in "The Story of the Cave of the Athi River and the Lumbwa Masai":

> There is a cave near the River Athi, which river is called by the Swahili the Hippopotamus River. It is believed that when Naiteru-kop brought the Masai in olden days from the district round about Kenya, and they arrived at Donyo Sabuk, some of them saw this cave and entered it. They journeyed for ten days and eventually reached a salt lake, where they came out of the earth again and settled.
>
> These people are the Lumbwa, who in appearance are like the Masai, but they till the earth.[30]

The Masai tribes were led by Naiteru-kop, the Beginner of the Earth. He is interchangeable with Eng-Ai or God in many Masai stories: in Masai accounts of the creation either God or Naiteru-kop descends from heaven. According to some narrators God put the god Naiteru-kop on the summit of Mount Kenya. God and his son Efé the Angel travel between heaven and earth in the legends of the Ituri Forest Pygmies. The terrestrial headquarters of the deity are associated in numerous Pygmy stories with the Mountain of the Moon. Little Mweiya, the first Masai medicine man, descended from heaven to the summit of Mount Ngong. Eng-Ai or God found the first man or Dorobo living on the Masai earth when

---

[30] A. C. Hollis, *The Masai*, p. 280.

he came down "to prepare the world." Efé returned to his people after his legendary visit to the celestial paradise of his father.

God or Naiteru-kop took the Pygmies' cattle and gave them to the Masai via the cowhide strip that a Pygmy archer shot with his hunting bow. Masai narrators frequently tack a rather outrageous ending onto this story: "Nowadays, if cattle are seen in the possession of Bantu tribes, it is presumed that they have been stolen or found, and the Masai say: 'These are our animals, let us go and take them, for God in olden days gave us all the cattle upon the earth.'" The Masai use these garbled legends as their moral justification for rustling cattle from the Kikuyu and other Negro tribes whom they periodically massacred before the British came to Kenya. The Masai stories of the heavenly cattle are responsible in large part for the Masai belief that cattle-raising is the only good and godly way of life. The Masai fought many battles with their own Lumbwa tribes because the Lumbwa till the soil instead of raising cattle. The underworld cattle and ghostly characters who reside in the Pygmies' cave-world are commemorated in the East African story of the invisible Masai people and cattle who are supposed to dwell in a cave of Donyo Erok or Black Mountain.

"If you stand near its mouth, you hear the voices of people calling one another and also the lowing of cattle," say the Masai. Women take offerings of milk, honey and butter to the cave. The inhabitants of the cave are said to come during the night and eat these delicious offerings. The great Masai medicine man Mbatian was buried near the cave of Black Mountain. "Do not move from your country for I am about to die, and I will send you cattle from heaven," Mbatian told his people during the terrible cattle plague of the 1890's. Like every Masai medicine man, Mbatian was a direct lineal descendant of Mweiya, the Pygmy Moses who descended from heaven to the summit of Mount Ngong.

Sinai, the cavernous lunar mountain of Moses, was the refuge in which the prophet Elijah hid during a series of cataclysms. "Rock of ages, cleft for me, let me hide myself in thee," declares a modern Christian hymn. "Give ear, O ye heavens, and I will speak; and hear, O earth, the words of my mouth . . . Because I will publish the name of the Lord: ascribe ye greatness unto our God. He is the Rock . . . Of the Rock that begat thee thou art unmindful, and hast forgotten God that formed thee," Moses announced in the thirty-second chapter of Deuteronomy. "The God of my rock; in him will I trust: he is my shield, and the horn of my salvation, my high tower, and my refuge, my saviour," proclaimed that heroic harpist King David. The Efé people of the bow harp and the hunting bow define their mountain as the earthly abode or great throne of God. It is King David's "Rock of Israel." The rainbow is the bow of God, according to the Pygmies of Gabon and Cameroon. It is a bond or covenant between God and his people, the Pygmies. Jehovah made the rainbow covenant with Noah and his family after the Deluge, according to the book of Genesis.

The American Indians and the Eskimos did not inherit their treasury of Pygmy legends and their hunting bows from Cro-Magnon man, that tall European fossil who made a theoretical trek across conjectural bridges of land and ice. Another theory maintains that "the men who left skulls of Australoid or Melanesian type in the caves of South America reached that continent by a southern route across an Antarctic bridge of land and ice." Most anthropologists have dismissed this theory as "fantastic."[31] It is no more and no less fantastic than the theories of the first Americans' Arctic migrations from Pleistocene Europe and Siberia.

Like Cro-Magnon Man, the present-day tribes of Australia and Melanesia make spearheads, axes and other implements out of stone. They do not use hunting bows. There are Pygmy fossils and pygmoid tribes in Australia, New Guinea, and many islands of the Melanesian and Indonesian regions. The defunct Pygmies almost certainly used the bow, since the surviving Philippine Pygmies have bows and fifty or sixty types of arrows. The Polynesian people are equipped with bows, string pictures and Pygmy-style legends. Anthropological theories sometimes derive the Polynesians from Asia and sometimes from the Americas. Thor Heyerdahl tried to prove the latter theory by drifting on the Humboldt Current in the Kon-Tiki, a neo-Peruvian raft. If the Pygmies were the first Polynesians, which seems rather probable, they must have traveled in boats.

---

[31] Kenneth Macgowan and Joseph A. Hester, Jr., *Early Man in the New World*, p. 25.

The theoretical Cro-Magnon marchers to the Americas belonged to a larger group of European fossils known as the Aurignacians. On an Aurignacian kinsman of Cro-Magnon Man, *Early Man in the New World* says that "another specimen, the Grimaldi from the Riviera, is distinctly Negroid."[32] No ancient Negro bones have been found in equatorial Africa. There the tall fossils of the Upper Paleolithic period have all been assigned to the proto-Hamitic, Mediterranean or Caucasoid stock. Some of the Pygmies have the complexion of Mediterranean Caucasoids and the blue or gray eyes of Nordic Caucasoids. The long-haired white Pygmies of Ituri Forest legend are the "white elves" whom the Europeans identified with their ancestors of the ancient African Olympus. The present-day Europeans and African Pygmies are mutual descendants of those Caucasoid Archaeopygmies.

The bones of Cro-Magnon and Grimaldi Man do not reveal whether they, and the other Aurignacian residents of ancient Europe, had a white or black complexion. Like Cro-Magnon Man, some of the Australian "blackfellows" are over six feet tall. Others are pygmoid five-footers who hark back to the extinct Australian Pygmies. The blackfellows have the hairy skin and wavy tresses of the Caucasoids. Many children and a few adults have blond hair. The Australians' dark skins and broad noses are usually described as Negroid traits. The Melanesians are richly endowed with melanin or black pigment and often come equipped with noses of the Semitic variety.

These people are dark or black. They are not Negroes. The so-called Negritos or Asiatic Pygmies are little black folks with many Caucasoid traits. The Andamanese, for example, have predominantly Roman noses. The short-statured "aboriginal tribes" of southeastern Eurasia are very swarthy people. It is thus entirely possible that the Grimaldi and Cro-Magnon fossils of western Eurasia represent the remains of a tall black people whose bow-less culture and stone artifacts resemble the Melanesian-Australian equivalents.

The tall blacks may have mutated from the Asiatic Pygmies, who in turn may have mutated from the paler African Pygmy race.

---

[32] *Ibid.*, p. 102.

In his book *Les Pygmées,* Schebesta summarized the several theories of mutation or evolution from the Bambuti, a name he used for the African Pygmies in general, and the Far Eastern Negritos:

> For J. Kollmann, the Pygmies are a survival: their race is the infantile form of humanity; the tall people are the progressive form. Kollmann refers to their infantile traits, and he ranks them, by reason of the law of biogenesis, at the beginning, and not at the end, of an evolution. For him, all the races of tall stature are descended from Pygmaic races. The Reverend Father Schmidt, in his turn, in his celebrated work, defends the thesis of the Pygmies as a single race from which all the races of tall stature departed. H. Bryn says also that all the tall races descend from the Negritos-Bambuti by mutations, but he considers the Bambuti and Negritos as two races separated from the same first Archaeopygmy race.
>
> He defends energetically the racial originality of the Pygmies, and rejects categorically their degeneration. After having enumerated their distinctive characteristics, he adds: "All the traits that we note belong to this ensemble of particularities that the anthropologists call 'infantilism'; they show us very clearly that the Pygmy race represents the infant-type of humanity. Neither degeneration, undernourishment, nor etiolation can be evoked on these points. One must remember that all their characteristic traits can be found among the races of tall stature during the years of childhood."[33]

The scientists speak of physically infantile traits. Children have short legs, heads that are very large in proportion to their bodies, and other Pygmy-like traits. Some Ituri Forest Pygmies have well-bridged noses of almost Caucasoid type. Most Pygmies, like children, have very low-bridged noses. Our children echo the physique of our forefathers, or as Haeckel phrased it: "Ontogeny recapitulates phylogeny." There is, however, nothing infantile about the Pygmies' mentality and their very pleasant, peaceful way of life. War, murder and other forms of inhuman behavior were expressly forbidden in the commandments that a tall bearded black patriarch, God or the first man, gave to the ancestors of the Andaman Island Pygmies. He wears a coat of black pigment. Who is he? The Great White Father or Efé, the White Pygmy who gave the commandments to his children. And who are they? All men are his children,

---

[33] P. Schebesta, *Les Pygmées,* p. 189.

according to the Efé residents of Everyman's Lost Paradise, Purgatory and Hades.

The physical, psychological and cultural differences between the African Pygmies and the surrounding Negro tribes cannot be exaggerated. The lack of Negro fossils in equatorial Africa suggests both that the Negroes evolved elsewhere and that they subsequently invaded the territory of their remote Pygmy ancestors. Anthropologists of the "shrunken Negro" school describe the Pygmies as Negro degenerates, criminals and outcasts who dwindled and faded in the forest. A diametrically opposed theory maintains that the African Negroes evolved or mutated from the Pygmies:

> The negrillos or pygmies of central Africa are probably of ancient stock, and almost certainly sprang from a common source with the negritos of Oceania. There may be some basic relationship between negrillos and Bushmen, who share such features as dwarf stature, peppercorn hair, and steatopygia (the last two features are occasionally found in pygmies, commonly found in Bushmen). Possibly the Negro originated from negrillo ancestors in central Africa, or he may have evolved as the result of hybridization between negrillos (or perhaps proto-Bushmen) and some other early stock such as the proto-Hamites.
>
> In an attempt to explain the affinities between negrillos and Bushmen, and while admitting that the theory is hard to swallow, Hooton suggests that the ancestors of the Congo pygmies may have left Asia before the full development of either Mongoloid or Negroid features, carrying with them incipient tendencies towards both these specialized developments. The Congo pygmies then developed Negroid characters, while Mongoloid features appeared in Bushmen and Hottentots. The high incidence of B in both pygmy and Hottentot blood groups suggests an Asiatic origin, for the incidence of B is particularly high in this continent.[34]

The Andaman, Philippine and Malayan Pygmies are black people with very smooth skins. The "aboriginal tribes" of southern Asia echo their swarthy complexion. The Ituri Forest Pygmies are hairy-skinned people whose complexion ranges through the Caucasoid-Mongoloid-Amerindian-Polynesian spectrum that prevails over a much more extensive part of the globe. Their many proto-

---

[34] Sonia Cole, *The Prehistory of East Africa*, p. 114.

Caucasoid traits suggest that the ancient African Pygmies sired the Caucasoid stock which is "of very ancient origin in East Africa," as Dr. Cole remarked. The Archaeopygmy population of the Old White Africa offers equally plausible ancestors for the American Indians and the Polynesians, who possess many Caucasoid traits. Some Pygmies have a slightly Mongoloid cast of features that is much more pronounced in the yellow-brown Bushmen. In Gabon and Cameroon, the Negro tribes use the term "Yellow Pygmies" to describe Pygmy bands of a predominantly yellow-tan or even yellow-white complexion.

"In the beginning, when Nzamé, the Creator, made the first men, he created first of all the Pygmies of fair color," according to a Fang legend that Father Trilles mentioned in his book *The Soul of the African Pygmy*. Nzamé subsequently created chimpanzees, white men, gorillas and dark Pygmies. Then finally he made his masterpiece: he created "the Blacks, who are the most perfect of all, the others being only attempts or experiments." The Negro tribes continually ridicule and insult the Pygmy people, who are not "black and beautiful," so to speak. The Pygmies call themselves "the Great Race," tell anti-Negro jokes and even chant anti-Negro songs that revile "the sons of the night, black as the soot of a smoky house." The Negroes call the Pygmies by the equally unflattering epithet "stinking little beasts of the forest."

Dr. Cole described the Pygmies as members of the Negro stock and possible ancestors of the Negroes. R. Bourgeois, the former Lieutenant Governor of the Belgian mandate in the Central African nation of Rwanda, repudiated the theory that the Pygmies are Negroids. At the same time, however, he denied the ancestral character of the Pygmy people, who somehow managed to distribute their fossil bones and a vast number of Pygmoid tribes on every inhabited continent and many isolated islands:

> The Pygmoids do not form an ancestral link, but an aberrant branch, detached from the common human trunk that has, since its detachment, accentuated its Pygmy characteristics. To attach them simply to the Negroids is artificial; their dispersion speaks magnificently for their ubiquitous formation since they exist today from Gabon to New Guinea; their skeletons have been found in Mediterranean and Central Europe, as well as many points in America

(Argentina, Chile, Peru, Guiana, Guatemala). The pygmoid great-race can thus be conceived as the result of an essential ologenetic differentiation in the human species; the representatives of this great-race have been born over the extent of the earth.[35]

Bourgeois defined the Pygmies as an aberrant branch that sprouted from the trunk of the human family tree. He does not name any ethnic group as the trunk from which the Pygmy branch proceeded. He describes as a "branch" people who are "born over the extent of the earth." His Pygmies pop up like tulips in a Belgian garden. Did their pollen blow across the Atlantic Ocean from Gabon to Peru?

An astute African Negro expressed to Catholic missionaries his much more logical opinion that the Pygmies are "the root of the world."[36] Our remaining Pygmy legends may help us to discover the ultimate cause of the legendary cataclysms that occur when the world-tree is cut and the earth turns over. These stories originated as geophysical parables. They degenerated into the superstitions and dogmas that we dignify with the name of "religion."

---

[35] R. Bourgeois, *Banyarwanda et Barundi*, Vol. 1, p. 33.

[36] Henri Trilles, *The Soul of the African Pygmy*, p. 31.

The Beginning of the End

In the beginning, earth was above and heaven was below. Earth was crowded with people. Their camps covered the land. When the great famines came, God said to the lightning, 'Leap out of the earth!' The lightning split the earth with a deafening boom and sprang up to the sky. God followed, then the moon. That is how the world turned upside down."

My Pygmy friends at the Ebuya camp in the southeast Ituri told me this story. An Efé informant narrated to anthropologist Paul Schebesta: "In the beginning, the earth was on high and the sky below. During a famine, men demanded nourishment from God: the earth then descended with food and the sky mounted into the air." Schebesta obtained another version of this legend from Evadu, an Efé elder of the Oruendu region: "In the beginning, God, the moon and the lightning dwelled together and the earth was on high. Filth constantly fell into the food of the celestial hosts. God ordered the lightning to find 'up there' a place that would suit them. The lightning cracked the earth with a giant crash and sprang into the air. God followed and established himself there."[1]

"A great crash, the earth broke in two, and the lightning mounted to find another place" states the text that appears in Trilles' book *The Soul of the African Pygmy*. "Heaven and earth changed places" or "the world turned upside down," according to many Efé elders. "The lightnings flashed and the thunders roared terribly and all were afraid. Then the heaven burst and the fragments fell down and killed everything and everybody. Heaven and earth changed places. Nothing that had life was left upon the earth," declare the Indian legends of Brazil.[2] An Egyptian text called the Ipuwer papyrus laments the devastation caused when "Earth turned upside down" or "the earth turned over like a potter's wheel." The Harris papyrus describes a cataclysmic upheaval of fire and water that occurs when "the south becomes north, and the earth turns over."

Every great disaster of the past and future comes when the Andaman Pygmy deity breaks the supporting tree and the earth turns over. In some versions of the Efé deluge story, the tree is cut with a "lightning axe." The Greek double axe symbolized the thunderbolt of Zeus, the god of gods who punished man by sending floods and other cataclysms. The double axe and the hammer of Thor were both used "to represent thunder, which was accompanied by fire from heaven."[3] The Efé deity disciplines sinners by hurling bolts of lightning from the sky. To turn the world upside down, he sent or hurled the lightning out of the earth. "The Etruscans are said to have believed that thunderbolts came

---

[1] P. Schebesta, *Les Pygmées du Congo Belge*, pp. 307 and 320.

[2] Hans S. Bellamy, *Moons, Myths, & Man* (London: Faber & Faber, 1936), p. 80.

[3] H. R. Ellis Davidson, *Gods and Myths of Northern Europe*, p. 83.

not always from heaven, but sometimes from the earth; or, as some said, from the planet Saturn."[4]

Mantus, the Etruscan Hades, was credited with the power to hurl thunderbolts out of his subterranean abyss. Sethlans, the Etruscan Vulcan, wielded thunderbolts that apparently brought volcanic fire out of the earth. Hindu stories tell of "an unknown weapon, an iron thunderbolt, a gigantic messenger of death which reduced to ashes the entire race of the Vrishnis and the Andhakas. The corpses were so burned as to be unrecognizable. Their hair and nails fell out; pottery broke without any apparent cause, and the birds turned white. After a few hours, all foodstuffs were infected. The thunderbolt was reduced to a fine dust."[5]

The giant lightning bolt of the Efé legend presumably exterminated the famine-stricken mobs who crowded the earth with their camps. In the myth of the savior the people and cities of the ancient world were obliterated. The deluge solved the population problem by equally drastic means. "When the increase of population had been so frightful," Hindu legends relate, "the Earth, oppressed with the excessive burden, sank down for a hundred Yojanas. Suffering pain in all her limbs, and being deprived of her senses by excessive pressure, the Earth in distress sought the protection of Narayana, the foremost of the gods."[6]

Efé, the first man, was divinely commanded to beget children in the story of the forbidden *tahu* tree. Efé, the last man, repeoples the world after the cosmic cataclysms have eliminated the apparently excessive, decadent and overly urbanized population of the earth. Yima, the first man or first king of Persian legend, was told to multiply and govern the creatures of the Wise Lord, Ahura Mazda:

> Furnished with a ring (?) and a golden goad, he rules and
> spares his subjects the perils of foul weather, illness and death, with

---

[4] George Dennis, *The Cities and Cemeteries of Etruria,* Vol. 1, p. 32.

[5] Louis Pauwels and Jacques Bergier, *The Morning of the Magicians* (New York: Avon, 1968), p. 183.

[6] Donald A. Mackenzie, *Indian Myth and Legend* (Gresham Publishing Company, n.d.), p. 196.

the result that the human and animal populations outgrow the capacity of the earth. Three times Yima enlarges it with his magic instruments. This is the first solution to the problem of population that myth offers. In *Fargard* 2 of the *Videvdat* the second solution follows immediately on the account of the first. Here it is a question of reducing the population of the world, preserving only the finest specimens; this is brought about by a cataclysm which takes its pattern from the icy winters and torrential thaws of central Asia. The golden age cannot last forever. Ahura Mazda gives Yima warning that hardship will strike at the wickedness on earth and advises him to excavate an underground enclosure (*vara*) and to store there the seed of all species against the wrath to come in cataclysmic storm. All creatures will grow slowly, and men will reproduce themselves only once every forty years. After the cataclysm Yima, god on earth, re-emerges with his elect.[7]

The ring and golden goad of Yima are the metal rings and spears of Efé, the elite hero or nation. A predominantly black fowl, the sacred ibis, is the national bird of Efé. In some Pygmy territories, it is identified or confounded with the crow. The great Crow Father is confronted by the population problem in the legends of the Alaskan Eskimos. He creates all living creatures by the earth-modeling method that was used to produce the earthly incarnation of "Efé, the first man and father of all who came after." He teaches men how to build houses and boats, how to hunt and so forth, and then returns to the sky like the ascending Efé who resumed the role of lunar angel. The Eskimo Man in the Moon is, as we have seen, the heavenly hunting expert who is similar to "Efé, the Great Hunter of Heaven. The Crow Father wears wings and a bird mask that he can doff at will. His earthly descendants are crows:

> All vegetation springs from fragments of clay which the crow buries in soil on earth (earlier, in the sky, he seemingly went about things in the same way). With the same material he fashions animals and men. However, the emergence of the first four men, if not due to a sort of spontaneous generation, seems none the less independent of governing will. The Crow himself is astounded to see creatures emerge from husks, and so he fashions women for them,

---

[7] *Larousse World Mythology*, p. 200.

then other human beings to people the earth more quickly. However, the day comes when the earth, like the sky, is no longer large enough for its inhabitants: the latter make it bigger by throwing into the sea pieces of a gigantic monster which change into islands and weld themselves to the coasts.[8]

In the Pygmy myth of the savior a giant monster resolves the population problem; Efé carves up the monster after its task of destruction has been accomplished. According to the Pygmy legend of the world turned upside down, the sky and earth are rearranged by catastrophic means. "The Eskimos of Greenland are afraid that the support of the sky may fail and the sky fall down and kill all human beings; a darkening of the sun and the moon will precede such a catastrophe . . . The Eskimos of Greenland told missionaries that in an ancient time the earth turned over and the people who lived then became antipodes." In his book *Worlds in Collision* Immanuel Velikovsky cites many versions of this story, including the Andaman Pygmy legend of the turning earth, and remarked that "the versions of the tribes and peoples of all five continents include the same elements, familiar to us from the Book of Exodus: lightning and 'the bursting of heaven,' which caused the earth to be turned 'upside down,' or 'heaven and earth to change places.' " Regarding the Egyptian versions, he unhesitatingly declared, "The Papyrus Ipuwer, which says that 'the earth turned over like a potter's wheel' and 'the earth is upside down,' was written by an eyewitness of the plagues and the Exodus."[9]

Exodus 1:7 describes a serious population problem that afflicted the land of Egypt: "And the children of Israel were fruitful, and increased abundantly, and multiplied, and waxed exceeding mighty; and the land was filled with them." Velikovsky dated the exodus to the fifteenth century B.C. Not a single eyewitness of that era, or any other period in the history of dynastic Egypt, left any testimony that confirms the Biblical tale of the Israelites who filled up the land of Egypt and survived cataclysmic events that decimated the contemporary Egyptians.

"Behold, the Lord maketh the earth empty, and maketh it

---

[8] *Ibid.*, p. 201.

[9] I. Velikovsky, *Worlds in Collision*, pp. 131–32.

waste, and turneth it upside down, and scattereth the inhabitants thereof . . . The land shall be utterly emptied, and utterly spoiled: for the Lord hath spoken this word . . . The inhabitants of the earth are burned, and few men left . . . In the city is left desolation, and the gate is smitten with destruction . . . The earth is utterly broken down, the earth is clean dissolved, the earth is moved exceedingly," proclaimed the Old Testament prophet Isaiah.[10] "A problem the archaeologists will have to solve is that of clarifying whether the extermination of life in these regions of northwest America and northeast Asia, resulting in the death of mammoths, took place in the eighth and seventh or fifteenth century before the present era (or earlier)—in other words, whether the herds of mammoths were annihilated in the days of Isaiah or in the days of the Exodus," wrote Velikovsky.[11]

Spearheads have been found among the mammoth and other animal remains of the Alaskan-Siberian muck beds. According to the theories of early man's trip to the Arctic, the ancient Pygmies, and/or the controversial ancestors of the Eskimos, may have reached North America by 70,000 B.C. or even earlier. The first Americans have been accused by anthropologists of migrating toward the frozen wasteland during a remote prehistoric era of negligible population. The Pygmy doomsday legends tell a more convincing story of the overpopulated earth.

The human race "is always increasing at times, and at other times decreasing," the Egyptian priests informed Solon of Athens in Plato's story of the Atlantis cataclysms. The Ermitage papyrus tells of a rather radical decrease in population: "I show thee the land upside down . . . The sun is veiled and shows not in the sight of men. None can live when the sun is veiled by clouds . . . None knoweth that midday is there; the shadow is not discovered . . . Not dazzled is the sight when he [the sun] is beheld; he is in the sky like the moon."

The poles shift or "the south becomes north" when the Egyptian earth turns over. "The Egyptians pride themselves on being the most ancient people in the world. In their authentic

---

[10] Isaiah 24:1–19.

[11] I. Velikovsky, *Worlds in Collision*, p. 332.

annals," wrote the Roman scholar Pomponius Mela in his treatise *De Situ Orbis,* "one may read that since they have been in existence, the course of the stars has changed direction four times, and that the sun has set twice in the part of the sky where it rises today." Egyptian priests told the Greek historian Herodotus that four such changes of direction occurred during the 341 generations that followed the advent of their "first king." He calculated, on the basis of three generations per century, that the 341 generations spanned more than 11,000 years. "Four times in this period (so they told me) the sun rose contrary to his wont; twice he rose where he now sets, and twice he set where he now rises," reported Herodotus.

The first king reigned eleven or twelve thousand years before Herodotus visited Egypt during the fifth century B.C. The first king of this story was probably the slain and resurrected man-god Osiris. Balder, the murdered god of Germanic legend, is resurrected after the cataclysms that terminate every world-age. Yima, the first man or first king of Persian legend, returned after the cataclysms that close the world ages of Indo-Iranian cosmology. His Hindu counterpart, Yama, was represented as the progenitor of the human race. Four Hindu yugas or world-ages comprise a "great yuga" of twelve thousand years. Ahura Mazda, the Wise Lord, assigned a period of twelve thousand years to the age or duration of the Persian world.

"None can live" when the Egyptian world turns upside down. Herodotus' story implies that this fatal event occurred four times during the eleven- to twelve-thousand-year period that preceded his visit to Egypt. The Indo-Iranian legends suggest that four disasters instead terminated world-ages that endure for approximately twelve thousand years. The four major episodes of Pleistocene destruction are known as the glaciations of Günz, Mindel, Riss and Würm. In his theory of the Pleistocene, the English astronomer Sir John Herschel assigned an approximate duration of 10,500 years to each glacial and interglacial epoch.[12]

"Four times cataclysms descended on the world destroying all—or almost all—living creatures," according to many tribes of

---

[12] "Glacial Period," *Enclycopaedia Britannica,* 14th ed., Vol. 10, pp. 379–80.

South American Indians. The first disaster is frequently represented as a global conflagration. "The Apapocuva-Guarani Indians are convinced that this cataclysm, which took place at the beginning of time, will be repeated on the day that the creator removes the supporting struts from under the earth. The earth will catch fire, and everlasting night will descend upon the world. Then the creator will release the blue tiger to devour men."[13]

The earth turns over when the Andaman Pygmy deity breaks the giant tree that supports the earth from below and thereby removes the "struts" from under the Indian earth. The fiery lightning of the Efé legend turns the world upside down. The Efé deity sometimes punishes sinners by dispatching a man-eating leopard. The Apapocuva-Guarani creator released his "blue tiger." The first of the four Aztec world ages came to an end when ferocious cats devoured the residents of the earth and the sun disappeared. The first Aztec world-age or "sun" was called by the title *nahui ocelotl,* four tigers (as in ocelot). In some texts, the man-eating "tigers" attack at the end of the fourth Aztec world-age. Other texts describe a global flood as the climactic event of the fourth Aztec world age.

The man-eating leopard of Efé theology polishes off occasional sinners. The legend of the world turned upside down and the deluge story describe geophysical events that are said to terminate every world-age. The numerous American Indian systems of the four "suns" or world-ages arrange Pygmy legends in arbitrary schemes that differ from one locality to the next. The related cataclysms are separated and assigned to different eras. The Pygmy legends and concepts uniquely explain the otherwise incomprehensible symbolisms and events of the four Amerindian "suns" that correspond with the four world-ages of Hindu, Greek and Celtic cosmology.

The world-ages end with the four apparent polar shifts of Egyptian legend. "Have we of all mankind been deemed deserving that heaven, its poles uptorn, should overwhelm us? In our time has the last day come?" the fearful populace ask in *Thyestes,* a

---

[13] *Larousse World Mythology,* p. 490.

drama written by the Roman author Seneca during the first century A.D. No such disaster occurred during Seneca's time. "Behold,
the Lord maketh the earth empty, and maketh it waste, and
turneth it upside down . . . the inhabitants of the earth are
burned, and few men left," declared the prophet Isaiah. No such
mass extinction of mankind occurred "in the days of Isaiah," as
Velikovsky called the seventh or eighth century B.C. "The earth
shall reel to and fro like a drunkard, and shall be removed like a
cottage," warned Isaiah. The first man's hut is turned upside down,
to the tune of "a great noise resembling thunder," in the Masai
legend "Beginner of the Earth." The first man was the eponymous
ancestor of the pygmoid Dorobo people. Anthropological theories
that interpret the East African Masai as descendants of "early
Hebrews" omit the inconvenient or embarrassing Pygmies.

Efé and his motherly consort Matu repopulate the earth at
the beginning of every world-age. "After the fire had devastated
the earth, it was repeopled by a man and a woman who had
escaped the general conflagration by taking refuge in a hole,"
according to the Apapocuva-Guarani Indian tribes. Efé escapes
every disaster by entering a cavity, cave, cove, or *kovu*. The maze
of caverns in the lunar mountain lead to *kovu'iotani*, the "gigantic hole" or abyss of the Pygmy Hades. Efé hunted a giant black
hog that lured him into the caverns. He procured a liana rope
with the intention of hauling out the beast. Then the hog led him
through the caverns to the "gigantic hole." The Mundurucu Indian "companion of the creator" pursued an armadillo that
dragged him down to the underworld. The creator made the cotton
plant in order to fabricate a rope out of its fibers. He pushed the
rope through a hole that leads to the underworld. The ancestors
of the Mundurucu Indians climbed up the rope to the surface of
the earth. When the rope broke, a great many were forced to
remain underground.[14]

All of the characters in this South American story are forms
of Efé, the elite hero or nation that emerges from the "gigantic
hole" at the beginning of every world-age. The ancestors climbed

---

[14] *Ibid.*, p. 487.

up a grapevine to accomplish their exodus from the underworld, according to a North American story told by the Mandan branch of the Sioux:

> The whole nation resided in one large village, underground, near a subterranean lake. A grape-vine extended its roots down to their habitation, and gave them a view of the light. Some of the most adventurous climbed up the vine, and were delighted with the sight of the earth, which they found covered with buffalo, and rich with every kind of fruit. Returning with the grapes they had gathered, their countrymen were so pleased with the taste of them that the whole nation resolved to leave their dull residence for the charms of the upper region. Men, women, and children ascended by means of the vine, but, when about half the nation had reached the surface of the earth, a corpulent woman, who was clambering up the vine, broke it with her weight, and closed upon herself and the rest of the nation the light of the sun.

"Their belief in a future state is connected with this theory of their origin," remarked the American explorers Lewis and Clark, who recounted this legend in their book *Travels to the Source of the Missouri* (1811). "The myths of this North American Indian tribe tell how at some period their ancestors lived in a cave with a subterranean lake and that eventually after the period of disaster was over the ancestors of the tribe made their way to the surface and there set up their homes," Egerton Sykes says about the "creation legends" of the Sioux.[15] This story of the "origin" or "creation" instead describes the resurrection after the cataclysms that terminate the Amerindian world-ages.

Efé originated in the celestial paradise, according to the Ituri Forest legend of the forbidden tree. Efé returned to this ethereal region, and later came back to earth, by means of a long, long liana that passed through a hole in the vault of the sky: "The Warrau tribe of the Arawaks possess the following legend of their own origin and that of the Caribs. The Warraus originally dwelt in a pleasant region above the sky, where there were neither wicked men nor noxious animals. Okonorote, a young hunter, having wandered far in pursuit of a beautiful bird, dis-

---

[15] Egerton Sykes, *Everyman's Dictionary of Non-Classical Mythology*, p. 195.

charged an arrow at it which missed its mark and disappeared. While searching for it he found a hole through which it had fallen, and on looking through it, descried the lower world. He made a rope, down which he led the Warraus to the earth, but a corpulent women, as in several of the North American myths, remained fixed in the aperture, and filled it up."[16]

The Arawak and Sioux ancestors came to earth, in mirror-image stories, through the celestial and terrestrial holes of Pygmy cosmology. The holes lead to the corresponding sectors of the Egyptians' doubly-hidden underworld. According to the ancient Chinese philosophers, "At the highest point of the heavens there was a gap, *lie-k'iue*, through which lightning flashed. Beyond that gap the sky ended, there was absolutely nothing more. The same thing happened on the horizontal plane; at the edge of the cosmos there was neither sky nor earth, only a gaping void."[17]

Efé brought three iron spears down through the heavenly hole. His father, the sky-smith, forged the spears in the celestial paradise. Otu or "Grandfather," as he is called, is said to strike sinners dead by hurling bolts of lightning. Efé used the spears in the story of his resurrection through the maze-like mountain caverns that lead to the underworld kingdom of the dead. Tinia, the head of the Etruscan pantheon, was armed with three thunder-bolts. The retinue of the "sacred king" carried three spears in the Etruscan vase picture of the resurrection through the Troy-town maze. *Atli*, meaning "grandfather," was an epithet of Thor, the thundering Germanic sky-smith and earthly prince of Asgard-Troy.

Efé wields three iron spears in the myth of the savior. Matu, his mother, talks and behaves like a woman. A chaste widow gave birth to Mexitli, the Aztec god of lightning who was armed with four divine war-spears. Efé emerged through a hole in the foot of Matu the Mountain Mother. In the story of the hero's resurrection from the kingdom of the dead, Efé brought all kinds of treasures back through the mountain. "They also related that

---

[16] Marian Edwardes and Lewis Spence, *A Dictionary of Non-Classical Mythology*, p. 45.

[17] *Larousse World Mythology*, p. 277.

Maiso, a stone woman, produced all living beings and all rivers.
Even the domestic animals and iron tools of the whites are borne
by this original mother," according to the Paressi tribe of the
Arawak Indian nation.[18]

Efé made round-trip journeys through the hole in the foot
of the mountain and the hole in the vault of heaven. Yima, the
terrestrial god of light, accomplished the former trip by traveling
through a cave in the Persian mountains. His heavenly twin was
Mithra, the god of light or the sun. The Egyptian light-god Ra
was said to go every night into the mouth of the goddess Nut,
whose arched body comprised the star-spangled vault of the sky.
Ra emerged every morning from a hole at the other end of her
body. Nut and the other "sycamore ladies" stood in the branches
of the southern sycamore tree, pouring down water from their
jugs. Matu the Mountain Mother stands in the forest and sends
the waters of the Albertine Nile down from her summit. Nut, according to many Egyptian texts, was the mother of Ra and Osiris.
"He who is between the thighs of Nut is the Pygmy," proclaims
the pyramid text of Ra-Meri or Pharaoh Pepi the First. Ra, Osiris
and all of the great Egyptian gods were represented on the Metternich Stele by a portrait of the Pygmy god Bes.

Efé, the Pygmy, does not depart every evening and return
every morning through the holes of heaven and earth. Yima and
the other resurrected heroes entered the mountain cave or underworld abyss in the evening of a world-age, sat out the cosmic
cataclysms, and returned in the morning of a succeeding world-
age. "During the night the sun goes backward over his daily
route, but so high in the sky that one cannot see him," an Efé
elder told Schebesta.[19] Other Pygmies say that the sun reverses
his course during the "long dark night" of the past and future
disasters. Egyptian, Greek, Aztec, Mayan and other globally distributed legends describe appalling cataclysms that occur when
the sun changes or reverses his route through the sky. All directions are apparently reversed when the Pygmies' world turns over
or upside down.

---

[18] Edwardes and Spence, *A Dictionary of Non-Classical Mythology*, p. 45.

[19] P. Schebesta, *Les Pygmées du Congo Belge*, p. 319.

"Sun, stand thou still upon Gibeon; and thou, Moon, in the valley of Ajalon," commanded Moses' successor, the Hebrew warrior Joshua. "And the sun stood still, and the moon stayed, until the people had avenged themselves upon their enemies." This event supposedly occurred during the Israelites' invasion of Palestine. The Lord bombarded the Israelites' enemies with hailstones or "great stones from heaven," according to Joshua 10:11. "The earth quaked and trembled from the noise of Thy thunders. Thou didst pursue them in Thy storm, Thou didst consume them in the whirlwind," declares a prayer attributed to Joshua. Kingdoms tottered and the Lord destroyed "all the princes of the earth." The Israelites' prior exodus from Egypt is assigned by conventional critics to a period no later than the fifteenth century B.C. The contemporary Egyptians, Babylonians and company somehow failed to notice the cataclysms of Exodus and Joshua. Their history continued, unperturbed by the Biblical cataclysms that destroyed all the princes or kingdoms of the earth.

Five Amorite kings—the kings of Jerusalem, Hebron, Jarmuth, Lachish and Eglon—fled from Joshua's Israelites and "hid themselves in a cave at Makkeda." Joshua said, "Roll great stones upon the mouth of the cave, and set men by it for to keep them." After the children of Israel made "a very great slaughter" of their enemies, the kings were taken out of the cave. "And afterward Joshua smote them, and slew them, and hanged them on five trees: and they were hanging upon the trees until the evening. And it came to pass at the time of the going down of the sun, that Joshua commanded, and they took them down off the trees, and cast them into the cave wherein they had been hid, and laid great stones in the cave's mouth, which remain until this very day."[20]

The doomsday events of Joshua are echoed in the New Testament accounts of the crucifixion. The twenty-third chapter of Luke describes a perturbation that affected the sun: "And it was about the sixth hour, and there was a darkness over all the earth until the ninth hour. And the sun was darkened, and the veil of the temple was rent in the midst. And when Jesus had cried with

---

[20] Joshua 10:5–27.

a loud voice, he said, 'Father, into thy hands I commend my spirit,' and having said thus, he gave up the ghost." The twenty-seventh chapter of Matthew explains how the veil of the temple was rent: "Jesus, when he had cried again with a loud voice, yielded up the ghost. And, behold, the veil of the temple was rent in twain from the top to the bottom; and the earth did quake, and the rocks rent; and the graves were opened; and many bodies of the saints which slept arose, and came out of the graves after his resurrection, and went into the holy city, and appeared unto many." Jesus' body was placed in a cavernous tomb and the entrance was sealed with a rock. "And behold, there was a great earthquake: for the angel of the Lord descended from heaven, and came and rolled back the stone from the door, and sat upon it. His countenance was like lightning, and his raiment white as snow," according to the twenty-eighth chapter of Matthew. The resurrected Jesus was "carried up into heaven," according to the twenty-fourth chapter of Luke.

The historic records of the first century A.D. do not describe the geophysical events or miracles of the crucifixion. The prophet Elijah survived a series of cataclysms by hiding in a cave of Mount Sinai. He was carried up into heaven by means of a whirlwind or a chariot of fire. The legends of Charlemagne install Elijah on the summit of a paradisaical mountain at the source of the Nile. A cave or cleft in the mountain leads to the abyss of Hades. The Malayan Pygmies describe a cavernous rock that stands on the shores of a river at the center of the earth above a subterranean abyss. The dead will be resurrected from this abyss, the Andaman Pygmy Hades, when the earth turns over and the living are annihilated by the ensuing disasters. Efé, the Pygmy hero or nation, returned and may once again be resurrected from the "gigantic hole" or kingdom of the dead through the Troy-town maze of caverns in the Mountain of the Moon at the source of the Nile. Efé, the first man and last man, survives every disaster. Thousands of Old and New World stories echo the Efé legends of the hero's apparent demise, resurrection, miraculous birth, trips to the sky, combats with giant monsters, enlightened laws and teachings, cultural inventions and so forth. The national "histories" of the Israelites and many other ethnic groups are crammed with so many pseudohistorical heroes and events that one cannot determine where legend leaves off and history begins.

Geoffrey of Monmouth's *History of the Kings of Britain* describes King Arthur as an historic personality whose reign terminated in 542 A.D. Lord Raglan commented in his study *The Hero:*

> There is not a word in Geoffrey which is more reliable than his account of Arthur's Continental campaign of which Sir John Rhys writes that "it appears on the whole that Arthur's subjugation of the west of Europe was directly or indirectly founded on the mythic invasion of Hades by him in the character of a Culture Hero," yet it is upon Geoffrey that those stories and poem are based which have given rise to a belief in Arthur's historicity . . .
>
> There were three eminent prisoners, but a greater was Arthur, who was thrice for three nights in magic prisons. He pursued with his whole army a magic sow from Wales to Cornwall; he fought with giants and monsters, the latter including a huge cat. He had a magic sword and various other articles of magical equipment. He is the wild huntsman, and as we have seen, the knight who sleeps in a cave . . . Arthur has certainly been identified with the raven, and also with the chough . . . "Arthur has none but mythological relatives," says Mr. Briffault, "his father is the dragon Uther, his sister the goddess Anu, his wife the 'White Lady,' his mistress or sister Morgana, the fairy."[21]

The thirteenth-century French romance "Huon of Bordeaux" describes a visit to the land of Morgana's son Oberon, the king of the fairies. Huon, the nephew of the Pope, travels to Arabia and enters a forest. There he meets Oberon, a "beautiful dwarf" whom he at first mistakes for a five-year-old child. "I hold my power from the God you adore, whose faithful servant I am, as well as you," declares Oberon. Then he narrates, concerning his parentage: "Julius Caesar, going by sea to join his army, was driven by a storm to take shelter in the island of Celea, where dwelt the fairy Glorianda. From this renowned pair I draw my birth. I am the heritor of that which was most admirable in each of my parents: my father's heroic qualities, and my mother's beauty and magic art . . . The power which I derive from my

---

[21] Lord Raglan, *The Hero*, pp. 77–81.

mother I use sometimes for my own diversion, but always to promote justice and to reward virtue."[22]

Glorianda was another name of Morgana the Fairy. Her heroic mate, Julius Caesar, was not a bona-fide member of King Arthur's elfin family. He was an historic personality (c. 100–44 B.C.) equipped with a pseudohistoric pedigree that traced his descent from Julius the son of Aeneas the Trojan. Aeneas' mother, the goddess Aphrodite or Venus, had a diminutive son named Cupid. Caesar's family connections with Cupid, the first and oldest of the gods, probably explain why the French romance associates "the noblest Roman of them all" with the virtuous dwarf Oberon and the other "good little people" of European legend. The Orphic creation story of Greece maintains that Cupid was hatched from the silver egg of the moon and dwelled in a cave with his mother, the black-winged goddess Night. The Greek philosopher Aristotle wrote about the "little men" or Pygmies who dwell in caverns at the source of the Nile. Huon of Bordeaux met King Oberon in the territory of the Egyptians' Pygmy god Bes, who was associated with Arabia, Punt and the "land of trees and spirits at the foot of the mountains of the moon." Bes = Oberon = Arthur = Efé, the once and future king of Everyman's Camelot-Eden-Olympus-Asgard-Troy.

Efé, the Great Hunter, chased the giant hog that the "wild huntsman" Arthur pursued with his army from Wales to Cornwall. After Efé killed the hog, it came back to life and lured the hero to the abysmal kingdom of the dead. There Efé was incarcerated for three months and part of a fourth month. Arthur was three times forced to spend three nights in magic prisons. "Spend the night with me, darling," the ghost of Matu said to Efé. "I have been three times resident in the castle of Arianrhod . . . I have been three periods in the prison of Arianrhod," Little Gwion/ Merlin/Taliesin declares in the versions of the Welsh riddle-poem Hanes Taliesin.

Merlin buried himself alive in a subterranean tomb under a cavernous mountain that stands in the center of a forest. An ecclesiastical tradition maintains that "Arthur visited St. Padarn

---

[22] "The Legends of Charlemagne," *Bulfinch's Mythology*, p. 651.

and coveted his tunic, whereupon the saint caused the earth to open and swallow Arthur, and keep him a prisoner till he apologized."[23] The earth swallowed the paradisaical Athenians after their war with Atlantis. A troop of Greek heroes descended to the abyss of Tartarus as a result of their battles with the moon goddess' magic boar.

Arianrhod's prison or Spiral Castle was associated with the constellation of Corona Borealis. Efé traveled to the celestial paradise beyond the hole in the vault of the sky. There the hero fought giant monsters, was embraced by the ladies of heaven, remained for an indefinite period of time, and returned to earth with the aid of his father, God, the cosmic power who wields or distributes the life force from his post in the celestial paradise. "I have been on the Galaxy at the throne of the Distributor," proclaims the poem of Hanes Taliesin. Efé, the immortal hero, is the benevolent lawgiver and poet who transmits his knowledge to the people of every world age. "I have been teacher to all intelligences, I am able to instruct the whole universe, I shall be until the day of doom on the face of the earth," declared the divine bard Little Gwion/Merlin/Taliesin.

Thoth, the Egyptian god of knowledge, was sometimes pictured as an ibis-headed man. The sacred ibis is the national bird of Efé, the lunar hero or nation. This predominantly black fowl is associated or confounded in some Pygmy territories with the crow. King Arthur was identified with the chough, a kind of crow, and the raven. All-Father Odin was pictured with a pair of wise ravens called Huginn and Muninn. Sigurd, Earl of Orkney, is said to have had a raven banner that brought victory to his troops. Bran, the Raven, traditionally led the Celts into battle. The Celtic hero-god Cuchulainn was equipped with a sacred cloak of raven's feathers. The Great Crow or Crow Father of the Eskimos has feathers and a mask that he can doff at will. He is the creator and omniscient teacher who returned to the sky. He is Efé, Thoth or the Eskimo Man in the Moon.

The Eskimos tell many stories concerning a first or ancestral race of very diminutive stature. In Alaska, for example, the Es-

---

[23] Lord Raglan, *The Hero*, p. 78.

kimos of the Cape Denbigh area say that a "little chief" and his people left the artifacts and ruins of an ancient village that was excavated by archaeologist J. Louis Giddings. He argued with a group of Eskimos, trying to convince them that "there were no miniature people." The Eskimos insisted. "The first men in America, whenever they came and whoever they were, and all of those who descended from them, were most likely full-sized people— no larger, no smaller, than the tall and short people we know today," declared Giddings. After a moment of silence, an Eskimo named Nakarak politely replied, "We thank you for explaining all these things to us. We do read a little, and we go to Bible School in the winter, but no one has ever explained these things to us before." Then he added, "We understand those things better now. The world has had big people and small people—and we think it must be true that the little chief was one of the smallest, all right, and we think all the other people in this village were pretty small, too!"[24]

Forty-two Venezuelan Pygmy fossils recently confirmed the Eskimo tradition that the first Americans were pretty small people. A nineteenth-century anthropologist, R. Andree, maintained that the Eskimos borrowed their cat's-cradle pictures from "Nordmen" or early Scandinavian voyagers. The Eskimos still possess an Efé string figure, "The Mouse," that is equally well remembered by the residents of the British Isles. The diminutive ancestor-gods of Celtic and Germanic legend were relegated to the category of folklore when Christian missionaries arrived. The Philippine Pygmies while away their leisure time with string figures and inscribed dice. The rectangular *bili* or tablet dice of the Efé Pygmies rather curiously resemble the wooden billets that the Druids of the old British forests inscribed with messages written in the Ogham version of the alphabet:

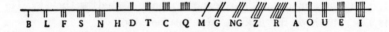

B L F S N H D T C Q M G NG Z R A O U E I

---

[24] J. Louis Giddings, *Ancient Men of the Arctic* (New York: Alfred A. Knopf, 1967), pp. 3–8.

Efé *bili* is English *billet*, a written note or an heraldric figure that represents a rectangular block of wood. French *billet*
and *billette* are the note and the wooden block. In English, one
can send or spend a bill. The legendary treasures of the Germanic
Aesir or Elder Gods and the Celtic Tuatha De Danaan include
"Golden Tablets" inscribed with historic records.[25] The Aesir and
the People of Danaan were both identified with the dwarfs, elves
or fairies. All-Father Odin obtained the Runic alphabet after he
hung on the World Ash Tree, according to the Norse poem of
Havamal.

"I know I hung on the windswept Tree, through nine days
and nights. I was stuck with a spear and given to Odin, myself
given to myself. They helped me neither by meat nor drink. I
peered downward, I took up the runes, screaming, I took them—
then I fell back," Odin declares in this poem. H. R. Ellis Davidson commented, "It was thought at one time that this image of
the suffering god hanging from the tree must have been derived
from the Christian Crucifixion. But despite certain resemblances,
it would seem that here we have something whose roots go deep
into heathen thought, and which is no late copy, conscious or
unconscious, of the central mystery of the Christian faith. By
hanging on a tree, Odin is not sharing in the suffering of the
world or saving men from death, he is there to win the secret of
the runes."[26]

Toré or God hangs on a tall tree in the Pygmy legend of the
Satanic bird-man who brought death to the world. Toré's son Efé,
the first man and last man on earth, comes out of a hole in the
tree or the forest after the flood. Efé receives all kinds of treasures during his sojourn in the "gigantic hole" or infernal kingdom
of the dead. Efé returned with his treasures through the holes
or caverns of the Troy-town maze in the mountain.

Thor, the father-son of Odin, was the Germanic tree and
sky god. Odin hung on the World Ash Tree at the center of the
earth. The world is repeopled by living men who come out of the

---

[25] Egerton Sykes, *Everyman's Dictionary of Non-Classical Mythology*, pp.
202 and 214.

[26] H. R. Ellis Davidson, *Gods and Myths of Northern Europe*, pp. 143–44.

World Ash Tree or Hoddmimir's Grove after the great deluge of Ragnarok. Odin's son Balder is resurrected from the infernal land of hell at the beginning of every world-age. The ancestors of the American tribes bring cultural tools or "treasures" back from the underworld or the cave in the mountain. The survivors apparently return with the written tablets of Germanic-Celtic legend when they emerge from the Heaven Mountain at the center of the earth in the paradisaical land of Asgard or Troy. "I was in Africa before the building of Rome, I am come now here to the remnants of Troia," Little Gwion/Merlin/Taliesin affirmed in the Welsh poem of Hanes Taliesin. His people came from Troy to the land of Trojanova, Trinovantum or London.

The Polynesians tell many stories of the "little people." Like the Pygmies, the Polynesians are equipped with bows, string figures and a lost system of writing on wooden tablets. A few of the Easter Island tablets survive. What happened to the rest?

> As happened in Africa and in South America, the first missionaries to arrive on Easter Island took steps to remove all traces of a dead civilization. At the foot of the statues there were wooden tablets covered with hieroglyphics: these were all burned or dispatched to the Vatican Library which houses many secrets. Was this done to destroy all traces of ancient superstitions, or to remove what could have been evidence of some Unknown Power? A record of the presence on the Earth of other beings—visitors from Elsewhere?
>
> The first Europeans to visit Easter Island discovered that the inhabitants included a race of white men, with beards. Where did they come from? The descendants, perhaps, of some degenerate race, in existence for many thousands of years and today completely submerged? There are references in legends to a Master Race of Teachers, of great antiquity, fallen from the skies.[27]

All-Father Efé descended from the sky, modeled his earthly incarnation out of earth, gave his laws and teachings to his children, and returned to the heavens. The earthly nation of Efé possesses many proto-Caucasoid traits including beards. Missionaries have in general burned documents, artworks and artifacts

---

[27] Louis Pauwels and Jacques Bergier, *The Morning of the Magicians* (New York: Avon Books, 1968), pp. 172–73.

in order to eradicate "heathen superstitions." They have then tried to indoctrinate the heathens with the supremely superstitious belief that they will somehow be "saved" if they believe that a Jewish carpenter of divine origin died on the tree of the crucifixion, that his mother was a virgin, that he walked on the waters, that the Israelites walked through the waters, that Noah survived the deluge in an ark full of animals, ad infinitum. Down through the centuries the missionaries have explained that the similar stories of the heathens are sheer coincidence, borrowings from earlier missionaries or apostles who made imaginary voyages, fabrications of the devil, or divine revelations that prove the literal truth of the Judeo-Christian scriptures. The heathen evidence proves to the contrary that the Old and New Testaments contain exceedingly recent, local and corrupt stories derived from a profoundly meaningful cycle of legends. Here is an outstanding example:

> The Californian Indians had a flood legend, and believed that the early race was diminutive; and the Athapascan Indians of the north-west professed to be descendants of a family who escaped the deluge. Indeed, deluge myths were widespread in the "New World."
>
> The American belief that the first beings who were created were unable to live on earth was shared by the Babylonians. According to Berosus the first creation was a failure, because the animals could not bear the light and they all died. Here we meet the germs of the doctrine of the World's Ages, which reached its highest development in Indian [Hindu], Greek, and Celtic (Irish) mythologies.[28]

The diminutive ancestors of the Indians and Eskimos are legendary, not mythical characters. "Pygmies Before Australoids in the New World?" asked Macgowan and Hester. The answer is yes. The Babylonian historian Berosus maintained that the "light" somehow killed the animals of the first creation. The Cashinaua tribes of Brazil say that all living creatures were annihilated when the lightnings flashed, the thunders roared, and "heaven and earth changed places." The Apapocuva-Guarani tribes maintain

---

[28] Donald A. Mackenzie, *Myths of Babylonia and Assyria*, p. 198.

that the earth caught fire and the first world-age ended when the struts were removed from under the earth. According to the Eskimos the earth turned over.

Gbala, the Efé lightning, is represented as the power that turned the world upside down or caused heaven and earth to change places. Both Gbala and the magic bird-man are said to steal the sacred fire. Some Pygmies say that the lightning repeats the original theft whenever he flashes through the sky: "Each time, it is the lightning who profits from the stolen fire; while the Pygmies dance around it, he springs down to earth and seizes a brand for himself. Since then, the lightning has always possessed the fire."[29] Gbala and the magic bird-man are brother-sons of Efé and God. The bird-man usurped the wings or shape of the Pygmies' national bird in order to steal the sacred fire.

The Eskimo Crow Father is supposed to have stolen the sun from mankind. His elder brother took the sun back and returned it to mankind. The Athapascan descendants of the diminutive race say that their ancestor Yetl, the Raven, gave the fire to mankind. Yetl is the thunderbird: "The Athapascan Indians of Northwest America attribute the creation to the raven Yetl, a bird with fiery eyes, which produced thunder from its wings, a common enough conception among American tribes. On passing from heaven to the sea the plane of earth arose from the waters. From this being the Athapascans trace their descent, that is, they regard the raven as their totem, or eponymous ancestor. Yetl saved their ancestors from the flood and, like Prometheus, brought them fire from heaven."[30]

Prometheus, aided by Athena, stole the fire that Zeus withheld from mankind. The theft led to the advent of death and every other misery. Wekwek the Falcon dropped the stolen fire on the earth, or an evil spirit named Sahte caused the world conflagration, according to the Tuleyone Indians of California. Gbala, the Efé lightning, leaped out of the earth and ascended to the sky. "Then Porphyrion leaped into Heaven from the great pyramid of rocks which the giants had piled up, and none of the gods

[29] P. Schebesta, *Les Pygmées du Congo Belge*, p. 315.

[30] Edwardes and Spence, *A Dictionary of Non-Classical Mythology*, p. 45.

stood his ground. Only Athena adopted a posture of defense," according to the Greek legend of the giants' revolt. The giants attacked the gods in the style of erupting volcanoes: "Without warning, they seized rocks and fire-brands and hurled them upwards from their mountain tops, so that the Olympians were hard pressed."[31]

Doru flew to the forest and fought with the deity. "His brutish ass-head touched the stars, his vast wings darkened the sun, fire flashed from his eyes, and flaming rocks hurtled from his mouth. When he came rushing towards Olympus, the gods fled in terror to Egypt, where they disguised themselves as animals: Zeus becoming a ram; Apollo, a crow; Dionysus, a goat; Hera, a white cow; Artemis, a cat; Aphrodite, a fish; Ares, a boar; Hermes, an ibis, and so on. Athene alone stood her ground, and taunted Zeus with cowardice until, resuming his true form, he let fly a thunderbolt at Typhon, and followed this up with a sweep of the same flint sickle that had served to castrate his grandfather Uranus. Wounded and shouting, Typhon fled to Mount Cassius, which looms over Syria from the north, and there the two grappled."[32]

Athena alone stood her ground when Porphyrion leaped up like the Pygmies' lightning and when Typhon attacked like the Pygmies' magic bird-man. Matu, the mother of the Pygmy nation, uniquely survived the onslaught of the giant swallowing monster. Athens was "compelled to stand alone," deserted by her allies, according to Plato's story of Atlantis. The war was climaxed by violent earthquakes, floods and tempests. Then the Athenians "in a body sank into the earth, and the island of Atlantis in like manner disappeared beneath the sea." Greek ghosts customarily "sank into the earth" to accomplish their trip to the infernal kingdom of Hades. A number of living Greek heroes embarked on Efé's round trip to the "gigantic hole" of the Pygmy Hades.

Efé returned either through a hole in the mountain or through a hole in the foot of the Mountain Mother. In another story, the Pygmy adversary of giant monsters or dragons comes

---

[31] Robert Graves, *The Greek Myths*, Vol. 1, p. 131.

[32] *Ibid.*, p. 134.

back from the celestial paradise through a hole in the vault of heaven. His father, the supreme deity, is stationed above or beyond the hole. Chinese cosmology locates the hole "at the highest point of the heavens." Babylonian legends identify the supreme deity with Polaris, the North Star, and the deity's son with the dragon-fighting hero Merodach or Marduk:

> The seemingly steadfast Polar Star was called "Ilu Sar," "the god Shar," or Anshar, "star of the height," or "Shar the most high." It seemed to be situated at the summit of the vault of heaven. The god Shar, therefore, stood upon the Celestial mountain, the Babylonian Olympus. He was the ghost of the elder god, who in Babylonia was displaced by the younger god, Merodach, as Mercury, the morning star, or as the sun, the planet of day; and in Assyria by Ashur, as the sun, or Regulus, or Arcturus, or Orion. Yet father and son were identical. They were phases of the One, the "self power" . . .

> It is possible that the Babylonian idea of a Celestial mountain gave origin to the belief that the earth was a mountain surrounded by the outer ocean . . . In India this hill is Mount Meru, the "world spine," which "sustains the earth;" it is surmounted by Indra's Valhal, or "the great city of Brahma." In Teutonic mythology the heavens revolve around the Polar Star, which is called "Veraldar nagli," the "world spike;" while the earth is sustained by the "world tree" . . . The Babylonian temple towers were apparently symbols of the "world hill" . . .

> Now Polaris, situated at the summit of the celestial mountain, was identified with the sacred goat, "the highest of the flock of night."

> Tammuz, like Anshar, as sentinel of the night heaven, was a goat, as was also Nin-Girsu of Lagash. A Sumerian reference to "a white kid of En Mersi (Nin-Girsu)" was translated into Semitic, "a white kid of Tammuz." The goat was also associated with Merodach. Babylonians, having prayed to that god to take away their diseases or their sins, released a goat, which was driven into the desert. The present Polar star, which was not, of course, the Polar star of the earliest astronomers, the world having rocked westward, is called in Arabic Al-Jedy, "the kid." In India, the goat was connected with Agni and Varuna; it was slain at funeral ceremonies to inform the gods that a soul was about to enter heaven. Ea, the Sumerian lord of water, earth, and heaven, was symbolized as a

"goat fish." Thor, the Teutonic fertility and thunder god, had a chariot drawn by goats. It is of interest to note that the sacred Sumerian goat bore on its forehead the same triangular symbol as the Apis bull of Egypt.[33]

Polaris was the "world spike" or "world nail" of Germanic legend. Efé *apili* and *pilisi,* arrow-point and needle: Anglo-Saxon *pil*, arrow, dart, javelin, spike, nail, pointed object in general. Norwegian *pil* and *pila*, arrow and pillar. Latin *pilum* and *pila*, javelin and pillar. Greek *palton* and *polos*, javelin and pole. English *pillar*, *pole*, and *Polaris*. An old Egyptian legend described four pillars or four gods, the Children of Horus, who held up the sky from their stations at the four cardinal points. The legends of the Norse Eddas station four sky-supporting dwarfs called North, South, East, and West, at the four cardinal points. A very fragmentary Efé legend says that four Pygmy elders were drowned in a great flood or deluge. This story is connected, like other Pygmy legends, with the epic disasters of the Pleistocene. Efé *apili* is a form of *api*, arrow, pointed stick, pointer. This word may be related to Egyptian *hapi,* the god of the north cardinal point, who was sometimes identified with Osiris.

Polaris was obscurely associated with a sacred goat. The Greek goat-god Pan was represented as the son of Hermes and hence of the Egyptian moon-god Thoth. The god Pan and a goat were worshiped in the Lower Egyptian cities of Hermopolis and Mendes. The goat was known at the "Ram of Mendes." The Pygmy god Bes wears "the horns of Amen or of the Ram of Mendes" in his Metternich portrait. Etruscan tomb paintings show bearded "dwarfs" teaching youths how to play the panpipes. Efé, the Pygmy inventor of wind instruments, plays flutes and trumpets of several varieties. Efé or Aré'bati, the Angel of the Moon, is the eldest son and principal servant of the deity. The lunar angel sent a goat down to earth; the goat gave birth to all of the animals and returned to the sky. The Efé represent the moon as the celestial power that gives fertility to plants, animals and people. The Mountain of the Moon is a form of Matu, the "maternal" parent of Efé. The people of every world-age are sired by Efé,

---

[33] Donald A. Mackenzie, *Myths of Babylonia and Assyria*, pp. 330–33.

the first man and last man. *Mémé* or *méma*, the goat, is the *ema* or "mother" of the Efé animals: Greek *mamme* and *mamma*, grandmother and mother. English *mammal*, *mama* and *ma*. Sumerian *ama*, Hebrew *em*, mother.

The Efé Pygmies did not borrow from any outside source their legends of the sacred goat, the vault of heaven and the cosmic mountain that stands on the eastern edge of the Ituri Forest. Efé enters the Troy-town maze in the mountain at the end of every world-age. The lightning is the "bad" or destructive power that achieves the end by turning the world upside down. The lightning is a tool of the Pygmies' deity. He directs the activities of the personified lightning, hurls bolts of lightning, or produces the lightning and thunder out of himself: "The lightning comes when the divinity opens his mouth and his eyes; the thunder is the voice of God. Thunder and lightning are under his control," Schebesta commented on Efé theology.[34]

"Hear attentively the noise of his voice, and the sound that goeth out of his mouth. He directeth it under the whole heaven, and his lightning unto the ends of the earth. After it a voice roareth: he thundereth with the voice of his excellency; and he will not stay them when his voice is heard. God thundereth marvellously with his voice; great things doeth he, which we cannot comprehend," declares the Old Testament book of Job.[35]

God the Grandfather hurls lightning bolts at sinners. In numerous Pygmy stories his angelic son Efé wields the weapons of his father. The lightning is their tool or a form of their wicked, destructive brother-son. Many Greek and Egyptian stories describe Set-Typhon, the brother of Horus the Elder and of Osiris, as the supremely evil source of lightning, earthquakes, tempests and all cataclysmic phenomena that modern insurance policies define as "acts of God." The Satanic destroyer's foremost Greek adversary, Zeus, hurled thunderbolts and disciplined mankind by causing world-wide cataclysms.

Typhon attacked Olympus and imprisoned Zeus in a cave. Efé was incarcerated in the abyss; Efé or his son returned through

[34] P. Schebesta, *Les Pygmées du Congo Belge*, p. 321.

[35] Job 37:2–5.

the hole in the Mountain Mother and vanquished the giant swallowing monster. Zeus was released from the cave and defeated Typhon, the father of the infamous water serpent Hydra. Zeus's son Apollo emerged from the mountain-island of Delos that was raised above the waters of the flood, and on the fourth day of his life, conquered the giant serpent Python. The hero-god was "imprisoned" in the underworld kingdom while his tool or secret ally, the geophysical destroyer, annihilated the population of the earth.

In the story of the forbidden tree, God sends his son Efé from the celestial paradise to the earthly paradise. There, according to the Kango Pygmies, "God" worked in his smithy and taught smithcraft to the ancestors. God the Grandfather throws his son Gbala down to earth in the form of Efé lightning bolts. Zeus hurled his son Hephaestus down from the sky or the summit of Olympus. The Greek god of smithcraft and fire broke both of his legs when he struck the earth at Lemnos, an island in the Aegean Sea, and thereafter had to wear golden braces on his legs. Hephaestus' thieving and deceitful enemy Prometheus descended to earth, modeled the first man out of clay, taught smithcraft, and brought disaster to mankind when he stole the forbidden fire of Zeus from the Olympian smithy of Hephaestus.

Hephaestus, not Prometheus, should have modeled the first man in the creative style of Efé. Prometheus, not Hephaestus, should have been hurled down to earth in the style of the Pygmies' thieving lightning. Doru, the magic bird-man, is the alternate thief of fire. Dante's *Divine Comedy* describes a Roman eagle or thunderbird of Zeus that plummeted down from the heavens and struck the tree, cross or chariot pole on the paradisaical summit of the purgatorial mountain. "The Mountain of Purgatory, the only land in the southern hemisphere, to which Dante now comes, was formed when Lucifer fell by the earth rushing up to escape him. It is the exact antipodes of Jerusalem and Mount Calvary," Edmund Gardner maintained in his edition of Dante's epic poem (p. 147). Satan, the so-called fallen angel, makes a pyrotechnic descent from heaven to the infernal abodes in the first book of Milton's *Paradise Lost:* "Him the Almighty Power hurld headlong flaming from th'Ethereal Skie, with hideous ruine and combustion down to bottomless perdition, there to dwell in Adamantine Chains and penal Fire."

Gbala is the Efé name of the lightning. *Bali,* the sacred name of fire, is an absolute synonym for God. The latter word is also used as a title of Efé, the divine father-son of the Ituri Forest legend cycle. Matu, the enigmatic lady whom the Pygmies do not define as a goddess, tends the sacred fire and is said to be as bright as the sun:

Babylonian *Gibil,* the fire of heaven, the fire at the heart of the earth, the fire of the altar, the sacrificial fire, the god of smithcraft, the messenger of Marduk or intermediary between God and Man. Phyrgian *Cybele,* the great mother of the gods. Babylonian *bel* and *belit,* god and goddess. Hebrew *baal,* god or lord; *baalim,* heathen gods or idols. Syro-Phoenician *baal,* Carthaginian *bal,* god or lord. Tyrian *Baal,* the god of fire and the sun. Scottish *Baal* and Irish *Beli,* the god of the Celtic "Beltane" fires. Western Pygmy *Bali,* God as the source of fire, heat, light, and life. Old Norse *bal,* Swedish *bal,* Norwegian *bal,* Anglo-Saxon *bael,* English *bale:* fire, flame, bonfire, sacrificial fire, funeral fire, balefire. Germanic *Balder,* the god of the balefires, the god of light, a son of Odin and brother of Thor. *Balder's Balar,* "Balder's Balefires," ceremonial fires that are still lighted periodically in some parts of rural Scandinavia. The light-god Balder was traditionally resurrected from the underworld kingdom of hell after the cataclysms of Ragnarok or Götterdämmerung, the twilight of the gods. Bel Marduk, "God Marduk," and/or the Mesopotamian deity Tammuz likewise accomplished Efé's trip to the abyss.

Gbaragé and *gbalagé* are forms of the Efé word for a bolt of lightning or thunderbolt. The Pygmies very commonly drop the consonant *g* before *b,* as Schebesta remarked. *Baragé* and *balagé* are thereby produced: Hebrew *barak,* a flash of lightning, splendor, to send forth lightning; *balag,* to cause to flash up, to burst forth in splendor. Arabic *bark,* Persian *barq,* lightning. Sanskrit *bhargas,* radiance; *bhraj,* to shine. Dutch *blaken,* to burn or glow; *bliksem,* lightning. Swedish *blixt,* Czech *blesk,* Polish *blyskawica,* German *blitz,* lightning.

Efé *balagé* is still remembered by the Andaman Island Pygmies, whose language is ostensibly unrelated to any human tongue: "Puluga, the Deity, who has the form of fire, is a god of the storm whose voice roars like thunder and who hurls the lightnings like fire brands . . . His righteous wrath punishes the men who ignore his commandments. One can sin in many fashions against Puluga; the principal faults are lying, theft, adultery, aggression and murder."[36] Greek *Phlego,* I flash, burn, shine, flame, or blaze; *phloga,* fire or phlogiston. Latin *Fulgeo,* I flash, lighten or shine; *fulgor,* lightning, flash, brightness, splendor; *fulgur,* lightning or thunderbolt.

Bali and *bari* are variant forms of the fire word: Anglo-Saxon *bael,* the balefire; *baernan,* to burn. Old Norse *bal,* the balefire; *baela,* to consume by fire. Finnish *palaa,* to burn; *palo,* fire or conflagration. Greek *pyro-,* pertaining to fire, as in pyromaniac; *pyr,* fire, lightning or blaze; *pyra,* a place where fire is kindled, a funeral pyre, a burial place; *pyramis,* an Egyptian tomb or pyramid. Greek *pyro-* approaches Efé *boru,* which Schebesta gave as a variant form of the sacred fire word: English *burn,* French *brûler,* to burn. Old Norse *bruni,* burning, heat or fire. Dutch *brand,* fire or fire brand; *branden,* to burn. German *brennen,* Yiddish *brenen,* Norwegian *brenne,* Old Norse *brenna,* Swedish *brinna,* to burn, as in Efé *bari* or *boru.*

Schebesta defined the *boru'é'i* constituent of the Efé personality as the "pulse" and equated it with the soul. The "pulse" definition is Sua Pygmy usage. In Efé, this word refers to the spiritual fire, essence or life force of human beings and the deity. It is also used to designate a spiritual being or "spirit" in general. (There are different categories of spirits, as in medieval angelology.) The sacred fire is a subdivision of the vital force with which the deity animates the universe. Animals do not use fire, say the elders, or possess the fiery essence.

"According to all appearances, this principle returns to God (Toré), in the sky, where it becomes a star, since the stars are the souls of the departed, the hosts of the celestial deity's kingdom," Schebesta commented on the glorious post-mortem apotheosis of the Efé *boru'é'i.*[37] The elders say to the children, "Look at those twinkling stars! They are the Pygmy people of the sky. If you are a good little boy and live your life as an honorable man, your star will be one of the brightest. If you are a coward or

---

[36] P. Schebesta, *Les Pygmées,* p. 161.

[37] P. Schebesta, *Les Pygmées du Congo Belge,* p. 331.

a cruel man, your star will be so dim that no one will be able to see it." The child's eyes shine like stars as he says, "Oh, I will always be good! My star will be the brightest!"

The Babylonians maintained that "the stars are all spirits, the host of heaven." Anthropologists call the globally distributed versions of this belief by the savage-sounding title of "star totems." The ancient astronomers have been denigrated because their people cherished the idea that the soul, or some part of the personality, is transformed into a twinkling star.

> That astronomy had humble beginnings in Greece as elsewhere is highly probable. The late Mr. Andrew Lang wrote in this connection: "The very oddest example of the survival of the notion that the stars are men and women is found in the *Pax* of Aristophanes. Trygaeus in that comedy has just made an expedition to heaven. A slave meets him, and asks him: 'Is not the story true, then, that we become stars when we die?' The answer is, 'Certainly!' and Trygaeus points out the star into which Ion of Chios has just been metamorphosed." Mr. Lang added: "The Eskimos, Persians, Aryo-Indians, Germans, New Zealanders, and others had a similar superstition.[38]

Western Pygmy ghosts dwell for an indefinite length of time with their friends and relatives. They do good deeds in the style of invisible Boy Scouts until they "no longer recognize people." Then what happens? "Having rejoined the Creator in the form of shooting stars, they are on high, very high, brilliant, in the luminary."[39] The ghosts of the Bantu and Sudanese tribesmen who surround the Pygmies are not transformed into stars, meteors or heavenly bodies of any variety. The people of Pythagoras, Anaxagoras and the other Greek astronomers instead shared a "primitive superstition" with Homer's Pygmies. Egyptian pictures of two dwarfs were associated with the belief that the deceased would turn into a star. The Eskimo descendants of the diminutive race, the Germanic progeny of the elves, the Polynesian members of the Pygmies' string-picture club, and a host of globally distributed peoples have echoed the "primitive superstition" that is very inti-

---

[38] Donald A. Mackenzie, *Myths of Babylonia and Assyria*, pp. 319–20.

[39] Henri Trilles, *The Soul of the African Pygmy*, p. 180.

mately connected with the star pictures of the constellations and the zodiac.

Toré the Star-Maker does not traffic in Efé "souls" that represent immaterial versions of the deceased or his total personality. The fiery constitutent of the deceased returns to the celestial lord of the sacred fire. Up until the past few generations, this apotheosis was achieved by a very remarkable ceremony. The deceased was laid out on a funeral pyre, along with his bow, arrows, musical instruments and other worldly goods. Prayers were intoned, a burning brand was touched to the pyre, and while all the members of the community wept and keened like mourners at a Irish wake, the sacred fire of the deceased ascended in smoke to the sky. The lunar angel received the fire and transmitted or reflected it to his father Toré in the celestial paradise.

A few Efé bands in the depths of the forest retain the fiery funeral that has been supplanted in most territories by the recently introduced custom of burial. The deceased is now interred in a shallow grave. The members of his community mourn him with prayers, songs, keening and paroxysms of weeping that make the funeral an almost unbearably moving experience. Every person, male or female, young or old, is laid to rest and mourned in these rituals. Bereaved women throw themselves into the grave and have to be forcibly removed by the men. The surrounding Negro tribes formerly buried only chiefs and wealthy men; the ordinary dead were traditionally exposed to hyenas, jackals and other scavengers. Today, most of the Negro tribes bury all their dead, with a minimum of ceremony.

The traditional funeral pyres of the older Efé ceremony are, as ever, unparalleled among the modern Bantu and Sudanese invaders of the Ituri Forest. Fire, the "vital spark," was the "principle of life which was manifested by bodily heat" in the Indo-European religion of ancient India. "The Aryan fire worshippers cremated their dead so that the spirits might be transferred by fire to Paradise," scholars have remarked.[40] The recently suppressed custom of suttee obliged the Hindu widow to mount the funeral pyre of her husband. No person was ever permitted, much

---

[40] Donald A. Mackenzie, *Myths of Babylonia and Assyria*, pp. 49–50.

less forced, to commit suicide on the Pygmy funeral pyres. The Efé make incense fires out of aromatic leaves and special wood; the ascending smoke "delivers a prayer" to the deity, as in many religions (Christianity included) that feature the burning of incense. The Efé do not make burnt offerings of sacrificial animals and humans. They are not "fire worshipers."

The traditional funeral fire "separates the parts of a person," say the elders. The human components are released like the elements of a chemical compound. An Efé person and his elements do not have the same properties. The compound person represents a unique combination of the elements. These elements cannot be equated with a soul, which is represented as an immaterial version of the deceased person. A living Efé person possesses a soul, as we usually conceive of it. This soul or personality does not survive the process of death. The Pygmies' Negro neighbors believe that the spirits of the dead wander about their natal villages, hounding the living with their incessant demands. "The Pygmies are free from those nagging ghosts because they do not share in that most persistent of all primitive beliefs, the survival of the soul," I wrote in *Congo Kitabu*. Here I used the word "primitive" in the sense of crude or unsophisticated.

The Pygmy concept that fire "separates the parts of a person" would be appreciated by the Greek philosopher Heraclitus (c. 540–470 B.C.): "As Anaximenes had chosen Mist as his First Principle, Heraclitus chose Fire. He was the philosopher of change. His doctrine has been summed up in the phrase *Everything flows;* but his choice of Fire as his First Principle was probably not due, as is often said, to its being the most impermanent of things, but to its being the active agent which produces change in so many technical and natural processes."[41] The flaming pyres of the Homeric heroes and the "Vikings' funerals" of northern Europe are outstanding examples of an Efé-style cremation ceremony. The early Etruscans, many American Indian tribes and the great majority of early historic peoples cremated their dead: "This method of disposal of the dead was the general practice of the ancient world with the important exceptions of Egypt, where bodies were embalmed,

[41] B. Farrington, *Greek Science* (Penguin Books, 1949), Vol. 1, p. 35.

Judaea, where they were buried in sepulchres, and China, where they were buried in the earth. Cremation is still practiced over a great part of Asia and America, but not always in the same form. Thus, the ashes may be stored in urns, or buried in the earth, or thrown to the winds, or (as among the Digger Indians) smeared with gum on the heads of the mourners."[42]

Greek *pyro-*, the fire of the traditional funeral pyre, approaches the "burning" *boru* variant of Efé *bali*, the sacred fire or a title of the ancestral deity. Old Norse Bur, the first man, emerged from the melting ice of the Germanic beginning. His son Bor was the father of Thor's father or son Odin. Thor's murdered brother Balder, the god of light, was cremated with the aid of *bal*, the "balefire" or funeral pyre. Then Balder went to the land of Hell whence he is resurrected after the great disasters of Ragnarok. The several forms and titles of Efé account for the weird genealogy of Balder, Odin, Thor and company. "This was the place for the fire which was never allowed to go out. This they called the sacred fire," the *Kjalnesinga Saga* comments on the fire that burned in the temple of Thor. The Efé congregation of Toré or "God" retain the strictest possible version of the perpetual fire custom---they do not use artificial fire-making apparatus of any variety.

Balder went to the underworld after his Viking's funeral; then he was resurrected from the depths of Hell. Efé and many other living heroes accomplished a round-trip expedition to the infernal abode of the ghosts. Bali, the fiery title of the ancestral deity, might easily be confused with *balimo*, the disembodied spirit or ghost that goes after death to the Efé kingdom of the dead. The *balimo* is represented as the spiritual essence of the sacred fire or intellectual component of the total person. The Egyptian person was composed of Pygmy-style elements that included the spirit, the soul, the heart, the shadow, the double, and so forth. Khu, the spirit or intelligence, was defined as a "shining, impalpable and immaterial" entity that more or less corresponds with the Efé "ghost."

The *balimo* is much more humanoid in character than the so-called soul that the celestial deity turns into a star. The ghosts, for example, behaved like people during the hero's trip to Hades;

---

[42] "Cremation," *Encyclopaedia Britannica*, 14th ed., Vol. 6, p. 665.

they conversed and enjoyed Efé's musical performance. Deceased members of many early European tribes alternately turned into stars and descended to the land of the ghosts. The Germanic hell, in its most archaic form, was not a place of punishment. The ghosts or souls of sinners were chastised in the Greco-Roman abyss of Tartarus; thus, when the living hero Orpheus descended to Tartarus, his music soothed the savage heart of Zeus's brother Hades and temporarily suspended the "tortures of the damned."

The Efé *balimo* is not an underworld version of the total person. The *balimo* is not responsible for the sins, crimes or follies of the deceased. In territories where the Pygmies have been grossly corrupted by the feudal system, this concept of the ghost has been mingled with Bantu and Sudanese beliefs about the malevolent spirits of the dead. The traditional Efé *balimo* does not behave like the ghosts or evil spirits of Black Africa, the ghosts who haunt European castles, or the ghosts who send messages at séances where their bereaved relatives are exploited by phony "spiritualists." The *balimo* does not retain any memories of its earthly existence; it is like a computer whose banks have been cleared. When a child is begotten, a *balimo* leaves the land of the ghosts and joins the other components that the lunar angel traditionally assembles to produce a new human being. The Pygmies are perfectly aware of the role that the human father plays in begetting a child; the lunar angel is the heavenly father who regulates the process and, according to many Pygmies, allots a span of life and decides whether the child will be a boy or a girl. "What if all the elements of a person are rejoined? Does that person live again?" I asked the Efé elder Mwenua. He replied, "It is possible that the same combination may be repeated once in a while. Such a person would still be new. He would not know what the former person had seen and felt."

Here we see the germ of the reincarnation belief. The total person of Efé philosophy cannot, however, be reincarnated: he is the irreproducible result of all his elements combined with his experiences. Some of the elders maintain that the *balimo* dwells with the dwarfs during its sojourn in the kingdom of the dead; others say that the *balimo* inhabits the body of a dwarf until its return. The dwarfs correspond with the "dark elves" of the Germanic underworld, the *menehune* or black dwarfs who dwell beneath the Hawaiian earth, and many similar characters who are usually interpreted as earth spirits. The mischief-working dwarf and the giant swallowing monster of the Western Pygmy underworld are "spirits of night" and "spirits of cold." Their original homeland in the faraway frozen countries of legend matches the Germanic hell in the quick-frozen Europe of the last Pleistocene glaciation.

Efé, a living hero, apparently died and returned to life by taking a trip through the Mountain of the Moon. The *balimo* or "ghost" goes back and forth to the kingdom of the dead through the Troy-town maze in the mountain. The Egyptian deceased was "an Osiris" who traditionally repeated or emulated the experiences of the slain and resurrected hero Osiris. The pottery figurines of Ptah-Seker-Osiris, the triune god of the resurrection, represent the deity as a Pygmy or "dwarf." The Egyptian kings were direct descendants of the gods. The Egyptian practice of burying deceased kings in mountainous pyramids and in the labyrinth at Crocodilopolis rather strongly suggests that confused versions of Pygmy legends and concepts are responsible for the Egyptian embalming customs and belief in the resurrection of the dead. The residence of Osiris, the god of the moon and the god of the Nile, was located in the funeral mountain of Amentet, which we have identified with the Pygmies' lunar mountain at the source of the Nile. "After a long life of toil, the pious Egyptian embarked in Amen's barge to delve into the dark kingdom of Anumbis. Terrific ordeals had to be overcome before he could reach the luminous shores of the Amenti where a new life awaited him."[43]

This voyage is paralleled by a very significant custom of the early Germanic people who did not embalm or mummify the dead:

> By the early Iron Age, the ship was also in use as a funeral symbol. Graves in Gotland and elsewhere were carefully made in the shape of a boat, the outline marked out in stones around the burned or buried remains of the dead. By about A.D. 600, the dead were buried or burned inside real boats, or parts of boats . . . Whether in heathen

---

[43] Paul Ghalioungui, *Magic and Medical Science in Ancient Egypt* (London: Hodder and Stoughton, 1963), p. 156.

times a dead man was ever launched on a ship which formed his funeral pyre as it sailed, slowly burning, out to sea is something which we cannot know. Such a rite was said to have formed part of Balder's funeral . . . Ship funeral could have been presented as a re-enactment of the departure in the mythical past of the founder of the race over the sea to the Other World . . . It is a very ancient funeral symbol, for in ancient Egypt ships were placed in graves beside some of the pyramids in the Old Kingdom, while model ships were buried in the tombs of Tutankhamen and other rulers of the New Kingdom.[44]

The medieval legends of Charlemagne and many other European stories specifically locate the entrance to Hades at the source of the Nile. Balder was cremated by the traditional Efé funeral that returns the sacred fire to the celestial deity; then Balder went to the Efé land of the ghosts that is reached through the Troy-town maze in the Mountain of the Moon. Down to modern times, British children danced the Troy-town dance that the Athenian king Theseus supposedly brought to Europe after he sailed to Crete and traveled through the "death-maze." The Cretans denied the existence of a Cretan labyrinth or "death-maze." Theseus accomplished an alternate trip through the cavernous kingdom of Hades.

The Metternich Stele shows the Pygmy god Bes holding the sovereign emblems of Osiris, the Egyptian god of the dead. "I am not dead," Efé, the Pygmy, repeatedly declared during his sojourn in the abyss. Efé, the living hero or nation, was "resurrected" or returned from the infernal kingdom of legend. The Egyptian concept of the resurrection is intimately related to the fallacious, superstitious or wistful Christian belief that the dead body of Christ came back to life, and that the buried remains of his devout followers will be miraculously reanimated. "There can be little doubt that the practice of cremation in modern Europe was at first stopped, and has since been prevented in great measure, by the Christian doctrine of the resurrection of the body; partly also by the notion that the Christian's body was redeemed and purified," the *Britannica* remarks in its article entitled "Cremation." The practice of cremation was an almost universal custom among the

---

[44] H. R. Ellis Davidson, *Gods and Myths of Northern Europe*, pp. 133–37.

Old and New World representatives of early historic man. Anthropological theories nevertheless describe burial in graves as the source of the globally distributed legends about the subterranean kingdom of Hades:

In the "Descent of Ishtar" the Babylonian Underworld is called Cuthah. This city had a famous cemetery, like Abydos in Egypt, where many pious and orthodox worshippers sought sepulture . . .

In Nether Cuthah, as Ea-bani informed Gilgamesh, the worm devoured the dead amidst the dust and thick darkness.

It is evident that this Underworld was modelled on the grave. In early times men believed that the spirits of the dead hovered in or about the place of sepulture. They were therefore provided with "houses" to protect them, in the same manner as the living were protected in their houses above the ground . . .

Among the ancient Romans the primitive belief survived that the spirit of the dead "just sank into the earth where it rested, and returned from time to time to the upper world through certain openings in the ground (mundi), whose solemn uncovering was one of the regular observances of the festal calendar.[45]

This author described, in another context, Gilgamesh's journey to the tremendous mountain of Mashi: "The mountain peak rose to heaven, and its foundations were in Aralu, the Underworld. A dark tunnel pierced it and could be entered through a door . . ." Gilgamesh went through the door, groped for "twice twelve hours" through a tunnel that was twelve miles long, emerged from the tunnel into an "enchanted garden," and went to the palace of the sea lady Sabitu on the shores of the Sea of Death. Gilgamesh accomplished this journey by invoking the "divine protection" of the moon god. Efé, the earthly son of the lunar angel, traveled through the Troy-town maze in the Mountain of the Moon to the groves and forests on the shores of the underworld river, met the hag-like ghost of Matu, and then paid a forced visit to the house of Doru and Matu, or Greek palace of Hades and Persephone in the abyss of Tartarus.

Anthropological theories maintain that mazes originated as sepulchers. Theseus, the hero of the Greek maze legend, was incarcerated on Hades' underworld chair. Efé played his harp and told

[45] Donald A. Mackenzie, *Myths of Babylonia and Assyria*, pp. 206–7.

stories while seated on the stool in the village of the ghosts. Efé is Bes, the harp-playing Pygmy god of the Egyptian musical arts. Orpheus played the harp of his father Apollo, the Greek god of the musical arts, during his trip to Tartarus. Apollo's priestess delivered prophecies while seated on a "sacred stool" or tripod in the "sacred chasm" at Delphi on the slopes of Mount Parnassus in Greece. A "sacred stone" called Omphalos, the Navel, marked the center of the earth at the famous Oracle of Delphi or Oracle of Mother Earth. Apollo was the ancestral "Homer," a title of the god's poets, musicians and dancers. Homer's Pygmies, ironically enough, tell the legend of Efé the Pygmy Homer and Egyptian Dancer of God who sat on the sacred stool of Everyman's Olympus-Hades at the center of the earth.

Another place called Omphalos was situated in the island of Crete, where Theseus supposedly made his trip through the Troy-town maze and Apollo's father Zeus spent his childhood years in a cave of the Aegean hill. The living hero Theseus made his legendary trip to the abyss of Tartarus through a cave of the Taenarum promontory in southernmost Greece. The ghost of Theseus' son Hippolytus descended to Tartarus where he was miraculously revived by Apollo's physician son Asclepius. Theseus allegedly cursed his son Hippolytus and caused his death by praying for the weird cataclysm that struck Hippolytus down while he was driving a chariot from Athens to Troezen, the Troy-like hometown of his father:

> As he drove along the narrow part of the Isthmus a huge wave, which overtopped even the Molurian Rock, rolled roaring shoreward; and from its crest sprang a great dog-seal (or, some say, a white bull), bellowing and spouting water. Hippolytus's four horses swerved towards the cliff, mad with terror, but being an expert charioteer he restrained them from plunging over the edge. The beast then galloped menacingly behind the chariot, and he failed to keep his team on a straight course. Not far from the sanctuary of Saronian Artemis, a wild olive is still shown, called the Twisted Rhachos—the Troezenian term for a barren olive-tree is *rhachos*—and it was on a branch of this tree that a loop of Hippolytus's reins caught. His chariot was flung sideways against a pile of rocks and broken into pieces. Hippolytus, entangled in the reins, and thrown

first against the tree-trunk, and then against the rocks, was dragged to death by his horses, while the pursuer vanished . . .

The Troezenians themselves deny that Hippolytus was dragged to death by horses, or even that he lies buried in his temple; nor will they reveal the whereabouts of his real tomb. Yet they declare that the gods set him among the stars as the Charioteer.[46]

Hippolytus apparently perished near a sanctuary of the moon-goddess Artemis. When his ghost descended to Tartarus, Artemis persuaded Apollo's son Asclepius to revive the hero. The Roman moon-goddess Diana was the patron saint of the sacred grove at Nemi, near the modern Italian town of La Riccia. There Hippolytus or Virbius, as the Romans called him, traditionally dwelled in the cave or grotto of Egeria. Every May Day solemn processions went to the grotto of the resurrected hero. The springtime Easter festivals of the old European tribes were the festivals of the Troy-town dance that Hippolytus' father Theseus brought to Europe after he returned from the Troy-town maze or the abyss of Hades.

The Romans supposedly clung to a "primitive belief" that the spirit of the dead "just sank into the earth where it rested, and returned from time to time to the upper world through certain openings in the ground (mundi), whose solemn uncovering was one of the regular observances of the festal calendar." Sir J. G. Frazer commented on Hippolytus in his study *The Golden Bough:*

> Some thought that he was the sun. "But the truth is," says Servius, "that he is a deity associated with Diana, as Attis is associated with the Mother of the Gods, and Erichthonius with Minerva, and Adonis with Venus." What the nature of that association was we shall enquire presently. Here it is worth observing that in his long and chequered career this mythical personage has displayed a remarkable tenacity of life. For we can hardly doubt that the Saint Hippolytus of the Roman calendar, who was dragged by horses to death on the thirteenth of August, Diana's own day, is no other than the Greek hero of the same name, who, after dying twice over as a heathen sinner, has been happily resuscitated as a Christian saint.[47]

---

[46] Robert Graves, *The Greek Myths,* Vol. 1, pp. 357–58.

[47] Sir J. G. Frazer, *The Golden Bough,* p. 5.

Hippolytus' metamorphosis from heathen sinner to Christian saint is a very unhappy example of the intellectual frauds that have expedited the rise to power and continuing survival of the organized Christian churches. The Romans identified Hippolytus with Erichthonius, the eponymous ancestor of the Erechtheids or royal family of Athens. Erichthonius was associated with Minerva, the Roman version of the Greek goddess Athena. Erichthonius' father Hephaestus was the gentleman founder of Plato's paradisaical Athens. The Athenians "sank into the earth" like ghosts descending to Hades, according to Plato's story of the cataclysms that sank Atlantis in the sea. The Romans identified Hippolytus with the murdered Greek god Adonis, a well-known equivalent of the Mesopotamian deity Tammuz who was "cast out with the flood" and the other pre-Christian versions of the New Testament Christ. Hippolytus was accused of having illicit sexual relations with Phaedra, his stepmother. Theseus indignantly expelled his son from Athens and the youthful hero met his apparent death in a watery disaster. After Hippolytus was revived in the kingdom of Hades, the moon goddess Diana or Artemis "disguised him as an aged man" and installed him in her Italian grotto. Does this story sound familiar?

The Theban prince Oedipus married his mother. King Laius tried to kill his son Oedipus by locking the infant in a chest and dumping it into the sea. Theseus buried the aged Oedipus in an undiscovered tomb. The people of Troezen repudiated the story that Theseus' son Hippolytus was buried in his temple and would not reveal the whereabouts of his "real tomb." Hippolytus, disguised as an old man, dwells in a sacred cave or grotto of the moon goddess Artemis-Diana. The bodies of King Arthur and a host of other hero-gods are buried in undiscovered or disputed tombs. Their people customarily cremated the dead. Merlin buried himself alive in a tomb that is reached through maze-like chambers in a towering mountain. "I was in Africa before the building of Rome," declared Little Gwion/Merlin/Taliesin. Arabic legends locate the tomb of the Great Hermes in the Central African Mountain of the Moon. "Saint Hippolytus" was involved in a tidal wave deluge and apparently returned from Hades via the resurrection cave in the mountain. The Great Hermes survived the deluge by retreating to the lunar mountain at the source of the Nile.

Hermes and his father Zeus were reputed fathers of a diminutive Greek deity who was represented in other stories as their ancestor, the first and oldest god. According to the Orphic creation legend Phanes, Eros or Cupid dwelled in a cave with his mother, the goddess Night. "Before this cave sat the inescapable mother Rhea, playing on a brazen drum, and compelling man's attention to the oracles of the goddess. Phanes created earth, sky, sun, and moon, but the triple-goddess ruled the universe, until her sceptre passed to Uranus."[48]

The Orphics were the devotees of Orpheus, the superlative poet and musician who was represented as the son of Apollo and identified with the god Dionysus. Apollo and Dionysus, the Greek versions of the Egyptian gods Horus and Osiris, were both associated with the Parnassus mountain of the "sacred chasm" at the Delphic navel of the earth. Apollo's father Zeus spent his childhood in a cave at the Cretan navel of the earth. Zeus's mother, the Titaness Rhea, sat at the entrance to Cupid's cave. She was identified with the Mountain Mother or Great Mother of the Gods and represented, in Plutarch's treatise on Isis and Osiris, as the mother of Isis, Osiris and Horus. Little Cupid apparently dwelled in the cave until his mother, the triple-goddess Night, relinquished her sovereignty.

The legends of Efé collectively explain that the Pygmy hero or nation goes through the hole in the foot of the Mountain Mother to the ghostly kingdom where Efé sojourns during "the long dark night," "the killer cold" and other disasters that occur when the world turns upside down. "After the 'Great Fire' came the 'Long Night,'" say the Apapocuva-Guarani Indians. "Men could not leave their homes. The majority died of hunger."[49] Famines preceded the earth-splitting lightning bolt of Efé legend. Man and beast could not find any room to live in the overpopulated world of Persian legend. "The earth was thereafter cloven with a golden arrow. Yima then built a refuge in which mankind and the domesticated animals might find shelter during a terrible winter."[50]

---

[48] Robert Graves, *The Greek Myths*, p. 30.

[49] *Larousse World Mythology*, p. 490.

[50] Donald A. Mackenzie, *Myths of Babylonia and Assyria*, p. 202.

Balder returned from the Germanic underworld after Fimbul-vetr, the Terrible Winter, and the associated disasters of Ragnarok. Balder's father, Odin, and/or the white elves of the Old White Africa have a fire shelter in the neighborhood of the Heaven Mountain that stands at the center of the earth in the lost paradise of Asgard or Troy. The Anglo-Saxon poem *Beowulf* describes a fiery winged dragon, "the aged dragon of darkness," that stands guard over "the great stronghold under the earth." An unknown man plundered the golden treasures of the infernal kingdom while the dragon slept. "Then did the resident spit forth embers, and burn up the bright dwellings; the flaming ray wrought mischief to men, for the enemy flying through the air would leave nothing alive . . . He encompassed the people of the land with burning, with fire and flame."[51]

An immense chameleon dragon guards the gate of Dan, the Western Pygmy underworld. During the daylight hours, the ghosts cling to the walls of the caverns and the dragon cannot be seen. He is invisible or hides himself from sight. On the very rare occasions that a chameleon is accidentally killed, the Western Pygmies burn the body on a miniature funeral pyre while they chant:

> Chameleon, to the one who sent you,
> Return with the greatest speed.
> Chameleon, chameleon!
> Your eyes are dead,
> Your ears hear no longer,
> Chameleon, chameleon!
> You have given your message,
> Return to the one who sent you.[52]

In the eastern Ituri, the Efé Pygmies recite a brief spontaneous prayer when they cremate an accidentally killed chameleon. "Father, we did not mean to harm the messenger of heaven. You know that. So forgive us," I have heard the Efé pray. The chameleon is the messenger of the lunar angel, Efé or Aré'bati. The chameleon is the most sacred but neither-totem-nor-taboo animal of Efé and God. The chameleon ceremony is not a "burnt offering"

---

[51] H. R. Ellis Davidson, *Gods and Myths of Northern Europe*, p. 159.

[52] Henri Trilles, *The Soul of the African Pygmy*, p. 165.

or sacrifice. It is intimately allied with the flaming human funeral that has been supplanted by the introduced custom of burial. The fiery winged dragon of *Beowulf* was just as closely associated with the funeral customs of northern Europe:

> The vivid description of the dragon in the Anglo-Saxon poem is to some extent corroborated by the dragon set on the king's great shield found in the Sutton Hoo ship-grave. The long teeth, folded wings, and pointed tail can be clearly made out in the stylized and yet powerful figure of the monster . . . Even after cremation of the dead was given up, there is reason to believe that there was ritual burning of the dead within the grave . . . The image of the dragon who is the source of fire in Old English literature may be an instance of a mythical figure who has emerged as a result of ritual at the grave . . . Both in England and Scandinavia the dragon came to be regarded as the guardian of the grave mound, watching over its treasures. Sometimes it is implied that he is to be identified with the dead man buried in the mound, and in some of the late legendary sagas it is said that a man after death became a dragon and guarded the treasure which he had taken into the howe with him.[53]

Icelandic traditions shed considerable light on the origin of the howe, barrow or burial mound. The residents of Thor's Ness were believed to pass, after death, into a sacred hill called Holyfell. *Eyrbyggja Saga* describes "the hill Holyfell standing open" and a Viking crew being welcomed inside by Thorolf, a disciple of Thor.[54] King Arthur and his knights will someday return from the caves of the British mountains. The greatest gods, heros or ancestors of the Old and New Worlds have returned or will someday return from local surrogates of the Efé Pygmies' Olympus-Hades at the source of the Nile. It is very difficult to believe that there is any factual basis to the Pygmy legends of the infernal kingdom and the globally distributed stories of the ancestors' sojourn in Hades. It is impossible to believe that these stories were separately contrived as idle myths that in many cases specifically locate Olympus-Hades in the land of the Efé Pygmies and identify the Pygmies, little peo-

---

[53] H. R. Ellis Davidson, *Gods and Myths of Northern Europe*, p. 161.

[54] *Ibid.*, pp. 158–59.

ple, elves, dwarfs or fairies as the ancestral heros of the Pleistocene resurrection.

The Pygmies' magic mountain towers over the central part of a gigantic fracture, the Rift Valley, that extends from Mozambique in southeast Africa to the lower spurs of the Taurus Mountains in Turkey. Ecologist Leslie Brown commented on the geology of the Rift Valley in general, the Western Rift on the edge of Efé territory, and the Efé Mountain of the Moon:

> It has been said of the Rift Valley that, although it may have its counterpart on another planet, there is nothing like it on earth. There are other rift valleys, but none of these is so great in extent and variety, nor can they be so easily studied, for other rift valleys of comparable size lie far below the oceans . . .
>
> Another branch of the Rift begins at Lake Albert in Uganda. This Western branch curves in a great arc to the Kivu Highlands, where it is blocked by an impressive group of high volcanic mountains, some of them still active. It continues, however, into the deep trough containing Lake Tanganyika, one of the largest lakes in the world and the second deepest. Here the floor of the Rift is 2,300 feet below sea level, and 4,730 feet under water . . .
>
> There are several exceptions to the general rule of vulcanism in the formation of mountains. The major one is the great Ruwenzori range, the famed Mountains of the Moon and one source of the Nile. Here there are six groups of snowy summits above fifteen thousand feet, culminating in Mount Stanley at sixteen thousand eight hundred feet. Certainly the Nile waters that originate in the glaciers of Ruwenzori come from a greater height than those coming from anywhere else.
>
> When one can see Ruwenzori—which is rare, for it is usually shrouded in dense cloud—it is at once obvious that it is not an isolated conical peak like Mount Kenya or Mount Elgon, but a range. It is actually about sixty-five miles long by thirty wide, and a series of peaks from a chain along its crest. Its formation has been entirely different from that of other high mountains.[55]

The unique geology of the region makes it possible to consider the possibility that there may be some kind of Hades-like country or infernal Shangri-la in the vicinity of the Ruwenzori

---

[55] Leslie Brown, *Africa: A Natural History*, pp. 248 and 268.

massif. Efé traveled through a hole in the foot of the mountain and a maze of cavern-tunnels that lead to the "gigantic hole" of the lush banana groves, forests, rivers, waterfalls, the village of the ghosts, the house of Doru and Matu, the magic stool and so forth. The Greek philosopher Aristotle associated Oi Pygmaioi with caverns at the source of the Nile. In the Greek legends of Hades or Tartarus the size of the Pygmies' ghostly kingdom appears to have been greatly exaggerated. "There is a chasm which is the vastest of them all, and pierces right through the whole earth," Socrates declares in Plato's dialogue *Phaedo*. "This is that chasm which Homer describes in the words, 'Far off, where is the inmost depth beneath the earth'; and which he in other places, and many other poets, have called Tartarus."

Socrates explains that the "four principal rivers" of the world, and many other streams, flow in and out of Tartarus. Oceanus is the greatest and outermost representative of the four rivers. Acheron "passes under the earth through desert places" to the Acherusian lake on whose shores "the souls of the many go when they are dead, and after waiting an appointed time, which is to some a longer and to some a shorter time, they are sent back to be born again as animals." Pyriphlegethon "flows into a vast region of fire, and forms a lake larger than the Mediterranean Sea, boiling with water and mud." The fourth principal river "falls first of all into a wild and savage region, which is all of a dark blue colour, like lapis lazuli; and this is that river which is called the Stygian river, and falls into and forms the Lake Styx, and after falling into the lake and receiving strange powers in the waters, passes under the earth, winding round in the opposite direction, and comes near the Acherusian lake from the opposite side to Pyriphlegethon."[56]

Medieval Arab geographers described the Mountain of the Moon as the source of the four Eden rivers and other great streams that were supposed to wind around or pass in and out of the earth. "At the distance of a few miles from Samarah stood a huge mountain, whose sides were swarded with wild thyme and basil, and its summit overspread with so delightful a plain that it might be taken

---

[56] Irwin Edman, *The Works of Plato* (New York: Modern Library, 1928), pp. 181–83.

for the paradise destined for the faithful . . . Four fountains, not less clear than deep, and so abundant as to slake the thirst of ten armies, seemed profusely placed here to make the scene more resemble the garden of Eden, which was watered by the four sacred rivers," wrote the English author William Beckford in his romance *Vathek*.[57] Beckford located the mountain of paradise near a city called "Samarah." On December 4, 1778, he penned a prose reverie about the mountain of "Amara." He imagined himself "in Africa, on the brink of the Nile beneath the Mountains of Amara." Then a guide led the author, who composed this reverie during "the full of the moon," to the Efé Pygmies' legendary caverns in the Mountain of the Moon: "I followed his steps thro' an infinity of irregular Vales, all skirted with Rocks and blooming with an aromatic vegetation, till we arrived at the hollow Peak and . . . a wide Cavern appeared before us . . . We entered the Cavern and fell prostrate before the sacred source of the Nile which issues silently from a deep Gulph in the Rock."[58]

Beckford's "Samarah" and "Amara" are rather obviously connected with Sumeru and Meru, which were alternate titles of the Olympian paradise where the four rivers flowed from the Hindu center of the earth. Milton's poem *Paradise Lost* locates Mount Amara "under the Ethiop line by Nilus' head." Professor John Livingston Lowes compared Beckford's "amazing reverie" to Coleridge's dream poem "Kubla Khan" and remarked that, " 'Caverns measureless to man' had been for twenty-three centuries associated with the legend of the Nile. It is little wonder, given what we now know about 'the sacred river,' that they turned up in the dream." The *Geographica Arabica Medicca*, he noted, declares that the plain of the Nile is "cavernous within" and "a region of mighty abysses."[59]

Samarah, the site of Beckford's Eden mountain, has been identified by critics with "a city of the Babylonian Irak, supposed

---

[57] William Beckford, *Vathek* (Boston: The Abbey Classics, n.d.), pp. 21–22.

[58] Lewis Melville, *The Life and Letters of William Beckford of Fonthill* (London, 1920), pp. 62–63.

[59] John Livingston Lowes, *The Road to Xanadu* (New York: Vintage Books, 1959), pp. 356 and 358.

to have stood on the site where Nimrod erected his tower."[60] Hebrew legends maintain that Nimrod, a cruel king of Babel, issued an edict: "When the days of a woman to be delivered are fulfilled, and the child is born, it shall be the duty of the midwife to kill it, if it be a boy." Seventy thousand infants were slaughtered. "It was about this time that Terah espoused the mother of Abraham and she was with child . . . When her time approached, she left the city in great terror and wandered toward the desert, walking along the edge of a valley, until she happened across a cave. She entered this refuge, and on the next day she was seized with the throes, and she gave birth to a son. The whole cave was filled with the light of the child's countenance as with the splendor of the sun, and the mother rejoiced exceedingly. The babe she bore was our father Abraham."[61]

The book of Genesis maintains that Abraham journeyed to Egypt during a time of famine that was followed by "great plagues." The book of Exodus claims that an unnamed Egyptian Pharaoh ordered the midwives to throw every male infant into the Nile. Moses was saved, grew to adulthood and led the exodus from Egypt. King Herod supposedly massacred "all the children that were in Bethlehem, and in all the coasts thereof, from two years old, and under." Jesus was saved when his parents fled to Egypt. The harried parents and miraculous sons of Judeo-Christian legend are all involved in pseudohistorical journeys that take them back and forth to the land of the Nile. The Arabic prophet Idrisi (alias Enoch-Thoth-Hermes-Am Kaam) went in time of disaster to the Mountain of the Moon at the source of the Nile. The Hebrew prophet Elijah survived a series of cataclysms by hiding in a cave of Sinai, the lunar mountain that Freud interpreted as an Arabian volcano. Who would take shelter in an erupting volcano?

Abraham's radiant countenance filled the cave with light "as the splendor of the sun." When he was only ten days old, Abraham "arose and walked about, and he left the cave and went along the edge of the valley." Efé, the earthly sun of the light-making god,

---

[60] William Beckford, *Vathek*, Notes, p. 197.

[61] Louis Ginzberg, *The Legends of the Jews* (Philadelphia: Jewish Publication Society of America, 1911), Vol. 3, pp. 90–94.

immediately turned into a man or emerged as a full-grown man from the cavernous foot of his mountainous mother. In the myth of the savior, Efé sojourned in the womb of Matu. The sun-god Apollo was born on the floating mountain-island of Delos and worshiped at Delphi on the slopes of Parnassus, the mountain of the "sacred chasm" at the Greek navel of the earth. Mother Earth hid Apollo's father Zeus in the mountain cave at the Cretan navel of the earth.

"Blessed art thou, Mary, for in thy womb thou hast prepared a habitation for the Lord. Behold, light from heaven shall come and dwell in thee, and through thee shall shine in all the world," according to the Gospel of Pseudo-Matthew. "The story is recounted everywhere; and with such striking uniformity of the main contours, that the early Christian missionaries were forced to think that the devil himself must be throwing up mockeries of their teaching wherever they set their hand," Joseph Campbell commented on this apocryphal text in his book *The Hero with a Thousand Faces.* Concerning the archetypal hero's homeland, he wrote: "The place of the hero's birth, or the remote land of exile from which he returns to perform his adult deeds among men, is the mid-point or navel of the world."[62]

Genesis locates the ancestral land of Eden at the source of Gihon-Nile. Abraham, Moses and Jesus were all involved in journeys that took them back and forth to the land of the Nile that for more than twenty-three centuries has been associated with Beckford's "hollow peak" and Coleridge's "caverns measureless to man." The Greek philosopher Aristotle described the caverns in the region of the Nile sources as the dwelling of the Pygmies. Efé, the Pygmy, is the ancestral hero who returns from Hades and sires mankind at the beginning of every world-age. Concerning the world-ages of India's Jain religion, Campbell reported:

> The descending series will terminate and the 'ascending' series (*utsarpini*) begin, when the tempest and desolation will have reached the point of the unendurable. For seven days then it will rain, and seven different kinds of rain will fall; the soil will be

---

[62] Joseph Campbell, *The Hero with a Thousand Faces* (New York: Meridian Books, 1956), pp. 309 and 334.

refreshed, and the seed will begin to grow. Out of their caves the horrible dwarf-creatures of the arid, bitter earth will venture; and very gradually there will be perceptible a slight improvement in their morals, health, beauty, and stature; until presently they will be living in a world such as the one we know today. And then a savior will be born, named Padmanatha, to announce again the eternal religion of the Jains; the stature of mankind will approach again the superlative, the beauty of man will surpass the splendor of the sun.[63]

The superlative men and women are supposed to be eight miles tall. The horrible dwarf-creatures probably correspond with the underworld dwarfs whom the Pygmies represent as physically hideous beings. Efé, the white elf, is forced to sojourn in their kingdom in the legend of the hero's trip to Hades. Balder the Beautiful returns from the underworld residence of the *svartálfar* or "swarthy elves." The *lichtálfar* or "light elves" are associated with the shelter at Gimlé in the neighborhood of the Germanic Heaven Mountain at the center of the earth in the southern continent of Muspelheim or Africa. Mweiya, the Pygmy Moses of East Africa, descended from heaven to the summit of Mount Ngong and founded the religion of the Nilo-Hamitic Masai. The Tamil legends of southern India describe a diminutive teacher named Agastya as the founder of the faith: "He had come, it was said, from the north, and had settled as a hermit at the top of Mount Podiyam, not far from Kodaikkanal; he was very small in stature; he would appear to have written a grammar, which is now lost, but which is said to be the source of all later Tamil grammars. His disciples were twelve grammarians, and in addition a few doctors, for he was very knowledgeable on all subjects."[64]

Odin, the god of poetry and knowledge in general, governed the twelve Elder Gods of the Germanic Heaven Mountain. His elfin colleagues are related to the twelve chieftains of Asgard-Troy, the twelve knights of Charlemagne and Arthur, the twelve Olympian gods, the twelve sons of Jacob or Israel, the twelve disciples of Jesus, and, in all probability, the twelve men of the jury and the

---

[63] *Ibid.*, p. 264.

[64] *Larousse World Mythology*, pp. 267–68.

twelve months of the lunar year. Numerous legends and poems of
northern Europe identify the paradisaical pinnacle with the Mountain of the Moon at the Central African source of the Nile. The
living but supposedly dead hero Efé was resurrected from Hades
through the Troy-town maze in the lunar mountain. Joseph Campbell defined the Christian holiday Holy Saturday as "the day between the Death and Resurrection of Jesus, who is in the belly of
Hell."[65] Jesus was resurrected from the cave-tomb at the Jerusalem
center of the earth. The living Athenian king Theseus came back
from the abyss of Hades or the maze at the Cretan center of the
earth. Balder returned from hell, Yima emerged with his elect from
the subterranean enclosure in the Persian mountains. The white
elves came out of the shelter in the African land of the Heaven
Mountain at the Germanic center of the earth.

Many crackpot theories of the "hollow earth" have been
derived from the globally distributed legends of Hades. "I declare
that the Earth is hollow and habitable in the interior," a retired
Ohio Infantry captain named J. Cleves Symnes proclaimed on April
10, 1818. His son, Americ Vespucius Symnes, predicted that the
Ten Lost Tribes of Israel would someday be discovered within the
hollow shell. The most reasonable Hades legends specifically locate
the cave-world in the geologically unique region of the Nile basin.
The Pygmy residents of this region are the white elves of Germanic
legend. "The real point of interest in this is that the tale goes back
to the onset of the last ice age which ended soon after 10,000 B.C.,
and must date back at least twenty thousand years before then,"
Egerton Sykes commented on the Terrible Winter of the Germanic
Ragnarok cycles.

The sacred status of the Biblical tales, the inviolable mysteries
of the Christian churches, the anthropologists' fallacious belief that
the so-called savages of the world must have borrowed their
legends from missionaries, and the Darwinian dogma of slow and
gradual evolution from brutish ancestors have all contributed to
the pseudohistory of mankind. On the last page of his book *The
Descent of Man*, Darwin expressed the opinion that he would
rather be descended from a monkey than from a "savage." He used

---

[65] J. Campbell, *The Hero with a Thousand Faces*, p. 249.

the words savage, low and degraded to describe the American Indians, the Andaman Island Pygmies and the representatives of almost every ethnic group whose physical appearance and culture differed from his own.

Dee Brown's tragic masterpiece *Bury My Heart at Wounded Knee* gives a truthful account of the savage treatment that the American tribes received from the Christian Europeans. E. H. Man's *History of Our Relations with the Andamanese* (Calcutta, 1899) describes the brutal exploitation of the Pygmy population by Darwin's British countrymen. During World War II, Japanese aircraft bombed the Andaman Pygmies. The Pygmies fought back by shooting arrows at the dive bombers. The government of India took over the Andaman Islands after the war. The little archipelago is now being deforested to produce quick timber revenues and farming land where a minute fraction of India's starving millions can be settled. The forests hold down a thin layer of topsoil on these very steep islands—the peaks of a subterranean mountain range—that are located in a region of torrential monsoons. After the forests have been destroyed, the soil will be washed into the Bay of Bengal and the Andaman Islands will be reduced to bare rock. The Pygmy population will "become extinct," a euphemism that describes the fate of many gentle folk who have been destroyed by our savage civilization. The population problem of India, which is packed with more than half a billion people, will not have been alleviated in the slightest by the destruction of the Andaman Islands, where no more than a thousand Pygmies currently survive.

The Sanskrit literature of ancient India maintains, ironically enough, that overpopulation causes or contributes to the catastrophic end of every world-age. Famine-stricken mobs crowd the land in the Efé legend of the earth-splitting lightning. Another Efé saga starts with a great famine and ends with the hero's escape in a boat. There are no famines in the ever-green Ituri. Far from sailing about in boats, the Ituri Forest Pygmies do not even build rafts of the most elementary variety. Some of the Andaman Pygmy bands dwell near the coast and traditionally make small dugout canoes, steadied by outriggers, that are used for offshore fishing. Most anthropologists say that the Andamanese must have borrowed their boats, probably from the Malayan pirates who used to raid the islands. It is, however, generally admitted that the Philippine Pygmies must have used boats to reach their present homeland, since it is not very practical to postulate a land bridge to the Philippines. The archipelago is surrounded by profound oceanic abysses such as the famous Mindanao Trench.

Forty-two Pygmy fossils (and many others) whose ancestors are believed to have come from Africa "by unknown means" were recently discovered in western Venezuela. Thor Heyerdahl and his crew recently tried to cross the Atlantic in a neo-Egyptian papyrus boat, the *Ra*. No party of anthropologists has ever attempted to prove the Bering Strait theory by walking for one or two thousand miles along the edges of the Antarctic icecap, using as their sole equipment the artifacts that they attribute to the Pygmies and Australoids of the Bering Strait theories. Such an experiment would determine the feasibility of early man's miraculous Arctic safari and benefit mankind by disposing of so-called scientists who defend their orthodox dogmas in the style of medieval bishops.

A band of Efé Pygmies, captained by All-Father Efé, cross a river by boat in a very remarkable legend. Then the immortal founder of the Pygmy nation makes a solo voyage in the boat. "What kind of a boat was it?" I have asked the elders of numerous territories. "It was bigger than a Negro canoe and it moved by itself," is the general consensus. "What made it move?" I asked. "We do not know," they replied. In Gabon, the local Pygmies told Father Trilles a "creation" legend about a great canoe that moved across the primordial waters. "What made the canoe go forward?" asked Trilles. "It is not known, our fathers did not tell us," the narrator replied. Schebesta's book *Les Pygmées* contains a version of the Efé boating legend.[66] Here is a very similar version I recorded in the southeast Ituri:

> When the great famine came, a Pygmy band rode across a river to a beautiful new land. They got out of the boat but before they went very far, Efé discovered that his headdress was missing. "What have you done with my headdress?" Efé asked his wife. "We must have forgotten it," she answered. Efé searched her basket, but the headdress was not there. When he failed to find it on the shore,

---

[66] P. Schebesta, *Les Pygmées*, pp. 39 and 40.

he said, "I must go back. I cannot dance the sacred dances without my headdress."

Efé rode back across the river and the boat returned to the opposite shore. After a long and difficult trip, Efé reached the old camp. There he was astonished to see a band of strangers dancing around a fire. One of the dancers was wearing Efé's own headdress. "That headdress is mine. Give it to me, please," said Efé. The strangers laughed and threatened to kill him. Efé was outraged by their behavior. He raised his bow and shot arrow after arrow into the crowd. Many men fell to the ground. They rolled around like stuck pigs, groaning in agony. While the survivors ran toward their weapons, Efé leaped onto the scoundrel who had refused to surrender his headdress, took the stolen property and slipped away into the bush.

The thieves tracked him with their horrible beast, a great dog with the head of a snake. "We will run him through with our spears! We will cut up his flesh and cook it in rolled-up leaves!" chanted Efé's pursuers. These creatures were not only thieves—they were cannibals!

Efé ran like an antelope toward the shore. The cannibals followed. The dog-snake caught up with Efé and opened its gaping jaws. "Do not touch me!" commanded the hero. "I am not the one you should hunt. I am the one who summoned you." The monster ran away. Then Efé climbed a tree and hid in the branches. After a while, the dog-snake led Efé's cruel pursuers to the tree. "We will cut up his flesh and cook it in rolled-up leaves!" the cannibals chanted while they danced around a fire at the base of the tree. Then they went to sleep beside the fire. They felt sure that the hero could not escape.

When they were all asleep and snoring loudly, Efé gathered an armload of fruit. He hurled the fruit at the sleepers, slipped down from the tree and ran toward the shore. The cannibals, stunned and confused, fought with each other. Every man thought he was fighting with Efé! Then they realized what they were doing and chased after the hero. "Send the boat!" Efé shouted to his wife on the other side of the river. The boat came sailing toward him. The great Efé archers meanwhile shot arrows across the river. The cannibals faltered as man after man was struck by arrows. Then Efé jumped into the boat and rode back across the river to the beautiful land.

"Then the Efé leaped into the boat. He was saved," ends the story told in Schebesta's book *Les Pygmées*. The author made no comment on the very remarkable boating legend told by the strictly pedestrian Pygmies of the eastern Ituri. Stanley's book *In Darkest Africa* contains a little glossary of Pygmy words. *Bwato* is given as the word for "boat." Some of the Efé elders define *bato* as the sacred boat of God and the lunar angel. This word should not be used, they say, to describe any other vessel: Norwegian *bat*, Anglo-Saxon *bat*, Old Norse *batr*, Swedish *bat*, French *bateau*, German *boot*, Dutch *boot*, English *boat*.

All-Father Efé rode back and forth in a boat that moved by itself. Scyld Sceafing, the father of the elder Beowulf, rode alone across the sea as a child in a treasure-laden ship "that was not propelled by oars or sail." The body of the aged Scyld and a choice collection of "tribal treasures" were laid in a ship that was set adrift. Balder, after his ship funeral, went to the infernal abodes. The ship funerals of northern Europe took the deceased to the same destination as the pious Egyptian's post-mortem voyage. An Icelandic story describes Thor's funeral hill of Holyfell standing open to receive a Viking captain and his crew. Efé and a band of Pygmies made the original voyage in the self-propelled boat; then the hero rode in the boat alone. Efé and Thor are the divine smiths of the earthly paradise. At the end of the Kango Pygmy creation story God the great smith went "down the river"; in some versions, the departing smith goes "up the river." Efé's voyages took him back and forth to the land of the Heaven Mountain in the lost Germanic paradise of Asgard or Troy.

The ancestral heroes of Greco-Roman legend sailed from Europe to the site of Troy and founded the city where the European ancestors paradoxically originated. Roman legends maintain that an Etruscan prince named Dardanus, the son of Zeus-Jupiter and/ or a king named Corythus, led a party of Etruscans from Italy to the traditional site of Troy in Asia Minor. Efé and a band of Pygmies made the original voyage. The hero's lost headdress led to the fight with the strangers. A tribe called Bebrycians tried to throw the invading Etruscans back into the sea. Then, according to the Roman legend, "Dardanus lost his helmet and, although his troops were in retreat, led them back to recover it. This time he was victorious, and founded a city named Corythus on the battlefield: as much in memory of his helmet (*corys*), as of his father."[67]

Efé fought alone. Before and after the battle, the immortal founder of the Pygmy nation made a solo voyage in the boat. The Athenians maintained that Zeus's son Dardanus sailed alone from Greece to the traditional site of Troy. He paddled a raft made of "an inflated skin which he had ballasted with four stones." There he was hospitably received by Teucer, a Greek who had previously migrated from the Athenian deme or district of Troes to the future site of Troy. Dardanus' grandson Tros founded the city of Troy. Dardanus founded the city of Dardania on the lower slopes of Mount Ida in the Phrygian sector of Asia Minor.

Another peak called Mount Ida was located on the island of Crete. Another story maintains that the Cretan hero Teucer led a migrant troop from their famine-stricken home in Crete to the land of Troy, where Teucer was hospitably received by the Greek or Etruscan hero Dardanus. Efé and his crew made the original voyage from the famine-blighted country to the "beautiful new land." Efé returned, fought the strangers, recovered his headdress and leaped into the boat. Teucer's Cretan father, Prince Scamander, led the migrants to Phrygia where they camped below a high mountain and called it Ida in honor of Zeus's Cretan home. After battling with the Bebrycian tribe from whom the Etruscan Dardanus recovered his helmet, Scamander leaped into a river that was named the Scamander in honor of the hero.

"I cannot dance the sacred dances without my headdress," said Efé, the hero who rode in the boat. It was a very large, canoe-like vessel, not a dinky little raft like Dardanus' contraption. Teucer is also said to have led the migration to Troy from Crete or the Athenian district of Troes. The Athenian king Theseus was born in the town of Troezen and voyaged to Crete in a ship that had sails and thirty oars. There he traveled through a legendary labyrinth and learned the Troy-town dance or dance of the crane. The crane was the bird of Hermes; the sacred ibis was the bird of Thoth, the Egyptian god of the moon. A coin of Knossos, the ancient capital of Crete, shows the new moon set in the center of

---

[67] Robert Graves, *The Greek Myths,* Vol. 2, p. 260.

a maze. The labyrinthine caves of Efé legend are located in the Mountain of the Moon. Theseus sailed to the island of Crete, a traditional site of the *omphalos* or navel of the earth; then he sailed back to Athens. His trip to Crete took him to the Germanic paradise of Asgard-Troy at the center of the earth. Beowulf's ancestor Scyld Sceafing rode back to Europe in the self-propelled boat of Pygmy and Germanic legend.

The Greco-Roman stories of Troy are pseudohistory at its worst. The Efé legend of the voyages is a complexly symbolic story of a boat that goes back and forth to the land of paradise. Efé makes a solo trip in the boat and overcomes a band of thieving cannibals. Zeus punished the cannibalistic sons of Lycaon, according to a Greek story that describes a very remarkable voyage. The villains murdered their brother Nyctimus, made soup out of his entrails, and tried to serve this "loathsome banquet" to Zeus. The god brought Nyctimus back to life, changed the cannibals into wolves, and disgustedly decided to destroy the human race by turning loose the waters of a global flood. Efé was accompanied by his wife during the original trip in the boat. A virtuous old couple named Deucalion and Pyrrha were divinely warned to build an ark out of oak. Then, according to this well-known counterpart of the Babylonian and Hebrew deluge stories, Zeus "broke up all the fountains of the deep, and opened the well springs of heaven, and it rained for forty days and forty nights continually." Not even those who fled to the hilltops were able to survive. A single mountain remained unsubmerged. "The ark rested on Parnassus, and when the waters ebbed the old couple descended the mountain and took up their abode in a cave."[68]

The self-propelled boat of Efé legend is represented as a means of transportation, not a shelter where people can survive the titanic cataclysms of the past and apocalyptic future. Deucalion's ark landed at Parnassus, the sacred mountain of Apollo-Horus and Dionysus-Osiris at the Delphi navel of the earth. Then the old man and his spouse went to the Hades caverns where so many godly ancestors of the Old and New Worlds survived the floods and other disasters that come at the end of every world-age.

---

[68] Donald A. Mackenzie, *Myths of Babylonia and Assyria*, p. 195.

Theseus rode in the boat to the Cretan navel of the earth. His son Hippolytus apparently perished when an enormous tidal wave with a water monster on its crest came roaring toward the shores of Greece. Then he was "resurrected" from the kingdom of Hades and disguised as an old man. He and his wife, the nymph Egeria, traditionally dwelled in the Roman moon-goddess' surrogate cave at the sacred grove of Nemi.

Pir-Napishtim, the Babylonian Noah, floated about in an immense flat-bottomed boat whose deck house was six stories high and contained nine apartments in each story. Pir-Napishtim loaded the ship with his wife, family, servants, workers, household goods, precious metals and the beasts of the field. Efé, his wife, and a band of Pygmies made the original trip in the boat. The Babylonian ship drifted "towards the country of Nitsir, and then it was held fast by the mountain of Nitsir." Pir-Napishtim and his wife were then installed in a mysterious abode "beyond the mouths of rivers." Gilgamesh visited his ancestor Pir-Napishtim by traveling through a tunnel in the tremendous mountain of Mashi to the land of the "nether garden" on the shores of the subterranean sea. Efé made Pir-Napishtim's voyage in one legend, and in another story accomplished Gilgamesh's journey by traveling to Hades through the Troy-town maze in the Mountain of the Moon.

Noah, his family and specimens of every animal in the world (including birds and "every creeping thing") drifted about in the Biblical ark that eventually landed "on the mountains of Ararat." The *Queen Mary* herself could not accommodate Noah's zoological collection or survive the gigantic tidal waves that sweep across the continents in many legends of the deluge. The Babylonian and Greek Noahs descended to the Hades caverns after their vessels landed on the mountains of Nisir and Parnassus. Genesis' story of the animal-cracker ark omits this rather important detail. The prophet Elijah, in another story, survives a series of cataclysms by hiding in a cave of Sinai, the mountain of the Babylonian moon-god Sin. Arabic legends maintain that Enoch-Thoth-Hermes-Idrisi-Am Kaam escaped the deluge by retreating to the Central African Mountain of the Moon.

Thoth is addressed as Temu in *The Book of the Dead*. Temu, the first man-god, released the waters of the great deep. Everyone drowned except the family or friends who rode in Temu's boat. The self-propelled ship of Efé legend is the sacred boat of the lunar angel and God. "The ark was a moon-ship and the feast was celebrated on the new moon nearest to the autumnal equinox, as a means of inducing the winter rains," Robert Graves commented on Pir-Napishtim's vessel and the Mesopotamian New Year festival that featured the outpouring of "sweet new wine." Noah was the Biblical inventor of wine. Deucalion, the Greek Noah and the god Dionysus-Osiris were alternately credited with the invention of wine. Deucalion rode in the lunar boat to Parnassus, a mountain associated with Dionysus-Osiris. His voyage took him to the Central African mountain of Osiris Moon, Horus Moon and Thoth Moon. The dwarfs or elves of the *Prose Edda* rowed about in boats and brewed the first mead or honey wine. Beowulf's ancestor Scyld Sceafing rode in the self-propelled boat of the Efé Pygmies or "little men" from the Mountains of the Moon.

All-Father Efé invented or taught the use of intoxicating, medicinal and poisonous plants of many different varieties. Efé instructed his children in the art of cooking and devised the first recipes. Zeus was understandably offended and sent the deluge after the sons of Lycaon offered him cannibal soup. "We will cut up his flesh and cook it in rolled-up leaves!" chanted the cannibals. (They utter the same threat in Schebesta's version.) Pygmy ladies cook chunks of meat and other food in rolled-up leaves; a similar method is used to make Greek grape-leaf roulades, Hungarian stuffed-cabbage rolls, and many other dishes. The cannibals planned to prepare Efé, the Julia Child of Ituri Forest cooking, by a favorite Pygmy technique. Anthropologists have not yet accused the Efé Pygmies of borrowing this story from Christian missionaries. Far from being a minor tale, it is an integral part of the legend cycle.

Zeus's son Tantalus cooked his own son, Pelops, and served the stew at a banquet to which he invited Zeus and the other Olympian gods. Zeus brought his grandson back to life, just as he revived Nyctimus, the murdered brother whom the sons of Lycaon cooked in their soup. Tantalus' other crimes include the theft of a "golden dog" that guarded the infant Zeus in the cave of Dicte at the Cretan naval of the earth. "Do not touch me! I am not the one you should hunt. I am the one who summoned you," Efé ordered the snake-headed dog. Cerberus, a three-headed or fifty-headed dog whose heads sprout serpents, guarded the shoreline of Hades' cavernous kingdom. Cerberus' father, the supreme monster Typhon, attacked Olympus and dragged Zeus into his cave. Efé and God secretly control these apparently evil monsters. The monsters bring retribution to sinners. The sinners are at fault, the monsters are not. Cerberus' Egyptian counterpart was Anubis, the jackal-headed god of the underworld. His alternate fathers were Set and Osiris, the Egyptian Satan and Christ.

Efé's dialogue with the dog-dragon occurred after the hero made a return trip in the boat to recover his headdress. Zeus's son Dardanus led his troops back to retrieve the lost helmet. Efé very politely requested his property; he said *kisi*, "Please." The strangers ridiculed and threatened him. Efé was morally outraged and shot a barrage of arrows at his antagonists; he did not however slay the villain who refused to return the headdress or *tsapo*. Efé's *tsapo*, like a crown, is an emblem of divine authority. Efé took the *tsapo* from the apparent leader of his impolite foes. The leader committed the crime of theft by refusing to surrender Efé's rightful property. His men supported him and thereby became accessories to the crime.*

This story does not reveal the identity of the thieving leader whose actions caused the massacre of his men, or explain why he was spared. Doru, the thieving antihero of the Efé legend cycle, brought death to mankind when he stole the forbidden fire and fruit. Doru, the brother-son of Efé and God, is the Promethean mentor of man. Like Prometheus, he is immortal; his human protégés are not. He is Man, they are men. Efé, the Pygmy, is immortal; individual Pygmies are not. Efé crossed the river with the Efé, left them in a safe place and returned to fight alone. Efé sprang on the principal villain and retrieved his *tsapo*. In another legend, Efé wrestles with the dwarf ghost of Doru for possession of an antelope which he has shot with his arrows and the villain attempts to steal. Doru's family support their thieving father. Doru is not, however, a truly wicked character. He is a good person who

---

* Efé *tsapo*, headdress or hat: Turkish *sapka*, Bulgarian *shapka*, French *chapeau*, Italian *capello*, headdress, bonnet, hat. English *chapeau* and *cap*.

sometimes succumbs to ignoble impulses. He is Set, the ambivalent brother of the "good" Egyptian gods; he has been grossly over-simplified in the Christian concept of Satan, the fallen angel or devil.

Efé had a confrontation with Doru after Efé's people crossed the river to a place of safety. The book of Genesis maintains that Jacob or Israel sent his family across a brook at the ford of Jabbok. Then the eponymous hero of Israel wrestled with an angel who wounded him in the hollow of the thigh. The Hottentot hero Tsui Goab wrestled with an evil spirit that wounded him in the knee. A Masai character called Il-Moruo, "the old man," wounded himself in the knee and gave birth to children through the orifice. Efé wounded the foot of his maternal parent and emerged through the hole. Efé *mara* or *mala* is an elder, chief or king: French *maire*, elder or mayor. Masai *moruo*, elder or old man. Arabic *malik*, Hebrew *melech*, king.

Doru's cohorts planned to make stuffed cabbage out of Efé; in another story, Doru sneaked into the forest and stole the fruit of the forbidden *tahu* tree. Before Zeus's son Tantalus cooked his cannibal banquet, he stole the nectar and ambrosia of the gods; then he shared the food of the gods with his mortal friends. Zeus's son Hercules persuaded the Titan Atlas to steal the golden apples of Hesperides. Doru, the thief of the fruit, is the thief of the fire. Atlas' brother Prometheus stole the forbidden fire of Zeus from the sun or the smithy of Olympus. "Tantalus, a physicist" was inter-preted by some early Greek scholars as a criminal who was pun-ished "for having proved that the sun is a mass of white-hot metal."[69] Tantalus as the cannibal cook served his stewed son to the gods. A single member of the Olympian pantheon unwittingly took a bite. Zeus' sister Demeter, the goddess of the fruitful har-vest, tasted Tantalus' obscene concoction. Famine afflicts the earth in the Efé legend of the cannibals.

All-Father Efé led the Efé from the famine-stricken country; then the divine hero returned, punished the villains and went back across the river. God the Father goes up or down the river at the

---

[69] Robert Graves, *The Greek Myths*, Vol. 2, p. 29.

close of the Kango Pygmy creation epic; then the plants and animals mysteriously dwindle and die. Hungry men wander through a dark, bitter-cold wilderness in the Western Pygmy legend of the "red beast," an epithet for fire. Then the leader of the band decides to invoke the deity. "He took his son and offered him to God, saying 'Creator, I call you.'" The deity inquires, "Who calls me?' The leader replies, "It is I, the chief of men"; He implores aid, saying, "I am hungry, I am cold." Then, according to this story, the Creator replies, "I will give you the red beast, the living creature, it will always be yours. You will no longer be hungry, you will no longer be cold. You alone will have the red beast: the other animals will fear it. With this companion in your house, they will no longer come to take your children. You will no longer fear the night, because the night will be like the day . . . I give you the red beast, and so that you will always know that it is I who give it to you, you will hear my thunder and see the fire cut the sky in two. I have spoken." Since that time, the narrator concluded, "whenever we offer the ordained sacrifice, the fire devours the beast that we offer . . . I, Atoum, the head of the Akye clan, I have said this."[70]

Men thought that they had received the greatest possible blessing when Doru gave them the stolen fire. Gbala, the lightning, split the earth and turned the world upside down when he leaped up to the sky. The fiery thunderer of the Western Pygmy legend cut the sky in two with his fire. Doru and Gbala are forms of the Destroyer, not the Creator. Efé religion absolutely condemns the worship of the Destroyer. Men may only worship the Creator or the total deity who uses and includes the Destroyer. The Efé never make burnt offerings by sacrificing animals; the chameleon ceremony and the traditional human cremation are funerals, like the cremations performed in present-day Europe and America. The "chief of men" offered his son to the deity in the Western Pygmy fire legend. The people who tell this story do not sacrifice children or adult human beings to any form of the deity. The surviving African and Asiatic Pygmies universally condemn and abhor human sacrifice, cannibalism, murder, war and aggressive be-

---

[70] Henri Trilles, *The Soul of the African Pygmy*, pp. 118–20.

havior in general. The "chief of men" who offered up his son is Doru, the antihero. The spurious Creator is Gbala, the lightning form of the Destroyer.

Jehovah, in the twenty-second chapter of Genesis, tells Abraham to give his son Isaac as a burnt offering. Abraham prepares to sacrifice his son on a mountaintop altar; at the last moment, "the angel of the Lord" tells him to refrain, saying "Now I know that thou fearest God, seeing thou hast not withheld thy son, thine only son from me." Many peoples of the Old and New Worlds have sacrificed human victims to gods of fire, lightning and/or the sun. The Aztecs offered vast numbers of victims to Mexitli or Huitzilopochtli, the miraculous son of a chaste widow and god of four divine war spears who was worshiped as the god of lightning and war. The heart and other parts of the victim were ceremonially eaten in many such rituals of human sacrifice. Efé the Son Avenger is the virtuous hero who uses the three divine lightning spears in the myth of the savior. It is supremely perverse to offer human sacrifice to Efé and to eat the victim in associated acts of ritual cannibalism.

By wearing Efé's headdress, Doru apparently posed as Efé and promulgated a false religion. Efé seized the emblem of his divine authority and massacred the criminals who followed in the footsteps of Doru, the Destroyer. Zeus's son Dardanus went back, like Efé, to retrieve his headgear. Zeus's son Tantalus killed his own son, Pelops, and served the cannibal stew to the gods. He is the "chief of men" who offered up his son in the Western Pygmy legend; he is also the leader of the uncouth cannibals who incurred Efé's righteous wrath. A man named Lycaon sacrificed a young boy to Zeus. The god of gods expressed his opinion of child sacrifice by striking Lycaon's house with lightning and turning him into *lycos*, a "wolf." When the sons of the first lycanthrope, or werewolf, stewed their brother and offered the "loathsome banquet" to Zeus, he turned them into wolves and sent a world-destroying deluge. The Western Pygmy lightning cut the sky in two. The earth-splitting lightning leaped up to the sky, at the command of God, and turned the Efé world upside down. The deity, in another legend, cuts a tree with his axe and releases the waters of the deluge. *Sa'e* is the Efé word for an axe: Middle English *sawe*, German *sage,* a saw. Greek *sagaris,* the double axe or thunderbolt of Zeus.

"I am the one who summoned you," Efé said to the dog-snake. Canine animals are classic symbols of hunger and privation. One can thus be "as hungry as a wolf" or "have the wolf at one's door." Wolves swallow the sun and moon at the end of every Germanic world-age. A wolf called Fenrir swallows All-Father Odin. The Midgard Serpent rises from the sea and fights with Odin's son or father, Thor. The Efé dog-snake is a symbol both of famine and of flood. Efé is God the Father. He sends these and other disasters to punish the criminals who violate his laws. He sends his people, the Efé, to a place of safety. After the earth has been purged, Efé vanquishes the monsters and the Efé repopulate the earth.

We have seen Efé fight the monsters with spears in the style of Horus versus Set. Now for the first time we see the hero fighting men and using his small-game weapon, the hunting bow, with which the "dwarf" Horus gods were armed. The diminutive Greco-Roman deity Cupid shot arrows of fire. A fabulous British hero named Robin Hood performed incredible feats of archery. He was said to dwell in Sherwood Forest and in many other forests of England, Scotland and Wales. He was associated with hills, caves and wells. He was the hero of May Day or "Robin Hood's festival." Cupid, the first god, dwelled in a cave during some phases of his career. Every May Day, Roman processions went to the moon-goddess' cave where Hippolytus dwelled, disguised as an old man. He was the hero who returned from the cave-world after the tidal-wave disaster. His father, the Athenian king Theseus, sat on Efé's magic stool in the abyss of Tartarus and returned from the cave-world or the Pygmies' legendary Troy-town maze in the Mountain of the Moon.

Robin Hood was represented as a robber. Efé forbids theft. Robin Hood usually stole from ecclesiastics and "seems to have held bishops, abbots, priests and monks, in a word, all the clergy, regular and secular, in decided aversion."[71] Efé tore his headdress from the head of Doru, the false and thieving counselor who led men astray. Jesus was the great antagonist of the corrupt and venal clergy. He was the heretic who argued with the Pharisees

---

[71] Lord Raglan, *The Hero,* p. 50.

and scribes. He was the Jewish Robin Hood who went into the temple of Jerusalem "and cast out all them that sold and bought in the temple, and overthrew the tables of the money-changers, and the seats of them that sold doves. And said unto them, 'It is written, My house shall be called the house of prayer; but ye have made it a den of thieves.' "[72]

Solomon, the son of Jesus' traditional ancestor David, built the first temple of Jerusalem as an annex to his palace. Concerning Solomon, "the Builder," the *Britannica* remarks: "Forced labor was exacted from the Canaanites. But though the boast is made that the Israelites were not treated as 'bond-servants,' the exactions made from them for the upkeep of the costly court and harem, and the expenses of building, must have reduced many of the poorer people to a condition hard to distinguish from slavery."[73] Efé's people have no priests or temples. The elders take the lead in saying prayers and performing religious ceremonies. They do not exploit their people in order to build Solomonic temples and Vatican palaces. Robin Hood, that fabulous British hero who supposedly "stole from the rich and gave to the poor," took back from the ecclesiastical thieves the property they had stolen from the poor. He was no robber—he was Efé, the divine hero who defends every man's right to his property and right to self-defense, as in the story of the virtuous bowman who massacred the criminals.

Efé single-handedly slew many men after they threatened to kill him. An elfin hero named Arthur slew 960 men at a single onset when he fought at Mount Badon, the field of his twelfth and final victory. Arthur subsequently sailed to Avalon, the apple-laden fairyland in the navel of the deep. After the battle, Efé rode away in the self-propelled boat. The medieval historian Nennius described Arthur as the "war leader" of the British people. Efé, the original Arthur, will only fight in a good cause. He resembles the Quaker hero played by Gary Cooper in the film *Friendly Persuasion*, who reluctantly took up arms to defend his family and property. Efé would unquestionably endorse the right of any "conscientious objector" to refrain from fighting for a cause he considered to be

---

[72] Matthew 21:12–13.

[73] *Encyclopaedia Britannica*, 14th ed., Vol. 20, p. 952.

morally corrupt or unjust. "What if a coward pretended to disapprove?" I have asked the elders. They replied, "Such a man is useless. Why try to force him? You cannot make a good hunting bow out of rotten wood."

Efé's massacre of the criminal "strangers" is paralleled by a very brief story that Schebesta called the "myth of the destruction of the human species." The hero of this story is called Ba'atsi, the "behorned one," a title of Efé, the lunar angel, and/or God. All horned animals are regarded as symbols of the Pygmies' lunar deity. The Ituri Forest animals are known in his honor as "the goats of God." Thor, the Germanic god of thunder and lightning, rode in a goat-driven chariot. His people wore horned helmets and venerated Thor's son or father Odin as the god of war. Athena, a Greek lady associated with the moon, was a very unusual goddess of war. She loathed war and tried in every way possible to achieve a just solution by peaceful means. When she had to fight, the divine mother of Plato's paradisaical Athens was unconquerable.

Here is the story of Ba'atsi's brief encounter with the strangers: "One fine day Ba'atsi encountered a number of men whom he did not know. He made a great massacre of them. He killed them with thrusts of his spear. When he emerged from his fury, he said to himself: 'If I kill all men, I shall have to be alone. That is not good.' He let the rest live. While traveling through the forest, he found bananas whose taste pleased him greatly. He gave them to his Pygmies. They said, 'Now we shall have good food.' Then Ba'atsi returned to the sky."[74]

Odin, the Spear-Brandisher, launched the first war by hurling his great spear Gungnir into the ranks of the Vanir. "May every field of battle be piled with your corpses, and may Odin let the spear fly according to my words," the Goths tell the Huns in a poem called "The Battle of the Goths and the Huns." Odin was intimately associated with the elves or dwarfs, the Vanir with men or people in general. The Pygmies associate iron spears and other metal weapons with lightning bolts. Their deity massacred mankind with his lightning spear. God the Grandfather is called Ba'atsi in Schebesta's story of the celestial parent who forged the

---

[74] P. Schebesta, *Les Pygmées du Congo Belge*, p. 314.

three iron spears—the three thunderbolts of the supreme Etruscan deity—that his son Efé brought down to earth. Efé is called Ba'atsi in Schebesta's story of the ancestral patriarch who went to visit his heavenly father before the sinners raided the forbidden tree. Matu, the first mother, shared the fruit with all of the Pygmies. The Pygmies and people in general both commit the original sins of Efé legend. Some of the elders say that Doru, a delinquent Pygmy, committed the sins first and that all subsequent sinners merely followed in his footsteps.

The ancient Pygmies committed the "original original sins," so to speak, during the legendary epoch when they lived in enormous camps and used wonderful tools. The Efé do not repeat the ancient Pygmies' errors. They are accordingly saved by the divine ancestor who took them across the river in his boat. The behorned one gave bananas to "his Pygmies." The ghost of Matu fed bananas to Efé when the hero arrived in the kingdom of Hades. Arthur sailed to the apple-land version of the Pygmies' infernal banana-land. Vergil's Elysium or apple-land was located in the cavernous kingdom of Hades.

Efé housewives dig *apa,* the wild potato, out of the Ituri Forest earth: Dutch *appel* and *aardappel,* apple and earth apple or potato. Anglo-Saxon *aeppel,* any kind of fruit, berry or nut, an apple. Algonquian *opin,* the potato, presumably originated in the Lost Paradise Across the Great Water. Efé *apa* and Sua *epa* are a wild potato and a father: Greek *patata* and *pateras,* potato and pater. Efé *apa* and *apulu* are the earth apple and the mole. The mole digs tunnels through the earth; in the myth of the savior, Efé cuts a path through the foot of a mountainous mother to accomplish his birth. A mountain labors and brings forth a mouse in Aesop's famous fable. Efé, in another story, returns from Hades through the maze-like caverns of the mountain. The mouse or thumb loop escapes through a net of holes at the grand climax of an Efé string trick that has been described as the world's most widely distributed string figure. Etruscan Aplu was a god whose name may mean "apple-man" according to some etymologists. He was apparently born underground. His sacred animal is the mouse. His sacred mountain is Parnassus at the navel of the earth. Greek Apollo and *aspalax,* the god and the mole.

"With respect to the Hawaiian cat's-cradle," wrote J. S. Emerson, "I have collected most carefully a considerable amount of valuable information, which I propose to publish as soon as I can get at it. The last bit of information with regard to the subject I came upon almost unexpectedly this morning at South Cape (Ka Lae). It was the last resting-place (in stone) of the famous rat that saved the human family from starvation when the god Makalii hung up the food in a net to a cloud in the heavens . . . There is no native now living who knows enough to give a full and connected story of this remarkable Hei, Koko or Makalii. Part of it comes from Iole, the home of the rat in Kohala. Part must be looked for in Waioli, Kanai, where the net was hung up to the cloud. And at last I have stumbled unawares upon the stars (Pleiades), the home of Makalii, his net, and the rat, all in the rock at South Cape."[75]

Efé-Apollo is the heroic mouse of the stone cat's cradle or Troy-town maze in the cosmic mountain at the center of the earth. Efé *musésé*, the little mouse, escapes at the end of the string-trick: Latin *mus*, English *mouse*. Greek *mys* and *megamys*, mouse and big mouse or rat. Efé brought food to his people through the maze in the mountain; food descends from the heavens in some accounts of the lightning disaster that turned the world upside down. Velikovsky interpreted the falling food as a hydrocarbon shower of Hebrew manna in his book *Worlds in Collision*. Heaven only knows what fell from the sky during the Pleistocene cataclysms. A vast number of Old and New World ancestors brought food, in the form of plants and animals, back from the cave-world after the legendary disasters. Yima, the Persian hero who saved the plants and animals in his underground enclosure, was the earthly twin of Apollo's kinsman Mithra, the cat-headed god of light or the sun. The great cat Ra and the cat-headed Pygmy god Bes were feline versions of the corresponding Egyptian deity. Efé, that sly old *pusu*, is the "puss" and mouse of world mythology.

Horus the Elder or Ra, the Egyptian Apollo, fought Set-Typhon with weapons of light. Efé slew the giant monsters of the sky and then returned to earth with his lightning spears. Matu refused to recognize her former husband; the story ended with an apparent

---

[75] Caroline Jayne, *String Figures and How to Make Them*, p. xviii.

reconciliation between Efé and her second husband, Doru, who had previously plundered the forbidden tree. Zeus's son Hercules conspired with the Titan Atlas to steal the golden apples of Hesperides. Zeus's son Tantalus stole the nectar and ambrosia of Olympus. He shared the food of the gods with his friends and then cooked his own son, Pelops, in the stew that he offered to the gods. Doru, far from reforming, descended to the lowest moral depths; he and his protégés refused to return Efé's property, threatened to murder the hero, and then planned to prepare a cannibal banquet.

In another story, Doru usurps the shape or wings of Efé's national bird and steals the sacred fire from the forest of God. The eagle-giant Thjazi flew to Asgard-Troy from his northern residence and stole the Germanic fruit of the gods. The eagle-giant Garuda flew to the Hindu Olympus and stole the nectar or ambrosia that assumed a golden body, like the sun. Prometheus stole the sacred fire from the sun or the smithy of Olympus. "Tantalus, a physicist" sinned by proving that "the sun is a mass of white-hot metal," according to some early Greek scholars.[76]

A cannibal physicist?

The leader of the would-be cannibals was Doru, the ingenious sinner who flew with the stolen wings or shape of Efé's national bird. His cohorts tried to kill and cook Efé. A demonic Athenian smith named Daedalus flew with artificial wings from the island of Crete to Cumae, near Naples. He then went to Sicily, where he erected "many fine buildings" for King Cocalus. Zeus's son Minos sailed from Crete to Sicily, determined to apprehend the fugitive criminal Daedalus. Aided by King Cocalus' daughters, Daedalus murdered Minos: "Daedalus led a pipe through the roof of the bathroom, down which they poured boiling water or, some say, pitch upon Minos, while he luxuriated in a warm bath. Cocalus, who may well have been implicated in the plot, returned the corpse to the Cretans, saying that Minos had stumbled over a rug and fallen into a cauldron of boiling water."[77]

Tantalus presumably cooked Zeus's grandson Pelops in some

---

[76] Robert Graves, *The Greek Myths*, Vol. 2, p. 29.

[77] *Ibid.*, Vol. 1, p. 314.

kind of cauldron. Zeus installed Minos, the boiled victim of
Daedalus, as the Chief Justice of the cavernous underworld where
he presides over the trials of ghosts who descend to Hades or
Tartarus. Minos, according to another story, consulted an oracle:
"The response was: 'Instruct Daedalus to build you a retreat at
Cnossos!' This Daedalus did, and Minos spent the remainder of
his life in the inextricable maze called the Labyrinth, at the very
heart of which he concealed Pasiphaë and the Minotaur."[78]

Chief Justice Minos alternately went to the cave-world and a
labyrinthine "retreat." Yama, the Hindu judge of the dead, departed for a paradise known as the Land of the Ancestors. Emma
or King Emma is the Japanese Buddhist judge of the dead who presides in the underworld kingdom of legend. Sanskrit literature
represents Yama as the deified first man. Yima, the first man or
first king, went to the underground enclosure whence he returns
with his elect after the "terrible winter" and other disasters of the
Persian Ragnarok.

So Daedalus' plot to boil Chief Justice Minos seems to have
failed. Doru and his cannibal chefs did not cook Efé, the first man,
who is the divine Giver, Defender and Enforcer of the Pygmy commandments. Minos concealed his wife Pasiphaë and her monstrous son, the Minotaur, in his labyrinthine retreat. The Minotaur
was fathered by a "dazzlingly white bull" that swam to the shore
of Crete. Pasiphaë-Athena fell in love with the bull. Daedalus
helped her to mate with the bull by building an upholstered wooden
cow. The lady climbed into the hollow cow, fitted her limbs into its
own, and was then mounted by the bull. The animal afterwards ran
amuck and devastated the whole island of Crete. Hercules caught
the bull and brought it to Greece where it was killed by Theseus,
the reputed son of Zeus's brother "Bull Poseidon." Minos had
prayed to Poseidon that a bull might emerge from the sea. When
Theseus prayed to Poseidon, the god sent a white bull that rode on
the crest of a towering tidal wave.

Poseidon's wife was a lady named Libya. This was an ancient
title of Africa in general. Libya was the daughter of Zeus's son
Epaphus. He was identified with the Egyptian "Apis" bull that was

---

[78] *Ibid.*, Vol. 1, p. 294.

believed to embody Hapi or Hapi-Osiris, the god of the Nile. The Roman author Pliny reported that the Apis bull was marked on the right side with a white crescent. Asar-Aah, Osiris Moon, was the title of Osiris as the god of the moon. The Apis bull of Memphis, the capital of Lower Egypt, was the lunar bull of the Nile. Epaphus, the Greek version of the Apis bull, was the son of Zeus and a lady named Io. The Argive Greeks called the moon Io, represented the moon as a cow, and regarded the moon as the source of all water. Zeus was accused of raping Io, a daughter of the Argive river-god Inachus and the granddaughter of Inachus' father, the Titan Okeanos-Nile. "I have never touched Io," Zeus insisted. Then he turned Io into a white cow. His sister-wife Hera imprisoned the cow. His son Hermes (the Egyptian moon-god Thoth) turned the cow loose. Then Hera sent a gadfly "to sting Io and chase her all over the world." The lunar cow galloped all the way to India, raced back to Arabia, and arrived in Ethiopia. What happened next?

"Thence she traveled down from the sources of the Nile, where the pygmies make perpetual war with the cranes, and found rest at last in Egypt. There Zeus restored her to human form and, having married Telegonus, she gave birth to Epaphus—her son by Zeus, who had *touched* her to some purpose—and founded the worship of Isis, as she called Demeter. Epaphus, who was rumored to be the divine bull Apis, reigned over Egypt, and had a daughter, Libya, the mother by Poseidon of Agenor and Belus."[79] According to some accounts, Io gave birth to Epaphus in a cave on the Aegean island of Euboea. Another story maintains that Io gave birth to Zeus's daughter Libya-Africa in Greece, fled to the land of Egypt, and was buried or disappeared at Mount Silpium in Armenia.

Zeus's daughter Athena had a traditional birthplace in Libya. Athena was identified with the moon and with Pasiphaë, the lady who got into Daedalus' upholstered cow and mated with the bull from the sea. In another story, Zeus transforms himself into a snow-white bull and kidnaps Europe, the granddaughter of "Bull Poseidon." The Zeus bull abducted Europe on the seashore near Tyre in Asia Minor; he swam with her to Crete, turned into an eagle and raped her under a tree. Their affair was consummated on the

---

[79] *Ibid.*, pp. 190–91.

island where Pasiphaë-Athena mated with the white bull from the sea. Europe's father, Agenor, had previously "left Egypt to settle in the Land of Canaan." Agenor's quasi-Biblical exodus took him to the Israelites' Promised Land of Canaan. His mother, Libya-Africa, was born either in Africa or in Greece; his daughter Europe was kidnapped in Asia. These legends mingle accounts both of the ancestors' migrations and of continents that were raped by "bulls from the sea."

Agenor's father, Bull Poseidon, was the husband of Libya-Africa. Poseidon was called Enosichthon, Earth Shaker, as the cause of earthquakes and floods. Plato's dialogue *Critias* describes Poseidon as the founding father of Atlantis, a nation that sank into the sea after violent earthquakes and floods:

> And Poseidon, receiving for his lot the island of Atlantis, begat children by a mortal woman, and settled them in a part of the island which I will describe. On the side toward the sea and in the center of the whole island there was a plain said to have been the fairest of all plains and very fertile. Near the plain again, and also in the center of the island at a distance of about fifty stadia, there was a mountain not very high on any side. There dwelt one of the earth-born natives of that country, named Euenor, and he had a wife named Leukippe, and they had an only daughter named Kleito. The maiden was growing up to womanhood, when her father and mother died; Poseidon fell in love with her and had intercourse with her, and breaking the ground inclosed the hill in which she dwelt all round, making alternate zones of sea and land larger and smaller encircling one another, two of land and three of water, which he turned as with a lathe out of the center of the island, equidistant in every way so that no man could get to the island, for ships and voyages were not yet heard of. He, being a god, easily effected special arrangements for the center island, bringing two streams of water under the earth, which he caused to ascend as springs, one of warm water and the other of cold and making every variety of food to spring up abundantly in the earth.
>
> He also begat and reared five pairs of twin sons, dividing the island of Atlantis into ten portions; he gave to the first-born of the eldest pair his mother's dwelling and the surrounding allotment which was the largest and best, and made him king over the rest; the others he made princes and gave them rule over many men and

a large territory. And he named them all; the eldest, who was the king, he named Atlas, and from him the whole island and the ocean received the name of Atlantis . . .

The palaces in the interior of the citadel were constructed in this wise: In the center was a holy temple dedicated to Kleito and Poseidon, which remained inaccessible, and was surrounded by an enclosure of gold; this was the spot in which they originally begat the race of the ten princes, and thither they annually brought the fruits of the earth in their season from all the ten portions, and performed sacrifices to each of them . . .[80]

The citadel of the gods is located in the "center island." The center island is not the whole island of Atlantis. The center island contains or comprises the mountain at the center of the whole island. Plato makes this distinction and elsewhere discusses the island in very ambiguous style. Now, where are the center island and the whole island located? The island-mountain at the center of the whole earth is represented in numerous Old and New World legends as the only mountain that remains unsubmerged or rises from the waters of the flood. Poseidon, the founding father of Atlantis, himself supported or raised the floating island-mountain of Delos to provide a refuge for Leto, the mother of Zeus's son Apollo. Deucalion sailed in the moon boat to Apollo's Parnassus mountain and descended to the cave or "sacred chasm" at the Delphic center of the earth. Many European legends and poems specifically identify the "hollow peak" of paradise with the Mountain of the Moon at the source of the Nile. The cavernous maze in the mountain leads to the Hades kingdom or citadel of the gods in the center island of the whole island.

The Efé Pygmies dwell at the foot of the lunar island-mountain in the center of Plato's Atlantis. The whole island of Atlantis comprises the islands or continents of the earth. The lunar island-mountain at the center of Atlantis is the entrance to the refuge in which the ancestor-gods survive the great floods that sweep over the whole earth or whole island of Atlantis at the end of every world-age. Plato's "whole island" of Atlantis had "an extent greater than that of Libya and Asia." A recent theory identifies Atlantis

---

[80] L. Sprague De Camp, *Lost Continents: The Atlantis Theme in History, Science, and Literature* (New York: Dover Publications, 1970), pp. 286–89.

with Thera, a little island in the Mediterranean Sea. Other theories have identified Atlantis with Crete, Malta, Ceylon, the British Isles, Belgium, the Netherlands, Palestine, Morocco, Tunisia, Carthage, Nigeria, Spain, France, Greenland, Mexico, Brazil, North America, Central America, North Africa, South Africa, a North Polar continent, a South Pacific continent, an Atlantic continent, ad infinitum. All of these theories have ignored or misinterpreted the problem of the "center island" and the "whole island." All of the theoreticians have inhabited—irony of ironies!—the "whole island" of Atlantis or island-continents of earth.

Atlantis was a paradise until its people broke the laws of "their kinsmen," the gods. Earth can be paradise wherever and whenever men live like intelligent human beings. The paradise or citadel of the gods is another affair. The decadent residents of Atlantis were defeated by the Athenian nation of Athena and Hephaestus, whom Plato described as a pair of siblings "sprung from the same father, having a common nature and being also united in the love of philosophy and art." Their father is described in many stories as Zeus. He sent the deluge of Deucalion and the deluge of Atlantis to punish the profligate residents of the whole earth and the whole island. His brother Poseidon undoubtedly assisted by shaking and flooding the earth. Atlantis "sank into the sea" and the victorious Athenian army sank into the earth, like Greek ghosts descending to Hades. The entrance to Hades is the lunar mountain of the original Athens in the center island of Atlantis. The characters and events of Plato's story are not new or unfamiliar. Plato's talk of the center island, the whole island and the island has merely confused the issue.

Poseidon mated with a lady who dwelled in the hill of the center island. Her first son, Atlas, was endowed with "his mother's dwelling and the surrounding allotment." Poseidon's several mates included a lady called Libya. Poseidon's reputed daughter Athena was born in Libya beside Lake Tritonis. The Libyan birthplace of the warrior goddess Athena was the traditional homeland of the warrior women called Amazons. Poseidon's reputed son Theseus, the hero-king of Athens, married the queen of the Amazons. The Greek historian Diodorus described the Amazons' African establishment in his treatise *The Library of History:*

We are told, namely, that there was once in the western parts
of Libya, on the bounds of the inhabited world, a race which was
ruled by women and followed a manner of life unlike that which
prevails among us. For it was the custom among them that women
should practice the arts of war . . .

As mythology relates, their home was on an island which,
because it was in the west, was called Hespera, and it lay in the
marsh Tritonis. This marsh was near the ocean which surrounds
the earth and received its name from a certain river Triton which
emptied into it; and this marsh was also near Ethiopia and that
mountain by the shore of the ocean which is the highest of those
in the vicinity and impinges upon the ocean and is called by the
Greeks Atlas. The island mentioned above was of great size and
full of fruit-bearing trees of every kind . . .

The Amazons dwelled at Hespera. Atlas fathered the three
ladies called Hesperides and built the stone walls that enclose the
Garden of Hesperides. Atlas' mountain is located on the shore of
the ocean. According to the very ancient Pelasgian Greek creation
legend, Atlas was the Titan of the moon. Homer's cranes flew to
"the streaming Ocean" and attacked the Egyptian's little men from
the Mountains of the Moon. The Efé Pygmies still dwell at the
lunar source of that grand old River Ocean, Father Nile, and tell
legends of an underworld river that flows through their kingdom
of the dead. Okeanos' daughter Styx was the goddess of the Stygian
river and the wife of the Titan Pallas. Homer described Pallas as
"the father of the moon." A giant named Pallas was the reputed
father of the goddess called Pallas or Pallas Athena.

Plato's dialogue *Critias* locates the temples of Athena and her
sibling Hephaestus on the summit of the Acropolis hill at Athens,
the first city that Athena founded. The Egyptian rock inscription
of Sahal describes the site of "the first city that ever existed" as the
island of Elephantine at the source of the Nile. "Moreover, there
were a great number of elephants in the island," Plato wrote of
Atlantis. He did not explain whether the elephants inhabited the
center island or the whole island. An enormous bull elephant called
Goru holds the sky upon his shoulders, according to the Pygmies
of Gabon and Cameroon. Bull Poseidon's son Atlas, the king of
Atlantis, was portrayed in other Greek stories as a towering giant

who holds up the sky. The Egyptian sky-goddess Nut was transformed into a huge cow; her legs were held in position by the four
children of Horus who stand at the four cardinal points of the
earth. The four cardinal points are intimately related to the pre-
Christian crosses of the terrestrial and celestial Olympus: the
mountain at the center of the earth and the mountain that comprises the vault of the heavens. The earthly Olympus is, in other
words, a miniature version of the celestial hemisphere. In *The
Library of History,* Diodorus described Atlas himself as the author
of this concept:

> After the death of Hyperion, the myth relates, the kingdom
> was divided among the sons of Ouranos, the most renowned of
> whom were Atlas and Kronos. Of these sons Atlas received as his
> part the regions on the coast of the ocean, and he not only gave the
> name of Atlantioi to his peoples but likewise called the greatest
> mountain in the land Atlas. They also said that he perfected the
> science of astrology and was the first to publish to mankind the
> doctrine of the sphere; and it was for this reason that the idea was
> held that the entire heavens were supported upon the shoulders of
> Atlas.

Atlas' father is described in this story as Ouranos or Uranus,
Father Sky. Uranus and Mother Earth were the parents of the
Titans, a group of gods who were related on the one hand to the
heavenly bodies and on the other to the earth-born giants. Hyperion
was the Titan of the sun. According to some accounts, Coeus was
the Titan of the moon. Atlas was variously described as a man, a
giant and the Titan of the moon. Kronos or Cronus was the Titan of
Saturn, the most remote planet known to the astronomers of early
historic times. Cronus fathered the original family of Olympian
gods: Zeus, Poseidon, Hades, Hera, Demeter and Hestia. Atlas and
Cronus are described in several legends as the principal powers
who stage the so-called war between the Titans and the gods.

The Titans fought the Olympian gods, according to the legend
of Atlas and Prometheus, immediately after the war between
Atlantis and Athens. The Athenians single-handedly defeated the
nation of Atlantis, "a kingdom with a precipitous coastline, bigger
than Africa and Asia put together." The Athenians won the war
with the "permission" of Zeus. "At the same time, the gods sent a

deluge which, in one day and one night, overwhelmed all Atlantis, so that the harbour works and temples were buried beneath a waste of mud and the sea became unnavigable. Atlas and Menoetius, who escaped, then joined Cronus and the Titans in their unsuccessful war against the Olympian gods. Zeus killed Menoetius with a thunderbolt and sent him down to Tartarus, but spared Atlas, whom he condemned to support Heaven on his shoulders for all eternity."[81]

Atlas had three brothers, according to this story: Menoetius, Prometheus and Epimetheus. Menoetius descended to the abyss of Tartarus when Atlantis was deluged. Another legend describes Prometheus' son Deucalion as a virtuous old man who rode in an ark to Parnassus and descended to a cave when the whole earth was deluged. Deucalion was accompanied by Pyrrha, his wife, who was the daughter of Epimetheus. Deucalion and Pyrrha went on a boat ride to the Delphic navel of the earth. Their kinsman Atlas had a residence at the center of Atlantis. His close human relatives descended to the cavernous kingdom of Hades when the earth or Atlantis was overwhelmed by disasters. The valiant Athenian warriors of Plato's *Timaeus* "in a body sank into the earth" when violent earthquakes and floods, followed by "a single day and night of rain" submerged Atlantis in the sea.

The legend of Atlas and Prometheus maintains that a continent larger than Africa and Asia combined was deluged "in one day and one night." What happened to the Athenians after the war with Atlantis? The legend does not say. Plato's *Critias* comments on the condition of Athens *prior* to the war with Atlantis: "Now the city in those days was arranged thus: in the first place the Acropolis was not as now. For the fact is that a single night of excessive rain washed away the earth and laid bare the rock; at the same time there were earthquakes and then occurred the third extraordinary inundation, which immediately preceded the great deluge of Deucalion." Here Plato tells us that the Acropolis hill of Athens was gravely eroded but apparently survived disasters that occurred during the era of 9600 B.C. Deucalion's deluge flooded the entire earth with the exception of a single mountain.

---

[81] Robert Graves, *The Greek Myths,* Vol. 1, pp. 143–44.

Plato's four great floods correspond with the disasters that terminate the four world-ages of Old and New World legend.

Atlas, the king of Atlantis, was represented in some stories as the lunar Titan and the founder of astronomy. Egyptian and Greek legends describe Thoth-Hermes as the founder of astronomy. Arabic legends portray the great Hermes as the primordial astronomer and universal scientific genius who survived the deluge by retreating to the Mountain of the Moon. Efé was the first astronomer, according to the Pygmy people who reside at the foot of Baba Tiba, "Mount Moon." The Greek scholar Diodorus, in *The Library of History,* referred to Atlas and the Saturnian Titan Cronus as the "most renowned" members of the Titan clan. Efé the Angel is said to have dwellings in the celestial lands of Tiba, the moon, and Bibi Tiba Abutsiua'ani, the star of nine moons or the planet Saturn. *Bibi* means a star or planet. The Saturnian Star of Nine Moons is also called Bibi Deba, the good or perfect star. Some Pygmies associate God the Grandfather with the moon and Saturn. Others locate his celestial paradise "somewhere in the stars."[82]

Heru, God or Horus, was the Egyptian god of the planet Saturn. Heru-Aah, Horus-Moon, was a title of Horus as the moongod. Horus and the lunar angel Thoth were combined as Heru-Tehuti, Horus-Thoth, which was a title of Osiris. Many scholars have described Horus as the first or oldest Egyptian deity. Of all the Egyptian gods, Horus was most closely associated with the Pygmies. Some pictures endow Bes, the Pygmy Dancer of God, with the attributes of Horus the Child. The Metternich Stele represents Bes as the father incarnation of Horus. During late dynastic times, remarked Sir E. A. Wallis Budge, "Bes was wholly merged in Horus." Pictures of Horus gods with "dwarf's legs" emphasize Horus' ethnic identity with Bes and his earthly kinsmen, the Pygmies.

Ba'atsi, the Behorned One, is a title of Efé the Angel and his father, God. Horned creatures and the crescent ornament are symbols of the deity who is associated with the moon and the Efé

---

[82] The Swahili names of the moon and Saturn are *mwezi* and *zahali.* I have never encountered a Bantu or Sudanese tribesman who credits Saturn with any moons, much less nine. Most Americans and Europeans are no better informed concerning the existence and number of Saturn's satellites.

Pygmies' Star of Nine Moons. Heru-Ka-Pet, "Horus, Bull of Heaven," was the Egyptian title of the planet Saturn. Horus wore the horns of the crescent moon as a lunar divinity; as the god of Saturn, he was likewise equipped with horns or horned headdress.

Efé uses iron lightning spears to behead the ogre, serpent and elephant manifestations of the giant monster. The divergent Horus gods used spears made from "iron of the god" in their combats with Set. Horus, the god of Saturn, beheaded the ogre and serpent forms of the god-demon Set. Sani, the planet Saturn, burned off the head of a god called Ganesha who dwells at Mount Meru or Sumeru, the Hindu Olympus at the center of the earth. Horus and Bes, the Dancer of God, are different forms of the same god. Efé himself dances the "sacred dances" in the legends of the Ituri Forest Pygmies. Nataraja, the King of the Dance, alternately burned off the head of Ganesha. Nataraja is a title of Siva, the Mahadeva or Great God. Hindu artworks show Siva dancing in a circle of fire while he holds in his hand the fire that will someday destroy the world. Siva rides on a bull called Nandi and wears a crescent moon in his headdress. The Egyptians called Saturn "Horus, Bull of Heaven." Horned creatures are symbols of Efé, the angel of the moon and the Star of Nine Moons.

Siva helps and heals the virtuous; Siva punishes the wicked. Brahma, Siva and Vishnu are forms of the same god: the Creator, Preserver and Destroyer. Efé the Angel plays all of those roles. Every anthropomorphic representation of the deity, including God the Grandfather, is a form of the divine hero Efé. God the Grandfather gave rings and spears to his beloved son Efé the Angel. The angel created or transformed himself into Efé the First Man and Father of All Who Came After. Yima, the Persian Adam, was equipped with a ring and a golden goad. His celestial twin, Mithra, is usually described as a sun-god. Scholars have however identified Mithra with Cronus or Saturnus, as the Greeks and Romans called Saturn.[83]

Efé wore the rings of Saturn and carried the iron spears of the Egyptian Horus gods when he returned to earth. "You will die if you see a ghost," warned Matu, the motherly prophetess who

---

[83] *Larousse World Mythology*, p. 203.

refused to recognize Efé. Ninip or Nirig, the Babylonian god of the planet Saturn, has been defined as "the ghost of the elder god" and "the black Saturn, the ghost of the dead sun, the demoniac elder god."[84] The ghost triggered the great deluge of Babylonian legend. "At the dawn of day I saw rising athwart the heavens a dark cloud, and in the midst of it Ramman thundered. Nebo and Merodach went in front, speeding like emissaries over hills and plains . . . Then Ninip, the tempest god, came nigh, and the storm broke in fury before him. All the earth spirits leapt up with flaming torches and the whole land was aflare. The thunder god swept over the heavens, blotting out the sunlight and bringing thick darkness. Rain poured down the whole day long, and the earth was covered with water; the rivers were swollen; the land was in confusion; men stumbled about in the darkness, battling with the elements."[85]

Ninip was associated with bulls, like his Egyptian colleague Horus, Bull of Heaven. They are forms of Efé or Ba'atsi, the Behorned One. Ba'atsi is the celestial "lord of the storm" and "lord of fire," as Schebesta reported. He massacres criminals or sinners with his fiery lightning-weapons. Ninip was the tempest god. Horus slaughtered the wicked followers of Set. Ninip touched off the great deluge that the Old Testament deity sent to punish sinners. Yima, the earthly twin of Mithra-Saturn, received advance warning and survived the cataclysmic storm of Persian legend. Cronus or Saturnus, as the Romans called him, sallied forth with his Titans in the classical legends of the deluge that drowned the decadent and aggressive residents of Atlantis. "Ninip resembled Kronos and Saturnus as a father, but he was also at the same time a son; he was the Egyptian Horus the elder and Horus the younger in one," according to a scholarly comparison of the Saturnian deities.[86]

Atlas and Cronus, the Titans of the moon and the planet Saturn, were represented as close collaborators. "This was the spearing of my foes," remarked the just lawgiver Thoth when Horus chastised the criminals. Thoth-Moon, Horus-Moon, and Horus the god of Saturn were forms of the same god. The Egyp-

---

[84] Donald A. Mackenzie, *Myths of Babylonia and Assyria*, p. 314.

[85] *Ibid.*, p. 192.

[86] *Ibid.*, p. 316.

tians represented the sacred ibis as the bird of Thoth. Efé's sacred ibis is identified or confounded in some Pygmy territories with the crow. The very name of "Cronus" has been derived from the title of the crow: "The later Greeks read 'Cronus' as *Chronos*, 'Father Time' with his relentless sickle. But he is pictured in the company of a crow, like Apollo, Asclepius, Saturn, and the early British god Bran; and *cronos* probably means 'crow,' like the Latin *cornix* and the Greek *corone*."[87]

The British god Bran has been interpreted as "the king of a crow or raven totem clan." The crow or raven was the bird of King Arthur. He was identified with a clan of Pygmy-like dwarfs, elves or fairies. So was All-Father Odin, the Germanic "god of ravens" who dwells with the white elves in the fire shelter of the far southern paradise. The Celtic bard-magician Merlin, a divergent form of the same ancient deity, warned in his apocalyptic prophecies that "Saturn the star" will massacre mankind after the "wonted course" of the heavenly bodies is confounded:

> The shining of the sun shall be dimmed by the amber of Mercury, and shall be a dread unto them that behold it. Stilbon of Arcady shall change his shield, and the helmet of Mars shall call unto Venus. The helmet of Mars shall cast a shadow, and the rage of Mercury shall overpass all bounds. Iron Orion shall bare his sword. Phoebus of the ocean shall torment his clouds. Jupiter shall trespass beyond his appointed bounds, and Venus forsake the way that hath been ordained unto her. The malignity of Saturn the star shall fall upon earth with the rain of heaven, and shall slay mankind as it were with a crooked sickle.[88]

The History of the Kings of Britain, by Geoffrey of Monmouth (c. 1100–1155 A.D.), says that Merlin was also called Ambrose or Ambrosius. *Bulfinch's Mythology* mentions Ambrosius as a title of King Arthur's father. In Book VII of Geoffrey's *History*, Ambrosius Merlin prophesies that Saturn the star will massacre mankind. Book VIII describes an ominous star that appeared when a king called Ambrosius or Aurelius Ambrosius died at the city of Win-

[87] Robert Graves, *The Greek Myths*, Vol. 1, p. 38.

[88] Geoffrey of Monmouth, *History of the Kings of Britain*, (New York: E. P. Dutton & Co., 1958), p. 151.

chester: "Whilst these things were being enacted at Winchester, there appeared a star of marvellous bigness and brightness, stretching forth one ray whereon was a ball of fire, spreading forth in the likeness of a dragon, and from the mouth of the dragon issued forth two rays, whereof the one was of such length as that it did seem to reach beyond the regions of Gaul, and the other, verging toward the Irish sea, did end in seven lesser rays."[89]

All who beheld the star were "stricken with wonder and fear." The king was "buried by the bishops of the land within the Giants' Dance, nigh the convent of Amesbury, according to the instructions he had given when alive." *The Ecclesiastical History of the English Nation,* a treatise composed by a British monk called Bede (c. 673–735) describes "Ambrosius, a man of Roman stock" or Ambrosius Aurelianus as "almost the only person of Roman race" to survive an extraordinary fire. Bede does not mention the appearance of a blazing star or the Giants' Dance, an edifice that is associated with Stonehenge. He tells us that the fire was kindled by English or Anglo-Saxon "pagans" who came to Britain from Germany around 449 A.D. The fire "carried on its burning from the eastern sea to the western, with no one to stop it, and covered almost the whole surface of the stricken island." After the conflagration, says Bede, the Anglo-Saxon army "returned home." He does not explain how they managed to avoid being incinerated in this Hiroshima-like holocaust. Led by Ambrosius Aurelianus, the Britons subsequently fought a series of battles that culminated in "the siege of Mount Badon, when they inflicted very great losses on the same enemy, in about the 44th year from their arrival in Britain." Why didn't the fireproof ancestors of the English people burn the Celtic Britons to a crisp with their pyrotechnic devices?

Lord Raglan described Bede's account of the Anglo-Saxon pagans as "a series of categorical falsehoods" contrived for religious or political purposes. "His introductory chapters are drawn from classical or ecclesiastical sources, and such facts as he mentions merely form a framework for accounts of conversions, persecutions, and martyrdoms; of the miracles of saints; and of the victories of the faithful over heretics and infidels," Lord Raglan

---

[89] *Ibid.,* p. 169.

astutely commented on this compendium of "pious frauds."[90]

Geoffrey's *History* says that the appearance of the fiery star betokened the coming birth of King Arthur. Many British traditions identify Arthur with another legendary hero whose birth was heralded by the appearance of a star. "The Star of Bethlehem was not Venus or any other planet, and neither was it an ordinary star. No definite scientific explanation is available; it may possibly have been a nova or supernova, while there is also a chance that it was a bright comet. My own theory is that a bright meteor (or possibly two meteors) was the source of the legend," commented Astronomer Patrick Moore.[91] He presumably referred to celestial prodigies or catastrophes that may have occurred during the very recent era assigned to Jesus' birth (8–4 B.C.). The *Britannica* remarks that "the celebration of the Birth of our Lord was fixed in the 4th century by enactment for December 25, thus consecrating the old Saturnalia of Rome to the new religion." The Saturnalia was the Roman festival of Saturn.

Merlin's prophecies rather strongly suggest that the ancient Celts identified "Saturn the star" with the celestial prodigy that preceded King Arthur's birth. The star appeared after the death of an elder sovereign, Aurelius Ambrosius. Sir J. G. Frazer remarked, concerning the king of the ancient Italian Saturnalia, that it may have been "the universal practice in ancient Italy, wherever the worship of Saturn prevailed, to choose a man who played the part and enjoyed all the traditionary privileges of Saturn for a season, and then died, whether by his own or another's hand, whether by the knife or the fire or on the gallows-tree, in the character of the good god who gave his life for the world."[92]

This Christ-like deity was represented as the wise civilizing hero who taught astronomy, navigation, agriculture and the other useful arts to his congregation, the first men or so-called "golden race." The Roman festival of the Saturnalia in late December was "popularly supposed to commemorate the merry reign of Saturn,

[90] Lord Raglan, *The Hero*, pp. 83–92.

[91] Patrick Moore, *The Observer's Book of Astronomy* (London: Frederick Warne & Co., Ltd., 1962), p. 185.

[92] Sir J. G. Frazer, *The Golden Bough*, p. 586.

the god of sowing and of husbandry, who lived on earth long ago as a righteous and beneficent king of Italy, drew the rude and scattered dwellers on the mountains together, taught them to till the ground, gave them laws, and ruled in peace. His reign was the fabled Golden Age: the earth brought forth abundantly: no sound of war or discord troubled the happy world: no baleful love of lucre worked like poison in the blood of the industrious and contented peasantry. Slavery and private property were alike unknown: all men had all things in common. At last the good god, the kindly king, vanished suddenly; but his memory was cherished to distant ages, shrines were reared in his honour, and many hills and high places in Italy bore his name."[93]

Cronus, the Greek Saturn, was the just god of the first men. The Cronian festival of the Basilai was "a very ancient seasonal festival of spring, which became attached to the vernal equinox when the sun and the critical dates of his annual course became important." Cronus' festivals fall usually "in the neighborhood of Christmas (the winter solstice) or of Easter (the vernal equinox) or at some season of carnival between these two dates." Cronus "stands for the cycle of reincarnation."[94]

The Christians borrowed both the Christmas and Easter festivals from the so-called pagans. The Christians then proceeded to denounce the pagan versions of the festivals, and the associated legends of the hero's return from the underworld, as wicked counterfeits contrived by the pagans. Ecclesiastical frauds of every variety were perpetrated to conceal the origin and meaning of the legends. Books and heretics were burned to safeguard the sacred mysteries and miracles of the Church. Merely to celebrate the Easter festival on an unauthorized date became an act of heresy, despite the plain fact that the New Testament and the writings of the apostolic Fathers nowhere mention the observance of an Easter festival.

A very ancient Greco-Roman legend sheds considerable light on the meaning of the Saturnalian festivals that the founders of

---

[93] *Ibid.*, p. 583.

[94] J. E. Harrison, *Epilegomena to the Study of Greek Religion* (New York: University Books, 1962), pp. 224, 253, 496.

the "new" religion converted into Christmas and Easter. During the December festival of the Saturnalia, the Romans gave Christmas presents of a rather significant nature: "All and sundry were greeted with *io Saturnalia,* and presents were freely exchanged, the traditional ones being wax candles and little clay dolls. Concerning these, the antiquaries had a quaint story that an old prophecy bade the earliest inhabitants of Latium send *phora* to Saturn and heads to Pluto; that they interpreted this as meaning human sacrifices, but that Hercules advised them to use lights (the word *phos* means 'light' or 'man' according to accentuation) and not human 'heads' (Macrob., *op. cit.,* 1, 7, 31)."[95]

Send lights to Saturn and men to the realm of the underworld deity whom the Greeks called Hades or Pluto. Many European legends and poems specifically locate the entrance to the underworld in a Central African mountain at the source of the Nile. Efé, the Pygmy hero or nation, went through the maze-like caverns of this mountain to the kingdom of the dead and then had to stay for three months and part of a fourth month. If the time of Efé's descent to the infernal abodes is identified with the winter Saturnalia, the Pygmy men return from the underworld at the time of the spring festival. *Dies Saturni,* Saturn's Day or Saturday, was the last day of the Roman week. The week began again with *Dies Solis,* Sunday. The world-age ends when Saturn or Efé the Angel massacres mankind. The world-age begins when his human kinsman, Efé the Pygmy, returns from the underworld like the resurrected Christian hero of Easter Sunday.

The Roman Saturn was armed with a sickle. An angel related to Christ, the Son of God or Son of Man, wields his sickle in the book of Revelation:

> And I looked, and behold a white cloud, and upon the cloud one sat like unto the Son of man, having on his head a golden crown, and in his hand a sharp sickle. And another angel came out of the temple, crying with a loud voice to him that sat on the cloud, Thrust in thy sickle, and reap: for the time is come for thee to reap; for the harvest of the earth is ripe. And he that sat on the cloud thrust in his sickle on the earth; and the earth was reaped.

---

[95] *Encyclopaedia Britannica,* 14th ed., Vol. 20, p. 7.

And another angel came out of the temple which is in heaven, he also having a sharp sickle. And another angel came out from the altar, which had power over fire; and cried with a loud cry to him that had the sharp sickle, saying, Thrust in thy sharp sickle, and gather the clusters of the vine of the earth; for her grapes are fully ripe. And the angel thrust in his sickle into the earth, and gathered the vine of the earth, and cast it into the great winepress of the wrath of God. And the winepress was trodden without the city, and blood came out of the winepress, even into the horse bridles, by the space of a thousand and six hundred furlongs.[96]

Merlin prophesied, "The malignity of Saturn the star shall fall upon earth with the rain of heaven, and shall slay mankind as it were with a crooked sickle." The Grim Reaper harvested the grapes of wrath with his sickle. Merry Christmas to all, and to all a good night. Your "Little Star of Bethlehem" is the planet of Horus, the Egyptian Saturn who acts as the just executioner in legends that date back to predynastic times. A divine Pygmy called Bes was "wholly merged in Horus," the oldest god of Egypt. Sir E. A. Wallis Budge calls this god "Bes-Horus" in his book *The Gods of the Egyptians*. *The Book of the Dead* lists Horus the Elder, Horus the Son of Isis, and Horus-Thoth as titles of Osiris. The index to *The Gods of the Egyptians* contains the terse equation "Osiris = Christ."

Merlin prophesied, concerning the events that will follow Saturn's massacre of mankind: "None hereafter shall return unto his wonted duty, but Ariadne shall lie hidden within the closed gateways of her sea-beaten headland."[97] Ariadne helped the Athenian hero Theseus to enter and return from the legendary "death maze" at the Cretan navel of the earth. When Ariadne closes her gateways, Little Gwion/Merlin/Taliesin is apparently forced to stay in the Welsh "prison" of a lady called Arianrhod. He was confined for three periods or three times incarcerated in this abode whence the hero is born, reborn and/or resurrected. "Although I am but little, I am highly gifted," the elfin sage declares in the Taliesin poems. "Three times have I been born, I know by medita-

---

[96] Revelation 14:14–20.

[97] Geoffrey of Monmouth, *History of the Kings of Britain*, p. 152.

tion; all the sciences of the world are collected in my breast, for I know what has been, and what hereafter will occur."[98]

Merlin was the omniscient lord of the little people. He and King Arthur were both associated with mountain caves and/or mazes. Near Bosinney, in Cornwall, there is a maze design carved upon a rock face: "The ravine where the maze was first noticed by Dr. Renton Green is one of the last haunts of the Cornish chough; and this bird houses the soul of King Arthur—who harrowed Hell, and with whom Bosinney is closely associated in legend."[99] Choughs, crows and ravens were closely associated with Cronus-Saturn, the god who stood for the cycle of resurrection. Merlin and Arthur are Welsh versions of Efé, the elfin hero who returns from the underworld as himself or his son.

Efé survived the war on earth and the war in heaven by taking refuge in his cavernous retreat. After a terrible war the little people of Irish legend departed to magnificent underworld dwellings that are visible to the human eye in the shape of mounds. During their career on earth, they were called the People of Dana. Now they are known as Aes sidhe, the Race of Mounds. The Irish mound of New Grange is rimmed by a circle of stones and contains a chamber that is reached by a tunnel about fifty feet long. A stone circle near Belfast is known as the Giants' Ring. Merlin ostensibly transported the stones of the Giants' Dance from the Mount of Killare in Ireland to the Mount of Amesbury in England. The Giants' Dance originated, however, in the African homeland of the little people whom the Greeks called Oi Pygmaioi. Concerning the stones of the Giants' Dance, Merlin himself declared, "Giants of old did carry them from the furthest ends of Africa and did set them up in Ireland what time they did inhabit there."[100]

The People of Dana slew the Fomors or giant monsters of Irish legend. After a later war, the People of Dana descended to the underground abodes where they dwell as the Race of Mounds. Geoffrey's History says that Brutus, the first king of Britain, led

---

[98] Bulfinch's Mythology, pp. 455–56.

[99] Robert Graves, The Greek Myths, Vol. 1, p. 346.

[100] Geoffrey of Monmouth, History of the Kings of Britain, pp. 164–65.

his people to an island called Albion which was formerly inhabited by giants. After the settlers dispatched the giants, Brutus renamed the island "Briton" and called his companions "Britons" to commemorate his name. During very recent times, "they were no longer called Britons but Welsh." The Irish legend of the elfin nation's retreat to the mounds is matched by Geoffrey's eminently pseudo-historical account of royal burials within the Giants' Dance.

A Dance of the Titans was performed at Knossos, the ancient capital of Crete, where Greek legends situate the Troy-town maze. The circling movement of the dancers "came to represent the annual courses of the heavenly bodies." Devotees of the "sky-bull cult" performed this version of the Troy-town dance.[101] "Horus, Bull of Heaven" was the Egyptian version of the Saturnian Titan Cronus. Bes-Horus united the deity with Bes, the god of the dance, and the Pygmy Dancers of God. Cronus' congregation, the first men, were represented as divine dancers whose spirits survive as the virtuous genii of "happy music retreats."

Greek legends associate Cronus, the "Elder Zeus" or father of Zeus, with a group of mountains called the Pillars of Cronus. The Rock of Gibraltar and a corresponding eminence on the African side of the Straits were known as the Pillars of Hercules and identified by some of the Greeks with Cronus' fabled pillars. Cronus' status as the god of the time cycle and the foremost representative of the seven Titans, suggest that his mountains were the sacred pillars of the planetary powers. Robert Graves remarked that "the Jews of Jerusalem worshipped a transcendant God, composed of all the planetary powers of the week: a theory symbolized in the seven-branched candlestick, and in the Seven Pillars of Wisdom. The seven planetary pillars set up near the Horse's Tomb at Sparta were said by Pausanius (ii. 20.9) to be adorned in ancient fashion, and may have been connected with the Egyptian rites introduced by the Pelasgians (Herodotus: ii. 57). Whether the Jews borrowed the theory from the Egyptians, or contrariwise, is uncertain; but the so-called Heliopolitan Zeus, whom A. B. Cook discusses in his *Zeus* (i. 570–76), was Egyptian in character, and bore busts of the seven planetary powers as frontal ornaments on

---

[101] Robert Graves, *The Greek Myths*, Vol. 1, p. 346.

his body sheath; usually, also, busts of the remaining Olympians as rear ornaments."[102]

The first two chapters of Revelation say that "one like unto the Son of man" holds seven stars in his right hand and walks in the midst of seven golden candlesticks. The heavenly throne of his parent, Jehovah, is described in Revelation 3:5: "And out of the throne proceeded lightnings and thunderings and voices: and there were seven lamps of fire burning before the throne, which are the seven spirits of God." The far more ancient pyramid text of Pepi the First associates the great throne of Osiris with the oldest known race of mankind. The Efé Pygmies identify the throne with the Mountain of the Moon or "funeral mountain" of Osiris. The lunar massif rears its snowy peaks in the Central African neighborhood of eight giant candlesticks, the Virunga volcanoes, which are surrounded by vast lava fields and hundreds of smaller craters.

Eight candles are lighted on eight successive days to celebrate a Jewish festival called Hanukkah, the Feast of Lights. Scholars have interpreted this holiday as "a primitive winter solstice festival."[103] Wax candles were a feature of the Roman Saturnalia or winter solstice festival. Cronus and Atlas, the Pelasgian Titans of Saturn and the moon, were represented as perennial collaborators. Atlas' mountain was alternately located in Libya-Africa and the center island of Atlantis. The first book of Homer's *Odyssey* says that Atlas "keeps the tall pillars that sunder earth and heaven." Cronus was involved with pillars and volcanoes.

Plutarch's treatise on Isis and Osiris represents Cronus as the father of the Egyptian god Set, whom Plutarch calls Typhon. Cronus' son Zeus supposedly buried Typhon under Mount Etna, a traditional residence of the Roman fire-god Vulcan. Zeus confined his father Cronus and the Titans in the abyss of Tartarus, or banished them to "a British island in the farthest west," according to a legend called "The Dethronement of Cronus." According to Geoffrey of Monmouth's *History of the Kings of Britain*, King

---

[102] *Ibid.*, p. 29.

[103] *Encyclopaedia Britannica*, 14th ed., Vol. 11, p. 166.

Arthur's British dominions included a far western island called Iceland. There are one hundred and seven volcanoes and thousands of craters on this pyrotechnic island. A region called Surtshellir is named after the formidable fire-giant Surt. "The first world to exist, however, was Muspell in the southern hemisphere; it is light and hot and that region flames and burns so that those who do not belong to it and whose native region it is not, cannot endure it. The one who sits there at land's end to guard it is called Surt; he has a flaming sword, and at the end of the world he will come and harry and will vanquish all the gods and burn the whole world with fire," declares the *Prose Edda*.

Surt and his cohorts attack from the sky, like Saturn and the wayward planets of Merlin's prophecies, in the *Prose Edda*'s account of the Ragnarok disasters that come at the end of the world: "In this din the sky will be rent asunder and the suns of Muspell ride forth from it. Surt will ride first and with him fire blazing both before and behind. He has a very good sword and it shines more brightly than the sun. When they ride over Bifrost, however— as has been said before—that bridge will break." Himinbjörg, the Heaven Mountain, is located "at heaven's end by the bridge-head where Bifrost joins heaven." Translation: the Heaven Mountain stands in a remote region of the southern continent where Bifrost, the rainbow bridge, joins heaven on earth with the celestial heavens or sky. Surt and the sons of Muspell break the connection between earth and heaven when they ride into battle at Ragnarok to fight "the kindly gods" in the plain of Vigrith. Cronus and the Titans, whose Homeric pillars sunder earth and heaven, meanwhile battle with the Olympian gods.

Surt's residence at land's end in the southern continent of Muspelheim is the home of those extraordinary giants who carried the stones of the Giants' Dance to Ireland from "the furthest ends of Africa." This event occurred during the dateless era of the beginning or the olden days. The end came when Gormund, the king of the Africans, sailed to Ireland and incinerated the dominions of Britain. Geoffrey's *History of the Kings of Britain* assigns this catastrophe to the reign of Careticus, the son of Malgo and ninety-sixth king of Britain:

Unto Malgo succeeded Careticus, a lover of civil wars, hateful
unto God and unto the Britons. The Saxons, having had experience
of his shiftiness, went unto Gormund, King of the Africans, in
Ireland, wherein, adventuring thither with a vast fleet, he had conquered the folk of the country. Thereupon, by the treachery of the
Saxons, he sailed across with a hundred and sixty thousand Africans into Britain, which in one province the Saxons by perjuring
their oath of fealty, and in another the Britons by continually
carrying on civil wars amongst themselves, were utterly laying
waste. Entering into covenant, therefore, with the Saxons, Gormund
made war upon Careticus, and after many battles betwixt them,
drove him fleeing from city unto city until he forced him into
Cirencester and did there beleager him . . . When Gormund at last
had taken and burnt the said city, he did battle with Careticus and
drove him fleeing beyond the Severn into Wales. Then he desolated
the fields, set fire to all the neighboring cities, nor did he stint his
fury until he had burnt up well-nigh the whole face of the country
from sea to sea; in such sort that all the colonies were battered to
the ground by rams, and all they that dwelt therein along with the
priests of the churches delivered up to the flashing of their swords
or the crackling of the flames. The residue of them that were
slaughtered in these dreadful visitations had no choice but to flee
unto whatsoever shelter might seem to promise safety.[104]

Bede's *Ecclesiastical History of the English Nation* describes
an identical fire, kindled by Anglo-Saxon pagans, that brought
divine retribution to British heretics and sinners who had cast away
"the light yoke of Christ." Bede says that "the fire kindled by the
hands of the pagans hastened on the just retributions of God on the
sins of the people, not unlike that fire which, kindled by the Chal-
deans, devoured the walls and indeed all the buildings of Jerusalem. For even so this fire, by the agency of the wicked conqueror,
or rather the disposition of the just Judge, depopulating the nearest
cities and fields, carried on its burning from the eastern sea to the
western, with no one to stop it, and covered almost the whole
surface of the stricken island. Public and private buildings crashed
together, priests on all sides were butchered at their altars, bishops
and their people, without any respect for their rank, were slain

[104] Pp. 239–40.

alike by the sword or the flames, and there was not anyone to give burial to those who had been cruelly killed.[105]

Ambrosius Aurelianus was almost the only person of Roman race to survive this disaster which Bede dates to the era of 449 A.D. Aurelius Ambrosius, the eighty-ninth king of Britain, was buried within the Giants' Dance when the fiery star of Geoffrey's *History* made its ominous appearance. Merlin prophesied that Saturn the star will massacre mankind when the planetary powers run amuck. Cronus and his Titans war with the Olympian gods in legends of the Atlantis disaster that Plato assigned to the era of 9600 B.C. Surt and the Sons of Muspell ride out of the sky and/or the southern continent of Muspelheim-Africa at the end of every Germanic world-age. King Gormund sailed out of Africa and incinerated well nigh the whole country, plus all of the colonies. The contemporary British dominions included, according to Geoffrey of Monmouth, "the six neighbor islands of the Ocean, to wit, Ireland, Iceland, Gothland, the Orkneys, Norway, and Denmark." Surt flings fire over the world at the grand climax of Ragnarok; then the land is overwhelmed by the sea. The fire devastated the kingdom of Britain; then the kingdom of Atlantis sank into the sea.

Ambrosius Aurelianus survived the great disaster of Bede's *Ecclesiastical History* by unexplained means. Geoffrey's *History* says that Aurelius Ambrosius, the eighty-ninth king of Britain, was buried within the Giants' Dance. He was succeeded by his brother, Uther Pendragon. When Uther died, he was buried within the Giants' Dance. *Bulfinch's Mythology* describes King Arthur's father as "Ambrosius, otherwise called Uther." Ambrosius Merlin himself declared that the stones of the Giants' Dance originated in Africa. Ambrosius Merlin set up the stones of the Giants' Dance at the Mount of Amesbury, where four hundred and sixty British princes had previously been buried "after Christian fashion" by Eldad, the Bishop of Gloucester. Eldad Ben Mahli, the author and hero of a ninth-century Jewish travel romance, set out to visit the Jews in Africa and discovered five lost tribes (Dan, Naphthali, Asher, Gad, and Levi) who had established

---

[105] Bede, *The Ecclesiastical History of the English Nation, Books I and II,* translated by Michael Maclagan (Oxford: Basil Blackwell, 1949), p. 69.

a kingdom in "the gold land of Havilla beyond Abyssinia."[106]

Geoffrey's *History* is packed with information that menaces the phony ecclesiastical histories of the medieval monks. Geoffrey would have been burned at the stake if he told the story in more forthright terms. His fabulous Bishop Eldad buried the British princes in "the church-yard that lieth about the monastery of Abbot Ambrius, who of yore had been the founder thereof." Is Ambrius our old friend Ambrose or Ambrosius Merlin? Geoffrey says that Merlin set up the stones of the Giants' Dance at the Mount of Amesbury. The name Amesbury has evolved from Ambresburia. Ambrius' mountain monastery was apparently equipped with an ambry. The ambry of medieval churches was a wall niche or recess near the altar. Sacred vessels and other ecclesiastical treasures were stored in the ambry. The elfin princes were buried at the Mount of Ambrius. The fairy "Race of Mounds" retreated to the magnificent underground dwellings of Irish legend. According to the Anglo-Saxon poem *Beowulf* the great stronghold under the earth is stocked with golden vessels and other wonderful treasures.

A German poem, the *Niebelungenlied,* describes the guardian of the treasure as an elf or dwarf called Oberon. The legendary history of the Merovingian dynasty represents Oberon as a Merlin-like magician, the brother of the Frankish king Merovee. The thirteenth-century French romance "Huon of Bordeaux" describes a visit to Oberon's older residence. "They took the route of the Red Sea, and entered Arabia. Their way lay through a region which Sherasmin described as full of terrors. It was inhabited by Oberon, King of the Fairies," declared the unknown author of this story. According to an ode written by the English poet Thomas Warton (1728–1790) King Arthur was healed when the Elfin Queen sprinkled on his wounds "dew from flowers that in Arabia grew"; the Elfin Queen bade her spirits to carry Arthur away "in Merlin's agate-axled car, to her green isle's enamelled steep, far in the navel of the deep." Geoffrey's *History* says that King Arthur was borne away "unto the Isle of Avallon" in 542 A.D. The isle that is now called Avalon was traditionally located in fairyland and/or the Welsh kingdom of the dead.

---

[106] *Encyclopaedia Britannica*, 14th ed., Vol. 8, p. 130.

Glorianda, Morgana and Viviane were some of the several names assigned to the Elfin Queen, Lady of the Lake, or fairy hostess of Avalon. Glorianda gave birth to Oberon, the king of the little people. Morgana played the role of King Arthur's sister and/or mistress. Merlin's mistress Viviane imprisoned the elfin prophet within "the strongest tower in the world." Charlemagne's knights visited Merlin's tomb by entering the maze-like caverns of a towering mountain, and visited the entrance to the underworld kingdom by traveling to a mountain at the source of the Nile.

Black poplars grow at the entrance to the Greek underworld in the Grove of Persephone beside the Ocean Stream. Black poplars shelter the "great cavern" of Calypso, the mistress of a famous Greek hero who was imprisoned in Calypso's abode. "My heart is torn for wise Odysseus, wretched man, who so long parted from his friends suffers on a seagirt isle at the very navel of the sea. On this forested isle dwells a goddess, daughter of crafty Atlas who knows the depth of every sea and keeps the tall pillars that sunder earth and heaven," the goddess Athena declares in the first book of Homer's *Odyssey*.

The hero was imprisoned or buried within the Giants' Dance that is formed by the African pillar-mountains of Cronus and Atlas, the Pelasgian Titans of Saturn and the moon. Some cremated remains have been unearthed at the Stonehenge version of the Giants' Dance. They were not the remains of Ambrosius Merlin, Aurelius Ambrosius, Uther Pendragon and King Arthur. These people are literary characters, blended out of legend and history. The hero of the original Giants' Dance and the Troy-town maze is a super-historical, not a pseudohistorical character. He is Efé, the Pygmy. He lives in the land of other people's legends. He has lived in this land since the earliest known times.

The elders say, concerning the kingdom of the dead, that there is "light of another kind" and eternally balmy weather. "We can live down there; other people become sick and quickly die," I was told by an old man named Mutuke. "Why?" I asked. Mutuke answered, "I do not know." We ourselves know very little about Pygmy physiology. The Pygmies are immune to many diseases that afflict the other races of mankind. If there really is a Hades kingdom, the Pygmies may well be uniquely qualified to survive the downstairs environment. The world-wide legends of the hero's trip to Hades render it impossible to believe that this story is a myth.

Most anthropologists and archaeologists portray early man as a savage simpleton who worshiped the sun. In 1901 Sir Norman Lockyer promulgated the still-surviving theory that Stonehenge was built for sun-worshiping purposes. Another theory credits early man with a much higher degree of intelligence and represents Stonehenge as a gigantic calendar device. We have shown that the Giants' Dance is related to the dance of the heavenly bodies and the pillar mountains of the planetary Titans. Now, here comes the grand finale:

The Greek historian Plutarch represented the Saturnian Titan Cronus as the father of Typhon, a demon associated with volcanoes. Typhon begat an enormous water serpent, the Hydra, that was equipped with eight mortal heads and one immortal head, "together making nine in honor of the moon goddess." The Efé Pygmies casually refer to Cronus' planet as "the Star of Nine Moons" and tell a story about a giant swallowing monster. Cronus himself swallowed the Olympian gods, according to a Greek legend called "The Dethronement of Cronus." According to the legends of the East African Masai, a hybrid Hamite nation that includes the pygmoid Dorobo, an heroic warrior liberated the swallowed victims of the nine-headed devil. Anthropologists have accused almost every people on earth of borrowing their swallowing-monster stories from the Old Testament tale of Jonah and the whale. The Biblical scriptures, as we have repeatedly seen, are superstitious myths derived from the monumental legends of the so-called pagans.

Saturn, the remote planet of Cronus, did not swallow the Olympian gods or any of the monsters' international victims. Cronus is not a whale or a sea serpent. Cronus ruled the "early earth-born race" as a sovereign lord of a kingdom that is "in quite a special way of the earth."[107] Rhea, the sister-wife of Cronus and Titaness of Saturn, was identified with the Mountain Mother and Mother Earth. Her Roman titles include Terra and Tellus, the terrestrial and tellurian names of our planet.

---

[107] J. E. Harrison, *Epilegomena to the Study of Greek Religion*, p. 496.

The medieval legends of Charlemagne locate "the mouth of the infernal abodes" in a mountain at the source of the Nile. Efé entered the mouth and traveled to the kingdom of Cronus' son Hades. Efé returned in the myth of the savior by cutting a path through the Mountain Mother's foot. The entrance had evidently been blocked or sealed during the hero's sojourn in the underworld. After Efé emerged, he fought an epic battle with Lulu, the giant swallowing monster whose gaping mouth had engulfed everyone in the world. Ituri Forest and Western Pygmy legends locate Lulu's principal residence in a somber cavern near the cataracts of the underworld river. Lulu is associated with water, like many similar monsters that produce floods.

Efé was swallowed by the earth and everyone else was swallowed by Lulu. The elite Athenians sank into the earth and the residents of Atlantis drowned in the sea. Cronus, the Saturn-Earth Titan who swallowed Efé, is not a true counterpart of Lulu or Jonah's whale as we supposed in an earlier chapter. The complexities of this story and the different types of symbolism render it susceptible to confusion of every conceivable variety. The Efé legend of the descent to the abyss says, for example, that the hero entered a hole or cavern. If the cavern is defined as the mouth of the underworld, he is swallowed up by the earth. Cronus and Rhea as Saturn-Earth Titans are male and female versions of the same concept. Cronus can regorge the hero through his mouth or Rhea can give birth to the hero through her genital orifice. Cronus as the civilizing hero is Efé, the great lawgiver and teacher. Lady Rhea is Matu, the Mother of God.

The legend of Cronus' dethronement says that Cronus successively swallowed the first five Olympian children that Rhea bore: Hestia, Hera, Demeter, Hades and Poseidon. Plutarch's treatise on Isis and Osiris says that Rhea successively gave birth to five Egyptian deities: Osiris, Horus the Elder, Set-Typhon, Isis and Set's wife Nephthys. Osiris and Horus the Elder were begotten by Helios, the sun. Osiris' titles include Horus the Elder. Bes-Horus combined the divine Pygmy Bes with the god of Saturn. So the sun fathered a Pygmy child associated with Saturn. The sun has nine planets; Saturn, the Pygmy sun, is equipped with nine moons. Osiris, the man-god, is the Pygmy. No people of early historic times possessed explicit knowledge of these nine moons and planets. The people of remote prehistoric times evidently possessed greater knowledge that survived in symbolic legends and that magnificent relic of the first astronomers, the Efé "Star of Nine Moons."

Now, returning to the Greek legend: To save her sixth and last child, Rhea bore Zeus "at dead of night" and tricked his gourmet parent Cronus into swallowing a stone. Rhea then entrusted Zeus to the custody of Mother Earth. The latter carried Zeus from Arcadia in Greece to the cave of the Aegean hill at the Cretan navel of the earth. When Zeus grew to manhood, he persuaded Cronus to drink an emetic potion. Cronus vomited up the stone and then the swallowed gods. Zeus set up the stone on the slopes of Parnassus, the mountain of the "sacred chasm," where it marks the Delphic navel of the earth. The regurgitated gods expressed their gratitude by asking Zeus to lead them into battle. The gods won the war, Zeus banished Cronus and his Titans to the underworld or to a remote British isle, and Atlas was condemned to hold the sky upon his shoulders.

All of the characters in this story are forms of the same cosmic-human characters: the Earth-Moon-Saturn Titans and Efé, the Pygmy. The stone is generally interpreted as a "thunder-stone," a symbol of the thunderbolt: "Hesiod tells us that, after Cronus had vomited forth the stone which he swallowed instead of his son, Zeus, entering on his reign, released from their bonds the brothers of Cronus, the Titans, who then gave Zeus the thunder and lightning. The unfettering of Cronus or Saturn appears to be a reflection of the custom at Saturnalian festivals of releasing prisoners and slaves—the mock subjects of the mock king of the feast, himself a prisoner or a slave."[108]

The Greek legend has been obscured by the customs of related festivals and the Titan-Titaness system. The Olympian gods were swallowed by a male or female form of the earth. The alternate legend of the Titan-Olympian war says that the Athenian heroes sank "in a body" into the earth. The residents of Atlantis sank— kerplunk!—into the sea. Efé supposedly resurrects the water- monster's victims by carving up the fiend; the grateful victims

---

[108] *Ibid.*, p. 224.

emerge and hail Efé as their savior and chief. The flood legend
informs us that everyone drowns with the sole exception of Efé,
the last man on earth, who then produces a new troop of
children. The living victims who emerge from the belly of the giant
water monster could not possibly survive this experience. The
Masai story of the nine-headed devil confirms this diagnosis by
resurrecting the victims through the devil's foot, i.e., through the
foot of the Mountain Mother. Hercules did not resurrect any victims when he carved up that hydraulic horror, the nine-headed
Hydra.

The pseudo-people who emerge from the belly of the watery
beast express their gratitude by installing Efé as their chief and
thereby agreeing to abide by his laws. They have been punished
and they have learned the error of their ways. Now they will honor
and respect Efé, the divinely ordained ruler of the world. This is
the moral of the swallowing-monster story, a parable that is not
factual or "true."

> In his book *The Story of Rome* Norwood Young makes the
> following comment about the pictures that adorn the walls of the
> Roman catacombs: The common picture of Jonah and the whale
> refers to the Resurrection. There was a great difference between
> Pagan and Christian burial. Although the Romans did not believe in
> the resurrection of the body, they thought that the shade, spirit, or
> soul, of the deceased would restlessly haunt the earth, if the body
> from which it came was not laid properly to rest. Hence the great
> respect extended to tombs and the liberty given to burial clubs.
> When the body had been cremated, and the ashes placed in an urn
> and buried, the place of interment became *religiosus,* under the
> protection of the pontiffs and the law . . . Believing in the resurrec-
> tion of the body, the Christians were even more particular than the
> Romans as to the interment of their dead . . . When the Christians
> grew in numbers, the *fossores* (diggers) having excavated all the
> soil immediately below the surface, and filled all the niches with
> corpses, could not extend their operations laterally in any direction
> because that would have taken them under a site belonging to the
> neighboring proprietor. They were obliged to excavate a second
> layer below the first, and then a third. As many as five layers have
> been found in one catacomb. Thus, though they do not extend
> beyond the third milestone from the walls of the city, the total

length of the galleries excavated is believed to amount to about 600 miles, and the number of graves to 2,000,000.[109]

Is there anything more pitiful than the spectacle of adult human beings who fearfully, sentimentally, or egotistically reject the simple fact of death?

The legends that the ancient Pygmies brought to every inhabited continent generated all of our "religions" or bodies of organized superstition. A great Italian philosopher, Giordano Bruno, was burned at the stake in the city of Rome on February 17, 1600. His crimes included the authorship of a book, *Spaccio della Bestia Trionfante*, which "exalts truth, prudence, wisdom, law and judgment, and at the same time scoffs at the mysteries of faith and places the Jewish record on a level with Greek myths."[110] An enlightened British theologian called Pelagius (c.360–c.420 A.D.) authored the Pelagian heresy by repudiating the Christian concepts of original sin and resurrection. Pope John IV denounced Pelagius' followers in a seventh-century letter to the Irish: "For who would not abhor their proud and wicked endeavor, saying that man can exist without sin of his own free will and not from the grace of God? And first indeed it is blasphemous folly to say man is without sin; because it can in no way be, save the one Mediator of God and Man, the man Jesus Christ, who was conceived and born without sin. For other men are born with original sin, and are known to bear the witness of the delinquency of Adam, even if they live without actual sin, according to the prophet, saying: Behold, I was shapen in wickedness and in sin hath my mother conceived me."[111]

Christ is a form of Horus, the oldest god of Egypt. Bes-Horus or Bes protected little children. He did not promulgate the dogma of infant damnation, and he did not condemn any man for sins committed by another. He was the god of dancing, music, mirth and every innocent pleasure. "Hail to the Dancer of God!" Pharaoh Pepi the Second saluted one of Bes' earthly kinsmen. "Those men

---

[109] Norwood Young, *The Story of Rome* (London: J. M. Dent, 1926), pp. 95–101.

[110] *Encyclopaedia Britannica*, 14th ed., Vol. 4, p. 287.

[111] Bede, *The Ecclesiastical History of the English Nation*, pp. 191–92.

were the so-called golden race, subjects of Cronus, who lived
without cares or labor, eating only acorns, wild fruit, and honey
that dripped from the trees, drinking the milk of sheep and goats,
never growing old, dancing, and laughing much; death, to them,
was no more terrible than sleep. They are all gone now, but their
spirits survive as genii of happy music retreats, givers of good
fortune, and upholders of justice," declares a Greek legend of
Cronus and the first men.[112] "In those days, God himself was the
shepherd," Plato said about the reign of Cronus, the god of the
first men.

Efé is still the spiritual leader of his people. A few thousand
Dancers of God survive in the equatorial forest. They are not all
gone. Not yet. The legends of Efé tell the story of a just and cour-
ageous hero whom all men should attempt to emulate. He is a
masterful hunter. He loves peace and he fights only in a good
cause. He is a great poet, musician and dancer. He is a *bon vivant*
who does not condemn any harmless pleasure. He is Oberon, the
good fairy king of the French romance "Huon of Bordeaux." Oberon
blew his ivory horn in this story and set a whole troop of monks
and nuns dancing on the grass. Then he explained to Huon, the
nephew of the Pope, that his horn would not have set the ecclesiastics dancing if their conscience had been pure.[113] "Robin Hood took
the bishop by the hand, and he caused the music to play; and he
made the old bishop to dance in his boots, and glad to get so
away," according to the British ballad of Robin Hood and the
Bishop of Hereford.[114]

Oberon staged his dancing party in the Arabian lands associated with the divine Pygmy, Bes. Little Bes holds Osiris' sovereign
emblems in his Metternich portrait. The Greeks identified Osiris
with Dionysus. He and his Roman counterpart Bacchus were represented as the pleasure-loving inventors of wine. Efé does not approve of *tsoi*, strong drink, beer or wine. The elders say that it is
debilitating, and they are right. Wherever alcohol has been introduced into Pygmy territories, the physical and moral health of the

---

[112] Robert Graves, *The Greek Myths*, Vol. 1, p. 36.

[113] *Bulfinch's Mythology*, pp. 650–51.

[114] *Ibid.*, p. 485.

community has been all but destroyed. The Efé bands of western Uganda, near Fort Portal, offer a particularly tragic example. Some are chronic alcoholics and most of them behave like hoodlums. Tourists who visit Uganda have gathered the very false impression that these grossly corrupted Efé bands are typical Pygmies. Since no conventional tour groups visit Zaïre, the Pygmies' reputation has grown steadily worse during the past decade.

To dispel this misunderstanding, I have for several summers led "Jean-Pierre Hallet's Congo Safaris" into the eastern Ituri and have introduced genuinely interested people to Pygmy bands who still follow their traditional and very beautiful way of life. There the Efé have hospitably introduced some of my companions to a relaxing and stimulating custom. The Efé have shared the "Pygmy peace pipe," as I call it, with their American guests.

The *tètè* is a bamboo water pipe used for smoking *djému*, hemp. The Sua, the Kango and other Pygmy populations throughout the equatorial forest smoke hemp, which is related to but somewhat stronger than marijuana. Far from being slowed down or stupefied, the Pygmy hemp smokers walk and run up to fifteen miles a day during their hunts and sometimes dance for hours in the evenings. They say that hemp "increases the vital force," a phenomenon which may be connected with their distinctive physiology. They suffer no ill effects whatsoever and do not have a psychological compulsion to smoke hemp. Their mental, emotional and physical condition is superb. The sick Pygmy alcoholics have cruelly but truthfully been described as "drunken bums."

An American presidential committee recently reported a fact that has been suspected for some time, namely, that cannabis plants have no harmful or addicting effects. Having been exposed to the prevalent European and American disapproval of cannabis, and having seen Negro tribesmen stupefied by excessive hemp smoking, I was at first shocked by the Pygmies' hemp smoking and deeply concerned lest this custom might injure their health. Since they currently obtain hemp from the Bantu and Sudanese tribes, I received the first impression that the Negroes had introduced the Pygmies to hemp.

"We have smoked hemp since the beginning of time," Efé friends subsequently informed me. "The Pygmies smoke hemp and the dwarfs smoke hemp. There are great fields of hemp in the kingdom of the dead. Those fortunate dwarfs!" declared the elder Mutuke. "God gave hemp to the Pygmies. Hemp keeps us healthy and happy," said an Efé hunter called Avi'oka, "Iron Man." All-Father Efé invented the pipe, according to the elders. I do not doubt this statement, since I have seen water pipes used by Pygmy bands who have not been in contact with Negroes, and I have never seen the Pygmy water pipe used by any Negroes except those who have been in direct contact with the Pygmies. Arabic legends associate hemp smoking with the ancestral paradise in the Mountains of the Moon. Sir Richard Burton described the pygmoid Bushmen as hemp smokers in his commentary on *The Arabian Nights:*

> The Arab Banj and Hindu Bhang (which I use as most familiar) both derive from the old Coptic Nibanj meaning a preparation of hemp and here it is easy to recognize the Homeric "Nepenthe." Al-Kazwini explains the term by "garden hemp" (Kinnab bostani or Shahdanaj). On the other hand not a few apply the word to the henbane (hyoscyamus niger) so much used in medieval Europe.
>
> The use of Bhang doubtless dates from the dawn of civilization, whose earliest social pleasures would be inebriants. Herodotus shows the Scythians burning the seeds (leaves and capsules) in worship and becoming drunken with the fumes, as do the S. African Bushmen of the present day. This would be the earliest form of smoking: it is still doubtful whether the pipe was used or not. Galen also mentions intoxication by hemp. Among Moslems, the Persians adopted the drink as an ecstatic, and about our thirteenth century, Egypt, which began the practice, introduced a number of preparations to be noticed in the course of The Nights.[115]

It is a crime to smoke cannabis plants in most countries of our Western world. The Pygmies have a much more enlightened view of criminal, sinful or unethical behavior. Their laws include a number of "ecological commandments," as I have described these statutes to my lecture audiences.

Wanton or unnecessary killing of the fauna is forbidden. Wasteful destruction of the flora is regarded as a crime. The sinner who wastes food of any kind is worse than a liar or an adulterer;

---

[115] Sir Richard Burton, *Love, War and Fancy: The Customs and Manners of the East* (New York: Ballantine Books, 1964), p. 261.

he depletes the natural resources of the community and thereby imperils the survival of all. Trapping is forbidden. It is wasteful as well as unmanly, according to the Pygmies. They explain that traps, snares, pits and deadfalls wound more animals than they catch. The wounded animals die for no useful purpose or turn into man-hating rogues. It is a sin to foul the Ituri Forest streams and rivers with excrement or refuse. People grow sick and may even die, say the elders, if they drink dirty water. The tall trees of the forest must never be cut. "The forest is our great house. We live in our great house; we sleep in the little huts. The trees are the great house of God. The tall trees belong to God. Efé told us that the tall trees must never be cut."

These are the principal "ecological commandments." Mwenua, the elder of Ebuya, told me that wasting food is a more grievous sin than lying, stealing and adultery. He defined cruelty to children and old people as the worst human crimes. To divide the meat unfairly among the participating hunters is a lesser but ethically contemptible crime. Another elder, Pukibili, ranked the sins of man in the following order: (1) cruelty toward children; (2) murder; (3) wanton slaughter of animals; (4) disrespect toward parent and elders; (5) failure to help a wounded or stray Pygmy from another territory; (6) wasting food; (7) fouling water; (8) sorcery; (9) adultery; (10) cowardly behavior during the hunt; (11) husband-beating;* (12) wife-beating; (13) cutting the tall trees; (14) blasphemy; (15) setting traps for animals; (16) theft; (17) eating eggs, which are like "seeds of life" or "babies in the womb"; (18) slander.

One cannot separate "ecological" from "ethical" command-

---

* The sin of husband-beating is unknown to other African communities. Pygmy women traditionally enjoy a degree of freedom and equality that makes them almost like members of our American Women's Lib. A Pygmy lady marries the man of her own choice, argues with him *ad libitum*, incessantly accuses him of flirting with young girls, and sometimes tries to beat him with a stick. She rarely administers more than a token tap. The little woman's shrewish behavior sometimes causes husbands to lose their tempers and commit the sin of wife-beating. The aggravated husband usually gives the wife more than a token tap. When he acts in self-defense, having received a prior tap, he does not commit a sin unless he uses unnecessary roughness and really injures the woman. A similar rule applies to scuffles between Pygmy men.

ments. The Pygmies' approach toward nature demonstrates the same causal and ethical thinking that typifies their views on human behavior and society. Their conservationist credo might be summarized as "Do unto nature as you would have nature do unto you." Their insistence that the truly ethical man must respect the natural world is echoed in the Egyptian commandments or "negative confessions" that the deceased made before Thoth and Osiris in the Hall of Double Law or Truth:

> I have not done iniquity to mankind. Not have I done harm unto animals . . . Not have I caused pain. Not have I made to weep. Not have I killed. Not have I made the order for killing for me . . . Not have I stolen from the orchard. Not have I trampled down the fields . . . Not have I captured the birds of the preserves of the gods. Not have I taken fishes with bait of their own bodies. Not have I turned back water at its season. Not have I cut a cutting in water running . . . not have I defiled the wife of a man . . . not have I harmed, not have I done evil . . . not have I fouled water . . . not have I cursed God . . . not have I borne false witness . . . I have given bread to the hungry, water to the thirsty, clothes to the naked, and a boat to the shipwrecked . . .[116]

We think that we invented the science of ecology. All-Father Efé gave his laws to the prehistoric ancestors of the ancient Egyptians. We preach but we do not practice the science of ecology. The Pygmies practice this science but unfortunately do not send missionaries abroad to preach their ethical "religion." Some ecologists give us less than fifty years. The earth, the air and the water will by then be poisoned to the point where human life, and virtually all life, may no longer be able to survive amid the swill of our pig-pen planet. Industrial profiteers who cannot see beyond this year's balance sheet sentence us to death by looting natural resources and spewing toxic residues out of their plants. Politicians who cannot see beyond this year's election sponsor the rape of the earth and play war games while the clock runs out. Religious leaders who cannot see beyond their damnable collection plates denounce ecologists as "alarmists" and exhort the faithful to "be fruitful and multiply" in a world where the famine-stricken children of the

---

[116] Sir E. A. Wallis Budge, *The Book of the Dead*, pp. 194–205.

faithful will devour each other like starving rats in a concrete cage.

Today Africa, the land of the first man, is dying with the rest of the earth. Overgrazing and overcultivation are killing the fragile soil. When the natural vegetation of the forests and savannahs is destroyed, the land turns into dust bowl and desert. The wildlife is vanishing, due to the rape of the land and the grand-scale slaughters perpetrated by man. The African cities are infested with slums and riot-prone mobs of unemployed workers. The new independent governments believe that industrialization will enable them to compete with America and Eurasia. This belief has already turned vast regions of the African continent into an ecological disaster area.

"Three of the greatest African rivers have recently been captured and domesticated by three of the greatest human building efforts made since the times of the pyramids: damming of the Volta in Ghana; the Zambesi between Zambia and Southern Rhodesia (Kariba dam); and the mighty Nile of East Africa, Sudan and Egypt by the Aswan dam," the eminent ecologist and parasitologist Dr. Donald Heyneman wrote in July of 1971. Some of the results:

> One of the more paradoxical but obviously planned results of the construction of the High Dam is the need for costly nitrate and phosphate plants (to be powered by energy from the dammed Nile) that will be required to replace the millions of tons of natural fertilizer formerly presented freely to man by the annual Nile floods, the basis of Egyptian civilization for well over 5000 years. Though double cropping is now possible everywhere below the dam, these crops must depend upon man's efforts for their enrichment. And that fertilization will add to a growing chemical pollution problem in the Nile and the Eastern Mediterranean which it feeds. For other reasons, too, the Mediterranean is permanently altered. The Nile's load of sediments are gone. So are the crustaceans and the fish that fed on them and supported in turn a major fishery for Egypt and coastal nations: 18,000 tons a year of valuable fish protein...
>
> Another impact, equally severe: *disease*. Familiar parasitic diseases, but enhanced, have been given a new intensity by the changed conditions that provide a far more efficient, concentrated mode of transmission. Human crowding, social unrest, malnutri-

tion, migration of nonimmune people through endemic foci of human or wild animal infection provide the basis for new and virulent outbreaks . . .

The results are tragically evident—hundreds of thousands more children with bilharzia-bloated livers. In certain areas of Nigeria affected by the Volta dam, thousands have been blinded by onchocerciasis, the river disease carried by blackflies. In other regions one finds the grotesquely swollen limbs or gonads of older persons with elephantiasis, the extreme manifestation of mosquito-borne filariasis. In the Sudan, new plagues from kala azar have been reported, attacking the same Wadi Halfans, forced from their homes and resettled into areas endemic with this lethal disease. Mosquito-borne malaria, the scourge of all the tropics, in some parts of Africa kills every other child before it reaches the age of three.

Most directly the result of human activity, however, is bilharzia, the modern plague of Egypt. Its spread is immediately attributable to damming the Nile, controlling the annual flood, and spreading its waters through a web of permanent irrigation canals. The disease is not limited to Egypt but has spread throughout Africa and today affects 200 millions around the world, probably the fastest spreading and most pathogenic parasitic disease of man . . . In Africa infection occurs wherever children play in the water, farmers irrigate by simple means, people wash their clothes, their water buffalos, or themselves, where they drink, carry water for cooking—and where they defecate or urinate egg-bearing wastes directly into the water. "He who drinks from the waters of the Nile shall return" is a warm and gracious Egyptian greeting. To take that hospitality literally today is an invitation one accepts at his peril.[117]

The annual inundation of the Nile has been dammed and the water has been grossly polluted. "Not have I turned back water at its season . . . Not have I fouled water at its season," the Egyptian deceased swore in the Judgment Hall of Osiris. It is against the law to foul the waters of the Ituri Forest streams and rivers. People get sick and may even die if they drink dirty water. It is against the law to kill animals and plant life without a valid purpose. It is

---

[117] Donald Heyneman, "Mis-aid to the Third World: Disease Repercussions Caused by Ecological Ignorance," from *The Canadian Journal of Public Health,* Vol. 62 (July–August, 1971), pp. 303–13.

against the law to cut the tall trees. Concerning the loss of ecological integrity in present-day Africa Dr. Heyneman remarks:

> It is reflected in the replacement of magnificently adapted native antelopes, the world's richest source of herbivore variety and productivity, with disease-susceptible livestock. Ecological loss is reflected in the miles of burning grasslands that are visible at any time in the central and east African veldt during the dry season; in meaningless deforestation, strip mining, labour exploitation, rabbit-warren urbanized settlements that have replaced widely scattered populations of highly mobile tribal groups. These dense concentrations of malnourished humans, under appallingly insanitary, exposed conditions, are fed upon by still higher densities of hookworms, *Ascaris* round-worms, blood flukes, pathogenic amoebae and other opportunistic parasites that now can multiply to densities unknown in their hosts when they were scattered in small groups and communities across the little-disturbed land.[118]

The Ituri Forest Pygmies dwell in shrinking islands of forest. Bantu and Sudanese plantations are engulfing the forest islands. Lumber operators chop down the tall trees on the edge of the forest islands. The plantations creep toward the center of the forest islands. The Pygmies have no place to go. They cannot leave the shady forest and dwell under the broiling equatorial sun, where many would be stricken by sunstroke and heat prostration. They have lived in the forest for untold millennia. A lengthy period of acclimation would be necessary to accomplish such a transition. And even if this could be arranged, where could the Pygmies go? They are surrounded by alien people who have taken over their land.

The Pygmies and the tall trees are dying together. The land will die with them. There are only four precious inches of topsoil in the equatorial forest. When the tall trees are cut, the torrential rainstorms of this region wash the topsoil into the rivers. The soil is already being eroded in deforested regions. The Ituri is being converted into a gullied wasteland that will be of no use to the Bantu and Sudanese tribes. Their population problem will be

---

[118] *Ibid.*, p. 310.

temporarily allayed by the destruction of the Ituri Forest; it will not be solved.

The Ituri is a remnant of the old equatorial forest belt; the Ituri itself consists of little forest remnants. The Ituri is like a jigsaw puzzle with many missing pieces; the surviving Pygmies of Africa and the Far East are like pieces of a human jigsaw puzzle that has been tattered by time, natural catastrophes and the oppression of less civilized races. All men are involved in this tragedy; all men will die if we permit this tragedy to reach its grand climax. We cannot cut down the tall trees, poison the oceans with filth, and hope to survive. The trees and the oceanic plankton make the oxygen that we breathe.

Between the years 1900 and 2000, scientists estimate, the carbon dioxide content of the air will have increased by 25 percent. Some authorities predict that this will cause drastic changes in climate, such as the melting of the Antarctic icecap. For all we know, our grand-scale tampering with the natural environment may itself trigger another glacial period.

"Do unto nature as you would have nature do unto you," is the magnificent moral of the Pygmy legend cycle. Conservationist groups have fought admirable battles to save the California redwood trees and animal species that are menaced by extinction. In Africa, more than one hundred fifty thousand square miles of national parks and game reserves are dedicated to the preservation of the flora and fauna. To date, not a single square mile has been set aside to aid the survival of Africa's oldest known people.

The Ituri Forest home of the Pygmies may have been reduced, at present, to some fifteen thousand square miles. This area comprises only 10 percent of the land reserved for the African animals. I believe that the Pygmies have the right to live in this small remnant of their original land. On June 25, 1972, I founded a nonprofit organization dedicated to the goal of securing for the Pygmies their Ituri Forest land. The organization is called The Friends of the Pygmies. With the help of good-hearted people, this humanitarian goal can and will be achieved.

The Pygmies have told us the story of every world-age. Death comes, in this story, to the men who plunder the land of All-Father

Efé and "his Pygmies." The story is told by the Pygmy people of Ta Neteru, the Egyptian "Land of the Gods." The Pygmies are men, not gods. Their tall trees make the air fit to breathe. Their great stream of ocean provides men with life-giving water. When the tall trees are cut and the water is fouled, death comes to mankind. These deeds are forms of the original sin committed by Adam or "man." These sins are now being repeated.

Efé's laws can really save people, unlike the superstitious dogmas derived from the Pygmy legends. Efé's laws command us to be ethical in our dealings with both man and nature. "If ye love me, keep my commandments," said Jesus. Efé's laws were inscribed in *The Book of the Dead* thousands of years before the era assigned to Jesus. Who is Efé? His name means "the Pygmy."

Index

About the Authors

JEAN-PIERRE HALLET was born in Louvain, Belgium, in 1927, but his roots are deep in African soil. His father, André Hallet, was a renowned painter whose landscapes and portraits are famous for their fidelity to African scenes. Jean-Pierre Hallet spent six years of his childhood in the Congo, and in 1948 returned to live and work among seventeen different African tribes. In 1957 he lived alone with the Efé Pygmies of the Ituri Forest for eighteen months, sharing completely their truly "ecological" way of life. During this time he gained a new personal and scientific knowledge of these little-known and most inspiring people. Since then, he has managed to revisit his adopted people every year, bringing back to America an increasing wealth of new facts on their amazing culture, philosophy and religion.

Mr. Hallet has compiled the first dictionary and grammatical study of the Efé language, the original Pygmy tongue, and has also photographed and filmed each aspect of their daily life. Mr. Hallet now lives in California, lectures extensively in the United States, and each summer leads his own safaris, a visit in depth of the Africa he knows. He is the author of the international best-sellers *Congo Kitabu* and *Animal Kitabu*.

Born and educated in New York, ALEX PELLE has worked as a writer since 1963 with Jean-Pierre Hallet. Having pursued informal studies in zoology and anthropology for more than ten years, she was well equipped to aid in the writing of *Congo Kitabu*, *Animal Kitabu* and *Pygmy Kitabu*. She now lives in San Pedro, California.

CENTRAL AFRICAN REPUBLIC

CAMEROON

MT. CAMEROON
13,353 ft.
• Yaoundé

GIELLI

• Bangui

Ubangi River

Zaire River

• Lisala

Ngbaka

Poto

• Isangi

□ Bata
RIO MUNI

EQUATOR

Mongo

Mbandaka

Tshuapa River

Lake Tumba

• Libreville

EQUATOR

GABON REPUBLIC

KWI

BONGO

KOA

Mbole

TSWA

REPUBLIC OF ZAÏRE
(FORMER CONGO-KINSHASA)

Lake Maji-Ndombe
1,040 ft.

Kasai River

Sankuru River

EASTER
KASA
TWA

Bandundu

• Mushenge

Kuba

Brazzaville

• Kinshasa

• Mweka

WESTERN-KASAI

ATLANTIC

ZAIRE

LOWER

CABINDA

• Mbanza-Ngungu

Matadi •

Kongo

BANDUNDU

Yaka

• Kikwit

Lulua

Kananga

• Mbuji-May

OCEAN

ANGOLA

Chokwe

Lunda

• Dilolo

Kamina •

Lulua River

Inset map

Limit of the territory now occupied by the Ituri Forest's Pygmies.

Isiro (Former Paulis) ⊙

○ Watsa

Nepoko

3,500 ft.

AKA

3,950 ft.

○ Wamba
2,500 ft.

Nava

Ngayu

SUA

Ndaye

EFÉ

○ Djugu

Aruwimi

KANGO

Ituri
Nia-Nia
○
2,050 ft.

2,300 ft.
Epulu

Epulu

Ituri

• Bunia

LAKE ALBERT
2,030 ft.

Lindi

Mambasa

Irumu
3,020 ft.

Bafwasende
1,770 ft.

SUA

Lenda

Ibina

EFÉ

Erengeti
Oicha ○

Semliki

• Fort Portal

Asumani ○

○ Kakoro

Mbau ×

RUWENZORI 16,763 ft.
MOUNTAINS OF THE MOON

Tshopo

Loya

Beni •
3,516 ft.

EQUATOR

Lubero

Butembo
5,900 ft.

LAKE GEORGE

Lindi

Lubero •
6,368 ft.

LAKE EDWARD
2,995 ft.

UGANDA

VIRUNGA (or Birunga) VOLCANOES

1. NYAMURAGIRA	10,026 ft.	⎤
2. NYIRAGONGO	11,384 ft.	⎬ Active
3. MIKENO	14,557 ft.	⎦
4. KARISIMBI	14,786 ft.	(the highest)
5. VISOKE	12,175 ft.	
6. SABYINYO	11,922 ft.	
7. GAHINGA	11,398 ft.	
8. MUHAVURA	13,540 ft.	

Kayna •
6,135 ft.

Rwindi •
3,200 ft.

Rutshuru •
4,190 ft.

Ishasha

1 2 3 5 6 7 8
4

Masisi ○

Goma ⊙
4,850 ft.

Gisenyi

LAKE KIVU
4,790 ft.

RWANDA

Kigali ⊙
4,495 ft.

TWA

⊕ Capital City
◉ Chief town of region (province)
◉ Chief town of sub-region (district)
⊙ Chief town of zone (territory)
○ Important locality

AKA Pygmy Group
2 300 ft. Altitude in feet

Bukavu ⊙

BURUNDI

|—————| 50 MILES

|———————| 0 miles 200

J. P. TREMBLAY